THE COMPLETE
CROSSWORD
SOLVER

THE COMPLETE
CROSSWORD
SOLVER

STEVE CURTIS

ARCTURUS

ACKNOWLEDGEMENTS

The compiler would like to thank Tessa Rose and Belinda Jones of Arcturus Publishing, and his friends Martin Manser and Andrew Hill JP for their valuable assistance with this project. Particular thanks are also due to his wife, Sally, who helped to type out the lists.

ARCTURUS

This edition published in 2009 by Arcturus Publishing Limited
26/27 Bickels Yard, 151–153 Bermondsey Street,
London SE1 3HA

ISBN: 978-1-84837-298-6
AD000116EN

Printed in the UK

Typeset by MATS, Southend-on-Sea, Essex

CONTENTS

ABBREVIATIONS ------------ 9
ACTORS/ACTRESSES -------- 20
AFRICA/AFRICAN ----------- 24
AGRICULTURE ------------- 27
AIRCRAFT ---------------- 31
AIR TRAVEL -------------- 33
ALPHABETS --------------- 36
AMERICA/AMERICAN -------- 38
ANIMALS ----------------- 43
ARCHITECTURE ----------- 50
ART --------------------- 54
ARTISTS ----------------- 58
ASIA/ASIAN -------------- 59
ASTRONOMY -------------- 60
AUSTRALIA/AUSTRALIAN ---- 64
BAD AND GOOD ------------ 66
BALLET ------------------ 73
BATTLES ----------------- 75
BIBLE ------------------- 77
BIRDS ------------------- 79
BODY -------------------- 84
BUILDINGS --------------- 89
BUSINESS ---------------- 93
BUTTERFLIES AND
  MOTHS ----------------- 99
CANADA/CANADIAN -------- 101
CAPITAL CITIES ---------- 102
CARS -------------------- 107
CATS -------------------- 111
CATTLE ------------------ 112
CHARACTERISTICS AND
  QUALITIES (non-physical) ----- 113
CHARACTERISTICS AND
  QUALITIES (physical) -------- 127
CHEESES ----------------- 132
CHEMISTRY -------------- 133
CHURCH ----------------- 137
CLOTHES ----------------- 138
COINS ------------------- 143
COLOURS ----------------- 144
COMPOSERS -------------- 146
COMPUTERS -------------- 148
CONTAINERS ------------- 152
COOKING ----------------- 154
COUNTIES ---------------- 156
COUNTRIES --------------- 158
CRICKET ----------------- 160
CRIME/CRIMINAL ---------- 162
CURRENCIES ------------- 165
DANCE ------------------- 168
DESERTS ----------------- 170
DICKENS ----------------- 171
DINOSAURS --------------- 173
DISEASE ----------------- 174
DOGS -------------------- 177
DRINK ------------------- 179
DRUGS ------------------- 181
EDUCATION --------------- 182
ELEMENTS (chemical) -------- 186
ENGINEERING ------------- 187
ENGLAND/ENGLISH -------- 194
ENTERTAINMENT ---------- 200
EUROPE/EUROPEAN -------- 203
EXPLORERS -------------- 206
FABRICS ----------------- 207
FEELINGS ---------------- 209
FILMS ------------------- 216
FISH -------------------- 219
FLOWERS ---------------- 223
FOOD -------------------- 225
FOOTBALL ---------------- 229
FRANCE/FRENCH ---------- 235
FRUIT ------------------- 240
FURNITURE --------------- 242
GAMES ------------------- 244
GEOGRAPHY -------------- 247
GEOLOGY ----------------- 250
GODS/GODDESSES --------- 252
GOLF -------------------- 257
GRAMMAR ---------------- 258
GROUPS ------------------ 260
HEALTH ------------------ 265
HERBS ------------------- 267
HORSES ------------------ 268
INSECTS ----------------- 270
INVENTORS -------------- 271
IRELAND/IRISH ----------- 272
ISLANDS ----------------- 274
JEWELS/JEWELLERY -------- 277
JOURNALISM ------------- 279

Contents

LAKES - 281
LANGUAGES - - - - - - - - - - - - - - 284
LAW/LEGAL - - - - - - - - - - - - - - - 286
LITERATURE/LITERARY - - - - - - 289
LONDON - - - - - - - - - - - - - - - - - 291
MACHINES/MACHINERY - - - - - 293
MATHEMATICS - - - - - - - - - - - - - 295
MEASUREMENT - - - - - - - - - - - - 298
MEDICINE/MEDICAL - - - - - - - - 301
METALS - - - - - - - - - - - - - - - - - - 304
MILITARY - - - - - - - - - - - - - - - - - 305
MOUNTAINS - - - - - - - - - - - - - - 313
MOVES - - - - - - - - - - - - - - - - - - - 316
MUSIC/MUSICAL - - - - - - - - - - - 319
MUSICIANS - - - - - - - - - - - - - - - - 325
MYTH/MYTHOLOGY - - - - - - - - 329
NAMES - - - - - - - - - - - - - - - - - - - 332
NAUTICAL TERMS - - - - - - - - - - 346
NEW ZEALAND - - - - - - - - - - - - 351
NOVELS - - - - - - - - - - - - - - - - - - 352
NUMBERS - - - - - - - - - - - - - - - - 356
OCCUPATIONS - - - - - - - - - - - - 358
OPERA - - - - - - - - - - - - - - - - - - - 370
PAINT/PAINTING - - - - - - - - - - - 372
PAINTERS - - - - - - - - - - - - - - - - 373
PHILOSOPHERS - - - - - - - - - - - - 376
PLANTS - - - - - - - - - - - - - - - - - - 377
POEMS/POETRY - - - - - - - - - - - - 382
POETS - - - - - - - - - - - - - - - - - - - 383
POLITICIANS - - - - - - - - - - - - - - 385
POLITICS/ PARLIAMENT - - - - - 390
PORTS - - - - - - - - - - - - - - - - - - - 394
PUBLISHING AND
PRINTING - - - - - - - - - - - - - - - - 396
RACE/RACING - - - - - - - - - - - - - 399
RELIGION/RELIGIOUS - - - - - - - 401
REPTILES - - - - - - - - - - - - - - - - 412
RIVERS - - - - - - - - - - - - - - - - - - 413
ROAD AND RAIL - - - - - - - - - - - 416
ROCKS AND MINERALS - - - - - - 418
ROYALTY - - - - - - - - - - - - - - - - 420
SAY/SPEAK/TALK - - - - - - - - - - 424
SCIENCE/SCIENTIFIC - - - - - - - 425
SCIENTISTS - - - - - - - - - - - - - - 429
SCOTLAND/SCOTTISH - - - - - - 431
SCULPTORS/SCULPTURE - - - - 435
SEAS - 436
SHAKESPEARE - - - - - - - - - - - - 438

SHIPS AND BOATS - - - - - - - - - - 446
SINGERS - - - - - - - - - - - - - - - - - 449
SNAKES - - - - - - - - - - - - - - - - - 452
SOUNDS - - - - - - - - - - - - - - - - - 453
SPACE - - - - - - - - - - - - - - - - - - - 455
SPICES - - - - - - - - - - - - - - - - - - 456
SPORT - - - - - - - - - - - - - - - - - - - 457
TELEVISION AND RADIO - - - - - 464
THEATRE - - - - - - - - - - - - - - - - 467
TOOLS - - - - - - - - - - - - - - - - - - - 474
TOWNS - - - - - - - - - - - - - - - - - - 477
TREES - - - - - - - - - - - - - - - - - - - 485
USA - 488
VEGETABLES - - - - - - - - - - - - - 491
VEHICLES - - - - - - - - - - - - - - - - 492
VOLCANOES - - - - - - - - - - - - - - 495
WALES/WELSH - - - - - - - - - - - - 496
WEAPONS - - - - - - - - - - - - - - - - 498
WEATHER - - - - - - - - - - - - - - - - 500
WINE - 503
WRITERS - - - - - - - - - - - - - - - - - 504

INTRODUCTION

The Complete Crossword Solver is a new and, hopefully, user-friendly attempt to solve the problem of helping people who would prefer not to be helped if they could possibly avoid it. It starts from the assumption that crossword solvers – the human, not the printed kind – want to do it by themselves. The pleasure of solving the clues and filling in the blanks is greatly increased, if you can manage it unaided.

But human crossword solvers are only human; their vocabularies only stretch so far, and their memories sometimes fail. Moreover, crossword setters are knowledgeable, wily and not always on exactly the same wavelength as the people they aim to entertain (or bedevil). As a result, the solvers sometimes get stuck.

The aim of this book is to get its users unstuck as quickly and painlessly as possible. To that end, the solutions it contains are listed under roughly one hundred and fifty key terms. These key terms have been selected because they occur with considerable frequency in crossword clues. To make things easier, the material for many key terms has been divided into different sections. Locate the relevant key term and section from the list at the front of the book, and Bob's your uncle!

Almost all the material is organized on the same principle. Words are listed in alphabetical order according to the number of letters they contain. Hyphenated words or words that have two or more parts are not, however, listed according to the total number of letters in them. If the solution is one that contains more than one word, most setters will show this as (2-2) and (2,2) respectively. Such words are listed at the end of each section under a heading '2+ words' and are simply listed alphabetically – to avoid situations where numbers could easily outnumber the words.

This book is aimed principally at people who do quick, non-cryptic crosswords. The compiler and publishers hope, however, that it will also prove useful in unlocking cryptic clues and as a source of general knowledge.

Steve Curtis

ABBREVIATIONS

1

b	born
C	Celsius, Centigrade, Conservative
c	cent(s), circa (around, approximately)
d	died, penny, pence (in old British money)
E	east, ecstasy
f	feminine, forte (loudly)
g	gram(s)
h	hour(s)
K	kelvin, kilobyte, thousand
L	lake, large, Latin, Liberal, learner
l	litre(s)
M	medium, Monsieur
m	married, masculine, metre(s), minutes, month
N	newton, north
p	page, penny, pence
q	query, question
R	royal, Regina (queen), Rex (king)
S	small, south
s	second(s)
V	volt(s)
v	versus, very
W	watt(s), west

2

AA	Alcoholics Anonymous, Automobile Association
AC	account, air conditioning, alternating current
AD	Anno Domini (in the year of Our Lord)
AI	artificial insemination, artificial intelligence
AK	Alaska
AL	Alabama
am	ante meridian (before noon)
AR	Arkansas
AS	Anglo-Saxon
AZ	Arizona
BA	Bachelor of Arts
BC	before Christ
BD	Bachelor of Divinity
BO	body odour
BS	Bachelor of Surgery, British Standard(s)
BT	British Telecom
Bt	Baronet
CA	California
ca	circa (around, approximately)
cc	carbon copy, cubic centimetres

CD	compact disc
CE	Church of England, common era
cf	compare
ch	chapter
cm	centimetre(s)
CO	Colorado, commanding officer
Co	company, county
c/o	care of
CT	Connecticut
CV	curriculum vitae
DA	district attorney (USA)
db	decibel(s)
DC	direct current, District of Columbia
DD	Doctor of Divinity
DE	Delaware
DJ	disc jockey, dinner jacket
DM	deutschmark
do	ditto
Dr	doctor
ed	editor
eg	for example (exempli gratia)
ER	Elizabeth Regina (Queen Elizabeth)
EU	European Union
ex	without, from
FA	Football Association
FC	Football Club
ff	fortissimo
FL	Florida
FM	frequency modulation
Fr	French, Friday
FT	Financial Times
ft	foot, feet
GA	Georgia
GB	Great Britain
Gb	gigabyte
GC	George Cross
Gk	Greek
gm	gram(s)
GM	genetically modified, George Medal
GR	Georgius Rex (King George)
Gr	Greek
Gt	great
HI	Hawaii
HM	Her/His Majesty
HP	hire purchase
hp	horsepower
HQ	headquarters
HR	human resources

hr	hour
Hz	hertz
IA	Iowa
ID	Idaho, identification
ie	that is (id est)
IL	Illinois
IN	Indiana
in	inch(es)
IQ	intelligence quotient
JP	justice of the peace
Jr	Junior
Kb	kilobyte
KC	King's Cousel
kg	kilogram(s)
km	kilometre(s)
KS	Kansas
Kt	knight
KY	Kentucky
LA	Los Angeles, Louisiana
lb	pound (libra)
Lt	lieutenant
MA	Massachusetts, Master of Arts
MB	Bachelor of Medicine
Mb	megabyte(s)
MC	master of ceremonies, Military Cross
MD	Doctor of Medicine, Maryland
ME	Maine, Middle English, myalgic encephalomyelitis
mf	mezzo forte
mg	milligram(s)
MI	Michigan
mm	millimetre(s)
MN	Minnesota
MO	medical officer, Missouri
MP	member of parliament, military police
Mr	Mister
MS	manuscript, Mississippi, multiple sclerosis
Ms	title for a married or unmarried woman
ms	manuscript
MT	Montana
Mt	Mount
MV	megavolt, motor vessel
NB	note well (nota bene)
NC	North Carolina
ND	North Dakota
NE	Nebraska, north east
NF	National Front
NH	New Hampshire
NJ	New Jersey

NM	New Mexico
no	number (numero)
nr	near
NT	New Testament
NV	Nevada
NW	north west
NY	New York
NZ	New Zealand
OE	Old English
OH	Ohio
OK	Oklahoma
OM	Order of Merit
op	opus
OR	Oregon
OT	Old Testament
oz	ounce(s)
PA	Pennsylvania, personal assistant, public address
PC	personal computer, police constable, politically correct
pd	paid
PE	physical education
pf	pianoforte
pl	plural
PM	prime minister
pm	post meridiem (after noon)
PO	post office
pp	by delegation to (per procurationem), pages, pianissimo
PR	proportional representation, public relations
PS	postscript
pt	pint
QC	Queen's Counsel
qr	quarter
qt	quarter
qv	which see (quod vide)
RA	Royal Academy
RC	Roman Catholic
Rd	road
RE	religious education
RI	Rhode Island
SC	South Carolina
SD	South Dakota
SE	south east
SF	science fiction
SM	sadomasochism, Sergeant Major
sq	square
Sr	senior
SS	steamship
St	saint, street
SW	south west

TA	Territorial Army
TB	tuberculosis
TN	Tennessee
TV	television
TX	Texas
UK	United Kingdom
UN	United Nations
US	United States
UT	Utah
VA	Virginia
VC	Victoria Cross
VD	venereal disease
vg	very good
VR	Victoria Regina (Queen Victoria)
vs	versus
VT	Vermont
vv	verses
WC	water closet
WI	Wisconsin
wt	weight
WV	West Virginia
WY	Wyoming
XL	extra large
yd	yard
yr	your

3

AAA	Amateur Athletic Association, American Automobile Association
ABC	alphabet, American Broadcasting Company
ADC	aide-de-camp
Adm	admiral
AGM	annual general meeting
aka	also known as
AOB	any other business
APR	annualized percentage rate
Apr	April
ATM	automatic teller machine
ATS	Auxiliary Territorial Service
Aug	August
aux	auxiliary
Ave	avenue
BBC	British Broadcasting Corporation
BDS	Bachelor of Dental Surgery
bhp	brake horsepower
BMA	British Medical Association
BNP	British National Party
Bro	Brother
BSc	Bachelor of Science

BSE	bovine spongiform encephalopathy
BST	British Summer Time
Btu	British thermal unit(s)
BVM	Blessed Virgin Mary
cap	capital
CBE	Commander of the British Empire (Order)
CBI	Confederation of British Indsutry
CBS	Central Broadcasting System (US)
CFC	chlorofluorocarbon
CIA	Central Intelligence Agency (US)
cif	cost, insurance, freight
CIO	Congress of Industrial Organizations
CIS	Commonwealth of Independent States
CJD	Creutzfeld-Jacob disease
CNN	Cable News Network (US)
COD	cash/collect on delivery
CPU	central processing unit
cwt	hundredweight
DBE	Dame Commander of the British Empire (Order)
DDT	dichlorodiphenyl trichlorocethane
Dec	December
DFC	Distinguished Flying Cross
DFM	Distinguished Flying Medal
DIY	do-it-yourself
DNA	deoxyribonucleic acid
DOS	disc-operating system
doz	dozen
DSC	Distinguished Service Cross
DSc	Doctor of Science
DSM	Distinguished Service Cross
DSO	Distinguished Service Order
DSS	Department of Social Security
DTI	Department of Trade and Industry
DUP	Democratic Unionist Party
EEC	European Economic Community
ENE	east north east
ESE	east south east
Esq	esquire
etc	etcetera
FBI	Federal Bureau of Investigation (US)
FCO	Foreign and Commonwealth Office
FDA	Food and Drug Administration (US)
Feb	February
fem	feminine
fig	figure
fob	free on board
FRS	Fellow of the Royal Society
gal	gallon(s)

GDP	gross domestic product
Gen	General
GHQ	general headquarters
GHz	gigahertz
Gib	Gibraltar
GMT	Greenwich mean time
GNP	gross national product
GOP	grand old party (US Republicans)
HIV	human immunodeficiency virus
HMS	Her/His Majesty's Ship
Hon	honorary, honourable
HRH	Her/His Royal Highness
hrs	hours
HRT	hormone replacement therapy
HSE	Health and Safety Executive
IBA	Independent Broadcasting Authority
IBM	intercontinental ballistic missile, International Business Machines
IBS	irritable bowel syndrome
ILO	International Labour Organization
IMF	International Monetary Fund
Inc	incorporated
INS	Immigration and Naturalization Service (US)
ins	inches
IOU	I owe you
IRA	Irish Republican Army
IRS	Internal Revenue Service (US)
ISA	individual savings account
ITV	Independent Television
IUD	intrauterine device
Jan	January
Jun	junior
KBE	Knight Commander of the British Empire (Order)
KGB	Russian secret service
KKK	Ku Klux Klan
kph	kilometres per hour
Lab	Labour
lbw	leg before wicket
LCD	liquid crystal display
LLB	bachelor of laws
LLD	doctor of laws
LSD	lysergic acid diethylamide
LSD	pounds, shillings and pence (librae, solidi, denarii)
LSE	London School of Economics
Ltd	limited
Maj	Major
Mar	March
MBA	Master of Business Administration
MBE	Member of the British Empire (Order)

MCC	Marylebone Cricket Club
MCP	male chauvinist pig
MEP	Member of the European Parliament
Mhz	megahertz
Mme	Madame
MOD	Ministry of Defence
MOT	Ministry of Transport
mph	miles per hour
MSc	Master of Science
MSP	Member of the Scottish Parliament
MSS, mss	manuscripts
MTV	Music Television
MWA	Member of the Welsh Assembly
NBC	National Broadcasting Company (US)
NCO	non-commissioned officer
NFU	National Farmers' Union
NHS	National Health Service
NNE	north north east
NNR	National Nature Reserve
NNW	north north west
nos	numbers
Nov	November
NRA	National Rifle Association
NSW	New South Wales
NUJ	National Union of Journalists
NUM	National Union of Mineworkers
NUS	National Union of Students
NUT	National Union of Teachers
NVQ	National Vocational Qualification
NYC	New York City
OAP	old age pensioner
OBE	Officer of the British Empire (Order)
Oct	October
OFT	Office of Fair Trading
OTC	Officer Training Corps
PBS	Public Broadcasting Service (US)
PFI	Private Finance Initiative
PhD	Doctor of Philosophy
PIN	personal identification number
plc	public limited company
PLO	Palestine Liberation Organization
PMS	premenstrual syndrome
PMT	premenstrual tension
pop	population
POW	prisoner of war
PPS	Parliamentary Private Secretary, post postscript
PTA	parent teacher association
PTO	please turn over

PVC	polyvinyl chloride
QED	that was to be demonstrated (quod erat demonstrandum)
RAC	Royal Automobile Club
RAF	Royal Air Force
RAM	random access memory
ref	referee, reference
rep	repertory, representative
Rev	Reverend
RIP	may he/she rest in peace (requiescat in pace)
RNA	ribonucleic acid
ROM	read-only memory
RSC	Royal Shakespeare Company
RSI	repetitive strain injury
RUC	Royal Ulster Constabulary
SAM	surface to air missile
SAS	Special Air Services
SAT	standard assessment test
SDP	Social Democratic Party
Sec	secretary
sec	second
Sen	senator
SMD	surface-mounted device
SME	small or medium-sized enterprise
SNP	Scottish National Party
Soc	society
SOS	distress signal
SS	steamship
SSE	south south east
SSW	south south west
STD	sexually transmitted disease, subscriber trunk dialling
tbs	tablespoon(s)
TGV	high-speed train in France (train grande vitesse)
TNT	trinitrotoluene
tsp	teaspoon
TUC	Trades Union Congress
UDA	Ulster Defence Association
UDI	unilateral declaration of independence
UFO	unidentified flying object
UHF	ultra-high frequency
UHT	ultra heat treated
UNO	United Nations Organization
USA	United States of America
USS	United States Ship
VAT	value-added tax
VDU	visual display unit
VHF	very high frequency
VIP	very important person
viz	namely (videlicet)

vol	volume
VSO	Voluntary Service Overseas
WNW	west north west
WPC	woman police constable
WSW	west south west
WTO	World Trade Organization
WWF	Worldwide Fund for Nature

4

AIDS	acquired immune deficiency syndrome
asst	assistant
Bart	baronet
Bros	Brothers
BUPA	British United Provident Association
Capt	Captain
chap	chapter
Corp	corporal,
dept	department
DfEE	Department for Education and Employment
FTSE	Financial Times Stock Exchange
GATT	General Agreement on Trade and Tariffs
GCHQ	Government Communications Headquarters
GCSE	General Certificate of Secondary Education
GNVQ	General National Vocational Qualification
html	hypertext markup language
http	hypertext transfer protocol
ibid	in the same source (ibidem)
inst	of the present month (instant)
ISBN	international standard book number
Mlle	Mademoiselle
MusB	Bachelor of Music
MusD	Doctor of Music
NASA	National Aeronautics and Space Administration (US)
NATO	North Atlantic Treaty Organization
OECD	Organization for Economic Cooperation and Development
OHMS	On Her/His Majesty's Service
OPEC	Organization of Petroleum Exporting Countries
Oxon	of Oxford
PAYE	pay as you earn
PDSA	People's Dispensary for Sick Animals
Prof	professor
PSBR	public sector borrowing requirement
recd	received
Regt	regiment
RIBA	Royal Institute of British Architects
RSPB	Royal Society for the Protection of Birds
RSVP	please reply (répondez s'il vous plaît)
Sept	September

Serg	Sergeant
STOL	short takeoff and landing
TEFL	teaching English as a foreign language
TGWU	Transport and General Workers' Union
USAF	United States Air Force
USSR	Union of Soviet Socialist Republics
WASP	white Anglo-Saxon Protestant
YMCA	Young Men's Christian Association
YWCA	Young Women's Christian Association

5

ANZAC	Australia and New Zealand Army Corps
ASCII	American Standard Code for Information Interchange
assoc	association
Dlitt	Doctor of Letters
Lieut	lieutenant
NAAFI	Navy, Army and Air Force Institutes
NSPCC	National Society for the Prevention of Cruelty to Children
RSPCA	Royal Society for the Prevention of Cruelty to Animals
UNHCR	United Nations High Commission for Refugees
VSTOL	very short takeoff and landing

6

Cantab	of Cambridge
Messrs	Messieurs
Ofsted	Office for Standards in Education
UNESCO	United Nations Educational, Scientific and Cultural Organization
UNICEF	United Nations International Children's Emergency Fund

ACTORS/ACTRESSES

An actor
Famous actors and actresses

AN ACTOR

3
ham

4
diva
lead
mime
star

5
extra
lovie

6
luvvie
mummer
player

7
actress
artiste
farceur
starlet
trouper

8
comedian
thespian

9
performer
principal
superstar
tragedian

10
comedienne
improviser
understudy

2+ words
leading lady
leading man
spear-carrier
stand-in

FAMOUS ACTORS AND ACTRESSES

3
Bow (Clara)
Day (Doris)
Eve (Trevor)
Fox
(Emilia/Edward/James/
Michael J.)
Fry (Stephen)
Hay (Will)
Law (Jude)
Lee (Bruce/Christopher)
Lom (Herbert)
Loy (Myrna)
Mix (Tom)
Ray (Aldo)
Rix (Brian)
Roc (Patricia)
Sim (Alastair)

4
Alda (Alan)
Ball (Lucille)
Bara (Theda)
Burr (Raymond)
Caan (James)
Cage (Nicholas)
Chan (Jackie)
Cher
Cobb (Lee J.)
Cole (George)
Cook (Peter)
Dean (James)
Depp (Johnny)
Dors (Diana)
Dunn (Clive)
Ehle (Jennifer)
Faye (Alice)
Ford (Glenn/Harrison)
Gere (Richard)

Gish (Lillian)
Hawn (Goldie)
Hird (Thora)
Holm (Ian)
Hope (Bob)
Hurt (John)
Kaye (Danny)
Kean (Edmund)
Keel (Howard)
Kerr (Deborah)
Ladd (Alan)
Lake (Veronica)
Laye (Evelyn)
Lisi (Verna)
Lowe (Arthur)
Marx
(Chico/Groucho/Harpo)
More (Kenneth)
Muni (Paul)
Page (Geraldine)
Peck (Gregory)
Penn (Sean)
Pitt (Brad)
Raft (George)
Reed (Oliver)
Rees (Angharad)
Reid (Beryl)
Rigg (Diana)
Sher (Anthony)
Soul (David)
Syms (Sylvia)
Thaw (John)
Todd (Richard)
Torn (Rip)
Tree (Sir Herbert
Beerbohm)
West
(Mae/Sam/Timothy)
Wray (Faye)
York (Susannah)

5
Allen (Woody)
Annis (Francesca)
Baker
(Colin/Stanley/Tom)
Bates (Alan)
Bloom (Claire)

Bolam (James)
Booth (Edwin)
Boyer (Charles)
Burke (Kathy)
Caine (Michael)
Caron (Leslie)
Clift (Montgomery)
Close (Glenn)
Conti (Tom)
Cosby (Bill)
Cross (Ben)
Crowe (Russell)
Damon (Matt)
Dance (Charles)
Davis (Bette)
Dench (Judi)
Derek (Bo)
Donat (Robert)
Evans (Edith)
Finch (Peter)
Flynn (Errol)
Fonda (Henry/Jane/Peter)
Gable (Clark)
Gabor (Zsa Zsa)
Garbo (Greta)
Grant
(Cary/Hugh/Richard E.)
Greco (Juliette)
Gwynn (Nell)
Hanks (Tom)
Hardy (Oliver/Robert)
Hawes (Keeley)
Hodge (Patricia)
Ifans (Rhys)
Imrie (Celia)
Irons (Jeremy)
Johns (Glynis/Mervyn)
Keith (Penelope)
Kelly (Grace)
Kline (Kevin)
Lange (Jessica)
Leigh (Janet/Vivien)
Lloyd (Harold)
Loren (Sophia)
Lorre (Peter)
Madoc (Philip)
Mason (James)
Miles (Bernard/Sarah)

Mills (John)
Moore
(Demi/Dudley/Roger)
Nimoy (Leonard)
Niven (David)
Nolte (Nick)
Novak (Kim)
O'Neal (Ryan/Tatum)
Power (Tyrone)
Pryce (Jonathan)
Quick (Diana)
Quinn (Anthony)
Segal (George)
Smith (Maggie)
Stamp (Terence)
Tandy (Jessica)
Terry (Ellen)
Topol
Tracy (Spencer)
Tutin (Dorothy)
Wayne (John)
Welch (Raquel)

6

Alleyn (Edward)
Atkins (Eileen)
Bacall (Lauren)
Bannen (Ian)
Bardot (Bridget)
Beatty (Warren)
Bergen (Candice)
Bisset (Jacqueline)
Bogart (Humphrey)
Brando (Marlon)
Briers (Richard)
Bujold (Genevieve)
Burton (Richard)
Cagney (James)
Callow (Simon)
Carrey (Jim)
Chaney (Lon)
Cleese (John)
Coburn (James)
Cooper (Gary/Gladys)
Cotton (Joseph)
Cruise (Tom)
Curtis (Jamie Lee/Tony)
Dalton (Timothy)

Durbin (Deanna)
Ekberg (Anita)
Ekland (Britt)
Farrow (Mia)
Fields (Gracie/W.C.)
Finlay (Frank)
Finney (Albert)
Foster (Jodie)
French (Dawn)
Gambon (Michael)
Garson (Greer)
Gaynor (Mitzi)
Grable (Betty)
Harlow (Jean)
Harris (Richard)
Havers (Nigel)
Hedren (Tippi)
Heston (Charlton)
Hiller (Wendy)
Howard (Leslie/Trevor)
Hudson (Rock)
Hunter (Tab)
Irving (Henry)
Jacobi (Derek)
Keaton (Buster/Diane)
Keitel (Harvey)
Kemble (John)
Kendal (Felicity)
Kidman (Nicole)
Lamarr (Hedy)
Lamour (Dorothy)
Laurel (Stan)
Lemmon (Jack)
Lesser (Anton)
Lipman (Maureen)
Lugosi (Bela)
Lumley (Joanna)
Macnee (Patrick)
Malden (Karl)
Mature (Victor)
McEwan (Geraldine)
McKern (Leo)
Merman (Ethel)
Midler (Bette)
Mirren (Helen)
Monroe (Marilyn)
Moreau (Jeanne)
Morley (Robert)

Mostel (Zero)
Murphy (Eddie)
Neagle (Anna)
Neeson (Liam)
Newman (Paul)
Oberon (Merle)
O'Toole (Peter)
Pacino (Al)
Porter (Eric)
Quayle (Anthony)
Reagan (Ronald)
Robson (Flora)
Rogers
(Ginger/Roy/Will)
Rooney (Mickey)
Sallis (Peter)
Scales (Prunella)
Sharif (Omar)
Sinden (Donald)
Snipes (Wesley)
Spacek (Sissy)
Streep (Meryl)
Suchet (David)
Suzman (Janet)
Swayze (Patrick)
Taylor (Elizabeth)
Temple (Shirley)
Turner (Kathleen)
Voight (John)
Warner (David)
Weaver (Sigourney)
Welles (Orson)
Wilder (Gene)
Winger (Debra)
Wolfit (Donald)

7

Ackland (Joss)
Agutter (Jenny)
Andrews (Julie)
Astaire (Fred)
Bennett (Hywel)
Bergman (Ingrid)
Blakely (Colin)
Blessed (Brian)
Bogarde (Dirk)
Branagh (Kenneth)
Bridges (Beau/Jeff/Lloyd)

Bronson (Charles)
Brynner (Yul)
Burbage (Richard)
Calvert (Phyllis)
Chaplin
(Charles/Geraldine)
Colbert (Claudette)
Collins (Joan)
Connery (Sean)
Costner (Kevin)
Cushing (Peter)
Douglas (Kirk/Michael)
Fricker (Brenda)
Gardner (Ava)
Garland (Judy)
Garrick (David)
Gielgud (John)
Gingold (Hermione)
Gleason (Jackie)
Goddard (Paulette)
Granger (Stewart)
Hancock (Sheila/Tony)
Hawkins (Jack)
Hayward (Susan)
Hepburn
(Audrey/Katharine)
Hoffman (Dustin)
Hopkins (Anthony)
Hordern (Michael)
Hoskins (Bob)
Houston (Donald/Glyn)
Jackson (Barry/Glenda)
Jacques (Hattie)
Johnson (Celia)
Karloff (Boris)
Kendall (Kay)
Langtry (Lily)
Lombard (Carol)
Madonna
McCowen (Alec)
McQueen (Steve)
Milland (Ray)
Nettles (John)
Olivier (Laurence)
Perkins (Anthony)
Pertwee (Bill/John)
Plummer (Christopher)
Poitier (Sidney)

Redford (Robert)
Robards (Jason)
Roberts (Julia/Rachel)
Robeson (Paul)
Roscius
Sellers (Peter)
Shatner (William)
Shearer (Moira)
Siddons (Sarah)
Simmons (Jean)
Steiger (Rod)
Stewart (James)
Swanson (Gloria)
Ullmann (Liv)
Ustinov (Peter)
Walters (Julie)
Windsor (Barbara)
Winters (Shelley)
Withers (Googie)

8

Ashcroft (Peggy)
Bancroft (Anne)
Bankhead (Tallulah)
Basehart (Richard)
Basinger (Kim)
Blackman (Honor)
Campbell (Mrs Patrick)
Christie (Julie)
Crawford (Joan)
Dietrich (Marlene)
Dreyfuss (Richard)
Eastwood (Clint)
Fontaine (Joan)
Grenfell (Joyce)
Griffith (Hugh/Kenneth)
Guinness (Alec)
Harrison (Rex)
Hayworth (Rita)
Lansbury (Angela)
Laughton (Charles)
Lawrence (Gertrude)
Lockwood (Margaret)
Maclaine (Shirley)
McGregor (Ewan)
McKellen (Ian)
Mercouri (Melina)
Minelli (Lisa)

Phillips (Siân)
Pickford (Mary)
Redgrave
(Corin/Lynn/Michael/
Vanessa)
Reynolds (Debbie)
Robinson (Edward G.)
Scofield (Paul)
Stanwyck (Barbara)
Stephens (Robert)
Stallone (Sylvester)
Thompson (Emma)
Whitelaw (Billie)
Williams
(Emlyn/Kenneth/Robin)
Woodward
(Edward/Joanna)

9
Barrymore
(Ethel/John/Lionel)
Bernhardt (Sarah)
Betterton (Thomas)
Cardinale (Claudia)

Courtenay (Tom)
Depardieu (Gérard)
Fairbanks (Douglas)
Greenwood (Joan)
Hampshire (Susan)
Knightley (Keira)
Lancaster (Burt)
Mansfield (Jayne)
Nicholson (Jack)
Pleasence
(Angela/Donald)
Plowright (Joan)
Stevenson (Juliet)
Streisand (Barbra)
Thorndike (Dame Sybil)
Troughton
(Michael/Patrick)
Valentino (Rudolph)
Wanamaker (Sam/Zoe)
Waterston (Sam)

10
Carmichael (Ian)
Lanchester (Elsa)

Richardson
(Ian/Miranda/Ralph)
Rutherford (Margaret)
Sutherland (Donald)
Tushingham (Rita)
Woffington (Peg)
Zetterling (Mai)

11
Courtneidge (Cicely)
Mastroianni (Marcello)

12
Attenborough (Richard)

2+ words
De Niro (Robert)
De Vito (Danny)
Le Mesurier (John)
Zeta-Jones (Catherine)

AFRICA/AFRICAN

African animals
African cities
African countries
African rivers

AFRICAN ANIMALS

3
ape
bok
gnu

4
buck
ibex
kudu
lion
oryx

5
camel
civet
eland
hippo
hyena
hyrax
lemur
nyala
okapi
oribi
rhino

6
baboon
dassie
dik-dik
duiker
gerbil
impala
inyala
jackal
jerboa
koodoo
monkey
reebok

7
blesbok
buffalo
cheetah
gazelle
gemsbok
giraffe
gorilla
leopard
lioness
meerkat
warthog

8
aardvark
aardwolf
anteater
antelope
bontebok
bushbaby
bushbuck
elephant
mandrill
reedbuck
steinbok

9
porcupine
springbok
stonebuck
waterbuck

10
chimpanzee
hartebeest
rhinoceros
wildebeest

12
hippopotamus
klipspringer

AFRICAN CITIES
(* = capital city)

3
Fez (Morocco)

4
Giza (Egypt)
Oran (Algeria)

5
*Abuja (Nigeria)
Aswan (Egypt)
*Cairo (Egypt)
*Dakar (Senegal)
Lagos (Nigeria)
Luxor (Egypt)
*Rabat (Morocco)

6
*Asmara (Eritrea)
*Bamako (Mali)
*Banjul (Gambia)
*Bissau (Guinea-Bissau)
*Dodoma (Tanzania)
Durban (South Africa)
*Harare (Zimbabwe)
*Luanda (Angola)
*Lusaka (Zambia)
*Malabo (Equatorial
Guinea)
*Maputo (Mozambique)
*Maseru (Lesotho)
*Niamey (Niger)
Soweto (South Africa)
Tobruk (Libya)

7
Abidjan (Ivory Coast)
*Algiers (Algeria)
*Conakry (Guinea)
*Cotonou (Benin)
*Mbababne (Swaziland)
Mansura (Egypt)
Memphis (Egypt)
Mombasa (Kenya)
*Nairobi (Kenya)
Tangier (Morocco)
*Tripoli (Libya)
*Yaoundé (Cameroun)

8
Bulawayo (Zimbabwe)
*Djibouti (Djibouti)

*Freetown (Sierra Leone)
*Gaborone (Botswana)
Ismailia (Egypt)
*Khartoum (Sudan)
*Kinshasa (Congo)
*Lilongwe (Malawi)
*Monrovia (Liberia)
*N'Djamena (Chad)
*Pretoria (South Africa)
Timbuktu (Mali)
Tangier (Morocco)

9
Bujumbura (Burundi)
Kimberley (South Africa)
Ladysmith (South Africa)
Marrakesh (Morocco)
*Mogadishu (Somalia)

10
Casablanca (Morocco)
*Libreville (Gabon)
Tananarive (Madagascar)

11
*Brazzaville (Congo)
Grahamstown (South Africa)

12
*Antananarivo (Madagascar)
Bloemfontein (South Africa)
Johannesburg (South Africa)

2+ words
*Addis Ababa (Ethiopia)
Cape Town (South Africa)
Dar es Salaam (Tanzania)
*Port Louis (Mauritius)
Port Said (Egypt)

AFRICAN COUNTRIES

4
Chad
Mali
Togo

5
Benin
Congo
Egypt
Gabon
Ghana
Kenya
Libya
Niger
Sudan

6
Angola
Gambia
Malawi
Rwanda
Uganda
Zambia

7
Algeria
Burundi
Eritrea
Lesotho
Liberia
Morocco
Namibia
Nigeria
Tunisia

8
Botswana
Cameroon
Djibouti
Ethiopia
Tanzania
Zimbabwe

9
Mauritius
Swaziland

10
Madagascar
Mauritania
Mozambique

2+ words
Burkina Faso
Cote d'Ivoire
Ivory Coast
Sierra Leone
South Africa

AFRICAN RIVERS

3
Hex
Kwa

4
Mooi
Nile
Prah
Vaal

5
Blood (River)
Congo
Habra
Kafue
Kowie
Niger
Shire
Volta
Welle
Zaire

6
Atbara
Gambia
Grande
Kagera
Kwanza
Lomami
Modder
Ogowai
Orange
Pungwe
Sunday

Tugela
Zontag

7
Buffalo
Calabar
Gamtoos
Gauritz
Kubango
Limpopo
Lualaba
Luangwa
Lugendi

Muluyar
Olifant
Sankuru
Semliki
Senegal
Zambezi

8
Gallinas
Itimbiri
Umvolosi

9
Crocodile
Umsimkulu
Umsimvubu

2+ words
Blue Nile
Great Kei
Great Fish
White Nile

AGRICULTURE

Terms used in agriculture

3

ark
awn
bin
BSE
cob
cod
cow
cub
dig
dip
ear
ewe
feu
hay
hip
hoe
hog
kex
kid
kip
lea
moo
mow
nye
pig
pip
ram
ret
run
rye
sow
ted
teg
tup
vat
vet

4

akee
arid
bale
barn
beam

beef
bent
boon
bran
bull
byre
calf
cart
clay
corn
cote
crib
crop
culm
curb
drey
dung
farm
flax
foal
fold
gait
gape
gate
grow
halm
harl
herd
hide
hind
holt
hoof
hops
hull
husk
kine
lamb
lime
loam
lyme
malm
mare
marl
mead
meal
milk
muck
neat

neep
nide
nowt
oast
oats
peat
pest
plot
pone
rabi
ragi
rake
rape
reap
rear
rick
rime
root
roup
runt
rust
ryot
sand
scab
seed
sere
shaw
silo
skep
sock
soil
soya
span
stot
stud
teff
toft
udal
vale
weed
wold
yean
zebu

5

aphid
baler
beans

biddy
borax
bosky
bothy
braxy
breed
calve
carse
cavie
chaff
churn
couch
croft
crone
crops
dairy
ditch
drill
drove
durra
ergot
farcy
field
fruit
fungi
glean
glebe
glume
grain
grass
graze
guano
halfa
hards
haugh
haulm
hedge
hilum
horse
humus
hutch
kulak
lande
llano
lobby
maize
mower
mummy

ovine
plant
raise
ranch
rumen
sheaf
shear
sheep
shoat
shote
shuck
spelt
spuds
stack
stall
stead
stock
stook
straw
swill
tilth
tithe
tuber
veldt
vimen
vomer
wagon
wheat
withe
withy
worms
yield

6
aerate
angora
animal
arable
arista
barley
basset
beeves
binder
bosket
bottle
butter
cattle
cereal

clover
colter
corral
cowman
cratch
cutter
digger
disbud
dobbin
drover
earing
eatage
ecurie
estate
fallow
farina
farmer
fodder
forage
furrow
garget
garlic
garner
garron
gather
gaucho
gluten
grains
grange
grower
harrow
heifer
hogget
hogsty
hopper
huller
hurdle
incult
inning
inspan
intine
linhay
llanos
manger
manure
mawkin
mealie
merino

milker
millet
mowing
nubbin
pampas
piglet
pigsty
plough
podzol
polder
porker
potato
punnet
raggee
rancho
reaper
roller
scythe
sheave
sickle
silage
slurry
socage
sowing
spread
spring
spruit
stable
steppe
stover
swathe
tiller
trough
turnip
turves
warble
weevil
yeoman

7
acidity
acreage
alfalfa
anthrax
binding
boscage
breeder
budding

bullock
buttery
cabbage
calving
combine
compost
coppice
coulter
cowherd
cowshed
crofter
demesne
digging
dipping
docking
drought
droving
eanling
erosion
farming
fencing
fertile
foaling
foldage
forcing
granger
grazier
grazing
harvest
hedging
herding
hogcote
holding
hunkers
implant
infield
innings
kibbutz
kidding
kolkholz
lambing
laniary
lucerne
marlite
milking
multure
murrain
organic

nursery
paddock
panicle
pannage
pasture
peonage
piggery
pinetum
pinfold
planter
polders
popcorn
poultry
prairie
praties
predial
pruning
pulping
pummace
radicel
raking
rancher
reaping
rearing
retting
rhizome
rundale
rustler
shearer
spancel
stacker
station
stooker
stubble
subsidy
subsoil
swinery
thwaite
tillage
tilling
tractor
trammel
trekker
trotter
vaquero
wagoner
windrow
yardman

8
agronomy
barnyard
branding
breeding
clipping
cropping
ditching
drainage
elevator
ensilage
farmyard
forestry
gleaning
grafting
hacienda
hayfield
haymaker
haystack
henhouse
haywagon
hopfield
irrigate
kohlrabi
landgirl
loosebox
milkcart
pedigree
praedial
rootcrop
rotation
shearing
vineyard
watering
wireworm

9
agrimotor
allotment
cornfield
cultivate

dairymaid
enclosure
farmhouse
farmstead
fertility
fungicide
gathering
grassland
harrowing
harvester
haymaking
horserake
husbandry
implement
incubator
livestock
pasturage
penthouse
phosphate
pitchfork
ploughing
screening
separator
shorthorn
swineherd
thrashing
threshing
trenching
winnowing

10
agronomist
cultivator
fertilizer (fertiliser)
harvesting
husbandman
irrigation
plantation
transplant
weedkiller
wheatfield

11
agriculture
cultivation
fertilizing (fertilising)
germination
insecticide
pastureland
reclamation

12
agribusiness
agricultural
fermentation
horticulture
insemination
smallholding

2+ words
battery hen
cattle cake
dairy farm
disc drill
feeding stock
fee-tail
foot rot
hay cart
hay rick
hop pole
market garden
milk can
motor plough
mould board
pig swill
poultry farm
rice field
rounding up
self-binder
set aside
sheep dip
stock taking
sugar beet
sugar cane
water trough
weed control

AIRCRAFT

Types and makes of aircraft
Parts of an aircraft
Crew of an aircraft
See also **AIR TRAVEL**

TYPES AND MAKES OF AIRCRAFT

3
jet
Mig
UFO

4
Avro
kite
STOL
VTOL

5
blimp
Comet
crate
jumbo
plane
Stuka

6
Airbus
Boeing
bomber
Cessna
Dakota
fanjet
Fokker
glider
Mirage
Nimrod
ramjet
rocket
tanker
Victor
Vulcan

7
airship
balloon
biplane
chopper
Dornier
Douglas
fighter
Harrier
Junkers
Mustang
Tornado
Trident
Tristar
trainer
Tupolev
twinjet
Typhoon
Valiant

8
airliner
autogyro
Catalina
Concorde
Hercules
Ilyushin
jetplane
Lockheed
Mosquito
seaplane
Spitfire
triplane
turbofan
turbojet
Vanguard
Viscount
warplane
zeppelin

9
aeroplane
dirigible
Hurricane
Lancaster
Liberator
Lightning
microlite

monoplane
spaceship
turboprop

10
helicopter
hovercraft
microlight
Shackleton
spacecraft
Sunderland

11
interceptor

13
Messerschmidt

2+ words
dive-bomber
delta-wing
fighter bomber
flying boat
Flying Fortress
hang-glider
jet fighter
jumbo jet
jump-jet
stealth bomber
stealth fighter
swing-wing
Tiger Moth

PARTS OF AN AIRCRAFT

3
fin
pod
rib

4
flap
hold
hull
nose
prop
wing

5
cabin
chock
flaps
float
frame
pylon
strut

6
basket
canopy
de-icer
elevon
engine
floats
galley
gasbag
intake
piston
rudder

7
aileron
airfoil
blister
cockpit
cowling
fairing
gondola
nacelle
trimtab
wingtip

8
aerofoil
airframe
airscrew
elevator
fuselage
joystick
longeron
throttle

9
altimeter
autopilot
empennage
propeller
tailplane

10
stabilizer

11
afterburner

14
undercarriage

2+ words
aero-engine
black box
ejector seat
flight deck
landing gear
tail fin

CREW OF AN AIRCRAFT

5
flier
flyer
pilot

6
airman

7
aircrew
co-pilot
steward

8
aeronaut
aviatrix

9
navigator

10
balloonist
stewardess

2+ words
air hostess
air steward
flight attendant
ground crew
test pilot

AIR TRAVEL

Airlines
Airports
Terms connected with air
travel and flying

AIRLINES

2
BA (UK)

3
BEA (UK)
CSA (Czech)
JAL (Japan)
JAT (Yugoslavia)
KLM (Holland)
LAN (Chile)
LAP (Paraguay)
LOT (Poland)
PIA (Pakistan)
SAA (South Africa)
SAS (Scandinavia)
SIA (Singapore)
TAP (Port)
THY (Turkey)
TWA (USA)
UAL (USA)
UTA (France)

4
BOAC (UK)

5
Delta (US)
FlyBe (UK)
Varig (Brazil)
Viasa (Venezuela)

6
Brymon (UK)
Iberia (Spain)
Qantus (Australia)
Sabena (Belgium)
Virgin (UK)

7
Braniff (US)
Finnair (Finland)
Olympic (Greece)
Ryanair (Ireland)

8
Aeroflot (Russia)
Alitalia (Italy)
EasyJet (Europe)
Emirates (UAE)
Swissair (Switzerland)

9
Britannia (UK)
Lufthansa (Germany)

2+ words
Aer Lingus (Ireland)
El Al (Israel)
Pan Am (US)

AIRPORTS

3
JFK (New York)

4
Dyce (Aberdeen)
Hurn (Bournemouth)
Luqa (Malta)
Lydd (Kent)
Orly (Paris)
Riem (Munich)
Seeb (Oman)

5
Kimpo (Seoul)
Logan (Boston)
Lungi (Freetown)
Luton
Luzon (Manila)
Mahon (Minorca)
O'Hare (Chicago)
Palam (Delhi)
Palma (Majorca)
Tegel (Berlin)

6
Changi (Singapore)
Deurne (Antwerp)
Dorval (Montreal)
Dulles (Washington)
Elmdon (Birmingham)
Ezeiza (Buenos Aires)
Filton (Bristol)
Findel (Luxembourg)
Gander (Newfoundland)
Haneda (Tokyo)
Juárez (Mexico City)
Kloten (Zürich)
Narita (Tokyo)
Lennon (John Lennon,
Liverpool)
Newark (New Jersey)
Okecie (Warsaw)
Subang (Kuala Lumpur)
Vantaa (Helsinki)

7
Arlanda (Stockholm)
Ataturk (Istanbul)
Athinai (Athens)
Barajas (Madrid)
Fornebu (Oslo)
Gatwick (London)
Kastrup (Copenhagen)
Kennedy (New York)
Larnaca (Cyprus)
Lyneham (Wilts)
Manston (Kent)
Mirabel (Montreal)
Ringway (Manchester)

8
Cointrin (Geneva)
Heathrow (London)
Hongqaio (Shanghai)
Leuchars (St Andrews)
Lulsgate (Bristol)
Malpensa (Milan)
Mehrabad (Teheran)
Prestwick (Ayr)
Rongotai (Wellington)
Schiphol (Amsterdam)
Stansted (Essex)

Thruxton (Andover)

9
Cranfield (Beds)
Downsview (Toronto)
Eastleigh (Southampton)
Fiumicino (Rome)
Schwechat (Vienna)
Templehof (Verlin)
Yeovilton (RAF,
Somerset)

10
Aldergrove (Belfast)
Hartsfield (Atlanta)
Hellenikon (Athens)
Ronaldsway (Isle of
Man)
Schonefeld (Berlin)
Tullmarine (Melbourne)

11
Fühlsbüttel (Hamburg)

12
Echterdingen (Stuttgart)
Metropolitan (Detroit)
Sheremetyevo (Moscow)

2+ words
Ben Gurion (Tel Aviv)
Benito Juárez (Mexico
City)
Biggin Hill (RAF, Kent)
Brize Norton (RAF,
Oxford)
Charles de Gaulle (Paris)
Dum Dum (Calcutta)
La Guardia (New York)
Le Bourget (Paris)
Le Touquet (Paris)
Marco Polo (Venice)

**TERMS CONNECTED WITH
AIR TRAVEL AND FLYING**

3
yaw

4
APEX
bank
buzz
dive
drag
kite
knot
land
lift
loop
roll
slip
slot
spin
taxi

5
apron
chock
crash
ditch
glide
pilot
plane
radar
stall
stunt

6
beacon
cruise
flight
ground
hangar
hijack
jetlag
refuel
runway

7
aircrew
airdrop
airlift
airline
airmiss
airport
airsick
airside
aviator
ballast
ceiling
charter
contact
descent
flyover
flypast
gliding
landing
pancake
payload
ripcord
retract
skyjack
take-off
taxiing

8
airborne
airfield
airspeed
altitude
approach
aviation
carousel
clearway
cruising
grounded
headwind
heliport
hijacker
landside
nosedive
pitching
seatbelt
sideslip
squadron

stopover
subsonic
tailwind
terminal
windsock

9
airworthy
jetlagged
overshoot
parachute
skywriter

10
aerobatics
aeronautic
airfreight
pressurize (pressurise)
slipstream
supersonic
turbulence

11
aeronautics
airsickness
parachutist
pressurized
retractable

12
airfreighter
depressurize
hedgehopping

2+ words
air lane
air pocket
barrel roll
bird strike
check-in
club class
control tower
co-pilot

crash landing
flight path
flight plan
flying speed
ground speed
in-flight
long-haul
mach number
short-haul
take off
touch down
vapour trail
victory roll

ALPHABETS

Letters of the Arabic alphabet
Letters of the Greek alphabet
Letters of the Hebrew alphabet
The phonetic alphabet

LETTERS OF THE ARABIC ALPHABET

2
ba
fa
ha
ra
ta
ya
za

3
ayn
dad
dai
jim
kaf
kha
lam
mim
nun
qaf
sad
sin
tha
waw
zay

4
alif
dhai
shin

5
ghayn

LETTERS OF THE GREEK ALPHABET

2
mu
nu
pi
xi

3
chi
eta
phi
psi
rho
tau

4
beta
iota
zeta

5
alpha
delta
gamma
kappa
omega
sigma
theta

6
lambda

7
epsilon
omicron
upsilon

LETTERS OF THE HEBREW ALPHABET

2
he
pa

3
ain
jod
mem
nun
tau
yod

4
ayin
beth
caph
heth
kaph
koph
resh
shin
teth
vain
zade

5
aleph
cheth
gimel
lamed
schin
zayin

6
daleth
samech
samekh
tzaddi

THE PHONETIC ALPHABET

A = ALPHA
B = BRAVO
C = CHARLIE
D = DELTA
E = ECHO
F = FOXTROT
G = GOLF

H = HOTEL
I = INDIA
J = JULIET
K = KILO
M = MIKE
N = NOVEMBER
O = OSCAR
P = PAPA
Q = QUEBEC
R = ROMEO

S = SIERRA
T = TANGO
U = UNIFORM
V = VICTOR
X = XRAY
Y = YANKEE
Z = ZULU

AMERICA/ AMERICAN

American English
American artists, authors,
architects and composers
American Indians (Native
Americans)
Countries of North and
South America
See also **CANADA/ CANADIAN, USA**

See also **CANADA/ CANADIAN, USA**

AMERICAN ENGLISH

Common terms in American English (with British equivalents in brackets)

3
car (carriage on train)
gas (petrol)
gum (glue)
Inc (plc)
mad (angry)
tab (bill, e.g. at restaurant)
tux (dinner jacket)

4
buck (dollar)
cart (trolley (e.g. in supermarket)
curb (kerb)
deck (pack of cards)
fall (autumn)
hood (bonnet of car)
mail (post)
math (maths)
robe (dressing gown)
soda (soft drink, fizzy drink)
vest (waistcoat)
yard (garden)

5
broil (grill)

candy (sweets)
check (bill, cheque)
chips (potato crisps)
diner (café, small restaurant)
flunk (fail)
fries (potato chips)
gizmo (gadget)
grade (mark)
ground (minced)
gumbo (type of stew)
jello (jelly)
jelly (jam)
movie (film)
pants (trousers)
purse (handbag)
shade (blind)
store (shop)
trash (rubbish)
truck (lorry)
trunk (boot of car)

6
casket (coffin)
closet (wardrobe)
cookie (biscuit)
diaper (nappy)
duplex (semi-detached house)
eraser (rubber)
faucet (tap)
fender (bumper)
gurney (hospital trolley)
period (full stop)
recess (playtime, break at school)
résumé (CV)
rubber (condom)
subway (underground)
teller (cashier)
tuxedo (dinner jacket)
wrench (spanner)

7
beltway (ringroad)
freeway (motorway)
garbage (rubbish)
highway (main road)

janitor (caretaker)
mailman (postman)
muffler (silencer on car)
oatmeal (porridge)
panties (knickers)
realtor (estate agent)
sneaker (trainer, plimsoll)
sweater (jumper, pullover)
takeout (takeaway)
trailer (caravan)
transit (public transport)

8
aluminum (aluminium)
barrette (hair slide)
bathrobe (dressing gown)
bathroom (toilet)
checkers (draughts)
downtown (town centre)
dumpster (skip)
eggplant (aubergine)
elevator (lift)
flapjack (pancake)
frosting (icing)
galoshes (Wellington boots)
gasoline (petrol)
pacifier (baby's dummy)
popsicle (ice lolly)
railroad (railway)
restroom (toilet)
rutabaga (swede)
scallion (spring onion)
sidewalk (pavement)
streetcar (tram)
vacation (holiday)
zucchini (courgette)

9
apartment (flat)
cellphone (mobile phone)
mortician (undertaker)
principal (headteacher)
thumbtack (drawing pin)

10
interstate (main road)
suspenders (braces)

undershirt (vest)
windshield (windscreen)

2+ words
back-up light (reversing light)
broad jump (long jump)
busy signal (engaged tone)
drug store (chemist's)
fanny pack (bum bag)
French fries (potato chips)
movie theatre (cinema)
tic-tac-toe (noughts and crosses)
trash can (dust bin)
zip code (post code)

AMERICAN ARTISTS, AUTHORS, ARCHITECTS AND COMPOSERS

3
Paz (Octavio, Mexican poet)

4
Agee (James, US novelist and poet)
Baum (L. Frank, US novelist)
Buck (Pearl S., US novelist)
Cage (John, US composer)
Capp (Al, US cartoonist)
Cruz (Juana, Mexican poet)
Hart (Moss, US dramatist)
Kern (Jerome, US composer)
Ives (Charles, US composer)
King (Stephen, US novelist)
Nash (Ogden, US humorist)
Roth (Philip, US novelist)

Tate (Allen, US poet)
West (Benjamin, US painter; Nathaneal, US novelist)

5
Adams (John, US composer)
Albee (Edward, US dramatist)
Barth (John, US novelist)
Benét (Stephen, US novelist and poet)
Crane (Hart, US poet; Stephen, US novelist)
Frost (Robert, US poet)
Glass (Philip, US composer)
Harte (Brett, US short-story writer)
Henry (O., US short-story writer)
Homer (Winslow, US painter)
Jones (LeRoi, US dramatist)
Kesey (Ken, US novelist)
Lewis (Sinclair, US novelist)
Mamet (David, US dramatist)
Moore (Marianne, US poet)
Odets (Clifford, US dramatist)
Plath (Sylvia, US poet and novelist)
Pound (Ezra, US poet)
Reich (Steve, US composer)
Sousa (John Philip, US composer)
Stein (Gertrude, US writer)
Stowe (Harriet Beecher, US novelist)
Twain (Mark, US novelist and humorist)

Wolfe (Thoman, US novelist)

6
Alcott (Louisa M., US novelist)
Atwood (Margaret, Canadian poet and novelist)
Barber (Samuel, US composer)
Bellow (Saul, US novelist)
Bierce (Ambrose, US writer)
Borges (Jorge Luis, Argentinian writer)
Bryant (William Cullens, US poet)
Calder (Alexander, US sculptor)
Capote (Truman, US novelist)
Carter (Elliott, US composer)
Cooper (James Fenimore, US novelist)
Fuller (Richard Buckminster, US architect)
Harris (Joel Chandler, US novelist; Roy, US composer)
Heller (Joseph, US novelist)
Holmes (Oliver Wendell, US essayist)
Irving (Washington, US short-story writer)
London (Jack, US novelist)
Lowell (Amy/James Russell/Robert, US poets)
Mailer (Norman, US novelist)
Millay (Edna St Vincent, US poet)
Miller (Arthur, US dramatist/Henry,

US novelist)
Neruda (Pablo, Chilean poet)
O'Neill (Eugene, US dramatist)
Parker (Dorothy, US humorist)
Piston (Walter, US composer)
Porter (Cole, US composer/Katherine Anne, US short-story writer)
Previn (André, US composer)
Ransom (John Crowe, US poet)
Rivera (Diego, Mexican painter)
Runyon (Damon, US humorist)
Singer (Isaac Bashevis, US novelist)
Thurber (James, US humorist)
Updike (John, US novelist)
Warhol (Andy, US painter)
Wilder (Thornton, US dramatist)
Wilson (Edmund, US critic)
Wright (Richard, US novelist)

7
Allende (Isabel, Chilean novelist)
Baldwin (James, US novelist)
Copland (Aaron Cole, US composer
Dreiser (Theodore, US novelist)
Emerson (Ralph Waldo, US philosopher and poet)
Grisham (John,

US novelist)
Hellman (Lillian, US dramatist)
Jeffers (Robinson, US poet)
Kaufman (George S., US dramatist)
Leacock (Stephen, Canadian humorist)
Lindsay (Vachel, US poet)
Menotti (Gian Carlo, US composer)
Nabokov (Vladimir, US novelist)
O'Keeffe (Georgia, US painter)
Pollock (Jackson, US painter)
Pynchon (Thomas, US novelist)
Sargent (John Singer, US painter)
Saroyan (William, US writer)
Stevens (Wallace, US poet)
Wharton (Edith, US novelist)
Whitman (Walt, US poet)

8
Anderson (Sherwood, US writer)
Bradbury (Ray, US novelist)
Chandler (Raymond, US novelist)
cummings (e.e., US poet)
Faulkner (William, US novelist)
Ginsberg (Allen, US poet)
Macleish (Archibald, US poet)
Marquand (J.P., US novelist)
McCarthy (Mary, US novelist)
Melville (Herman,

US novelist)
Mitchell (Margaret, US novelist)
Perelman (S.J. US humorist)
Salinger (J.D., US novelist)
Sandburg (Carl, US poet)
Sinclair (Upton, US novelist)
Spillane (Mickey, US novelist)
Vonnegut (Kurt, US novelist)
Whistler (James McNeill, US painter)
Williams (Tennessee, US dramatist/William Carlos, US poet)

9
Bernstein (Leonard, US composer)
Burroughs (Edgar Rice/William, US novelists)
Dickinson (Emily, US poet)
Feininger (Lyonel, US painter)
Hawthorne (Nathaniel, US novelist)
Hemingway (Ernest, US novelist)
Highsmith (Patricia, US novelist)
McCullers (Carson, US novelist)
Steinbeck (John, US novelist)

10
Fitzgerald (F. Scott, US novelist)
Longfellow (Henry Wadsworth, US poet)

AMERICAN INDIANS

3
Fox
Ute
Wea

4
Cree
Crow
Hopi
Hupa
Inca
Iowa
Maya
Sauk
Tupi
Zuni

5
Adena
Aztec
Caddo
Creek
Haida
Huron
Incas
Kaika
Kaska
Miami
Nazca
Omaha
Osage
Ponca
Sioux
Slave
Teton
Yaqui
Yurok

6
Abnaki
Apache
Apinai
Atoara
Cayuga
Dakota
Dogrib

Kayapo
Lenape
Mandan
Micmac
Mixtec
Mohave
Mohawk
Mojave
Navajo
Nootka
Ojiba
Pneida
Ottawa
Paiute
Pawnee
Quapaw
Salish
Santee
Seneca
Tanana
Toltec
Yakama

7
Arapaho
Araucan
Arikari
Beothuk
Catawba
Chinook
Choctaw
Choktaw
Hidatsa
Ingalik
Kutchin
Natchez
Quechua
Shawnee
Shuswap
Tlingit
Wichita
Wyandot
Zapotec

8
Cherokee
Cheyenne
Comanche

Delaware
Illinois
Iroquois
Kickapoo
Mesquito
Okanogan
Onondaga
Powhatan
Puebloan
Seminole
Shoshone
Sihasapa

9
Algonquin
Blackfoot
Chickasaw
Chipewyan
Chippeway
Menominee
Penobscot
Tahagmiut
Tillamook
Tsishian
Tuscarora
Winnebago

10
Algonquian
Kaviagmiut
Potawatomi

COUNTRIES OF NORTH AND SOUTH AMERICA AND THE CARIBBEAN

3
USA

4
Cuba
Peru

5
Chile
Haiti

6
Belize
Brazil
Canada
Guyana
Mexico
Panama
Tobago

7
Antigua
Bahamas
Bermuda
Bolivia
Ecuador
Jamaica
Uruguay

8
Barbados
Colombia
Dominica
Honduras
Paraguay

9
Argentina
Argentine
Guatemala
Nicaragua
Venezuela

10
Martinique
Montserrat

2+ words
Costa Rica
El Salvador

ANIMALS

Animals
Groups of animals
Homes of animals
Male and female animals
Parts of an animal's or
bird's body
The young of animals
See also **BIRD, FISH,**
INSECT, SEA, SNAKE

ANIMALS

2
ai
ox
zo

3
ape
ass
bat
bok
cat
cow
doe
dog
elk
ewe
gnu
goa
hog
kob
pig
ram
rat
sow
yak
zho

4
anoa
bear
boar
buck
bull
cavy

coon
deer
euro
eyra
gaur
goat
hare
ibex
kudu
lamb
lion
lynx
mice
mink
mole
mule
musk
orca
oryx
oxen
puma
seal
tahr
vole
wolf
zebu

5
addax
beast
biped
bison
camel
civet
coati
coypu
dhole
dingo
eland
fitch
fossa
gayal
genet
hippo
horse
hyena
hyrax
izard

koala
lemur
llama
manis
manul
moose
mouse
nyala
okapi
oribi
otter
ounce
panda
pekan
rasse
ratel
rhino
sable
sheep
shoat
shrew
skunk
sloth
stirk
stoat
swine
takin
tapir
tiger
urial
whale
zebra

6
agouti
alpaca
angora
aoudad
argali
auroch
baboon
badger
beaver
beluga
bharal
bobcat
cougar
coyote

cuscus
dassie
desman
donkey
dugong
ermine
duiker
fennec
ferret
gerbil
gibbon
gopher
grison
impala
inyala
jackal
jaguar
jerboa
kalong
koodoo
langur
mammal
margay
marmot
marten
monkey
nutria
ocelot
onager
ovibos
possum
rabbit
racoon
reebok
rodent
serval
simian
teledu
tenrec
vervet
vicuna
walrus
wapiti
weasel
wombat

7

aurochs

blesbok
buffalo
caracal
caribou
cattalo
chamois
cheetah
colobus
dasyure
dolphin
echidna
fitchet
fitchew
foumart
gazelle
gemsbok
giraffe
glutton
gorilla
grampus
grizzly
guanaco
hamster
jackass
lemming
leopard
lioness
macaque
mammoth
manatee
markhor
meerkat
miniver
mouflon
muntjak
muskrat
narwhal
nylghau
opossum
panther
peccary
polecat
potoroo
primate
raccoon
sealion
siamang
souslik

sunbear
tamarind
tarsier
wallaby
warthog
wistiti

8

aardvark
aardwolf
anteater
antelope
babirusa
bontebok
bushbaby
bushbuck
cachalot
capybara
chipmunk
dormouse
elephant
hedgehog
kangaroo
kinkajou
mandrill
marmoset
mongoose
musquash
pangolin
platypus
porpoise
reedbuck
reindeer
ruminant
squirrel
steinbok
suricate
talapoin
viscacha

9

armadillo
bandicoot
blackbuck
bunturong
carnivore
catamount
chickaree

dromedary	**10**	**2+ words**
groundhog	chevrotain	dik-dik
herbivore	chimpanzee	fallow deer
omnivore	chinchilla	flying lemur
orang-utan	coatimundi	giant panda
pachyderm	fieldmouse	grizzly bear
padamelon	hartebeest	Kodiak bear
phalanger	rhinoceros	mountain cat
porcupine	wildebeest	mountain lion
pronghorn		polar bear
quadruped	**11**	snow leopard
rearmouse	pipistrelle	water rat
sitatunga		water vole
springbok	**12**	
stonebuck	catamountain	
thylacine	hippopotamus	
tragelaph	klipspringer	
waterbuck		
wolverine		
woodchuck		

GROUPS OF ANIMALS

Collective names for different types of animal

animal	*group*
ants	army, colony
apes	shrewdness
asses	herd, pace
badgers	cete, colony
bears	sloth, sleuth
bees	hive, swarm
bitterns	sedge
boars	herd, sounder, singular
buffalo	herd
cats	clowder, cluster
cattle	drove, herd
choughs	chattering
colts	rag, rake
coots	covert
crows	murder
deer	herd, leash
dogs	kennel, pack
donkeys	herd, pace
doves	dole, dule, flight
ducks	flush (in flight), paddling (on water)
eagles	convocation
elephants	herd

elks	gang
falcons	cast
ferrets	business, fesnying
finches	charm, trembling
fish	school, shoal
foxes	lead, skulk
frogs	army, colony
goats	flock, herd, tribe
geese	gaggle
grouse	covey
gulls	colony
hares	down, leash, husk
herons	sedge, siege
horses	harras, herd, stable
hounds	kennel, pack
jays	band, party
kangaroos	herd, mob, troop
kittens	kindle, litter
lapwings	deceit, desert
larks	exaltation
leopards	leap, lepe
lions	pride
magpies	tiding, tittering
mares	stud
martens	richesse
moles	company, labour
monkeys	cartload, tribe, troop
mules	barren, pack, rake, span
nightingales	watch
otters	bevy, family
owls	parliament, stare
oxen	span, team, yoke
parrots	pandemonium
partridges	covey
peacocks	muster
penguins	colony, rookery
pheasants	bouquet, nye
pigs	herd, sounder
piglets	farrow, litter
plovers	congregation, wing
polecats	chine
porpoises	school
puppies	litter
rabbits	bury, colony
ravens	unkindness
rhinoceroses	crash
rooks	building, parliament, clamour
seals	bob, colony

sheep	drove, flock,fold, trip
snakes	den, nest, pit
starlings	murmuration
swans	wedge
swine	droylt, sounder
teal	coil, knob, raft, spring
thrushes	mutation
tigers	ambush
turkeys	rafter
turtles	dole, dule
wagtails	walk
walruses	herd, pod
whales	gam, herd, pod, school
widgeons	bunch, coil, company, knob
woodpeckers	descent
wolves	pack, rout
zebras	herd

HOMES OF ANIMALS

animal	*home*
badger	earth, set *or* sett
beaver	lodge
bee	hive
bird	nest
cattle	byre, cowshed
eagle	eyrie
fox	burrow, earth
hare	form
heron	heronry
horse	stable
insect eggs	nidus
otter	holt, lodge
penguin	rookery
pig	sty
rabbit	burrow, warren
rook	rookery
seal	rookery
sparrow	colony
squirrel	dray, drey
swan	colony
wild animal	den, lair

MALE AND FEMALE ANIMALS

species	*male*	*female*
antelope	buck	doe
badger	boar	sow
bear	boar	sow
buffalo	bull	cow

species (cont.)	male	female
camel	bull	cow
cat	tom	queen
cattle	bull, steer	cow, heifer
deer	buck, stag	doe, hind
dog	dog	bitch
donkey	jackass	jennyass
elephant	bull	cow
ferret	hob, jack	jill
fox	dog	vixen
goat	billy	nanny
hare	buck	doe
horse	stallion	mare
kangaroo	buck	doe
leopard	leopard	leopardess
lion	lion	lioness
panther	panther	pantheress
pig	boar	sow, gilt
rabbit	buck	doe
seal	buck	doe
sheep	ram, tup	ewe
walrus	bull	cow
weasel	boar	cow
whale	bull	cow
wolf	dog	bitch

PARTS OF AN ANIMAL'S BODY

3
fur
pad
paw

4
barb
beak
bill
claw
coat
frog
hock
hoof
horn
mane
ruff
rump
tail
tusk
wing

5
chine
crest
croup
flank
fleece
pouch
rumen
shank
snout
talon
trunk

6
cloaca
gaskin
gullet
muzzle

7
antlers
crupper
feather
fetlock
gizzard
pastern
whisker
withers

2+ words
hind quarters

THE YOUNG OF ANIMALS

animal	young
antelope	calf
bear	(bear)cub
cat	kitten
dog	pup
	puppy
ferret	kit
fox	(fox)cub
goat	kid
hare	leveret
horse	foal
kangaroo	joey
lion	(lion)cub
seal	pup
sheep	lamb

ARCHITECTURE

Architects
Architectural terms
See also **Building,**
Church

ARCHITECTS

4
Adam (Robert)
Kent (William)
Nash (John)
Shaw (Norman)
Wood (John)
Wren (Christopher)

5
Barry (Charles)
Dance (George)
Gaudi (Antonio)
Gibbs (James)
Jones (Inigo)
Levau (Louis)
Nervi (Pier)
Pugin (Arthur)
Scott (George Gilbert
and Giles Gilbert)
Soane (John)

6
Casson (Hugh)
Foster (Norman)
Paxton (Joseph)
Repton (Humphrey)
Rogers (Richard)
Smirke (Robert)
Spence (Basil)
Street (George)
Wright (Frank Lloyd)

7
Bernini (Lorenzo)
Gropius (Walter)
Latrobe (Benjamin)
Lutyens (Edwin)
Mansard (Francois)
Neumann (Balthazar)

Telford (William)

8
Bramante (Donato)
Jacobsen (Arne)
Palladio (Andrea)
Sullivan (Louis)
Vanbrugh (John)

9
Borromini (Carlo)
Hawksmoor (Nicholas)
Vitruvius

10
Mackintosh (Charles
Rennie)

11
Butterfield (William)
Michelangelo
(Buonarroti)

2+ words
Le Corbusier
van der Rohe (Mies)

ARCHITECTURAL TERMS

3
bar
bay
cap
cob
eye
hip
key

4
apse
arch
band
bead
boss
cowl
dado
dais
dike

dome
door
flag
fret
frog
gate
haha
hall
jamb
lath
lift
lock
loft
mews
moat
mole
nave
nook
ogee
pale
pier
pile
ramp
rink
roof
sash
sill
sink
site
slat
step
stoa
tige
tile
vane
wall
wing
yard

5
aisle
annex
arris
attic
block
brace
brick
court

crown
crypt
Doric
drain
eaves
entry
fence
floor
forum
gable
grout
gully
inlay
Ionic
joint
joist
latch
ledge
lobby
mitre
newel
niche
ogive
order
oriel
paned
panel
patio
plank
pound
putty
quoin
Roman
scape
sewer
shaft
shelf
shell
slate
socle
solar
spire
stack
stage
stair
stall
stand
steps

stone
strut
truss
Tudor
vault
verge

6
abacus
access
alcove
annexe
arbour
arcade
ashlar
atrium
aumbry
batten
belfry
canopy
cellar
cement
chevet
cintre
circus
coigne
column
coping
corbel
corona
coving
crenel
cupola
dagger
dentil
façade
fascia
fillet
finial
flèche
fresco
frieze
garret
gazebo
girder
Gothic
grille
grotto

gutter
header
impost
Ionian
lancet
lierne
lintel
loggia
louver
mantel
merlon
metope
mihrab
mitred
mortar
Norman
parget
paving
perron
plinth
Rococo
soffit
stucco
Tuscan
turret
volute
wattle
wicket
window

7
annulet
archway
balcony
Baroque
bastion
Bauhaus
butment
capital
ceiling
chateau
chevron
chimney
cistern
cornice
crocket
doorway
dovecot

fluting
gallery
gateway
joinery
keyhole
lantern
lattice
lunette
mansard
masonry
minaret
mullion
narthex
noggin
obelisk
pantile
parapet
plaster
portico
postern
pugging
pyramid
Regency
reredos
restore
roofing
rosette
rostrum
roundel
rotunda
scallop
shingle
staging
steeple
tambour
terrace
tracery
transom
trellis
vaulted
viaduct

8
abutment
acanthus
anteroom
baluster
banister

bartizan
basilica
basement
buttress
capstone
caryatid
casement
cincture
concrete
corridor
dovecote
entresol
epistyle
exterior
extrados
fanlight
frontage
fusarole
gargoyle
geodesic
grouting
hoarding
interior
intrados
keystone
kingpost
monument
moulding
orangery
outhouse
overhang
pavement
pavilion
pedestal
pediment
pilaster
restored
skirting
skylight
solarium
spandrel
transept
tympanum
verandah
vignette
wainscot

9
acropolis
aggregate
arabesque
belvedere
Byzantine
campanile
cartouche
colonnade
colosseum
composite
copestone
courtyard
Decorated
embrasure
escalator
fireplace
flagstone
flashings
gatehouse
hypocaust
inglenook
linenfold
mausoleum
mezzanine
oubliette
Palladian
pargeting
parquetry
partition
penthouse
peristyle
refectory
roughcast
rusticate
staircase
stonework
stretcher
triforium
vestibule

10
ambulatory
architrave
balustrade
bargeboard
cantilever
clerestory

Corinthian
drawbridge
foundation
pebbledash
proscenium
Romanesque
rusticated
undercroft

11
castellated
chinoiserie
columbarium
cornerstone
entablature
mantelpiece
Renaissance
restoration
rustication
tessellated
trelliswork

12
amphitheatre
chimneypiece
machicolated
substructure

13
machicolation
Perpendicular
specification

2+ words
Art Deco
bay window
corbel steps
Early English
fan vaulting
half-timbered
geodesic dome
lancet window
mock Tudor
oriel window
rose window
town planning

ART

Art
Terms used in art (the visual arts)
See also **FILM, LITERATURE, MUSIC, PAINTING, SCULPTURE**

5
batik
craft
knack
music
skill

6
method
mosaic
poetry

7
carving
drawing
etching

8
ceramics
painting
tapestry

9
engraving
sculpture
technique

10
literature

11
calligraphy
lithography
photography

3
hue
mat
oil
pen
sit

4
bust
copy
Dada
daub
draw
etch
gild
gilt
halo
icon
ikon
limn
line
nude
oils
show
tint
wash
work

5
batik
block
board
brush
cameo
chalk
craft
curio
draft
drawn
easel
frame
genre
glaze
gloss
grave
hatch

inlay
japan
lines
model
motif
mount
mural
paint
print
salon
scape
shade
smear
stamp
study
tinge
torso
trace
turps
virtu

6
artist
bedaub
canvas
colour
crayon
Cubism
depict
design
doodle
drawer
enamel
etcher
figure
fresco
garret
graven
Gothic
ground
incise
limner
medium
opaque
pastel
patina
plaque
poster

relief
Rococo
school
sculpt
shadow
sitter
sketch
statues
studio
symbol

7
academy
acrylic
aniline
artform
artwork
atelier
aureole
baroque
biscuit
cartoon
carving
collage
contour
Dadaism
Dadaist
daubing
diagram
diptych
drawing
engrave
etching
faience
Fauvism
gallery
gilding
glazing
gouache
graphic
imagism
impasto
lacquer
montage
mordant
moulded
outline
painter

palette
pattern
picture
pigment
plaster
plastic
portray
profile
realism
relieve
replica
remodel
scratch
scumble
shading
sketchy
spatula
stencil
stipple
support
tableau
tempera
texture
thinner
tracing
varnish
viewing
woodcut

8
abstract
academic
aesthete
anaglyph
aquatint
Barbizon
bohemian
ceramic
charcoal
chromism
designer
eggshell
emulsion
engraver
exposure
figurine
fixative
freehand

fretwork
Futurism
Futurist
graffiti
graphics
grouping
handling
hatching
inscribe
likeness
majolica
monotype
monument
mounting
negative
original
ornament
painting
panorama
pastiche
penumbra
portrait
positive
printing
repoussé
sculptor
seascape
sketcher
skyscape
statuary
symmetry
tachism
tapestry
tectonic
tincture
trecento
triptych
vignette

9
aesthetic
appliqué
aquarelle
aquatinta
asymmetry
blackware
blueprint
brushwork

cartridge
cartouche
chinaware
cityscape
cloisonné
colourful
colourist
damascene
enameller
engraving
facsimile
geometric
glassware
gradation
grisaille
grotesque
highlight
indelible
japanning
landscape
lithotint
Mannerism
Mannerist
marquetry
maulstick
mezzotint
miniature
modelling
modernism
modernist
oleograph
painterly
pictorial
portrayal
portrayer
primitive
represent
sculpture
scumbling
stippling
strapwork
symbolism
symbolist
technique
tenebrism
tenebrist
townscape
treatment

woodblock

10
achromatic
aesthetics
anaglyphic
anaglyptic
background
biomorphic
caricature
cerography
classicism
classicist
cloudscape
coloration
decoration
embossment
embroidery
enamelling
exhibition
foreground
illuminate
impression
lithograph
masterwork
mezzotinto
minimalism
minimalist
monochrome
naturalism
paintbrush
pastellist
pencilling
plasticine
plasticity
portcrayon
sculptress
serigraphy
silhouette
sketchbook
Surrealism
Surrealist
terracotta
tessellate
turpentine
waterscape

11
calligraphy
chiaroscuro
chinoiserie
composition
connoisseur
copperplate
draughtsman
eclecticism
enlargement
iconography
illuminator
lithography
marquetry
masterpiece
perspective
photography
picturesque
pointillism
pointillist
portraiture
primitivism
proportions
Renaissance
scenography
watercolour
woodcarving

12
caricaturist
illumination
illustration
lithographer
photographer
photomontage
reproduction

13
Expressionism
Expressionist
Impressionism
Impressionist
postmodernism
postmodernist

2+ words
art deco
art form

Art Nouveau
bas-relief
beaux arts
fine arts
full-length
half-length
lay figure

linseed oil
mock-up
modern art
objet d'art
objet trouvé
old master
Op art

pen and wash
pop art
Pre-Raphaelite
rough copystill life
silk screen
sketch pad
work of art

ARTISTS

See also COMPOSER,
PAINTER,
SCULPTOR, WRITER

2
RA

4
poet

6
Cubist
drawer
etcher
limner
master
writer

7
artiste
Dadaist
maestro
painter

8
composer
designer
musician
novelist
sculptor
virtuoso

9
colourist
craftsman
enameller
performer

10
cartoonist
ceramicist
pastellist

11
academician
draughtsman
entertainer
illuminator
illustrator
miniaturist
portraitist

12
caricaturist

ASIA/ASIAN

COUNTRIES OF ASIA

4
Iran
Iraq
Laos
Oman

5
Burma (Myanmar)
China
India
Japan
Korea (North and South)
Nepal
Qatar
Yemen

6
Bhutan
Brunei
Israel

Jordan
Kuwait
Syria
Taiwan
Turkey

7
Armenia
Bahrain
Georgia
Lebanon
Myanmar (Burma)
Vanuatu
Vietnam

8
Cambodia
Kiribati
Malaysia
Maldives
Mongolia
Pakistan
Thailand

9
Indonesia
Kazakstan
Singapore

10
Azerbaijan
Bangladesh
Kazakhstan
Kyrgyzstan
Tajikistan
Uzbekistan

11
Afghanistan
Philippines

12
Turkmenistan

2+ words
Saudi Arabia
Sri Lanka

ASTRONOMY

Astronomical terminology
Famous astronomers
Names of planets, moons
and asteroids
Signs of the zodiac
Stars
Constellations

ASTRONOMICAL TERMI-
NOLOGY

3
orb
Sol
sun
wax

4
belt
moon
nova
star
wane

5
comet
dwarf
epact
flare
giant
lunar
nadir
orbit
phase
solar
space
umbra

6
apogee
Apollo
astral
aurora
binary
Corona
galaxy

gnomon
lunary
meteor
nebula
octile
parsec
planet
pulsar
quasar
sphere
Viking
waning
waxing
zenith
zodiac

7
Cepheid
cluster
eclipse
equinox
gibbous
nebulae
nebular
perigee
quarter
radiant
sextile
spectra
sputnik
sunspot
transit

8
aerolite
aerolith
almagest
aphelion
asteroid
ecliptic
epicycle
Explorer
latitude
meridian
occulted
parallax
penumbra
quadrant

quartile
quintile
sidereal
solstice
spectrum
spheroid
universe
zodiacal

9
ascendant
ascension
astronomy
astrology
astronaut
celestial
cosmogony
cosmology
cosmonaut
elevation
epicyclic
firmament
longitude
magnitude
meteorite
meteoroid
parhelion
planetary
planetoid
Ptolemaic
reflector
refractor
satellite
starlight
sublunary
supernova
telescope
uranology

10
aberration
astrologer
astronomer
astronomic
atmosphere
brightness
Copernican
discoverer

earthshine
exaltation
opposition
perihelion
precession
prominence
refraction
retrograde
supergiant
trajectory

11
conjunction
declination
observatory
occultation
planetarium
terrestrial

12
astronautics
astrophysics
interstellar
spectroscope

2+ words
Big Bang
black hole
Halley's comet
lunar eclipse
lunar month
lunar probe
Milky Way
minor planet
North Star
Pole Star
red giant
shooting star
solar eclipse
solar flare
solar wind
spiral galaxy
white dwarf

FAMOUS ASTRONOMERS

4
Ryle (Martin)

5
Adams (John Couch)
Brahe (Tycho)
Hoyle (Fred)

6
Halley (Edmund)
Hubble (Edwin)
Lovell (Bernard)
Lowell (Percival)
Kepler (Johann)

7
Galileo (Galilei)
Huygens (Christiaan)
Ptolemy

8
Herschel (William)

9
Flamsteed (John)
Heaviside (Oliver)

10
Copernicus (Nicolaus)

2+ words
Van Allen (James)

***NAMES OF PLANETS,
MOONS AND ASTEROIDS***
*(A) = asteroid (M) = moon
(P) = planet*

2
Io (M)

4
Eros (A)
Hebe (A)
Juno (A)
Mars (P)
Rhea (M)

5
Ariel (M)
Ceres (A)

Dione (M)
Earth (P)
Mimas (M)
Pluto (P/A)
Regel (M)
Rigel (M)
Venus (P)
Vesta (A)

6
Deimos (P)
Europa (M)
Icarus (A)
Oberon (M)
Pallas (A)
Phobos (M)
Phoebe (M)
Saturn (P)
Tethys (M)
Triton (M)
Uranus (P)

7
Iapetis (M)
Jupiter (P)
Mercury (P)
Neptune (P)
Titania (M)
Umbriel (M)

8
Callisto (M)
Ganymede (M)

9
Enceladus (M)

SIGNS OF THE ZODIAC

3
Leo
Ram

4
Bull
Crab
Lion

5
Aries
Goat
Libra
Twins
Virgo

6
Archer
Cancer
Fishes
Gemini
Pisces
Scales
Taurus
Virgin

7
Scorpio

8
Aquarius
Scorpion

9
Capricorn

11
Capricornus
Sagittarius

2+ words
Water Bearer

STARS

4
Mira
Vega

5
Algol
Deneb
Hamal
Rigel
Spica

6
Altair
Castor
Pollux
Shaula
Sirius

7
Antares
Canopus
Capella
Lalande
Polaris
Procyon
Proxima
Regulus

8
Achernar
Arcturus
Denebola

9
Aldebaran
Bellatrix
Fomalhaut

10
Betelgeuse

Constellations

3
Ara
Cup
Leo
Ram

4
Apus
Argo
Bull
Crab
Crow
Crux
Grus
Hare
Lion

Lynx
Lyra
Lyre
Pavo
Swan
Vela
Wolf

5
Aries
Arrow
Cetus
Crane
Draco
Eagle
Hydra
Indus
Lepus
Libra
Mensa
Musca
Norma
Orion
Pyxis
Twins
Virgo

6
Aquila
Archer
Auriga
Bootes
Caelum
Cancer
Carina
Corvus
Crater
Cygnus
Dipper
Dorado
Dragon
Fishes
Fornax
Gemini
Hydrus
Indian
Lizard
Octans

Octant
Persei
Pictor
Pisces
Plough
Puppis
Scales
Scutum
Square
Taurus
Tucana
Virgin
Volans

7
Centaur
Cepheus
Columba
Dolphin
Furnace
Giraffe
Lacerta
Peacock
Pegasus
Perseus
Phoenix
Pleiads
Sagitta
Scorpio
Serpens

Serpent
Sextans
Unicorn

8
Aquarius
Circinus
Equuleus
Eridanus
Hercules
Herdsman
Pleiades
Scorpion
Sculptor
Triangle

9
Andromeda
Capricorn
Centaurus
Chameleon
Compasses
Delphonus
Monoceros
Ophiuchis
Reticulum
Swordfish
Telescope
Vulpecula

10
Atlantides
Cassiopeia
Charioteer
Greyhouds
Microscope
Triangulum
Watersnake

11
Capricornus
Sagittarius
Telescopium

2+ words
Big Dipper
Canis Major
Canis Minor
Charles's Wain
Great Bear
Great Dog
Little Bear
Little Dog
Noah's Dove
Southern Cross
Ursa Major
Ursa Minor

AUSTRALIA/ AUSTRALIAN

Australian animals, birds and plants
Australian towns and cities
Australian words
Famous Australians

AUSTRALIAN ANIMALS, BIRDS AND PLANTS

3
emu (bird)
gum (tree)

4
lory (bird)

5
bilby (animal)
dingo (animal)
galah (bird)
koala (animal)
mulga (shrub)
noddy (bird)

6
brolga (bird)
drongo (bird)
goanna (lizard)
kowari (animal)
numbat (animal)
possum (animal)
quokka (animal)
wombat (animal)

7
bettong (animal)
echidna (animal)
lorikeet (bird)
lyrebird (bird)
mulgara (animal)
potoroo (animal)
wallaby (animal)

8
coolabah (tree)

ironbark (tree)
kangaroo (animal)
platypus (animal)

9
bandicoot (animal)
cassowary (bird)
jacaranda (tree)
macadamia (tree)
marsupial (animal type)
pademelon (animal)

10
eucalyptus (tree)
kookaburra (bird)

2+ words
Tasmanian tiger

AUSTRALIAN TOWNS AND CITIES

5
Perth

6
Cairns
Darwin
Hobart
Mackay
Sydney

7
Geelong

8
Adelaide
Canberra
Ballarat
Brisbane

9
Fremantle
Melbourne
Newcastle

10
Kalgoorlie

Launceston
Palmerston
Woolongong

AUSTRALIAN WORDS

4
arvo (afternoon)
blue (fight)
bush (wild countryside)
daks (trousers)
dill (fool)
esky (cool box)
rapt (delighted, in love)

5
billy (pan for boiling water)
bluey (red-haired person)
crook (ill)
dunny (outside toilet)
tinny (can of beer)
yakka (hard work)

6
barbie (barbecue)
bonzer (great, excellent)
dinkum (honest)
furphy (rumour)
sheila (girl, woman)
sickie (day off work ill)
strine (Australian dialect or slang)
tucker (food)

7
chunder (vomit)
clobber (clothes)
jumbuck (sheep)
outback (wild countryside)
station (large farm or ranch)
strides (trousers)

8
shellack (defeat heavily, thrash)

9
billabong (pond in or near dried-up river)

FAMOUS AUSTRALIANS

4
Hoad (Lewis, tennis player)
Holt (Harold, politician)

5
Court (Margaret, tennis player)
Greer (Germaine, feminist, critic)
Kelly (Ned, outlaw)
Laver (Rod, tennis player)
Lyons (Joseph, statesman)
Melba (Dame Nellie, singer)
Nolan (Sidney, painter)
Shute (Neville, novelist)
Warne (Shane, cricketer)
White (Patrick, novelist)

6
Barton (Edmund, politician)

Benaud (Richie, cricketer)
Deakin (Alfred, politician)
Fadden (Arthur, politician)
Fraser (Malcolm, politician)
Gibson (Mel, actor)
Gorton (John, politician)
Harris (Rolf, painter, entertainer)
Howard (John, politician)
Kidman (Nicole, actress)
McKern (Leo, actor)
Miller (Ken, cricketer)

7
Brabham (Jack, racing driver)
Bradman (Donald, cricketer)
Everage (Dame Edna, 'entertainer')
Hinkler (Herbert, aviator)
Keating (Paul, politician)
Lindwall (Ray, cricketer)
McGrath (Glenn, cricketer)

Menzies (Robert, politician)
Minogue (Kylie, singer)
Roberts (Tom, painter)
Whitlam (Gough, politician)

8
Chappell (Greg/Ian, cricketers)
Drysdale (Russell, painter)
Keneally (Thomas, novelist)
Newcombe (John, tennis player)
Rosewall (Ken, tennis player)

9
Goolagong (Evonne, tennis player)
Humphries (Barry, entertainer)
Mackerras (Charles, musician)

10
Sutherland (Joan, singer)

BAD AND GOOD

Bad (of poor quality)
Bad (wrong/wicked)
Bad characteristic in a
person (vice)
The Seven Deadly Sins
Bad characteristic in a
thing
Bad person
Bad thing
Good (of high quality)
Good (virtuous)
Good quality in a person
Good quality in a thing
Good person
Good thing

BAD (OF POOR QUALITY)

3
ill
low
off

4
duff
grim
mean
poor
ropy
sour
weak

5
awful
cheap
flimsy
gross
lousy
mangy
manky
sorry
stale
tatty
worse
worst
yucky

6
abject
clumsy
coarse
crappy
crummy
faulty
feeble
filthy
flawed
grotty
grubby
measly
mouldy
patchy
putrid
rancid
rotten
shabby
shoddy
vulgar
woeful

7
abysmal
decayed
ghastly
harmful
noisome
noxious
pitiful
rubbish
ruinous
scruffy
squalid
unsound
useless
wanting

8
accursed
annoying
damaging
dreadful
grievous
hopeless
horrible
inferior

mediocre
pathetic
shocking
terrible
wretched

9
appalling
dangerous
defective
deficient
execrable
imperfect
unhealthy
worthless

10
abominable
lamentable
uninspired

11
incompetent
ineffective
inefficient
intolerable
substandard
undesirable

13
unsatisfactory

2+ words
cack-handed
ham-fisted
jerry-built
second-rate
third-rate

BAD (WRONG/WICKED)

4
base
foul
evil
rude
vile

5
crude
cruel
harsh
nasty
venal
wrong

6
amoral
brutal
greedy
guilty
impure
savage
sinful
shabby
shoddy
sleazy
sordid
stingy
unjust
unruly
wicked
wilful

7
abusive
beastly
boorish
caddish
corrupt
crooked
envious
harmful
heinous
jealous
illegal
immoral
miserly
naughty
selfish
uncouth
ungodly
vicious
violent
wayward
worldly

8
barbarous
churlish
covetous
criminal
depraved
egoistic
horrible
horrific
impudent
indecent
insolent
malicious
merciless
ruthless
shameful
shocking
spiteful

9
appalling
debauched
dishonest
dissolute
egotistic
malicious
mercenary
niggardly
offensive
shameless
unethical

10
abominable
avaricious
degenerate
delinquent
deplorable
despicable
egocentric
iniquitous
possessive
profligate
ungenerous
villainous
vindictive

11
acquisitive
disgraceful
disobedient
egotistical
mischievous
promiscuous
troublesome
undeserving
unendurable
unspeakable

12
contemptible
disagreeable
discourteous
disreputable
irredeemable
parsimonious
uncharitable
unmanageable
unprincipled
unscrupulous

13
discreditable
inconsiderate
materialistic
opportunistic
reprehensible

2+ words
cold-hearted
money-grubbing
self-centred
self-interested

Bad characteristic in a person (vice)

3
sin

4
envy
evil
lust
vice

5
greed
sloth

6
egoism
foible

7
avarice
egotism

8
impurity
iniquity
jealousy

9
amorality
blasphemy
carnality
depravity
indecency
turpitude
vulgarity

10
corruption
degeneracy
immorality
perversion
profligacy
wickedness

11
degradation
egocentrism
materialism

THE SEVEN DEADLY SINS

4
lust
envy

5
anger

greed
pride
sloth

12
covetousness

BAD CHARACTERISTIC IN A THING

3
bug

4
flaw
lack
snag
spot

5
error
fault
taint

6
defect

7
absence
blemish
failing
frailty
mistake

8
drawback
loophole
weakness

9
shortfall

10
deficiency
inadequacy

11
shortcoming

12
disadvantage
imperfection

BAD PERSON

3
cad
dog
hog
imp
pig
rat

4
hood
ogre
pimp
rake
thug

5
bitch
brute
bully
cheat
crook
devil
felon
fiend
ghoul
hussy
Judas
knave
louse
rogue
scamp
skunk
snake
thief
swine
whore

6
baddie
coward
egoist
hooker

killer
lecher
outlaw
rapist
rascal
robber
rotter
sadist
savage
sinner
tyrant

7
bastard
bounder
culprit
egotist
hoodlum
lowlife
monster
outcast
pervert
stinker
traitor
villain
wastrel
wrong'un

8
assassin
betrayer
criminal
evildoer
gangster
hooligan
murderer
offender
poisoner
profaner
quisling
recreant
renegade
Satanist
swindler

9
cutthroat
desperado

egomaniac
kidnapper
miscreant
racketeer
scoundrel
terrorist
wrongdoer

10
blackguard
blasphemer
degenerate
lawbreaker
malefactor
paedophile
profligate

11
rapscallion
undesirable

12
transgressor
troublemaker

2+ words
bad egg
bad lot
ne'er-do-well
self-seeker
snake in the grass

BAD THING

3
dud
ill

4
bane
flop
mess
miss
pain
pest
ruin

5
botch
farce
trial
worry

6
bother
bungle
burden
fiasco
hassle
turkey

7
blunder
debacle
failure
mistake
problem
tragedy
trouble

8
disaster
shambles

11
catastrophe

GOOD (OF HIGH QUALITY)

1
G

2
OK

3
ace
fab

4
able
cool
fair
fine

nice
plum

5
adept
brill
crack
dandy
great
sound
super
swell
valid

6
expert
lovely
master
spiffy
superb
wicked
wizard

7
capable
classic
genuine
notable

8
adequate
cracking
fabulous
pleasant
pleasing
salutary
smashing
splendid
superior
talented
terrific
thorough

9
agreeable
competent
efficient
enjoyable

excellent
exquisite
wholesome
wonderful

10
auspicious
beneficial
delightful
favourable
impressive
proficient
profitable
propitious

11
magnificent
respectable

12
accomplished
advantageous
praiseworthy
satisfactory

2+ words
first-class
first-rate
high-class
high-quality
top-notch
top-rate

GOOD (VIRTUOUS)

2
pi

4
holy
kind
pure

5
godly
lofty
moral
noble

pious
right
sober

6
benign
caring
chaste
decent
docile
honest
humane
humble
kindly
loving
modest
proper
worthy

7
angelic
ethical
helpful
liberal
perfect
saintly
sinless
upright

8
fatherly
friendly
generous
innocent
laudable
maternal
motherly
obedient
obliging
selfless
sisterly
spotless
tolerant
virtuous

9
admirable
blameless

brotherly
Christian
courteous
estimable
forgiving
fraternal
righteous
spiritual
unselfish

10
altruistic
beneficent
benevolent
charitable
chivalrous
honourable
idealistic
impeccable
munificent
solicitous
thoughtful

11
considerate
magnanimous
neighbourly
sympathetic

13
compassionate
disinterested
philanthropic

2+ words
above reproach
good-natured
kind-hearted
well-behaved
well-mannered
well-meaning
well-intentioned

***GOOD QUALITY IN A
PERSON***

4
duty

hope
love
pity

5
faith
grace
mercy
merit
skill
worth

6
honour
purity

7
charity
courage
decency
honesty
justice
probity

8
altruism
chastity
chivalry
civility
courtesy
goodness
goodwill
humanity
idealism
kindness
morality
prudence
sanctity

9
benignity
fortitude
innocence
integrity
obedience
principle
rectitude
tolerance

10
compassion
excellence
generosity
humaneness
kindliness
temperance
worthiness

11
benevolence
forgiveness
humaneness
magnanimity
munificence
uprightness

12
philanthropy
righteousness

***GOOD QUALITY
IN A THING***

3
use

5
asset
merit

6
profit
return
reward

7
benefit
calibre
quality

8
strength

9
advantage
soundness

10
excellence

11
distinction
superiority

GOOD PERSON

2
St

3
nun

4
hero
monk
prig

5
angel
goody
model
pearl
saint

6
martyr

7
paragon

8
altruist
treasure

2+ words
goody-goody
knight in shining armour
white knight

GOOD THING

3
gem
hit

4
boon
find
plus

5
asset
beaut
dandy
dilly
dream
jewel
peach
smash

6
corker
winner

7
benefit
godsend

8
blessing
knockout
treasure
windfall

9
advantage
humdinger

11
crackerjack
masterpiece

12
lollapalooza
masterstroke

2+ words
bee's knees
cat's whiskers
chef d'oeuvre
tour de force

BALLET

Ballets
Ballet dancers
Ballet movements and
other ballet terms
Choreographers

BALLETS

7
Corsair (the)
Giselle

8
Bayadère (la)
Coppelia
Firebird (the)

9
Petrushka
Sylphides (les)

10
Nutcracker (the)

2+ words
Daphnis and Chloe
Rite of Spring (the)
Romeo and Juliet
Sleeping Beauty
Swan Lake

BALLET DANCERS

4
Grey (Beryl)

5
Dolin (Anton)
Gable (Christopher)

ó
Ashton (Frederick)
Dowell (Anthony)
Sibley (Antoinette)

7
Bussell (Darcy)
danseur
Fonteyn (Margot)
Helpman (Robert)
Markova (Alicia)
Nureyev (Rudolf)
Pavlova (Anna)
Rambert (Marie)
Seymour (Lynn)
Ulanova (Galina)

8
coryphée
figurant
Nijinsky (Vaslav)

9
ballerina
figurante

2+ words
corps de ballet
de Valois (Ninette)

BALLET MOVEMENTS
AND OTHER BALLET
TERMS

3
pas

4
bras
demi
jeté
plié
pose
saut
tutu
volé

5
arqué
barre
battu
beats
brisé

collé
coupé
fondu
passé
piqué
pivot
porté
rosin
sauté
tendu

6
aplomb
attack
baissé
ballon
camber
chainé
change
chassé
croisé
écarté
effacé
entrée
épaulé
étoile
frappe
jarret
monter
penché
pointe
relevé
royale
tights

7
allongé
attaque
balancé
bourrée
deboulé
échappé
fouetté
glissée
leotard
maillot
sissone
soutenu

8
attitude
batterie
cabriole
cagneaux
glissade
pistolet
renversé
stulchik

9
arabesque
battement
développé
elevation
entrechat
pirouette
promenade
révérence

10
changement
enlèvement
épaulement
soubresaut

12
choreography

CHOREOGRAPHERS

6
Ashton (Frederick)
Cranko (Johnny)
Fokine (Michel)
Graham (Martha)
Petipa (Marcel)

7
Massine (Léonide)

9
Diaghilev (Sergei)

10
Balanchine (George)

BATTLES

Battle
Famous battles

BATTLE

3
war

4
duel
feud
fray

5
clash
fight
melee
scrap

6
action
combat
fracas
tussle

7
contest
crusade
scuffle

8
campaign
conflict
skirmish
struggle

9
encounter

10
engagement

FAMOUS BATTLES

3
Goa

Ulm

4
Acre
Alma (the)
Caen
Ebro (the)
Jena
Loos
Mons
Nile
Oran
Rome
Vimy

5
Aduwa
Alamo
Anzio
Arras
Boyne (the)
Bulge (the)
Cadiz
Crecy
Douro
Eylau
Issus
Lagos
Lewes
Ligny
Marne
Sedan
Selby
Sluys
Somme (the)
Texel
Valmy
Ypres

6
Actium
Arbela
Arnhem
Barnet
Cannae
Dieppe
Dunbar
Majuba

Maidan
Maldon
Midway
Minden
Naseby
Olmutz
Sadowa
Saigon
Shiloh
Tobruk
Towton
Verdun
Wagram

7
Aboukir (Bay)
Alamein (El Alamein)
Britain
Cassino
Colenso
Corunna
Dunkirk
Evesham
Flodden (Field)
Jutland
Leipzig
Lepanto
Magenta
Marengo
Matapan
Newbury
Okinawa
Plassey
Poltava
Preston
Salamis
Salerno
Taranto
Vitoria

8
Antietam
Ardennes
Atlantic (the)
Blenheim
Borodino
Bosworth (Field)
Culloden

Edgehill
Fontenoy
Hastings
Inkerman
Mafeking
Marathon
Navarino
Omdurman
Philippi
Poitiers
Quiberon (Bay)
Saratoga
Stirling
Talavera
Waterloo
Yorktown

9
Agincourt
Balaclava
Caporetto
Dettingen
Falklands
Gallipoli
Ladysmith
Lansdowne
Oudenarde
Pharsalus
Ramillies

Sedgemoor
Solferino
Steenkirk
Trafalgar
Vicksburg
Worcester

10
Austerlitz
Brandywine
Camperdown
Copenhagen
Gettysburg
Malplaquet
Paardeberg
Sevastopol
Shrewsbury
Stalingrad
Tannenberg
Tewkesbury

11
Bannockburn
Gualdacanal
Hohenlinden
Isandlwana
Prestonpans
Sheriffmuir
Thermopylae

12
Roncesvalles
Seringapatam

13
Killiecrankie
Magersfontein
Passchendaele

2+ words
Bull Run
Bunker Hill
Goose Green
Imjin River
Iwo Jima
Little Bighorn
Marston Moor
River Plate
Rorke's Drift
Spion Kop
St Albans
St Vincent
Tel-el-Kebir
Wounded Knee

BIBLE

Books of the Bible
Characters of the Bible
See also **CHURCH,**
RELIGION

BOOKS OF THE BIBLE
Ap. = Apocrypha;
NT = New Testament;
OT = Old Testament

3
Job (OT)

4
Acts (of the Apostles)
(NT)
Amos (OT)
Ezra (OT)
John (NT)
Joel (OT)
Jude (NT)
Luke (NT)
Mark (NT)
Ruth (NT)

5
Hosea (OT)
James (NT)
Jonah (OT)
Kings (OT)
Micah (OT)
Nahum (OT)
Titus (NT)
Tobit (Ap.)

6
Baruch (Ap.)
Daniel (OT)
Esdras (Ap.)
Esther (OT)
Exodus (OT)
Haggai (OT)
Isaiah (OT)
Joshua (OT)
Judges (OT)
Judith (Ap.)

Psalms (OT)
Romans (NT)
Samuel (OT)
Sirach (Ap.)

7
Ezekiel (OT)
Genesis (OT)
Hebrews (NT)
Malachi (OT)
Matthew (NT)
Numbers (OT)
Obadiah (OT)
Susanna (Ap.)
Timothy (NT)

8
Habakkuk (OT)
Jeremiah (OT)
Nehemiah (OT)
Philemon (NT)
Proverbs (OT)

9
Ephesians (NT)
Galatians (NT)
Leviticus (OT)
Maccabees (Ap.)
Zechariah (OT)
Zephaniah (OT)

10
Chronicles (OT)
Colossians (NT)

11
Corinthians (NT)
Deuteronomy (OT)
Philippians (NT)
Revelations (NT)

12
Ecclesiastes (OT)
Lamentations (OT)

13
Thessalonians (NT)

2+ words
Song of Songs
Song of Solomon

CHARACTERS OF THE BIBLE

3
Dan
Eli
Eve
Gad
Gog
Ham
Job
Lot

4
Abel
Adam
Ahab
Amos
Baal
Boaz
Cain
Esau
Ezra
Jehu
Joab
John
Joel
Jude
Leah
Levi
Luke
Magi (the)
Mark
Mary
Moab
Noah
Paul
Ruth
Saul
Shem

5
Aaron
Annas

Asher
Caleb
Cyrus
Dagon
David
Demas
devil
Enoch
Hagar
Herod
Hiram
Hosea
Isaac
Jacob
James
Jesse
Jesus
Jonah
Judah
Judas
Laban
Magog
Moses
Naomi
Nahum
Peter
Sarah
Satan
Silas
Simon
Titus
Uriah

6
Andrew
Balaam
Christ
Daniel
Darius
Elijah
Elisha
Esther
Gideon
Haggai
Isaiah
Israel
Jairus
Joseph

Joshua
Josiah
Judith
Martha
Miriam
Naboth
Nathan
Philip
Pilate
Rachel
Reuben
Salome
Samson
Samuel
Simeon
Thomas

7
Abraham
Absolom
Ananias
Delilah
Ephraim
Ezekiel
Gabriel
Goliath
Ishmael
Japhet
Jehovah
Jezebel
Lazarus
Lucifer
Malachi
Matthew
Meshach
Michael
Obadiah
Pharaoh
Raphael
Rebecca
Solomon
Stephen
Susanna
Timothy
Zebedee
Zebulun

8
Abednego
Barabbas
Barnabas
Benjamin
Caiaphas
Habakkuk
Hezekiah
Issachar
Jeremiah
Jeroboam
Jonathan
Matthias
Mordecai
Naphtali
Nehemiah
Philemon
Shadrach
Zedekiah

9
Bathsheba
Beelzebub
Nathaniel
Nicodemus
Thaddaeus
Zacchaeus
Zechariah

10
Belshazzar
Methuselah
Theophilus

11
Bartholomew

14
Nebuchadnezzar

2+ words
John the Baptist
Joseph of Arimathea
Judas Iscariot
Mary Magdalene
Pontius Pilate
Simon Magus
Simon of Cyrene

BIRDS

Birds
Male, female and young birds
See also **ANIMAL** (for names of groups and homes of birds and parts of the body)

BIRDS

3
auk
cob
daw
emu
hen
jay
kea
mew
moa (*extinct*)
nun
owl
pen
pie
roc (*mythical*)
tit
tui

4
chat
cirl
cock
coot
crow
dodo (*extinct*)
dove
duck
erne
eyas
guan
gull
hawk
hern
huia (*extinct*)
ibis
jack

kaka
kite
kiwi
knot
koel
lark
loon
lory
mina
monk
myna
nene
pern
poll
rail
rhea
rook
ruff
type
shag
skua
smee
smew
sora
swan
taha
teal
tern
wawa
weak
wren
yite

5
biddy
booby
capon
chick
colin
crake
crane
diver
drake
eagle
egret
eider
finch
galah

glede
goose
grebe
herne
hobby
homer
junco
macaw
madeg
mavis
merle
murre
mynah
nandu
nelly
noddy
ousel
ouzel
owlet
pewee
piper
pipit
polly
poult
quail
raven
reeve
robin
saker
scaup
serin
snipe
solan
squab
stare
stint
stork
swift
terek
twite
urubu
veery
wader

6
amazon
ancona
argala

auklet
avocet
bantam
barbet
bishop
bonxie
brahma
budgie
bulbul
canary
chewet
chough
chukar
cochin
condor
corbie
coucal
cuckoo
culver
curlew
cygnet
darter
dipper
drongo
duiker
dunlin
eaglet
falcon
fulmar
gambit
gander
gannet
gentle
gentoo
godwit
gooney
goslet
grouse
guinea
hermit
hoopoe
houdan
jabiro
jacana
kakapo
lanner
linnet
loriot

magpie
martin
merlil
missel
monaul
mopoke
motmot
oriole
osprey
oxbird
parrot
paster
peahen
peewee
peewit
petrel
pigeon
plover
pouter
puffin
pullet
ratite
redcap
roller
rumkin
runner
scoter
seamew
shrike
siskin
smeath
tercel
thrush
tomtit
toucan
towhee
trogon
turbit
turkey
turtle
weaver
wigeon
willet
yaffle

7
antbird
apteryx

babbler
beekite
bittern
bluecap
bluetit
boobook
bullbat
bunting
bushtit
bustard
buzzard
catbird
chicken
coaltit
colibri
corella
cotinga
courlan
courser
cowgirl
creeper
cropper
dorking
dottrel
dovekie
dunnock
fantail
finfoot
flicker
gadwall
gobbler
gorcock
gorcrow
goshawk
gosling
grackle
greyhen
greylag
haggard
halcyon (*mythical*)
harrier
hoatzin
icebird
jacamar
jackdaw
Jacobin
kestrel
lapwing

leghorn
mallard
manakin
marabou
martlet
minivet
Minorca
moorhen
noctule
oilbird
ortolan
ostrich
oventit
peacock
peafowl
pelican
penguin
phoenix (*mythical*)
pinnock
pintado
pochard
poulard
quetzal
redpoll
redwing
rooster
rosella
ruddock
sakeret
sawbill
scooper
seagull
seriema
skimmer
sparrow
squacco
sunbird
swallow
tanager
tattler
tiercel
tinamou
titlark
touraco
tumbler
vulture
wagtail
warbler

waxbill
waxwing
whooper
widgeon
woodhen
wrybill
wryneck

8
accentor
adjutant
alcatras
amadavat
baldpate
barnacle
bateleur
berghaan
blackcap
bluebird
bluewing
boatbill
boattail
bobolink
capuchin
caracara
cardinal
cargoose
cockatoo
cockerel
curassow
dabchick
didapper
dotterel
duckling
dundiver
falconet
fireback
firebird
flamingo
gamecock
garganey
greenlet
grosbeak
guachero
hackbird
hangbird
hawfinch
hernshaw

hornbill
kingbird
kingcrow
landrail
lanneret
lorikeet
lovebird
lyrebird
mannikin
megapode
moorcock
moorfowl
murrelet
nestling
nightjar
nuthatch
ovenbird
oxpecker
parakeet
peachick
pheasant
poorwill
popinjay
rainbird
redshank
reedbird
reedling
ringdove
screamer
shelduck
shoebill
silktail
snowbird
songbird
starling
thrasher
throstle
titmouse
tragopan
troupial
wheatear
whimbrel
whinchat
whipbird
whitecap
woodchat
woodcock
woodlark

zopilote

9
albatross
baltimore
beccafico
blackbird
blackcock
blackhead
bowerbird
brambling
broadbill
bullfinch
campanero
cassowary
chaffinch
chickadee
cockatiel
cormorant
corncrake
crossbill
currawong
dandycock
fieldfare
figpecker
firecrest
flutebird
francolin
friarbird
frogmouth
gallinule
gerfalcon
goldcrest
goldeneye
goldfinch
goosander
guillemot
guineahen
gyrfalcon
heathcock
heathfowl
honeybird
kittiwake
mallamuck
merganser
nighthawk
Orpington
ossifrage

partridge
peregrine
phalarope
pinefinch
ptarmigan
razorbill
riflebird
rockpipit
sandpiper
sapsucker
sheldrake
shoveller
snakebird
snowgoose
solitaire
spoonbill
stockdove
stonechat
stormcock
swordbill
thickhead
trochilus
trumpeter
turnstone
watercock
waterfowl
windhover
wyandotte

10
aberdevine
bluebreast
bluethroat
budgerigar
bufflehead
butterball
canvasback
chiffchaff
demoiselle
fledgeling
flycatcher
goatsucker
greenfinch
greenshank
honeyeater
honeyguide
kingfisher
kookaburra

meadowlark
nutcracker
pratincole
roadrunner
rockhopper
saddleback
sanderling
sandgrouse
shearwater
sicklebill
tailorbird
tropicbird
turtledove
wattlebird
weaverbird
woodgrouse
woodpecker
woodpigeon
woodthrush
yellowbird

11
butcherbird
cocksparrow
honeysucker
hummingbird
lammergeier
leatherhead
mockingbird
nightingale
scissorbill
sparrowhawk
treecreeper
whitethroat
woodswallow

12
capercaillie
whippoorwill
yellowhammer

2+ words
bald eagle
barnacle goose
barn owl
bee-eater
bell-bird
bird of paradise

black swan
blue-cap
blue jay
brent goose
brown owl
buff Orpington
Canada goose
carrier pigeon
carrion crow
eagle-owl
fish owl
frigate bird
golden eagle

grey owl
guinea fowl
hedge sparrow
herring gull
homing pigeon
house martin
marsh harrier
mistle thrush
more-pork
Muscovy duck
mute swan
oyster catcher
prairie hen

sand martin
secretary bird
snowy owl
storm(y) petrel
tawny owl
widow bird
wild goose
wild duck
wood pigeon
zebra finch

MALE, FEMALE AND YOUNG BIRDS

Species	Male	Female	Young
domestic fowl	cock/rooster/cockerel	hen	chick/poult
duck	drake	duck	duckling
eagle	eagle	eagle	eaglet
goose	gander	goose	gosling
hawk	hawk	hawk	eyas
peafowl	peacock	peahen	chick
pigeon	pigeon	pigeon	squab
swan	cob	pen	cygnet

The male of most species is called a cock, *the female a* hen *and the young bird a* chick.
In the early stages of its development a young bird may also be called a nestling *or a* fledgeling.

BODY

Body
Arteries and veins
Bones
Ear
Eye
Glands
Muscles
Parts of the body
Words relating to body
parts and processes
See also **ANIMAL**

BODY

5
build
torso
trunk

6
corpse
figure

7
anatomy
cadaver
carcass
8
physique

ARTERIES AND VEINS

5
aorta
iliac
renal
ulnar

6
radial
tibial

7
carotid
femoral
hepatic

jugular

8
brachial
cephalic
thoracic

9
pulmonary

10
innominate
mesenteric
subclavian
suprarenal

2+ words
hepatic portal
vena cava

BONES

3
jaw
rib

4
axis
ulna

5
anvil
costa
femur
hyoid
ilium
incus
pubis
skull
spine
talus
tibia
vomer

6
carpal
carpus
coccyx

cuboid
fibula
hallux
hammer
pelvis
rachis
radius
sacrum
stapes
tarsal
tarsus

7
cranium
humerus
ischium
jawbone
kneecap
kneepan
malleus
mastoid
maxilla
patella
phalanx
scapula
sternum
stirrup

8
backbone
clavicle
heelbone
mandible
scaphoid
shinbone
temporal
vertebra

9
anklebone
calcaneum
calcaneus
cheekbone
maxillary
phalanges
thighbone
wristbone
trapezium

10
astragalus
breastbone
collarbone
metacarpal
metacarpus
metatarsal
metatarsus

2+ words
cannon bone
floating rib
frontal bone
funny bone
haunch bone
shoulder blade
spinal column

EAR

4
lobe

5
anvil
helix
incus
pinna

6
concha
hammer
stapes
tragus

7
cochlea
eardrum
malleus
mastoid
saccule
stirrup
utricle

8
ossicles

9
endolymph
labyrinth
perilymph

2+ words
eustachian tube
inner ear
middle ear
oval window
round window
scala media
scala tympani
scala vestibuli

EYE

3
rod

4
ball
iris
lens

5
fovea
orbit
pupil
white

6
cornea
retina
sclera

7
choroid
eyeball
eyelash

9
sclerotic

11
conjunctiva

2+ words
aqueous humour
blind spot
optic nerve
tear duct
tear gland
yellow spot

GLANDS

5
liver
sweat

6
buccal
pineal
tarsal
thymus

7
adrenal
gastric
mammary
parotid
thyroid

8
ductless
exocrine
pancreas
prostate
salivary

9
endocrine
meibomian
pituitary
sebaceous

10
sublingual
suprarenal
vestibular

11
parathyroid

12
submaxillary

MUSCLES

5
psoas
sinew
teres

6
biceps
rectus
soleus
tendon
vastus

7
deltoid
gluteus
iliacus
triceps

8
anconeus
masseter
opponens
pectoral
peroneus
platsyma
postural
rhomboid
scalenus
serratus
skeletal
tibialis

9
depressor
iliopsoas
mylohyoid
obturator
popliteus
quadratus
sartorius
sphincter
supinator
trapezius

voluntary

10
brachialis
buccinator
epicranius
hyoglossus
quadriceps
stylohyoid
temporalis

11
orbicularis
sternohyoid

12
styloglossus

***PARTS OF THE HUMAN
BODY***

3
arm
ear
eye
gum
gut
hip
jaw
leg
lip
sac
toe

4
anus
back
bile
bone
brow
calf
chin
duct
fist
foot
gall
gene
hair

hand
heel
knee
lens
limb
lobe
lung
nail
nape
neck
node
nose
ovum
palm
pore
shin
side
skin
sole
vein
womb

5
ankle
aorta
belly
blood
brain
cheek
chest
colon
crown
cutis
digit
elbow
femur
gland
gonad
heart
hymen
ileum
joint
liver
lymph
molar
mouth
mucus
navel

nerve
ovary
penis
pubis
scalp
semen
sinew
sinus
skull
spine
teeth
thigh
thumb
tooth
trunk
vulva
waist
wrist

6
artery
breast
caecum
canine
corium
dermis
enzyme
finger
gamete
gullet
haunch
kidney
labium
larynx
muscle
nipple
palate
pelvis
phlegm
plasma
radius
rectum
retina
sacrum
spleen
temple
tendon
testis

thorax
throat
thymus
tissue
tongue
ureter
uterus
vagina
vessel

7
abdomen
bladder
buttock
eyebrow
eyelash
forearm
fraenum
gizzard
glottis
hormone
humerus
incisor
jejunum
keratin
knuckle
medulla
midriff
nostril
occiput
omentum
oviduct
pharynx
prostate
ribcage
scrotum
sternum
stomach
synapse
thyroid
toenail
trachea
urethra
viscera

8
alveolus
appendix

bronchus
cerebrum
cleavage
clitoris
duodenum
follicle
forehead
ganglion
genitals
ligament
membrane
pancreas
shoulder
skeleton
testicle
vertebra
windpipe

9
capillary
cartilage
corpuscle
diaphragm
digestion
epidermis
forebrain
hindbrain
intestine
mesentery
phagocyte
ventricle

10
bronchiole
cerebellum
epiglottis
fingernail
oesophagus
peritoneum

11
haemoglobin

2+ words
Adam's apple
bile duct
grey matter
umbilical cord

vocal cords
voice box

***WORDS RELATING TO
BODY PARTS AND
PROCESSES***

4
anal (anus)

5
nasal (nose)
optic (eye, sight)
renal (kidneys)

6
aural (ear, hearing)
dental (teeth)
dermal (skin)
facial (face)
labial (labia, lips)
lumbar (back)
neural (nerves)
pelvic (pelvis)
visual (sight)

7
adrenal (near kidneys)
cardiac (heart)
cranial (cranium)
femoral (femur)
gastric (stomach)
genital (sex organs)
hepatic (liver)
mammary (breast)
thyroid (thyroid gland)

8
auditory (hearing)
brachial (arm)
cerebral (brain)
duodenal (duodenum)
muscular (muscular)
pectoral (chest)
skeletal (skeleton)
thoracic (thorax)
tracheal (trachea)
urethral (urethra)
visceral (visceral)

9
abdominal (abdomen)
bronchial (bronchi)
laryngeal (larynx)
olfactory (smell)
pulmonary (lungs)
sebaceous (sweat)
umbilical (cord
connecting foetus to
uterus)
vertebral (vertebrae)

10
intestinal (intestines)
pancreatic (pancreas)
pharyngeal (pharynx)

11
respiratory (breathing)

BUILDINGS

Famous buildings and monuments
Parts of a building
Types of building

FAMOUS BUILDINGS AND MONUMENTS

6
Louvre (Paris)
Rialto (Venice)
Sphinx (Egypt)

8
Alhambra (Granada)
Escorial (Spain)
Pyramids (Egypt)

9
Acropolis (Athens)
Colosseum (Rome)
Hermitage (St
Petersburg)
Parthenon (Athens)

10
Stonehenge (England)
Versailles (France)

2+ words
Blenheim Palace
(England)
Brandenburg Gate
(Berlin)
Bridge of Sighs (Venice)
Brooklyn Bridge
(New York)
Eiffel Tower (Paris)
Empire State Building
(New York)
Golden Gate Bridge
(San Francisco)
Hagia Sophia (Istanbul)
Machu Picchu (Peru)
Notre Dame (Paris)
Sacré Coeur (Paris)

Sagrada Familia
(Barcelona)
Sears Tower (Chicago)
St Mark's (Venice)
St Paul's (London)
St Peter's (Rome)
Sistine Chapel (Rome)
Taj Mahal (India)
Tower of London

PARTS OF A BUILDING, INCLUDING ROOMS

3
bay
den
loo

4
door
exit
flue
hall
lift
lock
loft
pane
roof
sash
sill
site
step
tile
wall
wing

5
annex
attic
decor
diner
fence
floor
foyer
gable
grate
joist
ledge

lobby
newel
niche
panel
patio
plank
porch
salon
slate
stair
study
suite

6
alcove
atrium
batten
cellar
closet
façade
garret
gutter
hearth
larder
lintel
lounge
louver
mortar
office
pantry
rafter
recess
stairs
storey
studio
thatch
toilet
window

7
balcony
bedroom
boudoir
boxroom
buttery
canteen
ceiling
cesspit

chamber
chimney
cistern
cubicle
dinette
doorway
dungeon
fitting
fixture
gallery
keyhole
knocker
kitchen
landing
laundry
library
nursery
parlour
passage
plaster
shingle
veranda

8
anteroom
backdoor
backroom
ballroom
banister
basement
bathroom
corridor
doorpost
doorstep
entrance
fanlight
flooring
frontage
handrail
lavatory
playroom
pointing
scullery
showroom
skirting
skylight
thatched
upstairs

workroom
workshop

9
brickwork
doorframe
dormitory
escalator
extension
fireplace
flagstone
frontdoor
frontroom
guestroom
guttering
penthouse
refectory
roughcast
staircase
stairwell
stonework
storeroom
vestibule
wallpaper
whitewash

10
backstairs
balustrade
bargeboard
coachhouse
coalcellar
conversion
foundation
insulation
pebbledash
plastering
quadrangle
repointing
repository
ventilator

11
foundations
mantelpiece
mantelshelf
outbuilding
plasterwork

scaffolding

12
chimneypiece
conservatory
weatherproof

2+ words
common room
damp course
dining room
dormer window
draught excluder
dressing room
en-suite
entrance hall
finger plate
floor plan
ground plan
half-timbered
jerry-built
living room
load-bearing
parquet floor
party wall
picture rail
picture window
sash window
septic tank
solar panel
window frame

TYPES OF BUILDING

3
hut
inn
spa
sty

4
barn
byre
crib
farm
flat
fort
gaol

hall
home
jail
keep
mill
pile
ruin
semi
shed
shop
silo

5
abode
block
booth
bower
cabin
croft
dairy
depot
hotel
house
hovel
igloo
kiosk
lodge
manor
manse
ranch
shack
villa

6
arbour
asylum
aviary
belfry
bridge
castle
chalet
chapel
church
donjon
dugout
garage
gazebo
grange

grotto
hangar
hospice
hostel
museum
office
pagoda
palace
pigsty
prefab
priory
prison
school
shanty
smithy
studio
subway

7
college
convent
cottage
deanery
dovecot
edifice
eyesore
factory
foundry
gallery
granary
kennels
laundry
library
mansion
pergola
pillbox
pyramid
rectory
seawall
shelter
stadium
station
surgery
terrace
theatre
viaduct

8
aquarium
bungalow
causeway
cloister
detached
domicile
dovecote
dwelling
erection
hospital
hostelry
hothouse
monolith
monument
orangery
outhouse
pavilion
refinery
tenement
terminus
vicarage
windmill
ziggurat

9
almshouse
apartment
belvedere
boathouse
campanile
farmhouse
gatehouse
guildhall
gymnasium
homestead
infirmary
labyrinth
mausoleum
monastery
orphanage
parsonage
residence
structure
townhouse
warehouse

10

auditorium
dispensary
distillery
grandstand
greenhouse
habitation
laboratory
lighthouse
maisonette
sanatorium
skyscraper

12

amphitheatre
construction
semidetached

2+ words

bell tower
block of flats
clock tower
high-rise
lock-up
low-rise
power station
town hall

BUSINESS

2
CA
EU
FT

3
APR
bid
buy
c.i.f.
COD
cut
Dow
DTI
dun
ECU
EEC
EMU
fee
f.o.b.
GDP
GNP
IMF
job
lot
net
owe
par
pay
PIN
plc
put
SME
sum
tax
VAT
WTO

4
bank
bear
bill
bond

boom
bull
bust
call
cash
chip
City
cost
deal
debt
deed
dole
dues
dump
duty
earn
EFTA
euro
firm
fisc
FTSE
fund
gain
GATT
gilt
giro
glut
hire
idle
lend
levy
loan
long
loss
mart
memo
nett
OPEC
owed
paid
pool
post
PSBR
puff
punt
ramp
rate
rent

ring
sale
sell
sink
sold
spot
stag
tare
vend
wage

5
agent
angel
asset
audit
batch
board
bonus
books
brand
buyer
cargo
clear
clerk
costs
cover
crash
cycle
debit
draft
entry
float
funds
gilts
goods
gross
hedge
index
issue
lease
limit
offer
order
owing
paper
payee
payer

price
proxy
quota
quote
rally
remit
repay
rider
score
scrip
share
shark
short
sight
slump
stock
trade
trust
wages
worth
yield

6
accrue
advice
advise
agency
asserts
assign
bailee
bailor
banker
barter
bearer
borrow
bounce
bounty
bourse
branch
broker
bubble
budget
burden
buyout
cartel
cheque
client
corner

coupon
credit
dealer
debtor
defray
demand
docket
dot.com
drawee
drawer
equity
estate
excise
expend
export
factor
figure
fiscal
freeze
growth
holder
honour
import
income
indent
insure
jobber
labour
ledger
lender
liable
liquid
Lloyd's
margin
market
markup
mature
merger
minute
mutual
Nikkei
notice
office
offset
option
outbid
outlay
outlet

output
packet
parity
pledge
policy
profit
punter
quango
quorum
racket
rating
realty
rebate
recoup
redeem
refund
remedy
rental
report
resale
retail
return
salary
sample
saving
settle
shares
specie
spiral
spread
staple
stocks
stroke
supply
surety
surtax
tariff
teller
tender
trader
unload
unpaid
usance
valuta
vendee
vendor
volume

7

account
actuary
advance
allonge
annuity
arrears
auction
auditor
average
balance
banking
bargain
bidding
bonanza
bullion
cambist
capital
cashier
ceiling
certify
chamber
charter
company
consols
convert
crossed
customs
dealing
default
deficit
deflate
deposit
douceur
dumping
duopoly
economy
embargo
endorse
engross
entrust
expense
exploit
factory
failure
finance
forward
flutter

freight
funding
futures
gearing
haulage
hedging
holding
imprest
inflate
insured
interim
invoice
jobbing
killing
leasing
lending
limited
lockout
manager
minutes
nominal
package
partner
payable
payment
payroll
pension
premium
prepaid
pricing
produce
product
profits
promote
realize (realise)
receipt
reissue
renewal
reserve
returns
revenue
rigging
royalty
salvage
selling
service
shipper
solvent

squeeze
stipend
storage
subsidy
surplus
synergy
takings
tonnage
trading
traffic
trustee
utility
vending
venture
warrant

8

acceptor
accounts
agiotage
amortize (amortise)
antedate
appraise
assignee
assigner
auditing
bailment
bankbook
banknote
bankrupt
borrower
bottomry
carriage
cashbook
clearing
commerce
consumer
contango
contract
creditor
currency
customer
dealings
defrayed
delivery
director
disburse
discount

dividend
drawings
earnings
employee
employer
emporium
endorsee
endorser
entrepot
equities
estimate
evaluate
exchange
exporter
finances
goodwill
gratuity
hallmark
importer
increase
indebted
industry
interest
investor
manifest
maturity
merchant
monetary
monetize (monetise)
monopoly
mortgage
novation
offshore
ordinary
overhead
overtime
passbook
poundage
proceeds
producer
property
receipts
receiver
recovery
reinvest
reserves
retailer
retainer

scarcity
schedule
security
shipment
solvency
sterling
straddle
supertax
takeover
taxpayer
transfer
turnover
undercut
unquoted
variable
warranty
windfall

9

actuarial
aggregate
allotment
allowance
annuitant
appraisal
appraiser
arbitrage
arrearage
assurance
averaging
borrowing
brokerage
certified
chartered
clearance
commodity
debenture
deduction
defaulter
deflation
demurrage
depletion
depositor
dishonour
economics
economist
economize (economise)
emolument

endowment
exchequer
executive
fiduciary
financial
financier
flotation
foreclose
franchise
garnishee
globalize (globalise)
guarantee
guarantor
incentive
indemnify
indemnity
indenture
inflation
insolvent
insurance
inventory
leasehold
liability
liquidate
liquidity
marketing
middleman
mortgagee
mortgagor
outgoings
outsource
overdraft
overdrawn
overheads
packaging
paymaster
pecuniary
personnel
piecework
portfolio
preferred
principal
privatize (privatise)
profiteer
promotion
purchaser
quittance
quotation

recession
redundant
reflation
reimburse
repayable
repayment
resources
restraint
reversion
severance
speculate
statement
stockpile
subscribe
subsidize (subsidise)
surcharge
syndicate
trademark
tradesman
undersell
utilities
valuation
vendition
viability
warehouse
wholesale
workforce

10

acceptance
accountant
accounting
accumulate
adjustment
appreciate
assessment
assignment
auctioneer
automation
bankruptcy
bondholder
bookkeeper
capitalism
capitalist
capitalize (capitalise)
capitation
collateral
colporteur

commercial
commission
compensate
competitor
consortium
conversion
cumulative
defalcator
depreciate
depression
deregulate
employment
evaluation
forwarding
franchisee
franchiser
honorarium
indexation
industrial
insolvency
instalment
investment
lighterage
liquidator
management
mercantile
monetarism
monetarist
monopolize (monopolise)
moratorium
negotiable
overcharge
overpriced
percentage
preference
prepayment
production
profitable
prospector
prospectus
prosperity
prosperous
purchasing
recompense
redeemable
redemption
redundancy
remittance

remunerate
securities
settlement
speculator
statistics
subscriber
underwrite
unemployed
wholesaler

11

accountancy
acquittance
advertising
arbitration
beneficiary
bimetallism
bookkeeping
businessman
certificate
circulation
competition
competitive
consignment
consumption
convergence
cooperative
corporation
demutualize (demutualise)
devaluation
distributor
endorsement
expenditure
fluctuation
foreclosure
hypothecate
liquidation
manufacture
merchandise
nationalize (nationalise)
negotiation
outstanding
overpayment
partnership
realization (realisation)
reinsurance
restructure
revaluation

shareholder
speculation
stagflation
stakeholder
stockbroker
stockjobber
stockpiling
stocktaking
subsistence
supermarket
syndicalism
transaction
undercharge
underpriced
underwriter

12
amalgamation
amortization
(amortisation)
appreciation
compensation
deflationary
denomination
depreciation
deregulation
differential
distribution
econometrics
entrepreneur
inflationary
irredeemable
manufacturer
overcapacity
productivity
profiteering
receivership
redeployment
remuneration
remunerative
salesmanship
shareholding
underwriting
unemployment

13
appropriation
backwardation
globalization
(globalisation)
privatization
(privatisation)
profitability
restructuring
specification

2+ words
above the line
ad valorem
after tax
assembly line
asset-stripper
asset-stripping
at par
at sight
bad debt
balance sheet
bear market
bearer bond
before tax
below the line
bill of lading
blue chip
board meeting
book value
brand name
bull market
buy in
buy out
cash and carry
cash in hand
closing price
common market
cost of living
credit rating
cut-rate
day book
day trader
day trading

days of grace
del credere
Dow Jones
end user
enterprise zone
ex gratia
expense account
fixed costs
free market
free trade
human resources
in arrears
in the black
in the red
interest rate
labour market
laissez faire
loss leader
lump sum
mass-produce
mass-produced
on call
package deal
personal assistant
point of sale
postal order
pre-empt
premium bond
quarter day
Queer Street
raw material
sight bill
slush fund
spot cash
spot price
stock market
tax break
tax haven
tax-free
unit trust
way bill
write off
year end

BUTTERFLIES AND MOTHS

Butterflies
Moths

BUTTERFLIES

3
owl

4
blue
leaf
monk

5
argus
brown
comma
dryad
heath
joker
nymph
satyr
snout
white
zebra

6
acraea
Apollo
copper
diadem
glider
hermit
morpho

7
admiral
festoon
monarch
peacock
ringlet
skipper
sulphur
Vanessa

8
birdwing
cardinal
charaxes
cymothoe
grayling
milkweed

9
brimstone
cleopatra
commodore
hackberry
metalmark
swordtail

10
fritillary
gatekeeper
hairstreak
Parnassian
silverline

11
swallowtail

13
tortoiseshell

2+ words
Adonis blue
Artic blue
Bath white
cabbage white
Camberwell beauty
common blue
golden tip
hedge brown
large blue
orange tip
red admiral

MOTHS

2
Io

3
owl
wax

4
goat
hawk
puss

5
atlas
eggar
egger
fairy
gypsy
ghost
regal
swift
tiger
yucca

6
burnet
cactus
calico
carpet
ermine
lappet
tineid

7
bagworm
clothes
emperor
noctuid
pyramid
tussock
uranias

8
cecropia
cinnabar
forester
Hercules
peppered
silkworm

9
ailanthus
brahmaeid
carpenter
clearwing
geometrid
saturnid
underwing

11
hummingbird
olethreutid
pyromorphid

2+ words
death's head

CANADA/ CANADIAN

Canadian towns and cities
Canadian provinces and territories
Famous Canadians

CANADIAN TOWNS AND CITIES

6
Ottawa
Quebec
Regina

7
Calgary
Halifax
Toronto

8
Edmonton
Hamilton
Kingston
Montreal
Victoria
Winnipeg

9
Vancouver
Saskatoon

11
Fredericton

13
Charlottetown

2+ words
Niagara Falls
St Johns
Thunder Bay

CANADIAN PROVINCES AND TERRITORIES

5
Yukon

6
Quebec

7
Alberta
Nunavut
Ontario

8
Labrador
Manitoba

12
Newfoundland
Saskatchewan

2+ words
British Columbia
New Brunswick
Northwest Territories
Nova Scotia
Prince Edward Island

FAMOUS CANADIANS

4
Anka, Paul (singer, songwriter)
Burr (Raymond, actor)
Dion (Celine, singer)
Ford (Glenn, actor)
King (William, politician)

5
Adams (Bryan, singer)
Clark (Charles, politician)
Cohen (Leonard, singer, songwriter)

Gehry (Frank, architect)
Gould (Glenn, musician)
Myers (Mike, actor)
Osler (William, physician)

6
Atwood (Margaret, writer)
Bujold (Genevieve, actress)
Borden (Robert, politician)
Carrey (Jim, actor)
Cunard (Samuel, shipowner)
Durban (Deanna, actress)

7
Banting (Frederick, scientist)
Leacock (Stephen, humorist, writer)
Plummer (Christopher, actor)
Shatner (William, actor)
Shearer (Norma, actress)
Trudeau (Pierre, politician)

8
Anderson (Pamela, actress)
Chrétien (Jean, politician)
Mitchell (Joni, singer)

10
Sutherland (Donald/Kiefer, actors)
Villeneuve (Jacques, racing driver)

11
Diefenbaker (John, politician)

CAPITAL CITIES

CAPITAL CITIES OF THE COUNTRIES OF THE WORLD (AND SOME REGIONS)

Afghanistan	Kabul
Albania	Tirana
Algeria	Algiers (or El Djezair)
Andorra	Andorra La Vella
Angola	Luanda
Antigua and Barbuda	St John's
Argentina	Buenos Aires
Armenia	Yerevan
Ascension Is.	Georgetown
Australia	Canberra
Austria	Vienna
Azerbaijan	Baku
Bahamas	Nassau
Bahrain	Manama
Balearic Is.	Palma
Bangladesh	Dhaka (was Dacca)
Barbados	Bridgetown
Belarus	Minsk
Belau	Koror
Belgium	Brussels
Belize	Belmopan
Benin	Porto-Novo
Bermuda	Hamilton
Bhutan	Thimbu
Bolivia	La Paz
Bosnia-Herzegovina	Sarajevo
Botswana	Gaborone
Brunei	Bandar Ser Bagawan
Bulgaria	Sofia
Burkina Faso	Ouagadougou
Brazil	Brasilia (was Rio de Janeiro)
Bulgaria	Sofia
Burkina Faso	Quagodougou
Burma (now Myanmar)	Rangoon
Burundi	Bujumbura
Cambodia	Phnom Penh
Cameroon	Yaounde
Canada	Ottawa
Canary Islands	Las Palmas
Cape Verde	Praia
Central Africa Republic	Bangui
Chad	Ndjamena
Chile	Santiago

China	Beijing
Colombia	Bogota
Comoros	Moroni
Congo (Democratic Republic of Congo)	Kinshasa
Congo (People's Republic of Congo)	Brazzaville
Corsica	Ajaccio
Costa Rica	San José
Côte d'Ivoire	Yammoussoukro/Abidjan
Croatia	Zagreb
Cuba	Havana
Cyprus	Nicosia
Czech Republic	Prague
Denmark	Copenhagen
Djibouti	Djibouti
Dominica Is.	Roseau
Dominican Republic	Santo Domingo
Ecuador	Quito
Egypt	Cairo
El Salvador	San Salvador
England	London
Equatorial Guinea	Malabo
Eritrea	Asmara
Estonia	Tallinn
Ethiopia	Addis Ababa
Faeroe Is.	Thorshavn
Falkland Is.	Stanley
Fiji	Suva
Finland	Helsinki
France	Paris
Gabon	Libreville
Gambia	Banjul (was Bathurst)
Germany	Berlin (Bonn)
Ghana	Accra
Greece	Athens
Greenland	Godthab
Grenada	St George's
Guadeloupe	Basse-Terre
Guatemala	Guatemala
Guinea	Conakry
Guinea Bissau	Bissau
Guyana	Georgetown
Haiti	Port au Prince
Honduras	Tegucigalpa
Hungary	Budapest
Iceland	Reykjavik
India	New Delhi
Indonesia	Jakarta
Iran	Teh(e)ran

Iraq	Baghdad
Ireland, Republic of	Dublin
Israel	Jerusalem
Italy	Rome
Ivory Coast	Abidjan (or Yamoussoukro)
Jamaica	Kingston
Japan	Tokyo
Jordan	Amman
Kazakhstan	Astana (Akmola)
Kenya	Nairobi
Kiribati	Tarawa
Kuwait	Kuwait City
Laos	Vientiane
Latvia	Riga
Lebanon	Beirut
Lesotho	Maseru
Liberia	Monrovia
Libya	Tripoli
Liechtenstein	Vaduz
Lithuania	Vilnius
Luxembourg	Luxembourg
Madagascar	Antananarivo
Malawi	Lilongwe
Malaysia	Kuala Lumpur
Maldives	Malé
Mali	Bamako
Malta	Val(l)etta
Marshall Islands	Majuro
Martinique Is.	Fort de France
Mauritania	Nouakchott
Mauritius	Port Louis
Mexico	Mexico City
Micronesia	Palikir
Moldova	Kishinev
Mozambique	Maputo
Monaco	Monaco
Mongolia	Ulan Bator (or Ulaanbaatar)
Morocco	Rabat
Myanmar (was Burma)	Rangoon
Namibia	Windhoek
Naura	Yoren
Nepal	Kat(h)mandu
Netherlands	The Hague
New Zealand	Wellington
Nicaragua	Managua
Niger	Niamey
Nigeria	Abuja
Northern Ireland	Belfast

North Korea	Pyonyang
Norway	Oslo
Oman	Muscat
Pakistan	Islamabad (was Karachi)
Panama	Panama
Papua New Guinea	Port Moresby
Paraguay	Asuncion
Peru	Lima
Philippines	Manila
Poland	Warsaw
Portugal	Lisbon
Puerto Rico	San Juan
Qatar	Doha
Romania	Bucharest
Russia	Moscow
Rwanda	Kigali
St Kitts and Nevis	Basseterre
St Lucia	Castries
St Vincent	Kingstown
Samoa	Apia
San Marino	San Marino
Sao Tome and Principe	Sao Tome
Sarawak	Kuching
Sardinia	Cagliari
Saudi Arabia	Riyadh
Scotland	Edinburgh
Senegal	Dakar
Serbia	Belgrade
Seychelles	Victoria
Sicily	Palermo
Sierra Leone	Freetown
Singapore	Singapore
Slovakia	Bratislava
Solomon Islands	Honiara
Somalia	Mogadishu
South Africa	Pretoria
Spain	Madrid
Sri Lanka	Colombo
Sudan	Khartoum
Surinam	Paramaribo
Swaziland	Mbabane
Sweden	Stockholm
Switzerland	Berne
Syria	Damascus
Taiwan	Taipeh
Tajikistan	Dushanbe
Tanzania	Dodoma
Thailand	Bangkok

Tibet	Lhasa
Togo	Lomé
Tonga	Nuku'alofa
Trinidad and Tobago	Port of Spain
Tunisia	Tunis
Turkey	Ankara
Turkmenistan	Ashkabad
Tuvalu	Funafuti
Uganda	Kampala
Ukraine	Kiev
United Arab Emirates	Abu Dhabi
United Kingdom	London
United States of America	Washington
Uruguay	Montevideo
Uzbekistan	Tashkent
Vanuatu	Vila
Venezuala	Caracas
Vietnam	Hanoi
Wales	Cardiff
Western Sahara	Aaiun
Yemen	San'a
Yugoslavia	Belgrade
Zambia	Lusaka
Zimbabwe	Harare

CARS

A car
Makes of car
Parts of a car
Terms used in driving
See also **VEHICLE**

A CAR

4
auto
jeep
limo
mini

5
coupé
sedan

6
banger
estate
hotrod
jalopy
roller
saloon
wheels

7
compact
hardtop
softtop

8
drophead
fastback
roadster
runabout

9
cabriolet
hatchback
limousine
supermini

10
automobile

rattletrap

11
convertible

2+ words
beach buggy
estate car
people carrier
station wagon
stretch limo

MAKES OF CAR

2
MG
VW

3
BMW
Kia

4
Audi
Fiat
Ford
Lada
Opel
Saab
Seat

5
Buick
Dodge
Honda
Isuzu
Mazda
Rover
Skoda
Smart
Volvo

6
Austin
Daewoo
Humber
Lancia
Morris

Nissan
Jaguar
Proton
Subaru

7
Bentley
Bugatti
Citroen
Daimler
Ferrari
Hillman
Packard
Peugeot
Pontiac
Renault
Sunbeam
Triumph

8
Cadillac
Chrysler
Maserati
Mercedes
Vauxhall

9
Chevrolet
Landrover

10
Mitsubishi
Volkswagen

11
Lamborghini

PARTS OF A CAR

3
cam
cap
cog
fan
hub
key
nut

4
axle
belt
body
boot
bush
coil
dash
disc
door
drum
fuse
gear
hood
horn
jack
plug
pump
seat
sump
tail
tank
tyre
wing

5
alarm
brake
cable
choke
crank
float
gauge
grill
motor
pedal
rotor
servo
shaft
shift
spare
tread
valve
wheel
wiper

6
bonnet

bumper
clutch
dickey
dimmer
dynamo
engine
fender
gasket
grille
hubcap
mascot
mirror
pinion
pintle
piston
radial
satnav
spring
tappet
timing
towbar
winker

7
battery
bearing
blinker
chassis
exhaust
fanbelt
flasher
gearbox
kingpin
magneto
muffler
springs
starter
sunroof
toolkit
wingnut

8
armature
backseat
bodywork
brakerod
camshaft
crankpin

cylinder
dipstick
foglight
footpump
ignition
manifold
mounting
mudguard
odometer
radiator
roofrack
seatbelt
silencer
solenoid
tailpipe
throttle

9
brakeshoe
condenser
crankcase
dashboard
dipswitch
footbrake
gearshift
generator
handbrake
headlight
indicator
reflector
sidelight
stoplight
underseal
wheelbase

10
alternator
crankshaft
mileometer
suspension
upholstery
wheelbrace
windscreen
windshield

11
accelerator
accumulator

carburettor
distributor
immobilizer
(immobiliser)
interrupter
speedometer
splashboard
syncromesh
trafficator

12
differential
transmission

2+ words
air bag
big end
con rod
fuel tank
gear lever
ignition key
number plate
oil filter
radiator cap
petrol gauge
piston ring
radial tyre
rear mirror
rev counter
side mirror
spare tyre
sparking plug
tax disc
wing mirror

TERMS USED IN DRIVING

2
AA
cc
hp

3
MOT
mph
oil
pit
RAC

rev
run
ton

4
flat
hoot
idle
jack
lane
lock
pink
roll
skid
tour
veer

5
rally
route
speed
yield

6
bypass
camber
dazzle
detour
diesel
divert
fitter
garage
grease
idling
milage
octane
oilcan
petrol
signal
swerve
torque

7
blowout
bollard
carpark
carport
flyover

joyride
licence
mileage
misfire
mixture
offside
logbook
parking
pinking
reverse
roadhog
roadmap
roadtax
skidpan
touring
towrope
traffic
trailer

8
autobahn
backfire
clearway
declutch
driveway
gradient
gridlock
knocking
motoring
motorway
nearside
oncoming
overheat
overpass
overtake
overturn
puncture
roadside
speeding

9
autoroute
breakdown
chauffeur
crossroad
diversion
joyriding
insurance

lubricate
motorcade
overdrive
passenger

10
antifreeze
crossroads
horsepower
overtaking
roadworthy
roundabout
signalling

11
carriageway
compression
endorsement
lubrication
overheating

12
acceleration
registration

2+ words
bus lane
cut in
cut out
de-icer
fast lane

flat tyre
give way
Grand Prix
hit-and-run
lay-by
one-way
on tow
panel beater
pile-up
road rage
road sign
road test
rush hour
slip road
slow lane
top gear

CATS

A cat
Breeds of cat
Members of the cat family

A CAT

3
gib
kit
mog
tom

4
puss

5
kitty
moggy
pussy
queen
tabby

6
feline
kitten
mouser
ratter
tomcat

9
marmalade

13
tortoiseshell

BREEDS OF CAT

3
Rex

4
Abby
blue
Manx

5
cream
Korat
smoke

6
Birman
Havana
Somali

7
British
Burmese
Persian
Siamese
spotted
Turkish

8
Balinese

9
sealpoint
Tonkinese

10
Abyssinian
chinchilla
longhaired

11
shorthaired

12
colourpoint

2+ words
Cornish Rex
Devon Rex
Maine Coon
Red Self
Russian Blue
Scottish Fold
Turkish Angora
Turkish Van

MEMBERS OF THE CAT FAMILY

4
eyra
lion
lynx
puma

5
civet
genet
ounce
rasse
tiger
tigon

6
bobcat
cougar
jaguar
margay
ocelot
serval

7
caracal
cheetah
leopard

10
jaguarundi

CATTLE

BREEDS OF CATTLE

3
Gir

5
Devon
Kerry
Kyloe
Luing

6
Ankole
Dexter
Durham

Jersey
Sussex

7
Brahman
cattabu
cattalo

8
Alderney
Ayrshire
Friesian
Galloway
Guernsey
Hereford
Highland
Holstein

Limousin
longhorn

9
Charolais
Romagnola
shorthorn

10
Afrikander

2+ words
Aberdeen Angus
Red Poll
Welsh black

CHARACTER-ISTICS AND QUALITIES
(non-physical)

A characteristic
Characteristic

POSITIVE

Clever
Cleverness
Clever person
Courage
Courageous
Easy
Importance
Important
Kind
Kindness
Pleasant
Rich
Skilful
Skill
Skilled person

NEGATIVE

Boring
Difficult
Mad
Mad person
Poor
Poor person
Poverty
Stupid
Stupidity
Stupid person
Unimportant
Unkind
Unskilled
Unusual

SEE ALSO BAD AND GOOD

A CHARACTERISTIC

4
feel
mark
seal

5
brand
habit
idiom
label
mould
point
quirk
shape
smell
stamp
taste
token
touch
trait
trick

7
feature
flavour
quality
symptom

8
hallmark
property

9
attribute
mannerism
trademark

11
peculiarity
singularity

12
eccentricity
idiosyncrasy

CHARACTERISTIC (ADJECTIVE)

3
own

5
stock
usual

6
common
normal
proper
single
unique

7
average
routine
typical
special

8
discrete
distinct
orthodox
peculiar
personal
separate
singular
specific
standard

10
individual
particular

11
distinctive

13
idiosyncratic

14
representative

POSITIVE

CLEVER

3
apt
sly

4
able
sage
wily
wise

5
acute
canny
quick
sharp
smart

6
astute
brainy
bright
gifted
shrewd

7
cunning
erudite
knowing
learned
prudent
skilful

8
cerebral
rational
sensible
talented

9
brilliant
dexterous
ingenious
inventive
judicious

sagacious
scholarly

10
farsighted
perceptive
reasonable
streetwise
thoughtful

11
intelligent

13
intellectual
knowledgeable

2+ words
clued-up
quick-witted

CLEVERNESS

2
IQ

3
wit

4
nous

5
brain
flair
guile
sense
skill

6
acuity
acumen
brains
genius
talent
wisdom

7
insight
slyness

8
aptitude
sagacity
subtlety

9
acuteness
adeptness
alertness
canniness
dexterity
ingenuity
intellect
mentality
quickness
sharpness
smartness

10
astuteness
braininess
brightness
brilliance
shrewdness

12
incisiveness
intelligence

13
understanding

CLEVER PERSON

4
guru
sage

5
brain

6
genius
master

pundit
savant

7
egghead
scholar
thinker

8
academic
bookworm
highbrow
polymath

9
intellect

10
mastermind

COURAGE

3
vim

4
grit
guts

5
balls
pluck
nerve
spunk

6
bottle
daring
mettle
spirit
valour

7
bravery

8
audacity
backbone

boldness

9
gallantry

11
intrepidity

COURAGEOUS

4
bold

5
brave
gutsy
hardy
macho
tough

6
daring
feisty
heroic
plucky
spunky

7
doughty
gallant
valiant

8
fearless
intrepid
spirited
unafraid
valorous

9
audacious
dauntless
undaunted

10
undismayed
unshakable

11
indomitable
unflinching
unshakeable
unshrinking

EASY

5
clear
cushy
light
plain

6
facile
simple

8
downhill
painless

9
leisurely

10
accessible
effortless
elementary
manageable
simplified
uninvolved

11
comfortable
undemanding

12
intelligible

13
uncomplicated
unproblematic

15
straightforward

IMPORTANCE

4
mark
note
rank

5
merit
power
value
worth

6
degree
import
moment
repute
status
weight

7
account
gravity
primacy
urgency

8
eminence
emphasis
prestige
priority
standing

9
greatness
influence
magnitude
necessity
relevance
substance

10
notability
prominence
reputation
usefulness

11
consequence
distinction
materiality
paramountcy
seriousness
superiority
weightiness

12
memorability
significance

13
momentousness

IMPORTANT

3
big
key
top

4
main

5
chief
first
grand
grave
great
large
major
noted
prime
vital

6
summit
urgent

7
capital
central
crucial
eminent
leading

notable
pivotal
primary
radical
salient
serious
supreme

8
cardinal
critical
foremost
historic
material
relevant
superior
valuable

9
essential
memorable
momentous
necessary
paramount
principal
prominent
uppermost

10
imperative
meaningful
overriding

11
fundamental
influential
significant

12
considerable

13
consequential
indispensable
irreplaceable

2+ words
far-reaching

high-level
high-profile
high-ranking

KIND

4
good
mild
nice

6
benign
gentle
humane
kindly
tender

7
amiable
helpful
lenient

8
friendly
generous
gracious
obliging
selfless
tolerant

9
forgiving
indulgent

10
altruistic
beneficent
benevolent
charitable
forbearing
thoughtful

11
considerate
magnanimous
sympathetic

13
compassionate
philanthropic
understanding

2+ words
good-natured
tender-hearted
warm-hearted

KINDNESS

4
boon
care
help

6
favour
warmth

7
charity
concern

8
altruism
courtesy
goodness
goodwill
humanity
sympathy

9
tolerance

10
amiability
compassion
generosity
gentleness

11
beneficence
benevolence
forbearance

12
philanthropy

13
consideration

2+ words
good turn

PLEASANT

3
fun

4
cosy
good
kind
lush
nice
snug
soft
warm

5
cushy
fresh
juicy
sweet

6
divine
dulcet
genial
kindly
lovely
smooth

7
affable
amiable
cordially
genteel
helpful
idyllic
likable
lovable
restful

welcome

8
blissful
charming
fragrant
friendly
generous
heavenly
inviting
luscious
obliging
pleasing
relaxing
soothing
tasteful

9
agreeable
ambrosial
appealing
congenial
convivial
delicious
enjoyable
exquisite
luxurious
melodious
palatable
seductive
succulent
welcoming

10
acceptable
attractive
comforting
delectable
delightful
euphonious
gratifying
hospitable
refreshing
satisfying

11
comfortable
mellifluous

pleasurable
scrumptious
titillating

13
mouthwatering

RICH

4
deep
full
lush

5
fatty
flush

6
costly
loaded
ornate

7
moneyed
opulent
rolling
wealthy

8
abundant
affluent
precious
resonant

10
prosperous

12
indigestible

2+ words
in the money
quids in
rolling in it
well-heeled
well-off
well-to-do

SKILFUL

3
ace
apt

4
able
deft
good
neat

5
adept
agile
crack
handy
quick
ready
slick
smart
sound

6
adroit
clever
crafty
expert
fluent
nimble
shrewd

7
cunning
perfect
politic
skilled
stylish

8
artistic
finished
flexible
masterly
virtuoso

9
adaptable

competent
dexterous
efficient
ingenious
practised
versatile

10
diplomatic
proficient
scientific

11
industrious
magisterial
resourceful

12
accomplished
ambidextrous
professional

13
sophisticated

SKILL

3
art
use

4
ease
grip
nous

5
craft
dodge
flair
forte
grace
knack
touch
trick

6
aplomb

finish
metier
talent

7
ability
address
control
cunning
faculty
finesse
fluency
mastery
prowess
tactics

8
aptitude
artistry
capacity
deftness
delicacy
elegance
facility
neatness
wizardry

9
adeptness
execution
expertise
handiness
ingenuity
knowledge
sharpness
technique

10
adroitness
attainment
brilliance
capability
cleverness
competence
craftiness
efficiency
excellence
experience

expertness
perfection
specialism
speciality
suppleness
virtuosity

11
acquirement
flexibility
proficiency
skilfulness
versatility

12
adaptability

13
ambidexterity
craftsmanship
dexterousness

14
accomplishment
sophistication

SKILLED PERSON

3
ace
dan

4
diva
sage
seed
star

5
adept

6
expert
genius
master
wizard

7
acrobat
athlete
dabster
gymnast
maestro
prodigy

8
champion
graduate
handyman
virtuoso

9
craftsman

10
specialist

11
craftswoman

12
professional

2+ words
all-rounder
dab hand
past master

NEGATIVE

BORING

3
dry

4

arid
drab
dull
flat
slow

5
banal
plain
prosy
stale
trite

6
deadly
dreary
stodgy
stuffy

7
humdrum
insipid
prosaic
tedious
uniform

8
overlong
tiresome
wearying

9
laborious
soporific
wearisome

10
lacklustre
monotonous
pedestrian
repetitive
unexciting
unreadable

11
commonplace
repetitious
uninspiring

13
uninteresting

2+ words
long-winded

DIFFICULT

4
hard

5
heavy
steep
tough

6
knotty
severe
tricky
trying
uphill

7
arduous
complex
obscure
onerous
testing
unclear

8
abstruse
baffling
exacting
involved
puzzling
stubborn
toilsome

9
demanding
gruelling
Herculean
intricate
laborious
punishing
recondite
strenuous

10
convoluted
exhausting
impossible

oppressive
perplexing

11
challenging
complicated
problematic
troublesome

12
backbreaking
unmanageable

DIFFICULTY

4
snag

6
hurdle

7
problem

8
obstacle
severity

9
adversity
intricacy
obscurity

10
complexity
impediment

12
complication
disadvantage
technicality

2+ words
stumbling block

MAD

3
ape

4
bats
loco
nuts
wild

5
angry
crazy
dotty
loony
loopy
nutty
wacky
weird

6
absurd
cuckoo
insane
mental
raving
screwy

7
bananas
barking
bonkers
frantic
lunatic

8
cracked
demented
deranged
doolally
neurotic
peculiar
unhinged

9
disturbed
psychotic

senseless

10
irrational
unbalanced

11
certifiable

2+ words
mad as a hatter
mad as a March hare
not all there
off one's chump
off one's head
out of one's mind

MAD PERSON

3
nut

4
loon

5
crank
dummy
idiot
loony

6
maniac
nutter

7
lunatic
nutcase
oddball

8
crackpot
headcase
imbecile
neurotic

9
fruitcake

screwball

10
psychopath

POOR

3
bad

5
broke
needy
skint
stony

8
bankrupt
deprived
homeless
indigent

9
destitute
insolvent
penniless
penurious
underpaid

10
straitened

11
impecunious
necessitous
underfunded

12
impoverished

13
disadvantaged

15
underprivileged

2+ words
badly-off

down and out
hard up
low-paid
poverty-stricken

POOR PERSON

3
bum
Job

4
hobo

5
lazar
tramp

6
beggar
pauper

7
vagrant

8
bankrupt
indigent
squatter

9
insolvent
mendicant

10
Cinderella

POVERTY

4
lack
need
want

6
blight
misery
penury

8
distress
hardship

9
breadline
indigence
necessity
neediness
pauperism
privation

10
bankruptcy
depression

11
deprivation
destitution

STUPID

3
dim
mad

4
daft
dull
dumb
rash
slow
soft

5
barmy
crazy
dense
dopey
inane
loony
nutty
silly
thick

6
absurd
crazed

insane
lunatic
obtuse
simple
stolid
unwise

7
fatuous
foolish
idiotic
puerile
witless

8
childish
ignorant
immature

9
illogical
infantile
ludicrous
senseless

10
ridiculous
unthinking

11
nonsensical
thickheaded
thoughtless

12
irresponsible

13
unintelligent

2+ words
dim-witted
not all there
out to lunch

STUPIDITY

5
folly

6
idiocy

7
fatuity
inanity
vacuity

8
futility
hebetude

9
ignorance
puerility

10
imbecility
immaturity

12
illogicality

13
irrationality

STUPID PERSON

3
ass
mug
nit
oaf
sap

4
berk
bozo
burk
clod
clot
coot
dick

dolt
dope
dork
dupe
goon
jerk
nan
nerd
prat
twit
zany

5
bimbo
booby
chump
clown
crank
dumbo
dummy
dunce
goose
idiot
klutz
moron
ninny
noddy
prune
twerp
wally

6
buffer
cretin
dimwit
donkey
duffer
lummox
nitwit
noodle
sucker
stooge
thicko

7
airhead
buffoon
Charlie

dullard
fathead
halfwit
jackass
juggins
muggins
natural
palooka
pillock
pinhead
plonker
schmuck

8
bonehead
clodpoll
crackpot
dipstick
dumbbell
imbecile

9
birdbrain
blockhead
lamebrain
numbskull
simpleton

10
dunderhead
nincompoop

UNIMPORTANT

5
banal
light
minor
petty
small

6
little
slight
paltry
venial

7
minimal
nominal
trivial

8
fiddling
footling
marginal
niggling
nugatory
piddling
piffling
trifling
trumpery
twopenny

9
frivolous
parochial

10
immaterial
irrelevant
negligible

11
commonplace
dispensable
forgettable
ineffectual
inessential
lightweight
nondescript
superficial
unnecessary

12
nonessential

13
inappreciable
insignificant
insubstantial

14
inconsiderable

UNKIND

4
mean

5
cruel
harsh
nasty

7
beastly
callous
hateful
hostile
hurtful
inhuman

8
inhumane
spiteful
uncaring

9
malicious
unfeeling

10
malevolent
unfriendly

11
insensitive
thoughtless

13
inconsiderate
unsympathetic

UNPLEASANT

3
bad

4
cold
foul
vile

5
nasty

6
horrid
odious
shabby
sordid

7
irksome
painful
squalid

8
annoying
horrible

9
invidious
loathsome
obnoxious
offensive
repulsive
revolting
sickening
unsavoury
unwelcome

10
disgusting
nauseating
uninviting

11
displeasing
distasteful
unpalatable

12
disagreeable
unacceptable

13
objectionable.
uncomfortable

UNSKILLED

3
ham
lay
raw

5
crude
gawky
inept
unfit

6
callow
clumsy
gauche
unable

7
amateur
awkward
unhandy

8
bungling
fumbling
ignorant
inexpert
untaught
unversed

9
incapable
maladroit
untrained
untutored

10
amateurish
inadequate
uneducated
unequipped
uninformed
unseasoned

11
impractical

incompetent
ineffectual
inefficient
undeveloped
uninitiated
unpractised
unqualified

UNUSUAL

3
odd
rum

4
rare

5
alien
funny
novel
queer
weird

6
exotic
freaky
notable
quaint
quirky
scarce
strange
unique

7
amazing
bizarre
deviant
erratic
oddball
offbeat
special

8
aberrant
abnormal
atypical
freakish

peculiar
singular
uncommon
unwonted

9
anomalous
eccentric
grotesque
monstrous
remarkable

10
infrequent
marvellous
mysterious
noteworthy
outlandish
surprising
unexpected
unfamiliar
unorthodox

11
exceptional
incongruous

13
extraordinary
idiosyncratic

2+ words
out of the ordinary
way out

CHARACTER-ISTICS AND QUALITIES
(physical)

Beautiful
Big/Large
Fat
Small
Small person or thing
Strength
Strong
Thin
Ugly
Weak
Weakness
Weak person or thing

BEAUTIFUL

4
fair

5
bonny

6
comely
lovely
pretty
scenic

7
radiant

8
alluring
charming
gorgeous
handsome
pleasing
striking
stunning

9
appealing
beauteous
exquisite

glamorous
ravishing

10
attractive

11
picturesque

2+ words
good-looking

BIG/LARGE

1
L

2
OS
XL

4
huge
mega
tall
vast
wide

5
adult
ample
baggy
beefy
broad
bulky
elder
giant
great
gross
hefty
jumbo
large
lofty
roomy

6
goodly
mighty

7
immense
mammoth
massive
monster
outsize
titanic

8
colossal
enormous
generous
gigantic
imposing
sizeable
spacious
towering
whopping

9
capacious
extensive
ginormous
humungous
monstrous
overgrown
oversized
strapping

10
commodious
cumbersome
gargantuan
monumental
prodigious
stupendous
tremendous
voluminous

11
mountainous
substantial

12
astronomical

2+ words
king-size

FAT

2
OS

3
big

5
bonny
busty
buxom
dumpy
obese
plump
podgy
puffy
round
stout
thick
tubby

6
chubby
chunky
flabby
fleshy
portly
rotund

7
adipose
bloated
overfed
paunchy
swollen

9
corpulent

10
overweight

SMALL

3
toy
wee

4
baby
mini
poky
puny
thin
tiny

5
bijou
bitsy
brief
dinky
dwarf
minor
pygmy
scant
short
squat
teeny
weeny

6
bantam
humble
lesser
little
meagre
midget
minute
modest
paltry
petite
pocket
scanty
skimpy
slight
sparse
teensy
tiddly
titchy

7
compact
cramped
limited
minimal
scrawny

stunted
trivial

8
dwarfish
exiguous
shrunken
trifling

9
miniature
minuscule
undersize

10
diminutive
negligible
restricted
shrivelled

11
Lilliputian
microscopic

13
infinitesimal
insignificant

SMALL PERSON OR THING

3
dot
elf
jot
tot

4
atom
chit
drop
iota
mite
mote
runt
slip
spot
wisp

5
crumb
dwarf
fairy
fleck
gnome
midge
mouse
pygmy
scrap
speck
titch

6
bantam
midget
minnow
morsel
shorty
shrimp
sliver
sprite
squirt

7
minutia
snippet
tiddler

8
fragment
particle

STRENGTH

4
beef

5
asset
brawn
force
forte
might
power

6
muscle

sinews
vigour

7
courage
potency
stamina

8
backbone
firmness
tenacity
virility

8
beefiness
burliness
endurance
intensity
manliness
toughness

9
durability
resilience
resistance
resolution

10
muscularity

STRONG

3
fit
hot

4
neat
pure

5
beefy
burly
hardy
lusty
manly
rigid

solid
spicy
stout
tough

6
brawny
mighty
potent
robust
sinewy
sturdy
virile

7
durable
healthy
intense
piquant
pungent
staunch

8
muscular
stalwart
powerful
vigorous

9
Amazonian
fanatical
Herculean
resilient
resistant
strapping

10
compelling
convincing
formidable
persuasive

12
concentrated
intoxicating

2+ words
hard-wearing

heavy-duty
long-lasting

THIN

4
bony
fine
lean
slim
trim
weak
wiry

5
filmy
gaunt
gauzy
lanky
light
rangy
reedy
runny
sheer
spare
weedy

6
boyish
dilute
flimsy
light
narrow
scarce
skinny
slight
svelte
watery

7
diluted
girlish
scraggy
scrawny
shallow
slender
tenuous
willowy

8
anorexic
delicate
gangling
gossamer
skeletal

9
emaciated
sylphlike

10
attenuated
diaphanous

11
lightweight
translucent
transparent
underweight

13
insubstantial

2+ words
flat-chested
see-through

UGLY

4
drab
dull

5
dingy
dowdy
mousy
plain
tacky

6
coarse
common
garish
grisly
homely
horrid

tawdry
vulgar

7
hideous

8
deformed
gruesome
horrible
ungainly
unlovely
unseemly

9
contorted
inelegant
misshapen
monstrous
repellent
repulsive
unsightly

10
disfigured
unbecoming

11
distasteful
overdressed
threatening

12
unattractive

WEAK

3
dim
low

4
limp
puny
soft
thin

5
faint
frail
runny

6
feeble
flimsy
infirm
sickly
slight
unsafe
watery

7
anaemic
brittle
diluted
exposed
flaccid
fragile
insipid
rickety
tenuous
tottery

8
cowardly
decrepit
delicate
helpless
impotent

9
breakable
deficient
enervated
powerless
spineless
tasteless

10
inadequate
indecisive
irresolute
vulnerable

11
debilitated
defenceless
ineffectual
ineffective
unfortified
unprotected

12
unconvincing

WEAKNESS

4
flaw

5
fault

6
damage
defect
foible
liking

7
failing
frailty

8
debility
delicacy
drawback
fondness
penchant
puniness

9
cowardice
faintness
fragility
impotence
infirmity

10
feebleness
flaccidity
flimsiness
impairment
incapacity
indecision
partiality

11
shortcoming

WEAK PERSON OR THING

4
baby
drip
reed
weed
wimp

5
pansy
patsy
sissy
softy

6
coward
thread

7
chicken
doormat
invalid
milksop

8
eggshell
gossamer
pushover

9
dishwater

CHEESES

TYPES OF CHEESE

4

blue
Brie
curd
Edam
Feta
sage
Tome

5
cream
Derby
Gouda
Swiss

6
Dunlop
paneer
Tilsit

7
Boursin
Cheddar
cottage
Crowdie
Gruyère
Munster
ricotta
sapsago
Stilton

8
Auvergne
Cheshire
Cotswold
Emmental
Parmesan
Pecorino
Tilsiter
Vacherin

9
Caithness
Camembert
Gambozola
Jarlsberg

Leicester
Limburger
mousetrap
Provolone
Roquefort

10
Caerphilly
dolcelatte
Emmentaler
Gorgonzola
Lancashire
mascarpone
mozzarella

11
Wensleydale

2+ words
bel paese
double Gloucester
Pont l'Evêque
Port Salut
red Leicester
stinking bishop

CHEMISTRY

Chemicals and terms used in chemistry
See also **ELEMENTS**

CHEMICALS AND TERMS USED IN CHEMISTRY

2
mu
pH

3
DNA
EMF
fat
gas
ion
oil
ore
PVC
RNA
TCP
TNT

4
acid
atom
base
bond
cell
clay
cola
coke
keto
lime
mica
mole
neon
rust
salt
slag
soda
spin

5
aldol
alkyl
alloy
amide
amino
anion
anode
argon
azote
basic
beryl
borax
brass
chalk
ester
ether
ethyl
Freon
glass
group
inert
ionic
lipid
Lysol
metal
monad
noble
nylon
oxide
ozone
phase
radon
redox
resin
solid
steel
sugar
vinyl

6
acetal
acetic
acetyl
acidic
adduct
aerate
alkali
alkane
alkene
alkyne
amatol
ammine
atomic
barium
bleach
borane
borate
bronze
buffer
butane
casein
cerium
chrome
dipole
energy
enzyme
ethane
ferric
formic
galena
gangue
gypsum
halide
iodide
iodine
iodite
iodize (iodise)
isomer
liquid
litmus
methyl
octane
olefin
pewter
phenol
phenyl
potash
proton
quartz
raceme
reduce
refine
retort
ribose
silica
sinter
solute

starch
sterol
tannin
teepol
Teflon
thymol

7

acetate
acetone
acidity
aerosol
alchemy
alcohol
alumina
amalgam
ammonal
ammonia
aniline
antacid
aspirin
bauxite
benzene
bismuth
bonding
bromate
bromide
calomel
camphor
carbide
cathode
chloric
cocaine
codeine
cyanate
cyanide
diamond
dioxide
ebonite
element
entropy
ferment
fermium
ferrate
ferrous
formate
gallium
gelatine

glucose
halogen
hydrate
hydride
isotope
menthol
methane
mineral
neutral
neutron
nitrate
nitride
nitrite
nitrous
nucleon
nucleus
orbital
organic
osmosis
osmotic
oxidant
oxidize (oxidise)
peptise
perspex
plastic
polymer
propane
protein
pyrites
quantum
quinine
reagent
soluble
solvent
spectra
sucrose
titrate
toluene
tritium
valence
valency
veronal
vitamin
vitriol

8

actinide
aldehyde

alkaline
ammonium
antinomy
aromatic
asbestos
atropine
caffeine
carbolic
carbonic
carbonyl
catalyst
charcoal
chlorate
chloride
chromate
chromite
cinchona
corundum
covalent
cryolite
cyanogen
diatomic
diborane
didymium
disilane
dissolve
electron
emission
enthalpy
ethylene
fluoride
formalin
fructose
glucinum
glycerol
graphite
hematite
hydrated
hydroxyl
iodoform
kerosene
kinetics
litharge
magnesia
manganin
masurium
methanol
molecule

morphine
nichrome
nicotine
particle
periodic
peroxide
phosgene
reactant
reaction
refining
saturate
silicane
silicate
solution
spectrum
suboxide
sulphate
sulphide
sulphite
tartaric
unstable

9

acetylene
acylation
alchemist
alcoholic
aliphatic
allotrope
allotropy
aluminate
anhydrous
apparatus
brimstone
carbonate
carbonium
catalysis
cellulose
chokedamp
condenser
corrosion
diazonium
digitalin
duralumin
galvanize (galvanise)
haematite
histamine
homolysis

hydration
hydroxide
indicator
inorganic
insoluble
isomerism
limestone
limewater
magnetite
manganese
metalloid
molecular
monatomic
nitration
oxidation
palladium
permalloy
petroleum
phosphate
phosphide
polyester
polythene
polyvinyl
quicklime
reductant
reduction
resonance
stability
sulphuric
synthesis
synthetic
titration
vulcanite

10

bimetallic
catenation
chalybeate
chloroform
electronic
exothermic
flotation
hydrolysis
laboratory
lanthanide
molybdenum
neutralize (neutralise)
nucleotide

phosphorus
polymerize (polymerise)
saccharide
solubility
transition

11

acetylation
cholesterol
crystallize (crystallise)
dehydration
electrolyte
endothermic
equilibrium
hydrocarbon
naphthalene
paraldehyde
pitchblende
polystyrene
precipitate
quicksilver
radioactive
ribonucleic
sublimation
substituent
tautomerism

12

acetaldehyde
carbohydrate
chlorination
condensation
deliquescent
diamagnetism
disaccharide
displacement
dissociation
electrolysis
fermentation
formaldehyde
halogenation
hydrochloric
permanganate
sulphamonide

13

petrochemical
precipitation

radioactivity
semiconductor

2+ words
amino acid
atomic mass
atomic number

bell jar
carbon dioxide
carbon monoxide
chain reaction
ideal gas
latent heat
litmus paper

litmus test
marsh gas
periodic table
rock salt
specific gravity
test tube

CHURCH

Churches and other religious buildings
Parts of a church and objects found in churches
See also **RELIGION**

CHURCHES AND OTHER RELIGIOUS BUILDINGS

4
kirk

5
abbey
temple

6
chapel
mosque
priory

7
minster
nunnery
oratory

8
basilica

9
cathedral
monastery

PARTS OF A CHURCH AND OBJECTS FOUND IN CHURCHES

3
pew

4
apse
arch
dome
font
icon
jube
nave

5
aisle
altar
choir
crypt
niche
spire
tower
vault

6
adytum
belfry
chapel
column
corbel
cupola
fleche
fresco
pillar
pulpit
vestry

7
chancel
chantry
galilee
hassock
lectern
narthex
reredos
steeple

8
cloister
crossing
lichgate
sacristy
transept

9
campanile
sanctuary
triforium

10
clerestory
tabernacle
undercroft

12
chapterhouse

2+ words
Lady chapel
lych gate
organ loft

CLOTHES

*Clothes, clothing and
associated terms*
Hats
Shoes and footwear

CLOTHES

3
bib
boa
bra
hem
kit
lap
mac
rag
tie
tux
wig
zip

4
band
belt
body
cape
coat
cuff
duds
garb
gear
gown
hood
hose
kilt
mitt
muff
robe
ruff
sari
sash
slip
sock
spur
stud
suit

toga
togs
veil
vest
wrap

5
apron
burka
chaps
choli
cloak
clogs
clout
fichu
frock
gilet
glove
heels
jeans
lapel
liner
lungi
mitts
pants
parka
pleat
plume
teddy
thong
train
trews
tunic
weeds

6
afghan
anorak
basque
bikini
blazer
blouse
bodice
bolero
boucle
braces
briefs
buckle

burnet
bustle
button
caftan
capote
chador
chinos
coatee
collar
collet
corset
cravat
diaper
dickey
dirndl
dolman
edging
flares
fleece
gaiter
garter
girdle
gusset
hankie
jacket
jerkin
jersey
jumper
kaftan
khurta
kimono
kirtle
lining
mantle
mitten
muumuu
nylons
pleats
pompom
poncho
puttee
raglan
riband
ribbon
ruffle
samfoo
sarong
sequin

serape
sheath
shorts
slacks
sleeve
smalls
tabard
thongs
tights
tippet
trunks
tuxedo
tweeds
waders
whites

7
apparel
bandana
bandeau
batiste
blanket
blucher
burnous
cagoule
calotte
cantoon
capuche
cassock
casuals
challis
chemise
chimere
chlamys
chopine
chrisom
civvies
clobber
cockade
corsage
costume
djibbah
dornock
doublet
drawers
dupatta
fallals
falsies

flounce
gaiters
garment
glasses
gymslip
handbag
hosiery
layette
leotard
mantlet
muffler
necktie
nightie
overall
panties
parasol
puttees
pyjamas
rompers
shalwar
singlet
soutane
sporran
surcoat
surtout
sweater
topknot
twinset
uniform
wetsuit
wiggery
woollen
yashmak

8
bathrobe
bedsocks
bloomers
breeches
Burberry
burnoose
camisole
cardigan
codpiece
coiffure
corselet
culottes
dentures

dungaree
earmuffs
ensemble
flannels
footwear
frontlet
gauntlet
guernsey
hipsters
kerchief
knickers
knitwear
leggings
lingerie
mantelet
menswear
neckband
negligee
overalls
overcoat
pashmina
pinafore
playsuit
pullover
raincoat
sherwani
stocking
sunshade
swimsuit
tailcoat
trimming
trousers
umbrella
wardrobe
woollens
wristlet

9
bandolier
beachwear
bedjacket
brassiere
cheongsam
comforter
crinoline
dungarees
galoshes
gauntlets

glengarry
greatcoat
hairpiece
housecoat
loincloth
macintosh
neckcloth
nightgown
nightwear
overdress
pantaloon
patchwork
petticoat
quoiffure
separates
stockings
stomacher
strapless
sweatband
tracksuit
trousseau
underwear
waistband
waistcoat
wristband

10
bobbysocks
buttonhole
chemisette
coverchief
cummerbund
drainpipes
embroidery
legwarmers
nightdress
nightshirt
pantaloons
pinstripes
suspenders
sweatshirt
turtleneck
underpants
waterproof
windjammer

11
neckerchief

netherlings
regimentals
shoulderbag
slumberwear
windcheater

12
combinations
handkerchief
shirtwaister
underclothes

2+ words
Alice band
ankle socks
Aran jumper
bath wrap
bathing cap
bell bottoms
blue jeans
boat-neck
body belt
body stocking
boiler suit
boob tube
bow tie
bush jacket
bush shirt
business suit
court dress
cut-away
dinner jacket
divided skirt
diving suit
donkey jacket
dress clothes
dress coat
dress shoes
dress suit
dress tie
dressing gown
drip-dry shirt
duffle coat
Eton collar
Eton jacket
evening dress
false nails
fancy dress

feather boa
flared skirt
frock coat
fur coat
get-up
grass skirt
G-string
halter-neck
hand-me-downs
kid gloves
knee breeches
knee socks
lounge suit
lumber jacket
maxi skirt
mess jacket
midi skirt
mini skirt
monkey jacket
monkey suit
morning coat
morning dress
off-the-peg
opera cloak
Oxford bags
panty girdle
party dress
pea coat
pea jacket
pith helmet
plastic mac
plus-fours
polo neck
press stud
pret-a-porter
print dress
ready-to-wear
reefer jacket
riding habit
round-neck
sack dress
safety pin
sailor suit
scoop-neck
shell suit
ski pants
sloppy joe
sports coat

sports jacket
string vest
sun dress
sun suit
tennis skirt
terry nappy
thermal vest
top coat
trench coat
trouser suit
T-shirt
turn-ups
two-piece
V-neck
V-neck sweater
wedding dress
wing collar
wrap-around

HATS AND HEADGEAR

3
cap
fez
tam
wig

4
brim
coif
cowl
helm
hood
kepi
peak
topi

5
beret
busby
derby
hejab
hijab
mitre
shako
snood
tiara
topee

toque

6
beaver
boater
bonnet
bowler
castor
cloche
fedora
helmet
panama
topper
trilby
turban
wimple

7
biretta
cockade
homburg
skullcap
stetson
tricorn

8
bearskin
headband
mantilla
nightcap
skullcap
sombrero
tarboosh
yarmulka
yarmulke

9
balaclava
billycock
glengarry
stovepipe

11
deerstalker

2+ words
bobble hat
cheese-cutter

cloth cap
forage cap
mob-cap
mortar-board
opera hat
pill-box
pork-pie hat
slouch hat
sou'-wester
sun hat
tam o'shanter
ten-gallon hat

SHOES AND FOOTWEAR

3
dap

4
boot
clog
heel
lace
mule
pump
sole
vamp
welt

5
upper
suede
wedge
welly

6
brogan
brogue
galosh
insole
loafer
oxford
patten
sandal
toecap
waders

7
gumboot
gymshoe
slipper
sneaker
trainer

8
flipflop
footwear
jackboot
moccasin
overshoe
platform

plimsoll
sandshoe
shoelace
snowshoe
stiletto

9
slingback

10
espadrille
shoestring
wellington

2+ words
court shoe
Cuban heel
kitten heel
lace-up
slip-on
wedge heel

COINS

COINS OLD AND NEW

2
as (Rome)

3
bit
bob (UK)
écu (France)
sou (France)

4
anna (India)
cent (US, etc.)
dime (US)
mark (England, Germany)
peso (Spain, South America)
pice (India)
real (Spain, South America)

5
angel (England)
crown (England)
daric (Persia)
dinar (Middle East)
ducat (Europe)

franc (France, etc.)
frank (Europe)
groat (England)
liard (Europe)
noble (England)
obang (Japan)
penny (UK)
pound (UK)
royal (England)
scudo (Italy)

6
aureus (Rome)
bezant (Turkey)
byzant (Turkey)
dollar (US, etc.)
florin (UK)
guinea (UK)
gulden (Netherlands)
kopeck (Russia)
nickel (US)
obolus (Greece)
peseta (Spain)
rouble (Russia)
sequin (Italy, etc.)
shekel (Israel)
stater (Greece)
stiver (Netherlands)
talent (Bible)
tanner (UK)
tester (England)
thaler (Germany)

7
carolus (England)
drachma (Greece)
guilder (Netherlands, etc.)
ha'penny (UK)
moidore (Portugal)
pistole (Europe)
prindle (Scotland)
quarter (US)
solidus (Rome)

8
denarius (Rome)
doubloon (Spain)
farthing (UK)
groschen (Austria)
kreutzer (Germany)
maravedi (Spain)
napoleon (France)
sesterce (Rome)
shilling (UK)
sixpence (UK)
zecchino (Italy, etc.)

9
dandiprat (England)
halfcrown (UK)
halfpenny (UK)
sovereign (UK)

10
krugerrand (South Africa)

2+ words
Maria Theresa dollar (Austria)
piece of eight (Spain)
threepenny bit (UK)

COLOURS

3
bay
dun
dye
hue
jet
tan

4
anil
blue
buff
cyan
dark
dove
drab
ecru
fawn
gold
grey
iris
jade
lake
lime
navy
opal
pale
pied
pink
plum
puce
roan
rose
ruby
rust
sage
sand
saxe
tint
tone

5
amber
azure

beige
black
blond
blush
brown
camel
cocoa
coral
cream
delft
ebony
flesh
green
hazel
henna
ivory
khaki
lemon
lilac
lovat
mauve
mouse
ochre
olive
pansy
peach
pearl
sable
sepia
slate
straw
taupe
tawny
topaz
umber
white

6
auburn
bistre
blonde
bronze
canary
cerise
cherry
chrome
citron
claret

cobalt
copper
fallow
flaxen
indigo
madder
maroon
motley
orange
oyster
pastel
purple
russet
salmon
sienna
silver
sorrel
Titian
violet
yellow

7
apricot
avocado
biscuit
caramel
carmine
celadon
crimson
emerald
fuchsia
grizzle
heather
jacinth
magenta
mottled
mustard
neutral
saffron
scarlet

8
amethyst
burgundy
charcoal
chestnut
cinnamon
gunmetal

hyacinth
lavender
magnolia
mahogany
mulberry
mushroom
pistache
primrose
sapphire
viridian

9
aubergine
carnation
carnelian
champagne
chocolate
cochineal
tangerine
turquoise
vermilion

10
aquamarine
terracotta

11
ultramarine

2+ words
blood-red
brick-red
Cambridge blue
eau-de-nil
navy-blue
old gold
Oxford blue
pea-green
sage-green
slate-grey
sky-blue

COMPOSERS

FAMOUS COMPOSERS

3
Bax (Arnold)
Maw (Nicholas)
Suk (Joseph)

4
Abel (Karl)
Adam (Adolphe)
Arne (Thomas)
Bach (Johann Sebastian)
Bart (Lionel)
Berg (Alban)
Blow (John)
Bull (John)
Bush (Alan)
Byrd (William)
Cage (John)
Ives (Charles)
Kern (Jerome)
Lalo (Edouard)
Nono (Luigi)
Orff (Carl)
Part (Arvo)
Wolf (Hugo)

5
Adams (John)
Auber (Daniel)
Berio (Luciano)
Bizet (Georges)
Bliss (Arthur)
Boyce (William)
Brian (Havergal)
Dufay (Guillaume)
Dukas (Paul)
Elgar (Edward)
Falla (Manuel de)
Fauré (Gabriel)
Finzi (Gerald)
Glass (Philip)
Gluck (Christoph)
Grieg (Edvard Hagerup)
Haydn (Josef)
Henze (Hans Werner)

Holst (Gustav)
Ibert (Jacques)
Lehar (Franz)
Liszt (Franz)
Loewe (Karl)
Lully (Giovanni)
Parry (Hubert)
Ravel (Maurice)
Reger (Max)
Reich (Steve)
Satie (Eric)
Sousa (John Philip)
Spohr (Ludwig)
Suppé (Franz von)
Verdi (Guiseppe)
Weber (Carl von)
Weill (Kurt)
Widor (Charles)

6
Arnold (Malcolm)
Barber (Samuel)
Bartok (Bela)
Berlin (Irving)
Brahms (Johannes)
Bridge (Frank)
Busoni (Ferrucio)
Chopin (Frédéric)
Clarke (Jeremiah)
Coates (Eric)
Czerny (Karl)
Delius (Frederick)
Dvorak (Antonin)
Eisler (Hans)
Enesco (Georges)
Foster (Stephen)
Franck (César)
German (Edward)
Glinka (Mikhail)
Gounod (Charles)
Handel (George
Frederick)
Hummel (Johann
Nepomuk)
Kodaly (Zoltan)
Lassus (Orlando)
Ligeti (Gyorgy)
Mahler (Gustav)

Morley (Thomas)
Mozart (Wolfgang
Amadeus)
Porter (Cole)
Rameau (Jean-Philippe)
Rubbra (Edmund)
Schütz (Heinrich)
Tallis (Thomas)
Varese (Edgar)
Wagner (Richard)
Walton (William)
Webern (Anton)
Wesley (Samuel
Sebastian)

7
Albéniz (Isaac)
Bantock (Granville)
Bellini (Vincenzo)
Berlioz (Hector)
Borodin (Alexander)
Britten (Benjamin)
Campion (Thomas)
Cavalli (Francesco)
Copland (Aaron)
Corelli (Arcangelo)
Debussy (Claude)
Delibes (Léo)
Farnaby (Giles)
Galuppi (Baldassare)
Gibbons (Orlando)
Gorecki (Henryk)
Howells (Herbert)
Ireland (John)
Janacek (Leos)
Lambert (Constant)
Machaut (Guillaume)
Martinu (Bohuslav)
Menotti (Carlo)
Milhaud (Darius)
Nielsen (Carl)
Novello (Ivor)
Okeghem (Jean d')
Poulenc (François)
Puccini (Giacomo)
Purcell (Henry)
Quilter (Roger)
Rodgers (Richard)

Rodrigo (Joaquin)
Romberg (Sigmund)
Rossini (Gioacchino)
Roussel (Albert)
Ruggles (Carl)
Smetana (Bedrich)
Stainer (John)
Stamitz (Johann)
Strauss (Johann/Richard)
Thomson (Virgil)
Tippett (Michael)
Vivaldi (Antonio)
Warlock (Peter)
Weelkes (Thomas)
Xenakis (Yannis)

8
Albinoni (Tomasso)
Berkeley (Lennox)
Bruckner (Anton)
Chabrier (Emmanuel)
Cimarosa (Domenico)
Clementi (Musio)
Couperin (François)
Dohnanyi (Ernst)
Gabrieli
(Andrea/Giovanni)
Gershwin (George)
Gesualdo (Carlo)
Glazunov (Aleksandr)
Grainger (Percy)
Granados (Enrique)
Honegger (Arthur)
Ketelbey (Albert)
Kreisler (Fritz)
Mascagni (Pietro)
Massenet (Jules)
Messiaen (Olivier)
Musgrave (Thea)

Paganini (Niccolo)
Respighi (Ottorino)
Schubert (Franz)
Schumann (Robert)
Scriabin (Alexandr)
Sibelius (Jean)
Sondheim (Stephen)
Stanford (Charles)
Sullivan (Arthur)
Taverner (John)
Telemann (George
Philipp)
Victoria (Tomas)
Williams (John)

9
Addinsell (Richard)
Balakirev (Mili)
Beethoven (Ludwig van)
Bernstein (Leonard)
Buxtehude (Diderich)
Cherubini (Luigi)
Donizetti (Gaetano)
Dunstable (John)
Hindemith (Paul)
Hoddinott (Alun)
Meyerbeer (Giacomo)
Offenbach (Jacues)
Pachelbel (Johannes)
Pergolesi (Giovanni)
Prokofiev (Sergei)
Scarlatti
(Domenico/Alessandro)

10
Birtwistle (Harrison)
Boccherini (Luigi)
Ferrabosco (Alfonso)
Monteverdi (Claudio)

Mussorgsky (Modest)
Palestrina (Giovanni)
Penderecki (Krzysztof)
Ponchielli (Amilcare)
Praetorius (Michael)
Schoenberg (Arnold)
Stravinsky (Igor)
Waldteufel (Emile)

11
Charpentier (Gustave)
Dittersdorf (Karl)
Humperdinck
(Engelbert)
Leoncavallo (Ruggiero)
Mendelssohn (Felix)
Rachmaninov (Sergei)
Stockhausen (Karlheinz)
Szymanowski (Karol)
Tchaikovsky (Peter Russ)

12
Dallapiccola (Luigi)
Shostakovich (Dimitri)

13
Khatchaturian (Aram
Russ)

2+ words
Lloyd Webber (Andrew)
Rimsky-Korsakov
(Nikolai)
Saint-Saens (Camille)
Vaughan Williams
(Ralph)
Villa-Lobos (Heitor)
Wolf-Ferrari (Ermanno)

COMPUTERS

2
AI
IT
OS
PC
WP

3
AGP
Alt
ATM
BAK
BAT
bay
bit
BMP
BPS
bug
bus
CAB
CAD
CAM
CGA
CGI
com
CPU
CRT
Cut
DAC
DAT
DLL
DNS
DOS
DPI
DTP
DVD
EGA
end
ESC
EXE

FAQ
FAT
fax
FPU
FTU
hit
hub
ICQ
IDE
INI
IRC
IRQ
ISA
ISP
JPG
key
LAN
LCD
LED
log
LOL
MMX
NAP
net
NIC
OCR
OLE
PAL
pad
PCI
PDF
PIC
PIF
PIN
POP
PPM
PSU
PUB
RAM
ROM
RSI
RTF
Sig
SYS
Tab
Tag
URL
USB

VDU
WAV
WPM
WWW
XML
Y2K
Zip

4
ADSL
ANSI
BIOS
boot
byte
chip
CIFS
CMIS
code
copy
CTRL
data
disc
disk
down
drag
DRAM
drop
dump
echo
edit
exit
feed
file
font
hack
head
home
host
HTML
HTTP
icon
ISDN
ISOC
Java
JPEG
Kbps
link
load

LOGO
loop
MAPI
menu
MIDI
MIME
move
MPEG
node
ODBC
ODMA
page
path
perl
ping
port
POST
quit
RAID
save
scan
SCSI
SGML
site
SMTP
sort
spam
SRAM
surf
SVGA
TIFF
type
unit
UNIX
user
VESA
VRAM
VRML
WORM
WRAM

5
ABEND
alias
ASCII
ATAPI
BASIC
cache

click
clone
COAST
COBOL
CORAL
crash
debug
drive
email
enter
field
flame
frame
index
input
LINUX
macro
micro
modem
mouse
octal
parse
paste
pixel
print
proxy
queue
query
reset
route
SDRAM
shell
shout
slave
store
tower
trash
video
virus

6
access
analog
anorak
applet
archie
backup
banner

binary
bitmap
cookie
cursor
decode
delete
driver
escape
folder
format
gopher
hacker
indent
kermit
kernel
laptop
memory
Mosaic
newbie
online
output
packet
PASCAL
portal
QWERTY
reboot
record
return
router
screen
script
server
source
spider
subnet
syntax
telnet
thread
upload
usenet
visits
window

7
acronym
ActiveX
archive
booting

browser
circuit
command
compile
corrupt
default
density
digital
DirectX
dynamic
emulate
execute
gateway
graphic
imaging
install
integer
kilobit
mailbox
megabit
monitor
network
offline
pentium
pointer
printer
program
readout
recover
restore
scanner
spammer
storage
toolbar
utility
website
windows
WYSIWYG

8
activate
bookmark
capacity
databank
database
databits
diskette
document

download
emoticon
emulator
ethernet
extranet
facsimile
firewall
firmware
function
gigabyte
hardware
hotspots
internet
intranet
joystick
keyboard
kilobyte
livewire
megabyte
notebook
password
printout
protocol
recovery
scalable
shortcut
shutdown
software
spooling
swapfile
terabyte
terminal
topology
truetype
truncate
typeface
veronica
wildcard

9
backspace
bandwidth
cartridge
character
clipboard
directory
favourite
floptical

flowchart
groupware
highlight
hyperlink
hypertext
interface
mainframe
megahertz
microchip
overwrite
partition
processor
shareware
shockwave
signature
soundcard
uninstall
webmaster

10
controller
decryption
encryption
ergonomics
hypermedia
impression
JavaScript
multimedia
nanosecond
paintbrush
peripheral
programmer
resolution
subroutine
whiteboard
winchester
wraparound

11
compression
coprocessor
diagnostics
edutainment
gopherspace
hexadecimal
interactive
motherboard
nettiquette

programming
replication
spreadsheet
unformatted
workstation

12
housekeeping
multitasking
subdirectory

2+ words
active window
arrow key
aspect ratio
batch file
baud rate
beta version
Boolean logic
boot disk
cache memory
caps lock
CD ROM
chat room
chip set
circuit board
client server
clip art
clock speed
control key
CPU memory bus
cut and paste
daisy chain
default value
device driver

dialog box
disk cache
disk drive
display unit
domain name
dot matrix
dot.com
drag and drop
DVD ROM
e-commerce
fax modem
file format
file server
file type
flash ram
floppy disk
function key
game port
graphics card
hard disc
hard drive
home page
host computer
hot zone
image map
input device
laser printer
local bus
machine code
mail merge
mailing list
menu bar
menu-driven
mirror site
MS-DOS
news group

numeric pad
opt-in
output device
page layout
parallel port
plug and play
power cable
power supply
real time
response time
ribbon cable
ring network
screen filter
screen name
search engine
serial access
serial port
shift key
silicon chip
snail mail
space bar
system disk
time sharing
timed out
user-friendly
user ID
video card
virus scan
voice modem
warm boot
web browser
web page
word break
word wrap
World Wide Web

CONTAINERS

CONTAINERS

3
bag
bin
box
can
cup
hod
jar
jug
keg
mug
pan
pod
pot
tin
tub
tun
urn

4
bowl
butt
case
cask
dish
etui
ewer
hold
pail
poke
rack
sack
safe
sink
skin
skip
sump
tank
till
tray
trug
vase

5
basin
caddy
chest
churn
crate
creel
crock
cruet
cruse
flask
glass
gourd
joram
jorum
mould
pouch
purse
scoop
scrip
store
stoup
trunk

6
barrel
basket
beaker
boiler
bottle
bucket
bunker
carafe
carboy
carton
casket
coffer
drawer
eggbox
eggcup
flagon
goblet
hamper
icebox
inkpot
kettle
kitbag
larder

locker
noggin
oilcan
pallet
piggin
pipkin
pottle
punnet
salver
teacup
teapot
tureen
valise
vessel
wallet

7
amphora
ampoule
ashtray
canteen
capsule
chalice
cistern
dustbin
dustpan
freezer
handbag
holdall
panikin
pannier
pitcher
platter
roaster
sandbox
satchel
scuttle
tumbler

8
canister
cassette
cauldron
decanter
demijohn
gallipot
hipflask
jeroboam

jerrycan
knapsack
magazine
matchbox
meatsafe
reticule
snuffbox
soapdish
suitcase
wineskin

9
casserole
haversack
pepperpot
punchbowl

10
fingerbowl
pillowcase
pillowslip
repository

11
portmanteau

2+ words
butter dish
cat bowl
coal scuttle
dish rack
dog bowl
pipe rack
salt cellar
shoe box
slop basin
sugar bowl
water butt
work bag

COOKING

Cooking utensils
Terms used in cooking

COOKING UTENSILS

3
cup
hob
jar
jug
pan
pot
tin
wok

4
bowl
dish
ewer
fork
mill
oven
rack
spit
tray

5
basin
board
churn
flute
grill
knife
ladle
mixer
mould
plate
press
sieve
spoon
steel
stove
timer
tongs
whisk

6
beater
carafe
cloche
cooker
cooler
funnel
grater
jamjar
kettle
masher
mincer
mortar
peeler
pestle
saucer
shaker
shears
siphon
skewer
teapot
tureen

7
blender
broiler
chopper
drainer
dredger
griddle
ramekin
roaster
samovar
skillet
skimmer
spatula
steamer
stewpot
toaster

8
cauldron
colander
hotplate
saucepan
stockpot
teaspoon

9
cafetière
casserole
corkscrew
sauceboat
sharpener

10
chopsticks
liquidizer (liquidiser)
percolator
rotisserie
salamander
tablespoon

12
dessertspoon

2+ words
bain-marie
baking sheet
baking tin
baking tray
carving knife
chafing dish
chip pan
egg slice
egg timer
fish kettle
fish slice
food processor
frying pan
mixing bowl
palette knife
pastry brush
pastry cutter
rolling pin
serving dish
slow cooker

TERMS USED IN COOKING

3
fry
ice
mix
rub

4
bake
bard
beat
boil
bone
coat
chop
dice
draw
dust
fold
hash
lard
mash
pané
pare
peel
rare
roll
sear
sift
soak
stew
toss

5
broil
brown
brulé
brush
carve
chill
chine
cream
daube
devil
dress
flake
glaze

grate
knead
mince
pluck
poach
prove
purée
roast
sauté
scald
score
steam
stuff
sweat
truss
whisk

6
blanch
braise
confit
decant
dredge
fillet
flambé
fondue
freeze
gratin
grease
infuse
maison
mignon
paunch
pickle
reduce
render
scrape
seethe
simmer

7
clarify
crouton
drizzle
garnish
Marengo
parboil
refresh
suprême

8
barbecue
chasseur
duchesse
julienne
macerate
marinade
marinate
preserve

9
medallion
microwave

10
caramelize (caramelise)

2+ words
au gratin
deep-fry
pan-fry
pot-roast
shallow-fry
spit-roast
stir-fry
well done

COUNTIES

Counties of England
Counties of Ireland
Counties and regions of
Scotland
Counties of Wales

COUNTIES OF ENGLAND
* former county

4
Avon*
Beds
Kent

5
Berks
Bucks
Cambs
Devon
Essex
Hants
Herts
Lancs
Leics
Lincs
Notts
Salop*
Wilts
Yorks

6
Derbys
Dorset
Durham
Gloucs
Staffs
Surrey
Sussex

7
Cumbria
Norfolk
Rutland
Suffolk

8
Cheshire
Cleveland*
Cornwall
Somerset
Warwicks

9
Berkshire
Hampshire
Northants
Middlesex*
Wiltshire
Yorkshire

10
Cumberland*
Derbyshire
Humberside*
Lancashire
Merseyside*
Shropshire

11
Oxfordshire
Westmorland*

12
Bedfordshire
Lincolnshire
Warwickshire

13
Herefordshire
Hertfordshire
Staffordshire

14
Cambridgeshire
Leicestershire
Northumberland

15
Buckinghamshire
Gloucestershire
Huntingdonshire*
Nottinghamshire

16
Northamptonshire

COUNTIES OF IRELAND

4
Cork
Down (NI)
Mayo

5
Cavan
Clare
Kerry
Louth
Meath
Sligo

6
Antrim (NI)
Armagh (NI)
Carlow
Dublin
Galway
Offaly
Tyrone (NI)

7
Donegal
Kildare
Leitrim
Wexford
Wicklow

8
Kilkenny
Laoighis
Limerick
Longford
Monaghan

9
Fermanagh (NI)
Roscommon
Tipperary
Waterford
Westmeath

11
Londonderry (NI)

COUNTIES AND REGIONS OF SCOTLAND
* former county

3
Ayr*

4
Bute*
Fife*
Ross*

5
Angus*
Banff*
Moray*
Nairn*
Perth*

6
Argyll
Lanark
Orkney*

7
Berwick*
Borders
Central
Kinross*
Lothian
Peebles*

Renfrew*
Selkirk*
Tayside
Wigtown*
Zetland*

8
Aberdeen*
Ayrshire*
Dumfries*
Cromarty*
Grampian
Highland
Roxburgh*
Shetland
Stirling*

9
Caithness*
Dumbarton*
Inverness*

10
Kincardine*
Midlothian*
Sutherland*

11
Clackmannan*
Strathclyde

13
Kirkcudbright*

COUNTIES OF WALES
* former county

5
Clwd
Dyfed
Gwent
Powys

7
Gwynedd

8
Anglesey*

9
Glamorgan*
Merioneth

10
Flintshire*

11
Breconshire*
Radnorshire*

12
Denbighshire*

13
Cardiganshire*
Monmouthshire*
Pembrokeshire

15
Caernarfonshire*
Carmarthenshire*
Montgomeryshire*

COUNTRIES

COUNTRIES OF THE WORLD

2
UK

3
UAE
USA

4
Bali
Chad
Cuba
Fiji
Guam
Iran
Iraq
Java
Laos
Mali
Oman
Peru
Togo

5
Belau
Benin
Burma (Myanmar)
Chile
China
Congo
Cyprus
Egypt
Gabon
Ghana
Haiti
India
Italy
Japan
Kenya
Korea (North and South)
Libya
Malta
Nepal
Niger

Qatar
Samoa
Spain
Sudan
Timor
Wales
Yemen

6
Angola
Belize
Bhutan
Bosnia
Brazil
Brunei
Canada
Cyprus
France
Gambia
Greece
Guyana
Israel
Jordan
Kuwait
Latvia
Malawi
Mexico
Monaco
Norway
Panama
Poland
Russia
Rwanda
Serbia
Sweden
Syria
Taiwan
Tobago
Turkey
Tuvalu
Uganda
Zambia

7
Albania
Algeria
Andorra
Antigua

Armenia
Austria
Bahamas
Bahrain
Belarus
Belgium
Bermuda
Bolivia
Britain
Burundi
Comoros
Croatia
Denmark
Ecuador
England
Eritrea
Estonia
Faeroes
Finland
Georgia
Germany
Hungary
Iceland
Jamaica
Lebanon
Lesotho
Liberia
Moldova
Morocco
Myanmar (Burma)
Namibia
Nigeria
Romania
Rumania
Slovakia
Slovenia
Somalia
Sumatra
Surinam
Tunisia
Ukraine
Uruguay
Vanuatu
Vatican
Vietnam

8
Barbados

Botswana
Bulgaria
Cambodia
Cameroon
Colombia
Djibouti
Dominica
Ethiopia
Honduras
Kiribati
Malaysia
Maldives
Mongolia
Pakistan
Paraguay
Portugal
Scotland
Tanzania
Thailand
Trinidad
Zimbabwe

9
Argentina
Argentine
Greenland
Guatemala
Indonesia

Kazakstan
Lithuania
Macedonia
Mauritius
Nicaragua
Palestine
Singapore
Swaziland
Venezuela

10
Azerbaijan
Bangladesh
Kazakhstan
Kyrgyzstan
Luxembourg
Madagascar
Martinique
Mauritania
Micronesia
Montenegro
Montserrat
Mozambique
Seychelles
Tajikistan
Uzbekistan
Yugoslavia

11
Afghanistan
Netherlands
Philippines
Switzerland

12
Turkmenistan

13
Liechtenstein

2+ words
Bosnia and Herzegovina
Burkina Faso
Costa Rica
Cote d'Ivoire
Czech Republic
El Salvador
Holy See
Ivory Coast
New Guinea
New Zealand
San Marino
Saudi Arabia
Sierra Leone
South Africa
Sri Lanka
United Kingdom
United States of America

CRICKET

Cricketing terms
Famous cricketers

CRICKETING TERMS

2
in

3
bat
box
bye
cut
lbw
leg
MCC
MCG
net
off
out
run
six
tea

4
bail
ball
bowl
duck
edge
Oval
over
shot
slip
spin
test
walk
wide

5
catch
cover
drive
extra
Gabba
gully

Lords
lunch
point
snick
stump

6
beamer
bowled
bowler
caught
crease
glance
googly
howzat
keeper
maiden
onside
scorer
single
stumps
umpire
whites
wicket
yorker

7
batsman
batting
bouncer
bowling
declare
fielder
innings
legside
offside
spinner
stumped

8
boundary
chinaman
fielding
legbreak
offbreak
paceman
sledging

9
Edgbaston
midwicket
inswinger
scorecard

10
Headingley
outswinger
scoreboard

11
declaration

2+ words
cover point
fine leg
forward short leg
gully
leg-bye
leg slip
long leg
long off
long on
long stop
mid on
mid off
no-ball
not out
run-out
silly mid on
silly mid off
silly point
square leg
test match
third man
twelfth man
wicket keeper

FAMOUS CRICKETERS

4
Amis (Dennis)
Bird (Dickie)
Hall (Wesley)
Lamb (Allan)
Lara (Brian)
Khan (Imran)

Lock (Tony)
Snow (John)

5

Close (Brian)
Evans (Godfrey)
Gooch (Graham)
Gough (Darren)
Gower (David)
Grace (W.G.)
Greig (Tony)
Hobbs (Jack)
Knott (Alan)
Laker (Jim)
Lloyd (Clive)
Walsh (Courtney)
Warne (Shane)
Waugh (Mark/Steve)

6

Bailey (Trevor)
Bedser (Alec/Eric)
Benaud (Richie)
Border (Allan)

Botham (Ian)
Dexter (Ted)
Edrich (Bill/John)
Hadlee (Richard)
Hutton (Len)
Kanhai (Rohan)
Lillee (Dennis)
Miller (Keith)
Rhodes (Wilfred)
Sobers (Gary)
Statham (Brian)
Titmus (Fred)
Weekes (Everton)
Willis (Bob)

7

Ambrose (Curtley)
Boycott (Geoffrey)
Bradman (Donald)
Compton (Denis)
Cowdrey (Colin)
Hammond (Wally)
Hussain (Nasser)
Jardine (Douglas)

Larwood (Harold)
Stewart (Alec)
Thomson (Jeff)
Trueman (Fred)
Worrell (Frank)

8

Atherton (Michael)
Chappell (Greg/Ian)
Gavascar (Sunil)
Graveney (Tom)
Lindwall (Ray)
Marshall (Clive)
Richards (Viv)

9

D'Oliviera (Basil)
Sutcliffe (Herbert)
Underwood (Derek)

11

Constantine (Learie)
Illingworth (Ray)

CRIME/ CRIMINAL

Crimes
Criminal
Criminals

CRIMES

3
ABH
con
GBH
job
sin

4
foul
rape
riot
tort

5
arson
fraud
graft
heist
lapse
libel
theft
usury
wrong

6
bigamy
breach
delict
felony
incest
kidnap
murder
piracy
simony

7
assault
battery
bribery
cruelty
forgery
larceny
misdeed
mugging
neglect
offence
outrage
perjury
robbery
slander
treason

8
barratry
burglary
homicide
nuisance
poaching
regicide
sedition
stealing
trespass

9
abduction
blackmail
collusion
embracery
extortion
loitering
matricide
parricide
pilfering
violation

10
conspiracy
corruption
defamation
enticement
illegality
kidnapping
misconduct
negligence
peccadillo
wrongdoing

11
delinquency
infanticide
obstruction
subornation
trespassing

12
embezzlement
encroachment
infringement
intimidation
manslaughter
misbehaviour
misdemeanour
prostitution

13
housebreaking
transgression

2+ words
actual bodily harm
breach of the peace
breaking and entering
common assault
contempt of court
criminal damage
grievous bodily harm
inside job
ram raid
shop lifting

CRIMINAL

3
bad

4
bent
evil

5
fishy
shady
wrong

6
banned
guilty
sinful
unfair
unjust
wicked

7
corrupt
crooked
heinous
illegal
illicit
immoral
lawless

8
aberrant
culpable
unlawful

9
dishonest
felonious
forbidden
murderous
nefarious
negligent
unethical

10
antisocial
delinquent
fraudulent
indictable
iniquitous
outrageous
proscribed
punishable
scandalous
underworld

11
blameworthy
disgraceful

CRIMINALS

3
lag

4
hood
thug

5
crook
felon
fence
fraud
heavy
lifer
rough
thief
tough

6
abuser
bandit
coiner
dealer
forger
gunman
hitman
killer
looter
mugger
outlaw
pirate
rapist
robber
sinner
usurer
yardie

7
accused
brigand
burglar
convict
culprit
footpad
hoodlum

lowlife
Mafioso
mobster
outcast
poacher
ruffian
rustler
traitor
villain

8
abductor
arsonist
assassin
bigamist
evildoer
gangster
hooligan
jailbird
larcener
miscreant
murderer
offender
perjuror
peterman
prisoner
pilferer
receiver
smuggler
swindler

9
accessory
buccaneer
cracksman
embezzler
fraudster
kidnapper
larcenist
racketeer
terrorist
wrongdoer

10
bootlegger
delinquent
highwayman
lawbreaker

malefactor
pickpocket
recidivist
shoplifter
trafficker
trespasser

11
blackmailer
conspirator
perpetrator
safebreaker
safecracker

12
extortionist
housebreaker
transgressor

13
counterfeiter

2+ words
child molester
con man
confidence trickster
serial killer

CURRENCIES

Countries and their currencies

Country	Currency	Small unit
Afghanistan	afghani	pul
Albania	lek	qintar
Algeria	dinar	centime
Angola	kwanza	wei
Argentina	peso	austral
Armenia	dram	louma
Australia	dollar	cent
Austria	euro (formerly schilling)	cent (formerly groschen)
Azerbaijan	manta	gopik
Bahrain	dinar	fils
Bangladesh	taka	poisha
Belarus	rouble	kopek
Belgium	euro (formerly franc)	cent (formerly centime)
Bolivia	boliviano	centavo
Botswana	pula	thebe
Brazil	real	centavo
Bulgaria	lev	stotinka
Burma	kyat	pya
Cambodia	riel	sen
Canada	dollar	cent
Chile	peso	centavo
China	yuan (renminbi)	fen
Colombia	peso	centavo
Congo (both)	franc	centime
Costa Rica	colon	centime
Croatia	kuna	lipa
Cuba	peso	centavo
Cyprus	pound	cent
Czech republic	koruna	haler
Denmark	krone	ore
Ecuador	sucre	centavo
Egypt	pound	piastre
El Salvador	colon	centavo
Eritrea	nakfa	
Estonia	kroon	sent
Ethiopia	birr	cent
Finland	euro (formerly markka)	cent (formerly penni)
France	euro (formerly franc)	cent *or* centime
Germany	euro (formerly Deutchmark)	cent (formerly Pfennig)
Ghana	cedi	pesewa
Greece	euro (formerly drachma)	cent (formerly lepton)
Guatemala	quetzal	centavo

Country	Currency	Small unit
Guinea	franc	cauris
Haiti	gourde	centime
Honduras	lempira	centavo
Hungary	forint	filler
Iceland	krona	eyrir
India	rupee	paisa
Indonesia	rupiah	sen
Iran	rial	dinar
Iraq	dinar	fils
Ireland	euro (formerly punt)	cent (formerly penny)
Israel	shekel	agora
Italy	euro (formerly lira)	cent (formerly centesimo)
Jamaica	dollar	cent
Japan	yen	sen
Jordan	dinar	fils
Kenya	shilling	cent
Korea	whon	chon
Kyrgyzstan	som	tyin
Laos	kip	at
Latvia	lat	santimi
Lebanon	pound	piaster
Lesotho	loti	sente
Liberia	dollar	cent
Libya	dinar	dirham
Lithuania	litas	centas
Luxembourg	euro (formerly franc)	cent (formerly centime)
Macedonia	dinar	para
Malawi	kwacha	tambala
Malaysia	ringgit	sen
Malta	lira	cent
Mexico	peso	centavo
Moldova	leu	ban
Morocco	dirham	centime
Namibia	dollar	cent
Netherlands	euro (formerly guilder)	cent
New Zealand	dollar	cent
Nicaragua	cordoba	centavo
Nigeria	naira	kobo
Norway	krone	ore
Oman	rial	baiza
Pakistan	rupee	paisa
Panama	balboa	centésimo
Paraguay	guarani	centimo
Peru	sol	cent
Philippines	peso	centavo
Poland	zloty	grosz

Country	Currency	Small unit
Portugal	euro (formerly escudo)	cent (formerly centavo)
Romania	leu	ban
Russia	rouble	kopeck
Saudi Arabia	riyal	halala
Serbia	dinar	para
Singapore	dollar	cent
Slovakia	koruna	haler
Slovenia	tolar	stotin
Somalia	shilling	cent
South Africa	rand	cent
Spain	euro (formerly peseta)	cent (formerly centime)
Sri Lanka	rupee	cents
Sudan	dinar	
Sweden	krona	ore
Switzerland	franc	centime
Syria	pound	piaster
Taiwan	dollar	cent
Tajikistan	rouble	tanga
Tanzania	shilling	cent
Thailand	baht	satang
Tonga	pa'anga	seniti
Tunisia	dinar	millime
Turkey	lira	kurus
Turkmenistan	manta	tenge
Uganda	shilling	cent
UK	pound	pence
Ukraine	hryvyna	koplyka
USA	dollar	cent
Uruguay	peso	centésimo
Uzbekistan	sum	teen
Venezuela	bolivar	céntimo
Vietnam	dong	xu
Yemen	riyal	fils
Zambia	kwacha	ngwee
Zimbabwe	dollar	cent

DANCE

Dances and dance steps
Dancers
See also **BALLET**

DANCES AND DANCE
STEPS

3
bob
bop
hay
hey
hop
jig
pas
set
tap

4
alma
ball
frug
haka
hula
jive
pogo
prom
rave
reel
shag
trip

5
bebop
caper
conga
disco
fling
frisk
galop
gigue
glide
gopak
limbo
loure
mambo

mooch
pavan
polka
ragga
round
rumba
salsa
samba
shake
stomp
tango
twist
valse
volta
waltz

6
apache
ballet
batuta
bolero
boogie
Boston
branle
cavort
frolic
hustle
minuet
morris
nautch
pavane
prance
shimmy
smooch
valeta
veleta

7
beguine
bourrée
canario
carioca
ceilidh
coranto
courant
csardas
czardas
foxtrot

gavotte
hoedown
lambada
lancers
Ländler
lavolta
Madison
maypole
mazurka
measure
ragtime
rollick
roundel
routine
shindig
shuffle

8
ballroom
bunnyhop
bunnyhug
cachucha
cakewalk
chaconne
cotillon
courante
fandango
flamenco
galliard
habanera
hornpipe
moonwalk
rigadoon
rigaudon
saraband
snowball

9
allemande
bergomask
bossanova
ecossaise
eightsome
farandole
formation
gallopade
jitterbug
Kathakali

passepied
pirouette
polonaise
promenade
quadrille
quickstep
sarabande
siciliano

10
breakdance
carmagnole
charleston
corroboree
locomotion
masquerade
strathspey
tarantella

11
choreograph
contredanse
discothèque
Schottische

2+ words
ballroom dancing
belly dance
black bottom
body-popping
Boston two-step
break-dancing
can-can
cha-cha
cha-cha-cha
clog dance
country dance
country dancing
dosi-do

eightsome reel
excuse-me
fan dance
flip-flop
floral dance
foursome reel
furry dance
Gay Gordons
go-go dancing
hesitation waltz
highland fling
hoe-down
hokey-cokey
hunt-ball
invitation waltz
knees-up
Lambeth walk
lap dance
line dance
military two-step
morris dance
morris dancing
one-step
palais de danse
paso doble
Paul Jones
pole dance
Roger de Coverley
sand-dance
soft-shoe shuffle
split the willow
square dance
sword dance
tea-dance
thé dansant
trip the light fantastic
two-step
turkey-trot
Viennese waltz

DANCERS

3
lap (dancer)

4
pole (dancer)
rope (dancer)
taxi (dancer)

5
Caron (Lesley)
Kelly (Gene)

6
Duncan (Isadora)
geisha
hoofer
Rogers (Ginger)
Swayze (Patrick)

7
Astaire (Fred)

8
Buchanan (Jack)
corybant
coryphee

9
ballerina

DESERTS

Desert
Deserts of the world

3
rat

4
dump

5
leave
waste
wilds

6
barren
maroon
return
reward

7
abandon
forsake
scarper

8
badlands
desolate

9
wasteland

10
punishment
recompense
wilderness

11
comeuppance

DESERTS OF THE WORLD

4
Gila (USA)
Gobi (China)
Thar (India)

5
Nafud (Saudi Arabia)
Namib (Namibia)
Negev (Israel)
Ordos (China)
Sinai (Egypt)
Sturt (Australia)

6
Gibson (Australia)
Karroo (South Africa)
Mojave (USA)
Nubian (North Africa)
Sahara (North Africa)
Syrian (Syria)

7
Alashan (China)
Arabian (Egypt/Saudi Arabia)
Atacama (Chile)
Painted (USA)
Sechura (Peru)
Simpson (Australia)
Sonoran (Mexico)

8
Colorado (USA)
Kalahari (Botswana)

9
Anatolian (Turkey)

2+ words
An Nafud
Dasht-e-Lut (Iran)
Great Sandy (Australia)
Kara Kum (Russia)
Kyzyl Kum (Kazakhstan)
Death Valley (USA)
Nullarbor Plain (Australia)
Empty Quarter (Arabia)
Patagonian (South America)

DICKENS

Novels of Charles Dickens
Well-known characters
from Dickens's novels

NOVELS OF CHARLES DICKENS

Barnaby Rudge (BR)
Bleak House (BH)
Christmas Carol, A (CC)
David Copperfield (DC)
Dombey and Son (Dom)
Edwin Drood, The
    Mystery of (ED)
Great Expectations (GE)
Hard Times (HT)
Little Dorrit (LD)
Martin Chuzzlewit (MC)
Nicholas Nickleby (NN)
Old Curiosity Shop, The
    (OCS)
Oliver Twist (OT)
Our Mutual Friend
    (OMF)
Pickwick Papers (PP)
Tale of Two Cities, A (TC)

WELL-KNOWN CHARACTERS FROM DICKENS'S NOVELS
Abbreviations of novel titles
as above

2
Jo (BH)

3
Ada (BH)
Amy (OT)
Bet (OT)
Bud, Rosa (ED)
Jip (DC)
Joe (GE/PP)
Kit (OCS)
Pip (GE)
Tox, Miss (Dom)

4
Aged, the (GE)
Bray, Madeline (NN)
Dick, Mr (DC)
Fips, Mr (MC)
Fogg (PP)
Gamp, Sarah (MC)
Grip (BR)
Hawk, Sir Mulberry (NN)
Heep, Uriah (DC)
Jupe, Cecilia/Sissy (HT)
Tigg, Montague (MC)
Wade, Miss (LD)
Wren, Jenny (OMF)

5
Clare, Ada (BH)
Doyce, Daniel (LD)
Drood, Edwin (ED)
Fagin (OT)
Flite, Miss (BH)
Gills, Solomon (Dom)
Guppy, William (BH)
Hexam, Charlie/Lizzy
    (OMF)
Krook (BH)
Lorry, Jarvis (TC)
Nancy (OT)
Noggs, Newman (NN)
Pinch, Ruth/Tom (MC)
Price, 'Tilda' (NN)
Pross, Miss (TC)
Quilp, Daniel (OCS)
Rudge, Barnaby/Mary (BR)
Sikes, Bill (OT)
Smike (NN)
Toots, Mr (Dom)
Trent, Frederick/Nellie
    (OCS)
Twist, Oliver (OT)
Venus, Mr (OMF)

6
Badger, Dr Bayham (BH)
Barkis (DC)
Bitzer (HT)
Boffin, Nicodemus (OMF)
Bucket, Inspector (BH)

Bumble, Mr (OT)
Carker, James (Dom)
Carton, Sydney (TC)
Codlin, Thomas (OCS)
Darnay, Charles (TC)
Dartle, Rosa (DC)
Dennis, Ned (BR)
Dombey, Fanny/Florence/
    Louisa/Paul (Dom)
Dorrit, Amy/Edward/
Fanny/Frederick/William
    (LD)
Esther (BH)
Gordon, Lord George (BR)
Harmon, John (OMF)
Harris, Mrs (MC)
Hawdon, Captain (BH)
Jarley, Mrs (OCS)
Jasper, Jack (ED)
Jingle, Alfred (PP)
Lammle, Alfred (OMF)
Marley, Jacon (CC)
Merdle, Mr (LD)
Nipper, Susan (Dom)
Pancks (LD)
Pipkin, Nathaniel (PP)
Pirrip, Philip (GE)
Pocket, Herbert (GE)
Sawyer, Bob (PP)
Tapley, Mark (MC)
Toodle (Dom)
Tupman, Tracy (PP)
Varden, Dolly/Gabriel (BR)
Wardle, Emily/Isabella/
    Mr/Rachel (PP)
Weller, Sam/Tony (PP)
Wilfer, Bella (OMF)
Winkle, Nathaniel (PP)
Wopsle, Mr (GE)

7
Bardell, Mrs Martha (PP)
Blimber, Dr (Dom)
Chivery, John (LD)
Clenham, Arthur (LD)
Creakle (DC)
Dawkins, Jack (OT)
Dedlock, Sir/Lady (BH)

Defarge, Madame (TC)
Dodger, the Artful (OT)
Drummle, Bentley (GE)
Durdles (ED)
Estella (GE)
Gargery, Joe (GE)
Granger, Edith (Dom)
Grimwig, Mr (OT)
Jaggers, Mr (GE)
Jellyby, Caddy/Mrs/Peepy
        (BH)
Kenwigs, the (NN)
Manette, Dr/Lucy (TC)
Pipchin, Mrs (Dom)
Podsnap, Georgiana/Mr
        (OMF)
Scrooge, Ebenezer (CC)
Slammer, Dr (PP)
Slumkey, Hon Samuel (PP)
Sparsit, Mrs (HT)
Spenlow, Dora (DC)
Squeers, Fanny/Wackford
        (NN)
Trotter, Job (PP)
Wemmick (GE)

8
Bagstock, Major (Dom)
Brownlow, Mr (OT)
Boythorn, Lawrence
(BH)
Claypole, Noah (OT)
Cratchit, Belinda/Bob/
        Tiny Tim (CC)
Crummles, Vincent
(NN)
Havisham, Miss (GE)
Jarndyce, John (BH)
Magwitch, Abel (GE)
Micawber, Wilkins, Mr
(DC)
Nickleby, Clara/Mrs/
        Nicholas/Ralph
(NN)
Peggotty, Clara (DC)
Pickwick, Samuel (PP)

Traddles, Tom (DC)
Trotwood, Betsy (DC)
Wrayburn, Eugene (OMF)

9
Blackpool, Stephen (HT)
Bounderby, Mr (HT)
Cheeryble, Brothers/
        Frank (NN)
Gradgrind, Mr (HT)
Harthouse, James (HT)
Headstone, Bradley
        (OMF)
Lightwood, Mortimer
        (OMF)
Lillyvick, Mr (NN)
Mantalini, Mr & Mrs
        (NN)
Pecksniff, Seth (MC)
Riderhood, Rogue (OMF)
Smallweed,
Bartholomew/
        Joshua/Judy
(BH)
Snodgrass, Augustus
(PP)
Summerson, Esther
(BH)
Swiveller, Dick (OCS)
Tappertit, Simon (BR)
Veneering, Anastasia/
Hamilton (OMF)
Wickfield, Agnes (DC)
Woodcourt, Allan (BH)

10
Chuzzlewit, Martin
(MC)
Macstinger, Mrs (Dom)
Rouncewell, Mrs (BH)
Snevellici, Miss (NN)
Sowerberry (OT)
Steerforth, James (DC)
Tattycoram (LD)
Turveydrop, Prince (BH)
Wititterly, Julia (NN)

11
Copperfield, David (DC)
Marchioness, the (OCS)
Pumblechook, Uncle
(GE)
Tulkinghorn, Mr (BH)

2+ words
Aged P (BH)
La Creevy, Miss (NN)
Little Dorrit (LD)
Little Em'ly (DC)
Little Nell (OCS)
Tiny Tim (CC)

DINOSAURS

TYPES OF DINOSAUR

8
masosaur
sauropod

9
hadrosaur
iguanadon
nothosaur
oviraptor
pterosaur
stegosaur
trachodon

10
allosaurus
altispinax
ankylosaur
barosaurus
cotylosaur
dicynodont
diplodocus

dryosaurus
megalosaur
plesiosaur
pteranodon
stegoceras
titanosaur

11
anatosaurus
anchisaurus
apatosaurus
cetiosaurus
coelophysis
deinonychus
ichthyosaur
kritosaurus
monoclonius
polacanthus
pterodactyl
riojasaurus
saurolophus
scolosaurus
spinosaurus
stegosaurus
tarbosaurus

triceratops
tyrannosaur

12
ankylosaurus
brontosaurus
camptosaurus
ceratosaurus
chasmosaurus
deinocheirus
hylaeosaurus
kentrosaurus
lambeosaurus
megalosaurus
ornothominus
ouransaurus
plateosaurus
velociraptor

13
brachiosaurus
ichthyosaurus
tyrannosaurus

DISEASE

A disease
Diseases and other
complaints affecting humans
Diseases affecting animals

A DISEASE

3
bug
ill

5
virus

6
malady
plague

7
ailment
illness
scourge

8
disorder
sickness
syndrome

9
complaint
condition
infection

10
affliction
pestilence

DISEASES AND OTHER COMPLAINTS AFFECTING HUMANS

2
ME
MS
TB
VD

3
bug
cut
fit
flu
gyp
IBS
mal
pip
pox
RSI
tic
STD
wen

4
ache
acne
ague
AIDS
clap
gout
itch
rash
stye
wind
yaws

5
bends
chill
colic
cough
croup
fever
hives
lupus
mania
mumps
palsy
piles
polio
scald
shock
spasm
stone
ulcer
worms

6
angina
anuria
apnoea
asthma
ataxia
autism
bruise
callus
cancer
caries
chorea
dengue
dropsy
eczema
gravel
grippe
hernia
herpes
jetlag
megrim
myopia
nausea
oedema
otalgy
otitis
plague
quinsy
rabies
scurvy
sepsis
sprain
stitch
strain
stress
stroke
thrush
tumour
typhus

7
abscess
allergy
amnesia
anaemia
anthrax
aphasia
bulimia

catarrh
cholera
colitis
dysuria
earache
fistula
gumboil
leprosy
lockjaw
lumbago
malaria
measles
mycosis
otalgia
pinkeye
podagra
pyrexia
relapse
rickets
roseola
rubella
rupture
scabies
seizure
tetanus
typhoid
uraemia
variola
verruca
vertigo
whitlow

8
agraphia
alopecia
aneurysm
anorexia
apoplexy
backache
beriberi
botulism
bursitis
cachexia
calculus
clubfoot
coronary
cystitis
dementia

diabetes
dyslexia
embolism
enuresis
epilepsy
ergotism
erythema
fibrosis
fracture
gangrene
glaucoma
headache
hydropsy
hookworm
impetigo
insomnia
jaundice
mastitis
migraine
neuritis
neurosis
orchitis
pellagra
pleurisy
pruritis
ringworm
sciatica
scrofula
shingles
sickness
smallpox
syphilis
tapeworm
tinnitus
toxaemia
trachoma

9
arthritis
bilharzia
carcinoma
catalepsy
chilblain
chlamydia
cirrhosis
daltonism
diarrhoea
dysentery

dyspepsia
dystrophy
eclampsia
emphysema
enteritis
frostbite
gastritis
halitosis
heartburn
hepatitis
impotence
influenza
leukaemia
nephritis
neuralgia
nystagmus
paralysis
phlebitis
pneumonia
porphyria
psoriasis
psychosis
sclerosis
sunstroke
toothache
urticaria
vaginitis

10
alcoholism
Alzheimer's
asbestosis
bronchitis
chickenpox
concussion
depression
dermatitis
diphtheria
dipsomania
erysipelas
fibrositis
flatulence
gingivitis
gonorrhoea
hyperaemia
laceration
laryngitis
meningitis

nyctalopia
paraplegia
presbyopia
rheumatics
rheumatism
scarlatina
thrombosis
urethritis

11
consumption
haemophilia
haemorrhage
haemorrhoid
hydrophobia
hypothermia
indigestion
infertility
kwashiorkor
listeriosis
miscarriage
paratyphoid
peritonitis
pharyngitis
psittacosis
septicaemia
tachycardia
tonsillitis
trichinosis

12
appendicitis
collywobbles
constipation
encephalitis
fibrillation
haemorrhoids
hyperacidity
hypertension
hypochondria
incontinence
inflammation
malnutrition
neurasthenia
osteoporosis
parkinsonism
quadriplegia
thalassaemia
tuberculosis

13
elephantiasis
osteomyelitis
poliomyelitis
schizophrenia

2+ words
angina pectoris
anorexia nervosa
caisson disease
cardiac arrest
cystic fibrosis
delirium tremens
glandular fever
hay fever
heart attack
Hodgkin's disease
housemaid's knee
lassa fever
Legionnaire's disease
prickly heat
river blindness
scarlet fever
sleeping sickness
slipped disc
St Vitus's dance
tennis elbow
water on the brain
water on the knee
writer's cramp
yellow fever

*DISEASES AFFECTING
ANIMALS*

3
BSE
gid
haw
pip

4
gape
scab
wind

5
bloat
husks

mange
vives
worms

6
cowpox
garget
heaves
rabies
spavin
splint
thrush
warble

7
anthrax
footrot
hardpad
hoofrot
murrain
scrapie

8
blackleg
fowlpest
glanders
staggers
swayback

9
distemper
strangles

10
blackwater
rinderpest
swinefever

11
brucellosis
myxomatosis
psittacosis

2+ words
blue tongue
feline enteritis
foot and mouth (disease)
fur-ball
mad cow disease

DOGS

A dog
Breeds of dog
Some famous dogs

A DOG

3
cur
pup
toy

4
mutt
tike
tyke

5
bitch
brach
hound
pooch
puppy
whelp

6
bowwow
canine
gundog
lapdog
pariah
ratter
setter

7
mongrel

8
sheepdog
turnspit
watchdog

2+ words
guide dog
sniffer dog

BREEDS OF DOG

3
lab
pom
pug
pye

4
chow
peke
Skye

5
boxer
Cairn
corgi
dingo
husky
spitz

6
Afghan
basset
beagle
borzoi
cocker
collie
poodle
saluki
scotty
setter
yorkie

7
basenji
bulldog
griffon
lurcher
Maltese
mastiff
pointer
samoyed
Sharpei
Sheltie
spaniel
terrier
whippet

8
Airedale
Alsatian
Blenheim
chowchow
Doberman
elkhound
foxhound
keeshond
labrador
malemute
papillon
Pekinese
pinscher
sealyham
springer

9
boarhound
chihuahua
dachshund
Dalmatian
dobermann
greyhound
Pekingese
retriever
ridgeback
schnauzer
staghound
wolfhound

10
Bedlington
bloodhound
otterhound
Pomeranian
Rottweiler
schipperke

12
Newfoundland

13
affenpinscher

2+ words
Afghan hound
Border collie

Border terrier
bull terrier
Cairn terrier
clumber spaniel
cocker spaniel
Dandie Dinmont
Dandy Dinmont
German shepherd
golden retriever
Great Dane
Irish wolfhound
Jack Russell
King Charles spaniel
lhasa apso
pit-bull (terrier)
pug dog
pye dog
Pyrenean mountain dog
red setter
Scotch terrier
St Bernard
West Highland terrier

SOME FAMOUS DOGS

3
Jip (*David Copperfield*)

4
Asta (*Thin Man*)
Dash (Queen Victoria)
Nana (*Peter Pan*)
Toto (*Wizard of Oz*)

5
Argus (Ulysses)
Flush (*Barretts of Wimpole Street*)
Laika (first dog in space)
Pluto (Disney)
Snoopy (*Peanuts*)
Snowy (*Tintin*)
Timmy (*Famous Five*)

6
Lassie (films)
Nipper (HMV)

7
Diamond (Sir Isaac Newton)

8
Bullseye (*Oliver Twist*)
Cerberus (*Gk myth*)

2+ words
Jock of the Bushveld (childhood companion)
Greyfriars Bobby (faithful hound)
Rin-tin-tin (TV)
Mick the Miller (racing greyhound)

DRINKS

See also **WINE**

KINDS OF DRINK

3
ale
cha
gin
IPA
kir
nip
peg
pop
rum
rye
tea
tot

4
arak
beer
bock
brut
char
Coke
cola
dram
fino
fizz
flip
grog
half
hock
kava
mead
mild
milk
ouzo
pint
port
raki
rosé
sake
shot
slug
soda

swig
wine

5
bohea
broth
cider
cocoa
crush
cuppa
heavy
hogan
hooch
juice
julep
kvass
lager
latte
light
mocha
negus
perry
Pimms®
plonk
punch
sling
snort
stout
toddy
tonic
vodka
water

6
arrack
bitter
bracer
brandy
bubbly
bumper
cassis
caudle
chaser
claret
coffee
cognac
double
eggnog

gimlet
grappa
hootch
kirsch
kummel
liquor
malibu
mescal
nectar
noggin
pastis
Pernod®
porter
posset
poteen
quickie
scotch
shandy
sherry
spirit
squash
tipple
tisane
whisky

7
aquavit
bitters
bourbon
Campari®
chianti
Cinzano®
cobbler
collins
cordial
curacao
draught
koumiss
limeade
liqueur
Madeira
Martini®
mineral
oloroso
ratafia
retsina
sangria
scrumpy

seltzer
sherbet
sidecar
smoothy
snifter
tequila
whiskey

8
absinthe
advocaat
ambrosia
anisette
aperitif
armagnac
beverage
calvados
champers
cocktail
Drambuie®
Dubonnet®
espresso
gluhwein
highball
hollands
lemonade
mantilla
nightcap
schiedam

schnapps
snowball
souchong
spritzer
tincture
vermouth

9
applejack
champagne
chacolate
Cointreau®
firewater
grenadine
Manhattan
margarita
metheglin
moonshine
orangeade
slivovitz
sundowner

10
buttermilk
capuccino
chartreuse
maraschino
usquebaugh

11
amontillado
Benedictine®
screwdriver

12
sarsaparilla

2+ words
Adam's ale
bloody Mary
crème de menthe
Earl Grey
ginger ale
ginger beer
John Collins
old-fashioned
one for the road
pink gin
red-eye
root beer
rot-gut
slow gin
Tia Maria®

DRUGS

Medicinal drugs
Narcotic drugs

MEDICINAL DRUGS

4
pill

5
upper
senna

6
downer
emetic
opiate
potion
Prozak®
remedy
Valium®
Viagra®

7
anodyne
antacid
aspirin
bromide
cascara
chloral
codeine
ginseng
heparin
insulin
Librium®
menthol
Mogadon®
morphia
placebo
quinine
steroid
tylocin
veronal

8
antidote
barbital
caffeine

camomile
diazepam
laudanum
levodopa
medicine
morphine
Nembutal®
neomycin
sedative
sennapod
valerian
warfarin

9
analgesic
barbitone
cortisone
digitalis
ibuprofen
mepacrine
methadone
oestrogen
pethidine
phenazone
stimulant

10
antibiotic
belladonna
Benzedrine®
chloroform
depressant
medicament
medication
painkiller
penicillin
Terramycin®

11
amphetamine
anaesthetic
aphrodisiac
barbiturate
diamorphine
paracetamol
Thalidomide®

13
antihistamine

tranquillizer (*or*
tranquilliser)

2+ words
l-dopa
pep-pill

NARCOTIC DRUGS

3
fix
LSD
pot

4
coke
dope
hemp
snow
weed

5
bhang
crack
dagga
ganja
grass
horse
opium
smack
speed

6
heroin

7
cocaine
ecstasy
hashish

8
cannabis
mescalin
nicotine

9
marihuana
marijuana
mescaline

EDUCATION

Educational terminology
Famous schools
Oxford and Cambridge
colleges

EDUCATIONAL
TERMINOLOGY

2
BA
BD
IQ
KS
MA
PE
PT
RE

3
BEd
cap
CSE
DEE
don
EFL
ELT
fag
GCE
gym
gyp
HND
ICT
IEP
LEA
LSA
MBA
NLS
NUS
NUT
NVQ
OND
PhD
PTA
SAT
SEN

4
cane
coed
crib
dean
DfEE
digs
exam
fees
form
gate
GCSE
GNVQ
gown
hall
head
hons
hood
poly
prep
PSHE
quad
SATs
swot
TEFL
term
TESL
test

5
backs
bedel
board
break
chair
class
coach
Dip.Ed
DPhil
drill
expel
grant
house
lines
mixed
motto
MPhil
pupil

scout
SENCO
study
tawse
tutor

6
beadle
Bodley
bursar
course
degree
eights
fellow
finals
Hilary
incept
lesson
locals
locker
master
matron
Ofsted
optime
period
primer
reader
rector
regent
school
sconce
senate
supply
thesis
tripos
warden

7
academy
boarder
bulldog
burgess
bursary
captain
college
crammer
diploma
dominie

exclude
faculty
gestalt
grammar
honours
lecture
mid-term
monitor
nursery
prefect
proctor
project
provost
reading
scholar
science
seminar
student
suspend
teacher
torpids
Trinity
tuition
writing

8
academia
academic
backward
baseline
ceremony
doctoral
emeritus
examinee
examiner
freshman
graduate
guidance
holidays
homework
learning
lecturer
literacy
manciple
mistress
numeracy
remedial
research

semester
spelling
statutes
textbook
training
tutorial
vacation
wrangler

9
ancillary
bilateral
classroom
collegian
detention
doctorate
dormitory
exclusion
expulsion
inservice
pedagogue
playgroup
preceptor
prelector
president
principal
professor
refectory
registrar
scholarly
schoolboy
selection
sophomore
streaming
trimester

10
assessment
attainment
blackboard
chancellor
collegiate
coursework
exhibition
extramural
fellowship
foundation
graduation

headmaster
illiteracy
imposition
instructor
laboratory
Michaelmas
philosophy
playground
sabbatical
schooldays
schoolgirl
schoolmate
schoolroom
Sheldonian
suspension
university
vicegerent

11
certificate
coeducation
convocation
examination
headteacher
housemaster
matriculate
mortarboard
polytechnic
scholarship

12
congregation
dissertation
headmistress
kindergarten
postgraduate
schoolfellow
schoolmaster

13
coeducational
comprehension
comprehensive
matriculation
schoolteacher
undergraduate

2+ words
academic year
access fund
adult education
A-level
aptitude test
art school
common room
day boy
day release
day school
dining hall
dinner money
eleven plus
evening class
form teacher
grammar school
head boy
head girl
holiday task
ivory tower
Ivy League
key stage
league table
literacy hour
master of arts
mature student
O-level
post-doc
public orator
pupil-teacher
red-brick
regent master
roll call
scale post
school hours
school year
send down
single-sex
special needs
speech day
student loans
sub-rector
Sunday school
supply teacher
teach-in
three Rs
tuck shop

tuition fees
viva voce

FAMOUS SCHOOLS

4
Eton

5
Rugby
Stowe

6
Harrow
Oakham
Oundle
Radley
Repton

7
Alleyn's
Bedales
Clifton
Dulwich
Lancing
Malvern
Roedean

8
Ardingly
Benenden
Bluecoat
Downside
Gresham's
Oswestry

9
Blundell's
Cranleigh
Millfield
Sherborne
Tonbridge
Uppingham

10
Ampleforth
Haileybury
Shrewsbury

Stonyhurst
Winchester

11
Gordonstoun
Marlborough
Westminster

12
Charterhouse
Haberdashers'

***OXFORD AND
CAMBRIDGE COLLEGES***

3
BNC (= Brasenose O)
New (O).

4
Hall (The Hall = Trinity
Hall C)

5
Caius (C)
Clare (C)
Green (O)
House (The House =
Christchurch O)
Jesus (C and O)
Keble (O)
King's (C)

6
Darwin (C)
Exeter (O)
Girton (C)
Merton (O)
Queens' (C)
Queen's (O)
Selwyn (C)
Wadham (O)

7
Balliol (O)
Christ's (C)
Downing (C)
Linacre (O)

Lincoln (O)
Newnham (C)
Trinity (C and O)
Wolfson (C and O)

8
Emmanuel (C)
Gonville (C)
Hertford (O)
Homerton (C)
Nuffield (O)
Magdalen (O)
Pembroke (C and O)
Robinson (C)

9
Brasenose (O)
Churchill (C)
Magdalene (C)

Mansfield (O)
Templeton (O)
Worcester (O)

10
Peterhouse (C)
Somerville (O)
University (O)

11
Fitzwilliam (C)

12
Christchurch (O)

2+ words
All Souls (O)
Campion Hall (O)
Corpus Christi (C and O)

Hughes Hall (C)
Lady Margaret Hall (O)
New Hall (C)
Osler House (C)
Regent's Park (O)
Rewley House (O)
St Anne's (O)
St Antony's (O)
St Cross (O)
St Catharine's (C)
St Catherine's (O)
St Edmund Hall (O)
St Edmund's House (C)
St Hilda's (O)
St Hugh's (O)
St John's (C and O)
St Peter's (O)
Sidney Sussex (C)
Trinity Hall (C)

ELEMENTS

CHEMICAL ELEMENTS

3
tin (Sn)

4
gold (Au)
iron (Fe)
lead (Pb)
neon (Ne)
zinc (Zn)

5
argon (Ar)
boron (B)
radon (Rn)
xenon (Xe)

6
barium (Ba)
carbon (C)
cerium (Ce)
cobalt (Co)
copper (Cu)
curium (Cm)
erbium (Er)
helium (He)
indium (In)
iodine (I)
nickel (Ni)
osmium (Os)
oxygen (O)
radium (Ra)
silver (Ag)
sodium (Na)

7
arsenic (As)
bismuth (Bi)
bromine (Br)
cadmium (Cd)
caesium (Cs)
calcium (Ca)
fermium (Fm)
gallium (Ga)
hafnium (Hf)

iridium (Ir)
krypton (Kr)
lithium (Li)
mercury (Hg)
niobium (Nb)
rhenium (Re)
rhodium (Rh)
silicon (Si)
sulphur (S)
terbium (Tb)
thorium (Th)
thulium (Tm)
uranium (U)
wolfram (W)
yttrium (Y)

8
actinium (Ac)
antimony (Sb)
astatine (At)
chlorine (Cl)
chromium (Cr)
europium (Eu)
fluorine (F)
francium (Fr)
hydrogen (H)
lutetium (Lu)
nitrogen (N)
nobelium (No)
platinum (Pt)
polonium (Po)
rubidium (Rb)
samarium (Sm)
scandium (Sc)
selenium (Se)
tantalum (Ta)
thallium (Tl)
titanium (Ti)
tungsten (W)
vanadium (V)

9
aluminium (Al)
americium (Am)
berkelium (Bk)
beryllium (Be)
germanium (Ge)
lanthanum (La)

magnesium (Mg)
manganese (Mn)
neodymium (Nd)
neptunium (Np)
palladium (Pd)
plutonium (Pu)
potassium (K)
ruthenium (Ru)
strontium (Sr)
tellurium (Te)
ytterbium (Yb)
zirconium (Zr)

10
dysprosium (Dy)
gadolinium (Gd)
lawrencium (Lr)
molybdenum (Mo)
phosphorus (P)
promethium (Pm)
technetium (Tc)

11
californium (Cf)
einsteinium (Es)
mendelevium (Md)

12
praseodymium (Pr)
protactinium (Pa)

ENGINEERING

Engineering terms
Famous engineers

3
ace
amp
BHP
bit
cam
cog
dam
EMF
erg
fan
fit
gab
hob
hub
IHP
ion
key
lag
nut
ohm
oil
ram
rig
RPM
sag
tap
tie
UHF
VHF

4
arch
axle
beam
belt
bolt
butt
byte
cast
cone
cowl
flaw

flux
fuel
fuse
gear
glue
hasp
hook
hose
jack
kiln
lens
lift
link
lock
loom
main
mill
mine
nail
nave
oily
pawl
pile
pipe
plan
plug
pump
rack
rail
reel
road
rope
rung
rust
shop
skid
slag
slue
stay
stop
sump
tamp
tank
test
tire
tool
tram
tube

turn
tyre
unit
vane
vent
void
volt
weir
weld
wire
work
worm

5
alloy
anode
blast
braze
cable
chair
chase
civil
clamp
cleat
compo
crane
crank
crate
deuce
dowel
drill
drive
elbow
felly
flows
flume
flush
force
gauge
grace
helix
hinge
hoist
ingot
input
jenny
jewel
joint

joist
keyed
laser
level
lever
maser
miner
model
motor
mould
oakum
oiler
pedal
pivot
plant
power
press
pylon
quern
radar
radio
relay
resin
rigid
rivet
rough
rusty
screw
shaft
short
shunt
slack
slide
sling
smelt
spoke
spool
spout
stamp
steam
still
strap
strut
swage
taper
tools
tooth
train

valve
video
waste
wedge
wharf
wheel
wiper
works

6
analog
aerial
anneal
barrel
blower
bobbin
boiler
bridge
buffer
burner
camber
clutch
cotter
couple
cradle
damper
derail
duplex
dynamo
energy
engine
fitter
flange
funnel
geyser
girder
gutter
hinged
intake
jigger
kibble
lacing
ladder
lamina
latten
magnet
milled
mining

moment
monkey
nipple
nozzle
output
petrol
pinion
piston
pulley
rarefy
repair
retard
rigger
rocket
roller
rotary
rundle
sheave
siding
sleeve
sluice
smithy
socket
solder
spigot
static
stoker
strain
stress
strike
sucker
switch
swivel
system
tackle
tappet
temper
tender
thrust
tinned
toggle
torque
tripod
tubing
tunnel
uncoil
vacuum
washer

welded
welder

7
adapter
airfoil
artisan
battery
bearing
belting
booster
bracket
caisson
casting
cathode
chamfer
chimney
cistern
clacker
column
conduit
cuffing
derrick
digital
drawbar
drawing
dynamic
exciter
exhaust
eyebolt
factory
ferrule
firebox
forging
founder
foundry
fulcrum
furnace
gearing
gimbals
hydrant
inertia
jointer
journal
lagging
lockage
machine
magneto

manhole
milling
monitor
moulded
moulder
nuclear
pattern
pinhole
pontoon
program
railway
ratchet
reactor
refract
riveter
roadway
sawmill
seawall
shackle
shuttle
sleeper
smelter
spindle
stamper
statics
stopper
suction
support
syringe
tamping
tension
testing
thimble
tilting
tinning
torsion
tracing
tramcar
tramway
treadle
trolley
turbine
turning
unscrew
viaduct
voltage
voltaic
welding

wringer
wrought

8
acentric
annealed
aqueduct
axletree
balancer
ballcock
bevelled
bridging
camshaft
cassette
castings
chauffer
compound
computer
concrete
coupling
cradling
cryotron
cylinder
declutch
electric
elevator
engineer
enginery
fireclay
fireplug
flywheel
fracture
friction
galvanic
governor
gradient
hardware
ignition
injector
insulate
ironwork
irrigate
Jacquard
klystron
laminate
leverage
limekiln
linotype

magnetic
mechanic
momentum
monorail
monotype
moulding
movement
oilstone
operator
pendulum
penstock
platform
polarity
pressure
purchase
radiator
recharge
refinery
register
repairer
rheostat
rigidity
shearing
smelting
software
spinnery
stamping
standard
starling
stopcock
strength
stuffing
tapering
teletype
tempered
template
terminal
textbook
throttle
tinplate
tractile
traction
tractive
turbojet
turnpike
tympanum
uncoiled
unsolder

velocity
windmill
wireless
workable
workshop

9
acoustics
amplifier
artificer
baseplate
brakedrum
brakepipe
blueprint
clockwork
condenser
conductor
craftsman
crosshead
cyclotron
diaphragm
earthwork
eccentric
electrify
electrode
escalator
fishplate
floodgate
framework
funicular
galvanism
galvanist
galvanize (galvanise)
gasometer
gearwheel
hydraulic
hydrostat
induction
inductive
inertness
injection
insertion
insulated
insulator
ironsmith
ironworks
laminated
limelight

lubricant
lubricate
machinery
machinist
magnetist
magnetize
mechanics
mechanism
mechanize (mechanise)
millstone
perforate
pneumatic
programme
propeller
prototype
pulverize (pulverise)
radiation
rectifier
reflector
regulator
repairing
reparable
reservoir
resultant
rheomotor
roughcast
sandpaper
soldering
stanchion
stiffener
structure
superheat
telephone
tempering
transform
turntable
unscrewed
vibration
vulcanite
vulcanize (vulcanise)
watermark
winepress

10
accelerate
alternator
automation
automobile

cantilever
caseharden
centigrade
combustion
crankshaft
derailment
dielectric
discharger
drawbridge
efficiency
electrical
electronic
embankment
escapement
footbridge
galvanized
guillotine
horsepower
hydrophore
inflexible
instrument
insulating
insulation
irrigation
isodynamic
laboratory
lamination
locomotive
lubricator
macadamize (macadamise)
magnetizer (magnetiser)
mechanical
percolator
piledriver
pneumatics
powerhouse
programmer
refraction
rejointing
resistance
revolution
smokestack
stationary
stiffening
streamline
structural
telegraphy
telescopic

television
thermopile
thermostat
transients
transistor
tunnelling
unsoldered
voltaplast
watertight
waterwheel
waterwings
waterworks
windtunnel

11

accelerator
accumulator
aerodynamics
anelectrode
candlepower
carburettor
compression
computation
contrivance
diamagnetic
dynamometer
electrician
electricity
electrolyse
electrolyte
electronics
engineering
incinerator
laminations
lubrication
maintenance
manufactory
perforation
piledriving
rarefaction
reconstruct
retardation
revolutions
searchlight
superheater
switchboard
synchronism
synchronize (synchronise)

synchrotron
transformer
transmitter
underground
uninsulated
workmanship

12

acceleration
canalization (canalisation)
counterpoise
diamagnetism
differential
disintegrate
electrolysis
electromotor
hydrodynamic
installation
lubrifaction
magnetomotor
palification
polarization
(polarisation)
synchronized
(synchronised)
thermocouple
transmission

2+ words

air brake
alarm gauge
anti-friction
arterial road
artesian well
assembly line
atomic clock
balance wheel
bell founder
bell foundry
belt fastener
bevel gear
bevel wheel
blast furnace
cam wheel
cast iron
cast steel
coaxial cable
cog wheel

cotter pin
coupling box
coupling pin
crown wheel
cut-out
damask steel
Davy lamp
dead level
dead lift
dead weight
diesel engine
disc brake
disc coupling
disc wheels
dish wheels
disk brake
donkey engine
driving wheel
dry dock
endless belt
endless screw
engine driver
engine room
exhaust pipe
exhaust valve
fire brick
fire escape
fish joint
flange rail
floating dock
fluid drive
flying bridge
force pump
fuse box
fuse holder
gas fitter
gas gauge
gas holder
gas mains
gas turbine
gas works
H-beam
helical gear
high-pressure
idle wheel
iron filings
iron founder
iron foundry

Lewis bolt
Leyden jar
lock-nut
lynch pin
machine tool
make-and-break
non-conductor
oxy-acetylene
pig iron
pilot engine
piston rod
pressure pump
pug mill
ratchet wheel
Reaumur scale
ring bolt
road bed
road metal
rolling mill
rolling press
rolling stock
safety valve
safety-lamp
saw pit
slide rule
split pin
steam boiler
steam engine
steam gauge
steam hammer
steam turbine
steam whistle
stock lock
stoke hole
swing bridge
tail race
tappet valve
terminal post
test bay
tie bar
tie beam
tie rod
T-rail
train oil
trundle head
trunk line
tunnel pit
voltaic arc

voltaic pile
water supply
water tank
water tower
wave motion
welding heat
white heat
wind pump
wire drawing
working model
worm wheel
wrought iron

FAMOUS ENGINEERS

4

Ader (Clément)
Benz (Karl)
Eads (John Buchanan)
Otis (Elisha Graves)
Otto (Nikolaus August)
Tull (Jethro)
Watt (James)

5

Baird (John Logie)
Baker (Benjamin)
Evans (Oliver)
Gabor (Dennis)

6

Brunel (Isambard
Kingdom)
Cayley (George)
Dunlop (John)
Fokker (Anthony)
McAdam (John Loudon)
Rennie (John)
Savery (Thomas)
Singer (Isaac Merrit)
Taylor (Frederick
Winslow)
Wallis (Barnes)

7

Candela (Felix)
Curtiss (Glenn)
Daimler (Gottlieb)

Marconi (Guglielmo)
Siemens (Ernst)
Telford (Thomas)
Whittle (Frank)

8
Bessemer (Henry)

Brindley (James)
Crompton (Samuel)
Ericsson (John)
Koriolov (Sergei)
Maudslay (Henry)
Newcomen (Henry)
Sikorsky (Igor)

9
Armstrong (William
George)

10
Stephenson (George)
Trevithick (Richard)

ENGLAND/ ENGLISH

Rivers in England
Towns and cities in England
See also **COUNTY**

RIVERS IN ENGLAND

3
Aln
Axe
Cam
Dee
Don
Exe
Fal
Lee
Rye
Sid
Sow
Taw
Ure
Usk
Wey
Wye
Yeo

4
Adur
Aire
Arun
Avon
Bure
Chew
Cole
Coln
Dart
Dove
Eden
Isis
Lune
Mole
Nene
Ouse
Rede
Tees
Test
Wear
Yare

5
Brent
Camel
Colne
Deben
Fleet
Frome
Otter
Sheaf
Stort
Stour
Swale
Tamar
Teign
Trent
Tweed

6
Calder
Coquet
Crouch
Hamble
Humber
Irwell
Itchen
Kennet
Loddon
medina
Medway
Mersey
Monnow
Orwell
Parret
Ribble
Roding
Rother
Severn
Thames
Wandle
Weaver
Wensum
Witham

7
Chelmer
Derwent
Waveney
Welland

8
Beaulieu
Cherwell
Torridge
Wansbeck

9
Evenlode
Windrush

10
Blackwater

TOWNS AND CITIES IN ENGLAND

3
Ely
Rye

4
Bath
Bray
Bude
Bury
Clun
Deal
Diss
Eton
Hove
Hull
Hyde
Ince
Leek
Looe
Lydd
Ross
Ryde
Shap
Ware
York

5
Acton

Alton	Barnet	Morley
Bacup	Barrow	Naseby
Blyth	Barton	Nelson
Bourn	Batley	Neston
Calne	Battle	Newark
Chard	Bawtry	Newent
Cheam	Belper	Newlyn
Colne	Bodmin	Newton
Cowes	Bognor	Norham
Crewe	Bolton	Oakham
Derby	Bootle	Oldham
Dover	Boston	Ormsby
Egham	Bruton	Ossett
Epsom	Bungay	Oundle
Filey	Burton	Oxford
Fowey	Buxton	Penryn
Frome	Castor	Pewsey
Goole	Cobham	Pinner
Grays	Cromer	Pudsey
Hawes	Darwen	Putney
Hedon	Dudley	Ramsey
Hurst	Durham	Redcar
Hythe	Ealing	Ripley
Leeds	Eccles	Romney
Leigh	Epping	Romsey
Lewes	Exeter	Rugely
Louth	Goring	Seaham
Luton	Hanley	Seaton
March	Harlow	Selsey
Olney	Harow	Settle
Otley	Havant	Snaith
Poole	Henley	Stroud
Reeth	Hexham	Sutton
Ripon	Howden	Thirsk
Rugby	Ilford	Thorne
Selby	Ilkley	Totnes
Stoke	Ilsley	Walmer
Stone	Jarrow	Walton
Thame	Kendal	Watton
Tring	Leyton	Welwyn
Truro	London	Weston
Wells	Ludlow	Whitby
Wigan	Lynton	Widnes
	Lytham	Wigton
6	Maldon	Wilthon
Alston	Malton	Witham
Alford	Marlow	Witner
Ashton	Masham	Yeovil

7

Alnwick
Andover
Appleby
Arundel
Ashford
Aylsham
Bampton
Banbury
Barking
Beccles
Bedford
Belford
Berwick
Bewdley
Bexhill
Bickley
Bilston
Bourton
Bowfell
Brandon
Bristol
Brixham
Bromley
Burnham
Burnley
Burslem
Caistor
Cafford
Cawston
Chatham
Cheadle
Cheddar
Chesham
Chester
Chorley
Clacton
Crawley
Croydon
Datchet
Dawlish
Devizes
Dorking
Douglas
Dunster
Elstree
Enfield
Evesham

Exmouth
Fareham
Farnham
Feltham
Glossop
Gosport
Grimsby
Halifax
Hampton
Harwich
Haworth
Helston
Heywood
Hitchin
Honiton
Hornsea
Hornsey
Horsham
Ipswich
Ixworth
Keswick
Kington
Lancing
Langton
Ledbury
Leyburn
Lincoln
Malvern
Margate
Matlock
Molesey
Moreton
Morpeth
Mossley
Newbury
Newport
Norwich
Oldbury
Overton
Padstow
Penrith
Paulton
Prescot
Preston
Rainham
Reading
Redhill
Redruth

Reigate
Retford
Romford
Royston
Runcorn
Salford
Saltash
Sandown
Saxelby
Seaford
Shifnal
Shipley
Shipton
Silloth
Skipton
Spilsby
Staines
Stilton
Sudbury
Sunbury
Swanage
Swindon
Swinton
Taunton
Telford
Tenbury
Tetbury
Thaxted
Tilbury
Torquay
Twyford
Ventnor
Walsall
Waltham
Wantage
Wareham
Warwick
Watchet
Watford
Wickwar
Windsor
Winslow
Wisbech
Worksop

8

Abingdon
Alfreton

Alnmouth	Hinckley	Thornaby
Amesbury	Holbeach	Tiverton
Amthill	Hunmanby	Tunstall
Axbridge	Ilkeston	Uckfield
Aycliffe	Keighley	Uxbridge
Bakewell	Kingston	Wallasey
Barnsley	Lavenham	Wallsend
Berkeley	Lechlade	Wanstead
Beverley	Nantwich	Westbury
Bicester	Newhaven	Wetheral
Bideford	Nuneaton	Wetherby
Bolsover	Ormskirk	Weymouth
Brackley	Oswestry	Woodford
Bradford	Penzance	Woolwich
Brampton	Pershore	Worthing
Bridport	Peterlee	Yarmouth
Brighton	Petworth	
Bromyard	Pevensey	**9**
Broseley	Plaistow	Aldeburgh
Camborne	Plymouth	Aldershot
Carlisle	Ramsgate	Allendale
Caterham	Redditch	Alresford
Chertsey	Richmond	Ambleside
Clevedon	Ringwood	Ashburton
Clovelly	Rochdale	Avonmouth
Coventry	Rothbury	Aylesbury
Crediton	Saltburn	Blackburn
Dartford	Sandgate	Blackpool
Daventry	Sandwich	Blandford
Debenham	Sedbergh	Blisworth
Dedworth	Shanklin	Bracknell
Deptford	Shelford	Braintree
Dewsbury	Shipston	Brentford
Egremont	Sidmouth	Brentwood
Eversley	Skegness	Brighouse
Fakenham	Sleaford	Broughton
Falmouth	Southend	Cambridge
Foulness	Spalding	Carnforth
Grantham	Stafford	Castleton
Grantown	Stanford	Chesilton
Hadleigh	Stanhope	Chingford
Hailsham	Stanwell	Clitheroe
Halstead	Stockton	Congleton
Hastings	Stratton	Cranborne
Hatfield	Swaffham	Cranbrook
Helmsley	Surbiton	Crewkerne
Hereford	Tamworth	Cricklade
Hertford	Thetford	Cuckfield

Dartmouth
Devonport
Doncaster
Donington
Droitwich
Dronfield
Dungeness
Dunstable
Ellesmere
Faversham
Fleetwood
Gateshead
Godalming
Gravesend
Greenwich
Grinstead
Guildford
Harrogate
Haslemere
Haverhill
Hawkhurst
Hoddesdon
Holmfirth
Ilchester
Immingham
Kettering
Kingswear
Lambourne
Lancaster
Leicester
Lichfield
Liverpool
Longridge
Lowestoft
Lymington
Maidstone
Mansfield
Middleton
Newcastle
Newmarket
Northwich
Otterburn
Pembridge
Penistone
Pickering
Rochester
Rotherham
Salisbury

Saltfleet
Sevenoaks
Sheerness
Sheffield
Sherborne
Smethwick
Southgate
Southport
Southwell
Southwold
Stevenage
Stockport
Stokesley
Stourport
Stratford
Tavistock
Tenterden
Todmorden
Tonbridge
Towcester
Tynemouth
Ulverston
Upminster
Uppingham
Uttoxeter
Wainfleet
Wakefield
Warkworth
Weybridge
Whernside
Wimbledon
Wincanton
Wokingham
Woodstock
Worcester
Wymondham

10
Accrington
Altrincham
Barnstaple
Beaminster
Bedlington
Bellingham
Billericay
Birkenhead
Birmingham
Bridgnorth

Bridgwater
Bromsgrove
Broxbourne
Buckingham
Canterbury
Carshalton
Chelmsford
Cheltenham
Chichester
Chippenham
Chulmleigh
Coggeshall
Colchester
Cullompton
Darlington
Dorchester
Eastbourne
Eccleshall
Farningham
Folkestone
Gloucester
Halesworth
Hartlepool
Haslington
Heathfield
Horncastle
Hornchurch
Hungerford
Hunstanton
Huntingdon
Ilfracombe
Gillingham
Kenilworth
Launceston
Leamington
Leominster
Littleport
Maidenhead
Malmesbury
Manchester
Mexborough
Micheldene
Middlewich
Mildenhall
Nailsworth
Nottingham
Okehampton
Orfordness

Pangbourne
Patrington
Peacehaven
Pontefract
Portishead
Portsmouth
Ravenglass
Rockingham
Saxmundham
Shepperton
Sheringham
Shrewsbury
Stalbridge
Stowmarket
Sunderland
Teddington
Teignmouth
Tewkesbury
Thamesmead
Torrington
Trowbridge
Twickenham
Warminster
Warrington
Washington
Wednesbury
Wellington
Whitchurch
Whitehaven
Whitstable
Whittlesey
Willenhall
Winchelsea
Winchester
Windlesham
Withernsea
Woodbridge
Workington

11
Basingstoke
Berkhamstead
Bournemouth
Bridlington
Buntingford
Cleethorpes
Cockermouth
Glastonbury
Guisborough
Hatherleigh
Ingatestone
Leytonstone
Lostwithiel
Ludgershall
Lutterworth
Mablethorpe
Manningtree
Marlborough
Petersfield
Rawtonstall
Scarborough
Shaftesbury
Southampton
Stalybridge
Stourbridge
Tattershall
Wallingford
Walthamstow
Westminster

12
Attleborough
Chesterfield
Christchurch
Gainsborough
Huddersfield
Ingleborough
Loughborough
Macclesfield
Peterborough
Shoeburyness

13
Boroughbridge
Brightlingsea
Godmanchester
Kidderminster
Knareborough
Littlehampton
Middlesborough
Northallerton
Wolverhampton

2+ words
Bishop Auckland
Bognor Regis
Burton-on-Trent
Bury St Edmunds
Chipping Norton
Hemel Hempstead
Herne Bay
Higham Ferrers
King's Lynn
Kirkby Lonsdale
Kirkby Stephen
Lyme Regis
Lytham St Annes
Market Deeping
Market Drayton
Melton Mowbray
Milton Keynes
Newton Abbot
Potter's Bar
Saffron Walden
St Albans
St Austell
St Helens
St Ives
St Leonards
St Neots
South Shields
Tunbridge Wells

ENTERTAIN-
MENT

Entertain
Entertainer
Entertainment
Famous entertainers

ENTERTAIN

4
busk
jest
joke
quip

5
amuse
cater
cheer
clown
treat

6
divert
invite
please
ponder
regale

7
beguile
delight
harbour
imagine
receive

8
conceive
consider
distract
interest

9
wisecrack

11
accommodate

contemplate
countenance

ENTERTAINER

2
DJ
MC

4
foil
host
mime
star

5
actor
clown
comic
emcee
mimic

6
artist
busker
dancer
diseur
jester
mummer
player
rapper
singer
stooge
talent

7
acrobat
actress
artiste
buffoon
compère
diseuse
juggler
reciter
showman
starlet
tumbler

8
comedian
conjuror
humorist
magician
minstrel
musician
showgirl
stripper
thespian
virtuoso
vocalist

9
anchorman
ballerina
celebrity
hypnotist
performer
presenter
puppeteer

10
bandleader
comedienne
troubador

11
accompanist
broadcaster
illusionist

12
escapologist
impersonator

13
contortionist
impressionist
ventriloquist

2+ words
belly-dancer
dancing-girl
disc jockey
drag artist
fan dancer
fire-eater

knife-thrower
mind-reader
song-and-dance man
stand-up (comedian)
straight man
striptease artist
tap-dancer
tightrope walker
trapeze artist

ENTERTAINMENT

3
act
fun

4
ball
fête
play
show

5
cards
dance
disco
farce
opera
panto
party
radio
revue
rodeo
sport
video

6
casino
cinema
circus
comedy
masque
review
satire
sitcom
soirée
tattoo

7
cabaret
cartoon
concert
dancing
karaoke
musical
pageant
recital
showbiz
theatre
variety

8
barbecue
carnival
clubbing
festival
gymkhana
peepshow
pleasure
roadshow
serenade
waxworks

9
amusement
burlesque
diversion
enjoyment
fireworks
floorshow
melodrama
pantomime
reception
sideshow
spectacle

10
attraction
knockabout
performing
production
recreation
striptease
vaudeville

11
distraction
performance

12
extravaganza

2+ words
magic show
music hall
night-club
Punch and Judy
puppet show

FAMOUS ENTERTAINERS
See also ACTOR,
MUSICIAN, SINGER

3
Fry (Stephen)
Lee (Gypsy Rose)
Rix (Brian)

4
Bron (Eleanor)
Cook (Peter)
Gray ('Monsewer' Eddy)
Hall (Henry)
Hill (Benny)
Hope (Bob)
Lowe (Arthur)
Muir (Frank)
Reid (Beryl)
Swan (Donald)
Tate (Harry)
Took (Barry)
Wise (Ernie)

5
Adler (Larry)
Allen (Chesney/Dave)
Askey (Arthur)
Benny (Jack)
Borge (Victor)
Brice (Fanny)
Bruce (Lenny)
Burke (Kathy)
Burns (George)

Davis (Sammy)
Elton (Ben)
Frost (David)
Hardy (Oliver)
Horne (Kenneth)
James (Clive/Sid)
Jason (David)
Lloyd (Marie)
Moore (Dudley)
Palin (Michael)
Robey (George)
Sykes (Eric)
Wogan (Terry)
Worth (Harry)

6

Barker (Ronnie)
Barnum (P.T.)
Cleese (John)
Cotton (Billy)
Disney (Walt)
Fields (Gracie/W.C.)
Lauder (Harry)
Laurel (Stan)
Miller (Max)
Morley (Robert)
Mostel (Zero)

Norden (Dennis)
Savile (Jimmy)
Tilley (Vesta)

7

Bennet (Alan)
Bentine (Michael)
Blondin (Charles)
Chaplin (Charlie)
Chester (Charlie)
Corbett (Ronnie)
Enfield (Harry)
Feldman (Marty)
Hancock (Sheila/Tony)
Handley (Tommy)
Harding (Gilbert)
Houdini (Harry)
Jacques (Hattie)
Langtry (Lillie)
Marceau (Marcel)
Murdoch (Richard)
Rantzen (Esther)
Rushton (Willie)
Secombe (Harry)
Sellers (Peter)
Sherrin (Ned)
Ustinov (Peter)

8

Brambell (Wilfred)
Bygraves (Max)
Connolly (Billy)
Flanders (Michael)
Forsythe (Bruce)
Grenfell (Joyce)
Grimaldi (Joseph)
Milligan (Spike)
Robinson (Eric)
Williams (Kenneth)

9

Blackburn (Tony)
Chevalier (Maurice)
Humphries (Barry)
Lyttleton (Humphry)
Monkhouse (Bob)
Morecambe (Eric)

10

Whitehouse (Paul)

2+ words
La Rue (Danny)
Le Mesurier (John)

EUROPE/ EUROPEAN

Countries of Europe
European towns and cities

COUNTRIES OF EUROPE

5
Italy
Malta
Spain

6
Bosnia
Cyprus
France
Greece
Latvia
Monaco
Norway
Poland
Russia
Serbia
Sweden
Turkey

7
Albania
Andorra
Austria
Belarus
Belgium
Britain
Croatia
Denmark
Estonia
Finland
Germany
Hungary
Iceland
Moldova
Romania
Slovakia
Slovenia
Ukraine

8
Bulgaria
Portugal

9
Lithuania
Macedonia

10
Luxembourg
Montenegro

11
Netherlands
Switzerland

13
Liechtenstein

2+ words
Bosnia and Herzegovina
Czech Republic
San Marino
United Kingdom
Vatican City

EUROPEAN TOWNS AND CITIES
(excluding the United Kingdom and Ireland)
(* = capital city)

3
Aix (France)
Pau (France)

4
Albi (France)
Bari (Italy)
Bonn (Germany)
*Bern (Switzerland)
Breda (Netherlands)
Brno (Czech Rep.)
Caen (France)
Graz (Austria)
Kiel (Germany)
Kiev (Ukraine)
Köln (Germany)

Laon (France)
Linz (Austria)
Lodz (Poland)
Lvov (Ukraine)
Lyon (France)
Metz (France)
Nice (France)
Omsk (Russia)
*Oslo (Norway)
Perm (Russia)
*Riga (Latvia)
*Rome (Italy)
Tver (Russia)
Vigo (Spain)

5
Arhus (Denmark)
Arles (France)
Arras (France)
Basel (Switzerland)
Basle (Switzerland)
Brest (Belarus/France)
Cadiz (Spain)
Dijon (France)
Douai (France)
Essen (Germany)
Evian (France)
Genoa (Italy)
Ghent (Belgium)
*Hague, The (Netherlands)
Halle (Germany)
Kazan (Russia)
Liège (Belgium)
Lille (France)
Lyons (France)
Mainz (Germany)
Malmo (Sweden)
Milan (Italy)
*Minsk (Belarus)
Nancy (France)
Nimes (France)
Ostia (Italy)
Padua (Italy)
Palma (Majorca)
Parma (Italy)
*Paris (France)
Posen (Poland)

Pskov (Russia)
Reims (France)
Rieti (Italy)
Rouen (France)
Siena (Italy)
*Sofia (Bulgaria)
Split (Croatia)
Tours (France)
Trent (Italy)
Trier (Germany)
Turin (Italy)
Vence (France)
Verdun (France)
Vichy (France)
Worms (Germany)
Yalta (Ukraine)
Ypres (Belgium)

6

Aachen (Germany)
Amalfi (Italy)
Amiens (France)
Arnhem (Netherlands)
*Athens (Greece)
Bayeux (France)
Bergen (Norway)
*Berlin (Germany)
Bilbao (Spain)
Bochum (Germany)
Bremen (Germany)
Bruges (Belgium)
Calais (France)
Cannes (France)
Cassel (Germany)
Danzig (Poland)
Dieppe (France)
Erfurt (Germany)
Geneva (Switzerland)
Gdansk (Poland)
Hamlin (Germany)
Kassel (Germany)
Krakow (Poland)
Leiden (Netherlands)
Leyden (Netherlands)
*Lisbon (Portugal)
Lubeck (Germany)
Lublin (Poland)
*Madrid (Spain)

Malaga (Spain)
*Moscow (Russia)
Munich (Germany)
Nantes (France)
Naples (Italy)
Odense (Denmark)
Odessa (Ukraine)
Oporto (Portugal)
Orange (France)
Ostend (Belgium)
*Prague (Czech Rep.)
Rheims (France)
Samara (Russia)
Seville (Spain)
Skopje (Macedonia)
Tirana (Albania)
Toledo (Spain)
Toulon (France)
Treves (Germany)
Varna (Bulgaria)
Venice (Italy)
Verona (Italy)
Vienna (Austria)
*Warsaw (Poland)
*Zagreb (Croatia)
Zurich (Switzerland)

7

Ajaccio (France)
Alencon (France)
Antwerp (Belgium)
Auxerre (France)
Avignon (France)
Badajoz (Spain)
Bayonne (France)
Bologna (Italy)
Bolzano (Italy)
Bourges (France)
Breslau (Poland)
Coblenz (Germany)
Cordoba (Spain)
Cologne (Germany)
Corinth (Greece)
Corunna (Spain)
Donetsk (Ukraine)
Dresden (Germany)
Dunkirk (France)
Granada (Spain)

Hamburg (Germany)
Hanover (Germany)
Homburg (Germany)
Irkutsk (Russia)
Koblenz (Germany)
Kottbus (Germany)
Leipzig (Germany)
Limoges (France)
Lourdes (France)
Lucerne (Switzerland)
Messina (Italy)
München (Germany)
Münster (Germany)
*Nicosia (Cyprus)
Orleans (France)
Piraeus (Greece)
Potsdam (Germany)
Ravenna (Italy)
Rostock (Germany)
Salerno (Italy)
*Tallinn (Estonia)
Trieste (Italy)
Uppsala (Sweden)
Utrecht (Netherlands)
*Vilnius (Lithuania)
Yakutsk (Russia)

8

Alicante (Spain)
Augsburg (Germany)
*Belgrade (Serbia)
Bergerac (France)
Besancon (France)
Biarritz (France)
Bordeaux (France)
Boulogne (France)
*Brussels (Belgium)
*Budapest (Hungary)
Chamonix (France)
Chartres (France)
Chemnitz (Germany)
Dortmund (Germany)
Freiburg (Germany)
Goteborg (Sweden)
Grenoble (France)
Hannover (Germany)
*Helsinki (Finland)
Lausanne (Switzerland)

Mannheim (Germany)
Nijmegen (Netherlands)
Novgorod (Russia)
Nürnberg (Germany)
Pamplona (Spain)
Salonika (Greece)
Salzburg (Austria)
Schwerin (Germany)
Soissons (France)
Smolensk (Russia)
Syracuse (Italy)
Toulouse (France)
Trentino (Italy)
Valencia (Spain)
Zaragoza (Spain)

9
Abbeville (France)
Agrigento (Italy)
Amsterdam
(Netherlands)
Barcelona (Spain)
Brunswick (Germany)
Bucharest (Romania)
Cartagena (Spain)

Cherbourg (France)
Darmstadt (Germany)
Dordrecht (Netherlands)
Dubrovnik (Croatia)
Dunkerque (France)
Eindhoven
(Netherlands)
Frankfurt (Germany)
Innsbruck (Austria)
Magdeburg (Germany)
Marseille (France)
Nuremberg (Germany)
Rotterdam (Netherlands)
Santander (Spain)
Saragossa (Spain)
*Stockholm (Sweden)
Stuttgart (Germany)
Trondheim (Norway)
Wiesbaden (Germany)
Wuppertal (Germany)

10
*Bratislava (Slovakia)
*Copenhagen (Denmark)
Düsseldorf (Germany)
Gothenburg (Sweden)
Heidelberg (Germany)

*Luxembourg
(Luxembourg)
Maastricht (Netherlands)
Marseilles (France)
Montelimar (France)
Strasbourg (France)
Versailles (France)

11
Armentières (France)
Chelyabinsk (Russia)
Kaliningrad (Russia)
Montpellier (France)
Novosibirsk (Russia)
Saarbrücken (Germany)
Thessaloniki (Greece)

2+ words
Baden Baden (Germany)
Le Havre (France)
Le Mans (France)
St Etienne (France)
St Malo (France)
St Petersburg (Russia)
St Tropez (France)

EXPLORERS

4

Byrd (Richard)
Cook (James)
Dias (Bartolomeu)
Eyre (Edward John)
Gann (Thomas)
Park (Mungo)
Polo (Marco)
Ross (James Park)
Soto (Hernando de)

5

Anson (George)
Baker (Samuel)
Boone (Daniel)
Brown (William)
Bruce (James)
Burke (Robert O'Hara)
Cabot (John/Sebastian)
Clark (William)
Davis (John)
Drake (Francis)
Fuchs (Vivian)
Laird (McGregor)
Oates (Lawrence)
Parry (William)
Peary (Robert)
Scott (Robert Falcon)
Speke (John Hanning)
Sturt (Charles)
Wills (William John)

6

Alcock (John)
Baffin (William)
Balboa (Vasco)
Bering (Vitus)
Burton (Richard)
Cabral (Pedro)
Carson (Kit)
Conway (Martin)
Cortez (Hernando)
Duluth (Daniel)
Fraser (Simon)
Hudson (Henry)
Larsen (Kohl)
Nansen (Fridtjof)
Tasman (Abel)

7

Almeida (Lourenco)
Cartier (Jacques)
Dampier (William)
Doughty (Charles)
Fiennes (Ranulph)
Gilbert (Humphry)
Hawkins (John)
Hillary (Edmund)
Pizzaro (Francisco)
Raleigh (Walter)
Stanley (Henry Morton)
Wilkins (George)
Wrangel (Ferdinand)

8

Amundsen (Roald)
Columbus (Christopher)
Cousteau (Jacques)
Flinders (Matthew)
Franklin (John)
Humboldt (Alexander von)
Magellan (Ferdinand)
Marchand (Jean Baptiste)
Standish (Miles)
Vespucci (Amerigo)

9

Champlain (Samuel de)
Frobisher (martin)
Heyerdahl (Thor)
Mackenzie (Alexander)
Pausanias
Vancouver (George)
Velasquez (Diego)

10

Chancellor (Richard)
Clapperton (Hugh)
Richardson (James)
Shackleton (Ernest)
Willoughby (Hugh)

11

Livingstone (David)

12

Bougainville (Louis)
Younghusband (Francis)

2+ words
Da Gama (Vasco)
La Salle (Robert)

FABRICS

3
fur
kid
net
PVC
rep
tat

4
buff
calf
cire
coir
cord
down
drab
duck
ecru
felt
hemp
hide
jean
lace
lamé
lawn
rack
silk
vair
wool

5
arras
baize
braid
chino
cloth
crape
crash
crepe
denim
drill
flock
floss
gauze

gunny
kapok
khaki
laine
lapin
linen
lisle
lurex
moire
nylon
orlon
orris
piqué
plaid
plush
print
rayon
sable
satin
scrim
serge
sisal
stuff
suede
tammy
terry
tissu
toile
tulle
tweed
twill
voile

6
alpaca
angora
beaver
boucle
burlap
caddis
calico
camlet
canvas
chintz
cloque
cotton
crepon
crewel

dacron
damask
dimity
dowlas
dralon
duffel
durrie
ermine
fablon
frieze
jersey
kersey
lining
linsey
madras
merino
mohair
muslin
napery
oxford
poplin
ribbon
rubber
russet
samite
sateen
shoddy
tartan
tissue
tricot
velour
velure
velvet
vicuna
wincey

7
acrilon
acrylic
alamode
bagging
batiste
bombast
brocade
buckram
bunting
cambric
cantoon

caracal
catskin
challis
chamois
chiffon
cowhide
doeskin
drabbet
drugget
fishnet
flannel
foulard
fustian
gingham
grogram
hessian
Holland
jaconet
karakul
leather
mechlin
miniver
morocco
nankeen
netting
oilskin
organdy
organza
paisley
plastic
rawhide
romaine
sacking
satinet
suiting
taffeta
textile
ticking
tiffany
tussore
veiling
velours
viscose
viyella
wadding
webbing
woollen
worsted

8
buckskin
calfskin
cashmere
celanese
chambray
chenille
corduroy
cretonne
damassin
diamanté
duchesse
dungaree
goatskin
gossamer
homespun
indienne
jacquard
lambskin
lustrine
marocain
material
moleskin
moquette
musquash
nainsook
oilcloth
organdie
paduasoy
quilting
rickrack
sarcanet
sarsenet
sealskin
shagreen
shantung
tapestry
tarlatan
terylene
whipcord

9
astrakhan
bombazine
courtelle
crepeline
crinoline
crimplene

gabardine
georgette
grenadine
grosgrain
haircloth
horsehair
huckaback
patchwork
petersham
polyamide
polyester
sackcloth
sailcloth
satinette
sharkskin
sheepskin
snakeskin
stockinet
swansdown
tarpaulin
towelling
tricotine
velveteen
Worcester

10
candlewick
mackintosh
needlecord
polycotton
seersucker
winceyette

11
cheesecloth
flannelette
leatherette
stockinette

2+ words
American cloth
cavalry twill
chantilly lace
crepe-de-chine
lamb's-wool
shot silk

FEELINGS

A feeling
Anger/angry/be angry
Boredom/bored
Enthusiasm/enthusiastic
Fright/frighten/frightened/
be afraid
Happiness/happy
Hate/dislike
Indifference/indifferent
Love/loving/like
Unhappiness/unhappy
Want/wish

A FEELING

3
air

4
aura
feel
idea
love
mood
view

5
hunch
sense
touch

6
belief
notion
regard

7
concern
emotion
empathy
opinion

8
ambience
attitude
instinct

reaction
response
sympathy

9
affection
awareness
intuition
knowledge
sensation
sentiment
suspicion
transport

10
atmosphere
attachment
compassion
experience
foreboding
impression
perception

11
sensibility
sensitivity

12
presentiment

ANGER/ANGRY/
BE ANGRY

3
fit
ire
irk
mad
red

4
boil
burn
fret
fume
fury
heat
huff

lour
rage
rant
rave
rile
stew

5
anger
angry
annoy
chafe
cross
glare
growl
irate
livid
paddy
rabid
ratty
scowl
snarl
storm
tizzy
upset
wrath

6
choler
enrage
fierce
frenzy
fuming
glower
heated
ireful
madden
miffed
raging
savage
seethe
simmer
sizzle
snappy
temper

7
angered

annoyed
berserk
bluster
boiling
bristle
burning
enraged
explode
ferment
foaming
furious
hopping
incense
madness
outrage
passion
provoke
quarrel
rampage
stroppy
tantrum

8
agitated
choleric
ferocity
frenzied
incensed
irritate
outburst
outraged
paroxysm
sizzling
violence
wrathful

9
aggravate
annoyance
bellicose
crossness
explosion
indignant
infuriate
irritated
rampaging
vehemence

10
aggravated
aggressive
apoplectic
convulsion
exasperate
implacable
infuriated
irritation
resentment
sullenness

11
bellicosity
belligerent
exasperated
indignation
infuriation

12
belligerence
snappishness
wrathfulness

2+ words
bad-tempered
beside oneself
go berserk
go off the deep end
hit the roof
in high dudgeon
in a huff
in a stew
in a strop
kick up a fuss
lose it
make a scene
raise Cain
raise hell
raise the roof

BOREDOM/BORED

5
ennui
jaded
tired
weary

6
dreary
sullen
tedium

7
aridity
fatigue
languor
wearied

8
banality
fatigued
listless
longueur
monotony
restless
sameness
satiated

12
dissatisfied
uninterested

2+ words
fed up
sick and tired

ENTHUSIASM/
ENTHUSIASTIC

3
hot

4
agog
avid
keen
warm
zeal
zest

5
eager
gusto
ready

6
ardent

7
avidity
devoted
earnest
excited
fervent
fervour
intense
interest
passion
willing
zealous

8
aspiring
devotion
diligent
fervency
keenness
vehement
vigorous

9
assiduity
assiduous
dedicated
diligence
eagerness
energetic
fanatical
intensity
interested

10
dedication
passionate

12
wholehearted

FRIGHT/FRIGHTEN/
FRIGHTENED/BE AFRAID

3
cow

shy
wet

4
fear
flee
frit
funk

5
alarm
cower
daunt
deter
dread
jumpy
nervy
panic
quail
shake
shock
sissy
tense
timid
upset
worry

6
afraid
aghast
blench
cower
craven
dismay
fright
horror
menace
nerves
phobia
qualms
quiver
rattle
scared
shiver
shrink
terror
scared
unease

yellow

7
alarmed
anxiety
anxious
chicken
concern
fearful
gutless
horrify
jittery
nervous
panicky
petrify
rattled
stagger
startle
terrify
tremble
unnerve

8
browbeat
cowardly
disquiet
distress
timorous

9
agitation
cowardice
defeatist
misgiving
petrified
spineless
terrified
terrorize (terrorise)

10
foreboding
frightened
intimidate
misgivings

11
nervousness
trepidation

12
apprehension
apprehensive
butterflies
perturbation
timorousness

13
pusillanimous

2+ words
blue funk
bottle out
cold feet
faint-hearted
goose bumps
goose flesh
lily-livered
namby-pamby
on edge
the jitters
the willies
weak-kneed
yellow-bellied

HAPPINESS/HAPPY

3
gay
joy

4
glad
glee

5
bliss
cheer
jolly
merry

6
blithe
cheery
gaiety
jovial
joyful
joyous

7
content
delight
ecstasy
gleeful
pleased
rapture

8
blissful
cheerful
ecstatic
euphoria
euphoric
felicity
gladsome
pleasure

9
contented
delighted
enchanted
enjoyment
fortunate
merriment
opportune
overjoyed

10
captivated
enraptured
felicitous
prosperous

11
contentment
delectation
enchantment
exhilarated
intoxicated

12
exhilaration
intoxication

2+ words
in high spirits
in seventh heaven

on a high
on cloud nine
on top of the world
over the moon
pleased as Punch
tickled pink
tickled to death

HATE/DISLIKE

4
envy
gall

5
abhor
avoid
odium
scorn
spite
spurn
venom

6
detest
enmity
grudge
hatred
horror
loathe
malice
reject
revile
resent
spleen

7
condemn
despise
disgust
dislike
enmity
hatred
rancour

8
acrimony
aversion

distaste
execrate
jealousy
loathing

9
abominate
animosity
antipathy
avoidance
disfavour
disrelish
hostility
malignity
rejection
repulsion
revulsion
virulence

10
abhorrence
antagonism
bitterness
disapprove
discontent
execration
repugnance
resentment

11
abomination
detestation
disapproval
displeasure
malevolence

12
disaffection
spitefulness

INDIFFERENCE/
INDIFFERENT

3
lax

4
calm

cold
cool
lazy

5
aloof
blasé
inert
slack

6
apathy
casual
frosty
phlegm

7
deadpan
inertia
offhand
passive
unaware
unmoved

8
carefree
careless
detached
inactive
lethargy
listless
lukewarm
uncaring

9
apathetic
impassive
incurious
lethargic
oblivious
offhanded
passivity
unconcern
unfeeling
unruffled
untouched
withdrawn

10
detachment
dispassion
impersonal
insensible
insouciant
nonchalant
phlegmatic
unaffected
uninterest
uninvolved

11
disinterest
insensitive
insouciance
nonchalance
perfunctory
superficial
unconcerned
unemotional
unimpressed

12
noncommittal
uninterested
unresponsive

13
disinterested
dispassionate
lackadaisical
unsympathetic

2+ words
cold-blooded
cold-hearted
easy-going
half-hearted
laid-back
thick-skinned

LOVE/LOVING/LIKE

3
dig
fad
sex

4
care
dote
eros
fond
like
lust
pash
want
whim
wish

5
adore
amour
chase
court
craze
crush
Cupid
enjoy
fancy
fling
loyal
prize
shine
taste
yearn

6
admire
affair
ardour
choice
choose
desire
esteem
favour
liking
prefer
pursue
regard
relish
revere
savour
tender
warmth

7
amorous
approve
charity
cherish
devoted
empathy
idolize (idolise)
liaison
longing
passion
romance
smitten
worship

8
affinity
amicable
appetite
approval
attached
devotion
faithful
fondness
friendly
intimacy
maternal
motherly
paternal
penchant
platonic
sympathy
treasure
weakness
uxorious
yearning

9
adoration
affection
brotherly
fraternal

10
admiration
appreciate
attachment
attraction

charitable
friendship
partiality
preference
tenderness

11
amorousness
fascination
sentimental
sympathetic

12
affectionate

13
demonstrative
understanding

UNHAPPINESS/unhappy

3
low
sad
woe

4
blue
down
glum

5
blues
gloom
grave
moody
sorry
upset

6
bereft
dismal
gloomy
gutted
misery
morose
moving
pathos

sombre
sorrow
tragic
woeful

7
doleful
forlorn
painful
sadness
serious
tearful

8
dejected
desolate
dolorous
downcast
funereal
grievous
mournful
mourning
poignant
touching
wretched

9
cheerless
dejection
depressed
miserable
sorrowful
upsetting

10
crestfallen
deplorable
despondent
distressed
heartbroken
lamentable
melancholy

11
disconsolate
distressing
downhearted
inconsolable
regrettable
unfortunate

12
disheartened

2+ words
broken-hearted
grief-stricken
heart-ache

WANT/WISH

3
yen

4
hope
itch
lack
long
lust
miss
need
pine
wish

5
covet
crave
dream
fancy
yearn

6
demand
desire
hanker
hunger
pining
thirst

7
avidity
craving
longing
require

8
ambition
appetite
cupidity
fondness
penchant
voracity
weakness
yearning

9
eagerness
nostalgia

10
aspiration
partiality
preference

11
inclination

12
covetousness
homesickness
predilection

FILMS

Films
Film directors and producers
Terms used in films and
film-making

FILMS

2
AI
ET
If

3
Big
Hud
JFK
Kes
Ran

4
Babe
Diva
Gigi
Jaws
MASH
Rope

5
Alfie
Alien
Annie
Bambi
Dumbo
Evita
Fargo
Ghost
Giant
Klute
Marty
Rocky
Shane
Shoah
Twins
Wings
Yanks
Yentl

6
Batman
Gandhi
Grease
Harvey
Oliver
Psycho
Scream
Speed

7
Amadeus
Bullitt
Cabaret
Charade
Dracula
Platoon
Titanic
Tootsie
Vertigo
Witness

8
Fantasia
Oklahoma
Rashomon
Superman

9
Cleopatra
Genevieve
Gladiator
Manhattan
Moonraker
Octopussy
Nosferatu
Pinocchio
Suspicion
Viridiana

10
Casablanca
Cinderella
Goldfinger
Goodfellas
Moonstruck
Stagecoach

11
Bladerunner
Deliverance
Intolerance
Thunderball

12
Frankenstein
Ghostbusters

2+ words
Annie Hall
China Town
Citizen Kane
City Lights
Dr No
Dr Zhivago
Duck Soup
Easy Rider
Funny Face
Funny Girl
Gas Light
High Noon
King Kong
Raging Bull
Rear Window
Scar Face
Star Wars
Taxi Driver
The Big Sleep
The Birds
The Firm
The General
The Graduate
The Mask
The Misfits
The Queen
The Robe
The Sting
Tom Jones
Top Gin
Top Hat

FILM DIRECTORS AND PRODUCERS

3
Ray (Satyajit)

4
Ford (John)
Lang (Fritz)
Lean (David)
Reed (Carol)

5
Allen (Woody)
Capra (Frank)
Carné (Marcel)
Clair (René)
Hawks (Howard)
Kazan (Elia)
Korda (Alexander)
Losey (Joseph)
Lucas (George)
Mayer (Louis B.)
Wajda (Andrezj)

6
Altman (Robert)
Brooks (Mel)
Bunuel (Luis)
Disney (Walt)
Forman (Milos)
Godard (Jean-Luc)
Herzog (Werner)
Huston (John)
Renoir (Jean)
Welles (Orson)
Wilder (Billy)

7
Bergman (Ingmar)
Bresson (Robert)
Cameron (James)
Campion (Jane)
Chabrol (Claude)
Coppola (Francis Ford)
Fellini (Federico)
Goldwyn (Samuel)
Jackson (Peter)
Kubrick (Stanley)
Russell (Ken)

8
Anderson (Lindsay)
Berkeley (Busby)

Kurosawa (Akira)
Polanski (Roman)
Scorsese (Martin)
Selznick (David O)
Stroheim (Erich von)
Truffaut (François)
Visconti (Luchino)
Ziegfeld (Florenz)

9
Hitchcock (Alfred)
Peckinpah (Sam)
Preminger (Otto)
Spielberg (Steven)
Sternberg (Joseph von)

10
Bertolucci (Bernardo)
Eisenstein (Sergei)
Rossellini (Roberto)

2+ words
de Mille (Cecil B.)
de Silva (Vittorio)

*TERMS USED IN FILMS
AND FILM-MAKING*

3
can
cut
dub
DVD
MGM
pan
set

4
book
boom
cine
clip
crew
edit
epic
fade
gaff
mike

noir
reel
rush
shot
star
take
unit

5
BAFTA
extra
flick
focus
movie
Oscar
score
shoot
short
still
stunt
video

6
action
biopic
camera
cinema
direct
dubbed
editor
effect
gaffer
horror
lights
rushes
screen
script
sequel
silent
studio
talkie

7
cartoon
casting
chiller
clapper
credits

dubbing
feature
footage
musical
popcorn
prequel
preview
produce
release
stardom
starlet
trailer
western

8
animator
bioscope
Cinerama®
dialogue
director
festival
filmgoer
location
newsreel
pictures
premiere
producer
subtitle

thriller
typecast
wardrobe

9
animation
Bollywood
cameraman
cinematic
filmstrip
flashback
Hollywood
limelight
moviegoer
usherette

10
continuity
filmscript
microphone
production
screenplay
tearjerker
travelogue

11
Cinemascope
Technicolor

12
clapperboard
screenwriter
scriptwriter

2+ words
Academy Award
best boy
body double
box office
car chase
chick-flick
clapper boy
close-up
credit titles
cutting room
drive-in
horse opera
New Wave
second unit
silver screen
spaghetti western
stand-in
wide screen

FISH

Fishing
Types of fish

FISHING

3
bob
dun
fly
net
peg
rib
rod
tag
tip

4
bait
barb
cast
cran
gaff
hook
lead
line
lure
reel
shot
worm

5
angle
blank
catch
creel
float
floss
joker
leger
paste
quill
seine
shank
spoon
trawl
troll

6
angler
bobber
caster
hackle
maggot
marker
palmer
pinkie
priest
sinker
slider
spigot
squatt
strike
swivel
zoomer

7
antenna
bristle
dapping
drifter
dubbing
harpoon
plummet
spinner
trawler
waggler

8
freeline
legering
specimen
swingtip

9
bloodworm
disgorger
quivertip

2+ words
dry fly
keep net
landing net

TYPES OF FISH

3
ayu
bib
cod
dab
dar
eel
gar
ged
hag
ide
lob
lox
ray
tai

4
bass
blay
bley
butt
carp
chad
char
chub
cusk
dace
dory
drum
goby
hake
hind
huso
huss
kelt
keta
ling
luce
lump
moki
mola
mort
opah
orfe
parr
peal

pike
pope
pout
rudd
ruff
scad
scar
scup
shad
sild
snig
sole
tope
tuna

5
ablen
angel
apode
bleak
bream
brill
charr
cisco
coley
cuddy
danio
doree
dorse
elops
elver
fluke
gibel
grunt
guppy
loach
lythe
manta
moray
murry
perch
pilot
piper
pogge
porgy
powan
roach
roker

saury
scrod
sepia
sewen
sewin
shark
skate
skeet
smelt
smolt
smout
snoek
snook
sprat
squid
sudak
tench
torsk
trout
tunny
twait
witch

6
alevin
allice
angler
baggit
barbel
belone
beluga
bichir
blenny
bonito
bounce
bowfin
braize
burbot
caplin
conger
cuttle
darter
dipnoi
doctor
dorado
elleck
finnan
gadoid

ganoid
goramy
grilse
groper
gunnel
gurnet
kipper
launce
medusa
milter
minnow
morgay
mullet
nerite
plaice
pollan
porgie
poulpe
remora
robalo
salmon
samlet
sardel
sargus
sauger
saurel
sephen
shanny
shiner
sucker
tarpon
tautog
tomcod
turbot
twaite
urchin
weever
wrasse
zander

7
acaleph
actinia
anchovy
asteroid
batfish
bergylt
bloater

bluecap
boxfish
bummalo
capelin
catfish
cichlid
clupeid
codfish
codling
croaker
crucian
dogfish
echinus
eelpout
escolar
fiddler
finback
finnock
garfish
garpike
gourami
grouper
grunter
gudgeon
gurnard
gwyniad
haddock
hagfish
halibut
herling
herring
lampern
lamprey
mahseer
monodon
mooneye
morrhua
mudfish
oarfish
octopus
ophiura
piddock
pigfish
pinfish
piranha
pollack
polypus
pomfret

quinnat
redfish
rhytina
ripsack
ronchil
ronquil
rotchet
sardine
sargina
sawfish
schelly
scomber
sillago
skipper
skulpin
snapper
sockeye
spurdog
sterlet
sunfish
tiddler
torpedo
trepang
tubfish
vendace
vestlet
whipray
whiting

8

albacore
billfish
bluefish
boarfish
brisling
bullhead
coalfish
dragonet
drumfish
flatfish
flounder
forktail
frogfish
gilthead
goldfish
grayling
kingfish
lumpfish

lungfish
mackerel
menhaden
monkfish
nannygai
pickerel
pilchard
pipefish
rockfish
roncador
rosefish
sailfish
salmonet
sandfish
sardelle
siluroid
skipjack
solaster
sparling
spelding
speldrin
starfish
stingray
sturgeon
thrasher
toadfish
trevally
zoanthus

9

amberjack
angelfish
barracuda
blackfish
bulltrout
devilfish
globefish
houndfish
ichthyoid
jewelfish
kabeljouw
menominee
mudhopper
porbeagle
spearfish
stargazer
steenbras
stockfish

stonefish
swordfish
tittlebat
whitebait
whitefish
wobbegong

10
angelshark
anglerfish
archerfish
barramundi
butterfish
candlefish
coelacanth
cuttlefish
damselfish
demoiselle
dragonfish
fingerling
flutemouth
groundling
hammerhead
needlefish
paddlefish
parrotfish
sandhopper
silverside
suckerfish
yellowtail

11
hippocampus
stickleback
surgeonfish

2+ words
ale-wife
balloon fish
basking shark
blue shark
brown trout
carpet shark
conger eel
dolly varden
electric eel
electric ray
flying-fish
globe fish
great white (shark)
guitar fish
miller's thumb
pilot fish
rainbow trout
red bass
red drum
red-eye
sand-dab
sand-eel
sea-adder
sea-bass
sea-bat
sea-bream

sea-bun
sea-cat
sea-cock
sea-cow
sea-devil
sea-dog
sea-eel
sea-egg
sea-fox
sea-hog
sea-mink
sea-orb
sea-owl
sea-perch
sea-pert
sea-pig
sea-pike
sea-rat
sea-robin
sea-rose
sea-ruff
sea-slug
sea-tench
sea-trout
sea-wife
sea-wolf
thresher shark
tiger shark
trigger fish
zebra shark

FLOWERS

FLOWERS

3
may
rue

4
arum
flag
flax
iris
lily
musk
pink
rose

5
agave
aster
briar
broom
calla
canna
daisy
dilly
gowan
hosta
lilac
lotus
lupin
oxeye
oxlip
pansy
peony
phlox
poppy
stock
tulip
viola
yucca
yulan

6
azalea
camass

cistus
clover
crocus
cyphel
dahlia
jasmin
kowhai
mallow
mimosa
moutan
nerine
nuphar
orchid
scilla
shasta
squill
tagete
thrift
violet
yarrow
zinnia

7
aconite
althaea
anemone
banksia
begonia
campion
freesia
fuchsia
gentian
gladwyn
godetia
honesty
jasmine
jonquil
kingcup
lobelia
nigella
petunia
picotee
primula
rambler
rampion
seringa
shirley
syringa

verbena
vervain

8
agrimony
amaranth
asphodel
auricula
bluebell
buddleia
camellia
clematis
cyclamen
daffodil
dianthus
foxglove
gardenia
geranium
gillenia
girasole
gloxinia
harebell
hawthorn
hibiscus
hyacinth
japonica
larkspur
lavender
magnolia
marigold
myosotis
noisette
oleander
plumbago
primrose
snowdrop
tuberose
turnsole
wisteria
woodbine

9
buttercup
campanula
candytuft
carnation
cineraria
coltsfoot

columbine
dandelion
edelweiss
eglantine
forsythia
gladiolus
goldenrod
hellebore
hollyhock
hydrangea
impatiens
lavateria
narcissus
pyrethrum
saxifrage
speedwell
sunflower

10

agapanthus
amaranthus
cornflower
delphinium
frangipani
gypsophila

heliotrope
marguerite
montbretia
nasturtium
pennyroyal
periwinkle
poinsettia
polyanthus
snapdragon
stephanotis
wallflower

11

antirrhinum
gillyflower
honeysuckle
marshmallow

12

bougainvilia
rhododendron

13

chrysanthemum

2+ words

aaron's rod
busy lizzie
busy lizzy
canterbury bell
cup-rose
dog-brier
dog-rose
forget-me-not
gold-lily
guernsey lily
lady's mantle
lent-lily
love in the mist
michaelmas daisy
morning glory
red hot poker
sweet-pea
sweet william
tea-rose

FOOD

Food and meals
Types of food

FOOD AND MEALS

3
tea

4
chow
diet
eats
fare
grub
meal
menu
nosh

5
board
cheer
lunch
scoff
snack
table

6
brunch
dinner
fodder
supper
tiffin
viands

7
aliment
banquet
rations

8
delicacy
eatables
luncheon
victuals

9
appetizer (appetizer)
breakfast
nutriment
provender

10
provisions
sustenance

11
comestibles
refreshment

12
refreshments

TYPES OF FOOD

3
bap
bun
dip
egg
fat
ham
ice
jam
pie
poi
roe
soy

4
bean
beef
bran
cake
chop
chou
curd
fish
flan
fool
fowl
ghee
hare
hash

herb
kale
lamb
lard
lean
loaf
loin
meal
meat
melt
mint
mush
naan
oleo
olio
pâté
pork
puff
roll
rusk
sago
soup
stew
suet
taco
tart
veal
whey
yolk

5
aioli
aspic
bacon
balti
blini
bombe
brawn
bread
brose
broth
candy
clove
cream
crêpe
crust
curds
curry

dough
dulse
filet
flour
fruit
fudge
gravy
gruel
gumbo
heart
honey
icing
jelly
joint
kabob
kebab
liver
lolly
manna
matzo
melba
mince
pasta
paste
pasty
patty
pilaf
pilau
pilaw
pitta
pizza
prune
purée
roast
salad
sauce
scone
shape
spice
split
stock
sugar
sushi
sweet
syrup
taffy
toast
tripe

wafer
yeast

6
almond
batter
bisque
blintz
bonbon
borsch
brains
bridie
burger
butter
canapé
catsup
caviar
cereal
cheese
collop
compot
cookie
course
crowdy
cutlet
éclair
entrée
faggot
gillet
gammon
garlic
gateau
gelato
ginger
grease
greens
grouse
haggis
haslet
hotpot
humbug
hummus
jujube
jumble
junket
kidney
leaven
lights

mousse
muffin
mutton
noodle
nougat
oxtail
paella
panada
pastry
pepper
pickle
pilaff
pillau
polony
potage
potato
quiche
rabbit
ragout
raisin
rasher
relish
salami
samosa
simnel
sorbet
sponge
sundae
tamale
titbit
toffee
tongue
trifle
waffle
walnut
yogurt

7
bannock
biltong
biscuit
bloater
bouilli
brisket
broiler
brownie
burrito
cabbage

calipee
caramel
caviare
chicken
chicory
chowder
chutney
compote
cracker
crowdie
crumble
crumpet
currant
custard
dariole
dessert
falafel
fritter
galette
giblets
gnocchi
goulash
gristle
haricot
houmous
ketchup
lasagne
mustard
oatcake
oatmeal
pancake
paprika
polenta
popcorn
pottage
poultry
praline
pretzel
pudding
ramekin
rarebit
ratafia
ravioli
rhubarb
risotto
rissole
sapsago
sausage

savarin
saveloy
savoury
seafood
sherbet
sirloin
soufflé
strudel
tapioca
tartlet
teacake
tempura
terrine
tostada
treacle
truffle
venison
vinegar
Windsor
yoghurt

8
ambrosia
bouillon
chapatti
coleslaw
conserve
consommé
couscous
cracknel
crudités
doughnut
dripping
dumpling
escalope
fishcake
flapjack
flummery
frosting
frumenty
hazelnut
hotchpot
julienne
kedgeree
lollipop
macaroni
macaroon
marinara

marzipan
meatball
meatloaf
meringue
molasses
moussaka
mushroom
omelette
ossobuco
pastrami
pemmican
poppadum
porridge
preserve
quenelle
rollmops
salpicon
sandwich
seedcake
sukiyaki
syllabub
sparerib
stuffing
teriyaki
tortilla
turnover

9
antipasto
arrowroot
bubblegum
casserole
cassoulet
chipolata
colcannon
condiment
crackling
croquette
croustade
enchilada
forcemeat
fricassee
galantine
hamburger
honeycomb
jambalaya
lobscouse
macedoine

madeleine
margarine
marmalade
mincemeat
pepperoni
picalilli
potpourri
proveloni
rillettes
schnitzel
seasoning
shellfish
shortcake
spaghetti
succotash
sweetmeat
tabbouleh
vegetable
wholemeal

10
beefburger
blancmange
blanquette
bolognaise
cannelloni
chaudfroid
cheesecake
confection

cornflakes
estouffade
florentine
frangipane
hodgepodge
hotchpotch
jardinière
mayonnaise
minestrone
peppermint
salmagundi
sauerkraut
shortbread
sweetbread
tortellini
vermicelli

11
chimichanga
frankfurter
gingerbread
marshmallow
ratatouille
tagliatelle
vinaigrette

12
bouillabaisse
butterscotch

chateaubriand
mulligatawny
pumpernickel
taramasalata

2+ words
chop suey
chow mein
corned beef
cottage pie
fruit salad
hot cross bun
hot dog
humble pie
ice cream
Irish stew
jugged hare
jam tart
lardy cake
mince pie
olla-podrida
poached egg
pot roast
pound cake
shepherd's pie
toad in the hole
Welsh rarebit

FOOTBALL

Footballing terms
British football teams
European football teams
US Football teams
Famous footballers

FOOTBALLING TERMS

2
FA

3
box
cup
net
ref

4
area
away
back
ball
chip
dive
FIFA
foul
goal
head
home
kick
line
pass
post
save
shot
spot
trap

5
bench
cross
match
pitch
score
shoot
strip

6
corner
goalie
ground
handle
header
keeper
libero
nutmeg
onside
soccer
strike
tackle
winger

7
dribble
forward
kickoff
offside
penalty
referee
shinpad
striker
sweeper
whistle

8
crossbar
freekick
fullback

goalpost
halftime
handball
linesman
midfield
sidefoot
wingback

10
goalkeeper
midfielder
substitute

2+ words
centre back
centre circle
centre half
corner flag
corner kick
cup final
far post
five-a-side
flat back four
goal area
goal kick
left back
left half
inside left
inside right
near post
outside left
outside right
penalty area
penalty shootout
penalty spot
red card
right back
right half
six-yard area
yellow card

BRITISH FOOTBALL TEAMS

Team	Nickname	Ground
Aberdeen	Dons	Pittodrie Park
Aidrieonians	Diamonds, Waysiders	Broomfield Park
Aldershot	Shots	Recreation Ground
Alloa	Wasps	Recreation Park
Arbroath	Red Lichties	Gayfield Park
Arsenal	Gunners	Emirates stadium (formerly Highbury)
Aston Villa	Villa, Villans	Villa Park
Ayr United	Honest Men	Somerset Park
Barnet	Bees	Underhill Stadium
Barnsley	Colliers, Reds, Tykes	Oakwell Ground
Berwick Rangers	Borderers	Shielfield Park
Birmingham City	Blues	St Andrews
Blackburn Rovers	Blue and whites	Ewood Park
Blackpool	Seasiders	Blommfield Road
Bolton Wanderers	Trotters	Reebok Stadium
Bournemouth	Cherries	Dean Court
Bradford City	Bantams	Valley Parade
Brechin City	City	Glebe Park
Brentford	Bees	Griffin Park
Brighton & Hove Albion	Seagulls	Goldstone Ground
Bristol City	Reds, Robins	Ashton Gate
Bristol Rovers	Pirates	Memorial Stadium
Burnley	Clarets	Turf Moor
Bury	Shakers	Gigg Lane
Cambridge United	United	Abbey Stadium
Cardiff City	Bluebirds	Ninian Park
Carlisle United	Cumbrians, Blues	Brunton Park
Celtic	Bhoys	Celtic Park
Charlton Athletic	Addicks	The Valley
Chelsea Blues	Pensioners	Stamford Bridge
Chester City	Blues	Sealand Road
Chesterfield	Blues, Spireites	Recreation Ground
Clydebank	Bankies	Kilbowie Park
Colchester United	U's	Layer Road
Coventry City	Sky Blues	Highfield Road
Cowdenbeath	Cowden	Central Park
Crewe Alexander	Railwaymen	Gresty Road
Crystal Palace	Glaziers	Selhurst Park
Derby County	Rams	Baseball Ground
Doncaster Rovers	Rovers	Belle Vue Ground
Dumbarton	Sons	Boghead Park
Dundee	Dark Blues, Dee	Dens Park
Dundee United	Terrors	Tannadice Park
Dunfermline Athletic	Pars	East End Park
Everton	Blues (Toffees)	Goodison Park

Team	Nickname	Ground
Exeter City	Grecians	St James Park
Falkirk	Bairns	Brockville Park
Forfar Athletic	Sky Blues	Station Park
Fulham	Cottagers	Craven Cottage
Gillingham	Gills	Priestfield Stadium
Grimsby Town	Mariners	Blundell Park
Halifax Town	Shaymen	Shay Ground
Hamilton Academicals	Acces	Douglas Park
Hartlepool United	Pool	Victoria Ground
Heart of Midlothian	Hearts	Tynecastle Park
Hereford United	United	Edgar Street
Hibernian	Hibs	Easter Road
Huddersfield Town	Terriers	Leeds Road
Hull City	Tigers	Boothferry Park
Ipswich Town	Blues, Town	Portman Road
Kilmarnock	Killie	Rugby Park
Leicester City	Foxes	Walker Stadium (formerly Filbert Street)
Leyton Orient	O's	Brisbane Road
Lincoln City	Red Imps	Sincil Bank
Liverpool	Reds	Anfield
Luton Town	Hatters	Kenilworth Rd
Manchester City	Blues	City Stadium (formerly Maine Road)
Manchester United	Red Devils	Old Trafford
Mansfield Town	Stags	Field Mill
Middlesbrough	Boro'	Riverside Stadium
Millwall	Lions	The Den
Montrose	Gable Enders	Links Park
Morton	Ton	Cappielow park
Motherwell	Well	Fir Park
Newcastle United	Magpies	St James's Park
Northampton	Cobblers	Sixfields Stadium
Norwich	Canaries	Carrow Road
Nottingham Forest	Reds, Forest	City Ground
Notts County	Magpies	Meadow Lane
Oldham Athletic	Latics	Boundary Park
Oxford United	U's	Kassam Stadium
Partick Thistle	Jags	Firhill Park
Peterborough United	Posh	London Road
Plymouth Argyle	Pilgrims	Home Park
Portsmouth	Pompey	Fratton Park
Port Vale	Valiants	Vale Park
Preston North End	Lilywhites, North End	Deepdale
Queen of the South	Doonhammers	Palmerston Park
Queen's Park	Spiders	Hampden Park
Queen's Park Rangers	QPR, Rangers, R's	Loftus Road

Team	Nickname	Ground
Raith Rovers	Rovers	Stark's Park
Rangers	Gers	Ibrox Stadium
Reading	Royals	Elm Park
Rochdale	Dale	Spotland
Rotherham United	Merry Millers	Millmoor Ground
Scarborough	Boro'	Seamer Road
Scunthorpe United	Iron	Glanford Park
Sheffield United	Blades	Bramall Lane
Sheffield Wednesday	Owls	Hillsborough
Shrewsbury Town	Shrews, Town	Gay Meadow
Southampton	Saints	St Mary's (formerly The Dell)
Southend	Shrimpers	Roots Park
Stenhousemuir	Warriors	Ochilview Park
Stirling Albion	Albion	Annfield Park
St Johnstone	Saints	Muirton Park
St Mirren	Buddies, Paisley Saints	Love Street
Stockport County	County, Hatters	Edgeley Park
Stoke City	Potters	Victoria Ground
Stranraer	Blues	Stair Park
Sunderland	Rokerites	Stadium of Light
Swansea City	Swans	Vetch Field
Swindon Town	Robins	County Ground
Torquay	Gulls	Plainmoor Ground
Tottenham Hotspur	Spurs	White Hart Lane
Tranmere Rovers	Rovers	Prenton Park
Walsall	Saddlers	Feollws Park
Watford	Hornets	Vicarage Road
West Bromwich Albion	Baggies	Hawthorns
West Ham United	Hammers	Upton Park
Wigan Athletic	Latics	Wigan
Wolverhampton Wanderers	Wolves	Molineux
Wrexham	Robins	Racecourse Ground
York City	Minstermen	Bootham Crescent

EUROPEAN FOOTBALL TEAMS

4
Ajax (Netherlands)
Lens (France)
Roma (Italy)

5
Lazio (Italy)
Malmo (Sweden)

6
Monaco (France)
Napoli (Italy)

7
Benfica (Portugal)

8
Juventus (Italy)
Valencia (Spain)

9
Barcelona (Spain)
Feyenoord (Netherlands)
Sampdoria (Italy)

10
Anderlecht (Belgium)
Gothenburg (Sweden)
Olympiakos (Greece)

11
Galatasaray (Greece)

13
Panathinaikos (Gr)

2+ words
AC Milan (Italy)
Atletico Madrid (Spain)
Bayern Munich
(Germany)
Borussia Dortmund

(Germany)
Dynamo Kiev (Ukraine)
Herta Belin (Germany)
Inter Milan (Italy)
Moscow Dynamo (Russia)
Paris St Germain (France)
PSV Eindhoven
(Netherlands)
Rapid Vienna (Austria)

Real Madrid (Spain)
Red Star Belgrade
(Serbia)
Spartak Moscow
Sporting Lisbon
(Portugal)
Steava Bucharest
(Romania)

US FOOTBALL TEAMS

Home	Name
Atlanta	Falcons
Baltimore	Colts
Buffalo	Bills
Chicago	Bears
Cincinnati	Bengals
Cleveland	Browns
Dallas	Cowboys
Denver	Broncos
Detroit	Lions
Green Bay	Packers
Houston	Oilers
Kansas City	Chiefs
Los Angeles	Raiders
Los Angeles	Rams
Miami	Dolphins
Minnesota	Vikings
New England	Patriots
New Orleans	Saints
New York	Giants
New York	Jets
Philadelphia	Eagles
Phoenix	Cardinals
Pittsburgh	Steelers
St Louis	Cardinals
San Diego	Chargers
San Francisco	49-Ers
Seattle	Seahawks
Tampa Bay	Buccaneers
Washington	Redskins

FAMOUS FOOTBALL
PLAYERS AND MANAGERS

3
Law (Denis)

4
Best (George)
Dean (Dixie)
Figo (Luis)
Owen (Michael)
Pele
Rush (Ian)

5
Adams (Tony)
Banks (Gordon)
Busby (Matt)
Gazza (*see* Gascoigne)
Giggs (Ryan)
Henri (Thierry)
Hurst (Geoff)
Moore (Bobby)
Revie (Don)
Roony (Wayne)
Stein (Jock)

6
Clough (Brian)
Cruyff (Johann)
Ginola (David)
Haynes (Johnny)
Hoddle (Glen)
Keegan (Kevin)
Ramsey (Alf)
Robson (Bobby/Brian)
Wenger (Arsène)
Wright (Billy)
Zidane (Zinadine)

7
Beckham (David)
Cantona (Eric)
Greaves (Jimmy)
Klinsman (Jurgen)
Lineker (Gary)
McCoist (Ally)
Rivaldo
Ronaldo
Scholes (Paul)
Shearer (Alan)
Shilton (Peter)

8
Bergkamp (Denis)
Brooking (Trevor)
Charlton (Bobby/Jack)
Dalglish (Kenny)
Docherty (Tommy)
Ferguson (Alex)
Maradono (Diego)
Matthews (Stanley)

9
Beardsley (Peter)
Gascoigne (Paul)
Lofthouse (Nat)

10
Sheringham (Teddy)

11
Beckenbauer (Franz)

12
Blanchflower (Danny)

FRANCE/FRENCH

Famous Frenchmen and
Frenchwomen
French words and phrases
Rivers in France
Towns and cities in France

FAMOUS FRENCHMEN AND FRENCHWOMEN

3
Arp (Jean, sculptor)
Ney (Michel, general)
Sue (Eugène, novelist)

4
Dior (Christian, fashion designer)
Doré (Gustave, artist)
Dufy (Raoul, painter)
Foch (Ferdinand, World War I general)
Gide (André, novelist)
Hugo (Victor, poet, dramatist and novelist)
Loti (Pierre, novelist)
Piaf (Edith, singer)
Sade (Marquis de, novelist)
Sand (Georges, novelist)
Tati (Jacques, comic actor)
Weil (Simone, philosopher)
Zola (Emile, novelist)

5
Butor (Michel, novelist)
Camus (Albert, novelist)
Carné (Marcel, film director)
Clair (René, film director)
Corot (Camille, painter)
Curie (Pierre, physicist)
David (Jacques Louis, painter)
Degas (Edgar, painter)

Dukas (Paul, composer)
Dumas (Alexandre, novelist)
Fauré (Gabriel, composer)
Gabin (Jean, writer)
Genet (Jean, dramatist)
Henri (Thierry, footballer)
Jarry (Alfred, dramatist)
Laval (Pierre, politician, collaborator)
Manet (Edouard, painter)
Marot (Clément, poet)
Monet (Claude, painter)
Péguy (Charles, poet)
Petit (Roland, choreographer)
Ravel (Maurice, composer)
Rodin (Auguste, sculptor)
Sagan (Françoise, novelist)
Satie (Erik, composer)
Stael (Madame de, writer)
Verne (Jules, novelist)
Vigny (Alfred de, poet)

6
Ampère (André, physicist)
Artaud (Antoine, actor, theorist)
Balzac (Honoré de, novelist)
Bardot (Brigitte, actress)
Boulez (Pierre, composer)
Braque (Georges, painter)
Buffet (Bernard, painter)
Buffon (Georges, naturalist)
Cardin (Pierre, fashion designer)
Céline (Louis, poet)
Chanel (Coco, fashion designer)
Chirac (Jacques, president)
Danton (Georges, revolutionary)

Eluard (Paul, poet)
Fermat (Pierre, mathematician)
Fleury (André, cardinal, statesman)
France (Anatole, novelist)
Godard (Jean-Luc, film director)
Joffre (Joseph, World War I general)
Laclos (Pierre Choderlos de, novelist)
Moreau (Jeanne, actress)
Musset (Alfred de, dramatist and poet)
Nerval (Gérard de, poet)
Pascal (Blaise, mathematician, writer)
Pétain (Henri, general, Vichy leader)
Petipa (Marius, choreographer)
Proust (Marcel, novelist)
Racine (Jean, dramatist)
Réamur (René-Antoine, physicist)
Renoir (Jean, film director)
Renoir (Pierre, painter)
Sardou (Victorien, dramatist)
Seurat (Georges, painter)
Sartre (Jean-Paul, novelist and philosopher)
Valéry (Paul, poet)
Villon (François, poet)
Zidane (Zinadine, footballer)

7
Boileau (Nicolas, poet)
Cantona (Eric, footballer)
Cartier (Jacques, explorer)
Cézanne (Paul, painter)
Chénier (André, poet)
Claudel (Paul, dramatist)
Cocteau (Jean, writer and artist)

Colette (novelist)
Coulomb (Charles, physicist)
Diderot (Denis, writer and philosopher)
Duhamel (Georges, novelist)
Feydeau (Georges, dramatist)
Gautier (Théophile, writer)
Ionesco (Eugène, dramatist)
Labiche (Eugène, dramatist)
Lamarck (Jean-Baptiste, naturalist)
Laplace (Pierre, mathematician)
Lumière (Auguste, cinema pioneer)
Malraux (André, novelist)
Marceau (Marcel, mime)
Mauriac (François, novelist)
Merimée (Prosper, novelist)
Mistral (Frédéric, poet)
Molière (Jean-Baptiste Poquelin, dramatist)
Montand (Yves, actor)
Pasteur (Louis, chemist)
Platini (Michel, footballer)
Prévert (Jacques, novelist)
Queneau (Raymond novelist)
Rimbaud (Arthur, poet)
Rolland (Romain, novelist)
Romains (Jules, novelist)
Ronsard (Pierre de, poet)
Roussel (Raymond, novelist)
Scarron (Paul, dramatist)
Utrillo (Maurice, painter)
Watteau (Antoine, painter)

8
Aznavour (Charles, singer)
Barbusse (Henri, novelist)
Barrault (Jean-Louis, actor)
Beauvoir (Simone de, writer and philosopher)
Berlioz (Hector, composer)
Bernanos (Georges, novelist)
Blériot (Louis, aviator)
Constant (Benjamin, novelist)
Cousteau (Jacques, underwater explorer)
Daguerre (Louis-Jacques-Mandé, inventor)
Daladier (Edouard, politician)
Debussy (Claude, composer)
Flaubert (Gustave, novelist)
Goncourt (Edmond/Jules de, novelists)
Huysmans (Joris Karl, novelist)
Jacquard (Joseph-Marie, inventor)
Malherbe (François de, poet)
Mallarmé (Stéphane, poet)
Marivaux (Pierre, dramatist)
Napoleon (see Bonaparte)
Poincaré (Raymond, stateman)
Stendhal (Henri Beyle, novelist)
Truffaut (François, film director)
Verlaine (Paul, poet)
Voltaire (François-Marie Arouet, writer and philosopher)

9
Becquerel (Henri, physicist)
Bonaparte (Napoleon, emperor)
Chevalier (Maurice, singer)
Corneille (Pierre, dramatist)
Delacroix (Eugène, painter)
Descartes (René, philosopher)
Fernandel (comedian)
Fragonard (Jean, painter)
Froissart (Jean, chronicler)
Lamartine (Alphonse de, poet)
Lavoisier (Antoine, chemist)
Mitterand (Francois, president)
Montaigne (Michel de, essayist)
Richelieu (Armand, cardinal, statesman)

10
Baudelaire (Charles, poet)
Clemenceau (Georges, statesman)
Maupassant (Guy de, novelist)

11
Apollinaire (Guillaume, poet)
Montgolfier (Jacques-Etienne, balloonist)
Montherlant (Henry de, novelist)
Nostradamus (astrologer)
Robespierre (Maximilien, revolutionary)

12
Beaumarchais (Pierre, writer)

2+ words

de Gaulle (Charles, general and president)
La Fontaine (Jean de, poet)
Saint-Exupery (Antoine de, novelist)
Saint-Saens (Camille, composer)

FRENCH WORDS AND PHRASES

2

de – from, of
et – and
il – he
je – I
la – the (feminine)
le – the (masculine)
ou – or
sa – her
tu – you (informal)
un – a (masculine), one

3

bon – good
dix – ten
ils – they
les – the (plural)
moi – me
mon – my
par – by
qui – who
roi – king
rue – street
son – his
sur – on
thé – tea
toi – you
une – a (feminine), one

4

auto – car
avec – with
beau – beautiful (masculine)
café – café, coffee

cinq – five
bleu – blue
chez – at the house/home of
coup – success, coup d'état
dame – lady
dans – in
deux – two
elle – she, her
fils – son
gare – railway station
huit – eight
jour – day
mais – but
mari – husband
menu – set meal
midi – midday
Midi – south of France
neuf – nine
noir – black
nous – we
onze – eleven
plat – dish
pour – for
quel – what, which
quoi – what
roux – basis of white sauce
sept – seven
sous – under
très – very
vert – green
vous – you (formal)

5

année – year
belle – beautiful woman
blanc – white (masculine)
bonne – good (feminine)
daube – type of stew
douze – eleven
coupé – sporty two-door car
court – short
femme – wife, woman
fille – girl, daughter
grand – big, great
homme – man
jaune – yellow

mêlée – brawl, fray
merci – thank you
métro – underground
notre – our
petit – small
quand -when
rouge – red
route – road
sauté – quick-fried
trois – three
votre - your

6

cognac – brandy
dehors – outside
flambé – with brandy poured over it and ignited
gamine – boyish, tomboy
garcon– boy, waiter
maison – house
potage – soup

7

bonjour – hello, good day
comment – how
cuisine – cooking, kitchen
couture – dressmaking
petite – small (feminine)

8

coiffure – hairstyle
monsieur – gentleman, mister, sir
pourquoi – why

9

autoroute – motorway

2+ words

à la mode – fashionable
à propos – timely, to the point
bête noir – pet hate
billet doux – love letter
comme il faut – as it should be
cordon bleu – blue ribbon, top-quality

coup d'état – overthrow of a government
coup de foudre – sudden shock, love at first sight
coup de grâce – final blow, or merciful blow
coup de théâtre – unexpected and dramatic turn of events, especially in a play
de rigueur – required by custom or etiquette
de trop – superfluous, unwanted
en masse – all together
en passant – in passing
en route – on the way
entre nous – just between ourselves
haute couture – high fashion
laissez-faire – unrestricted, unregulated (capitalism)
nom de plume – pen name, writer's pseudonym
par avion – by airmail
poste restante – to be collected from the post office
raison d'être – reason for existing
répondez s'il vous plaît – please reply
savoir faire – the ability to do the right thing
tour de force – great achievement or performance
tour de France – cycle race around France
tout de suite – at once

RIVERS IN FRANCE

3
Ain
Ill
Lot
Lys
Var

4
Aire
Aube
Cher
Loir
Oise
Tarn
Vire

5
Adour
Agout
Aisne
Doubs
Isère
Loire
Marne
Meuse
Rance
Rhone
Saone
Seine
Somme
Yonne

6
Allier
Escaut
Sambre
Sarthe
Vienne

7
Durance
Garonne
Gironde
Mayenne
Moselle

8
Charente
Dordogne

TOWNS AND CITIES IN FRANCE

3
Aix
Pau

4
Albi
Caen
Laon
Lyon
Metz
Nice

5
Arles
Arras
Brest
Dijon
Douai
Evian
Lille
Lyons
Nancy
Nimes
Paris
Reims
Rouen
Tours
Vence
Verdun
Vichy

6
Amiens
Bayeux
Calais
Cannes
Dieppe
Nantes
Orange
Rheims
Toulon

7
Ajaccio
Alencon

Auxerre
Avignon
Bayonne
Bourges
Dunkirk
Limoges
Lourdes
Orleans

8
Bergerac
Besancon
Biarritz
Bordeaux
Boulogne

Chamonix
Chartres
Dunkerque
Grenoble
Soissons
Toulouse

9
Abbeville
Cherbourg
Marseille

10
Marseilles
Montelimar

Strasbourg
Versailles

11
Armentières
Montpellier

2+ words
Le Havre
Le Mans
St Etienne
St Malo
St Tropez

FRUIT

VARIETIES OF FRUIT

3
Cox
fig
haw
hip
nut

4
akee
crab
date
doum
gage
gean
kaki
kiwi
lime
pear
plum
pome
sloe
sorb
tuna
ugli

5
ackee
acorn
apple
berry
betel
eater
gourd
grape
guava
jaffa
lemon
logan
mango
melon
morel
morus
navel
olive

papaw
peach
prune

6
ananas
banana
banyan
cherry
citron
citrus
codlin
comice
cooker
damson
drupel
durian
lichee
litchi
loquat
lucama
lychee
mammee
medlar
muscat
orange
papaya
pawpaw
pippin
pisang
pomelo
pumelo
punica
quince
raisin
ramoon
rennet
russet
sharon
tampor
tomato
wampee

7
apricot
avocado
bouchet
bullace

coconut
codling
costard
cumquat
currant
genipap
golding
kumquat
leechee
mineola
morello
pomeroy
pompion
pumpkin
rhubarb
rosehip
ruddock
satsuma
shallon
sultana
tangelo
winesap

8
bergamot
bilberry
blenheim
bromelia
burgamot
calabash
faeberry
fenberry
honeydew
japonica
mandarin
mulberry
muscatel
pearmain
plantain
prunello
shaddock
sweetsop
victoria
windfall
xylocarp

9
blueberry

canteloup
cranberry
damascene
freestone
greengage
mirabelle
nectarine
ortanique
persimmon
pineapple
raspberry
tangerine
victorine

10
blackberry
breadfruit

cantaloupe
Clementine
clingstone
elderberry
gooseberry
granadilla
grapefruit
grenadilla
loganberry
mangosteen
redcurrant
strawberry
watermelon

11
boysenberry
chokecherry
huckleberry
pomegranate

12
blackcurrant
whitecurrant
whortleberry

2+ words
blood orange
cooking apple
crab apple
custard apple
navel orange
passion fruit
Seville orange
sugar apple

FURNITURE

PIECES OF FURNITURE

2
PC
TV

3
bar
bed
bin
cot
mat
pew
rug

4
bunk
crib
desk
form
lamp
seat
sofa

5
bench
bidet
chair
couch
divan
grate
light
piano
shade
shelf
stand
stool
suite
table
video

6
buffet
bureau
carpet

carver
caster
cheval
consol
cradle
drawer
fender
hearth
heater
locker
lowboy
pouffe
rocker
screen
settee
settle
stereo
teapoy
tester
throne
toilet

7
armoire
beanbag
boxseat
bunkbed
cabinet
campbed
charpoy
commode
console
counter
cushion
dresser
hammock
hassock
lounger
ottoman
tallboy
tambour
truckle
whatnot

8
armchair
bassinet
bedstead

bookcase
bookends
causeuse
credenza
cupboard
fauteuil
hatstand
loveseat
radiator
recliner
showcase
tabouret
wardrobe

9
bookshelf
bookstand
camp-stool
coatstand
davenport
deckchair
faldstool
footstool
garderobe
hallstand
headboard
lampstand
palanquin
radiogram
sideboard
washstand
workbench
worktable

10
candelabra
chandelier
chiffonier
escritoire
secretaire

12
chesterfield

2+ words
air bed
bedside table
box bed

chaise-longue
chest of drawers
cheval mirror
coffee table
console-table
dining table
dinner table
display cabinet
easy chair
filing cabinet
folding chair
four-poster
gate-leg(ged) table

leg-rest
linen press
loo table
magazine rack
music stool
night chair
night stool
occasional table
piano stool
pier table
put-u-up
reading desk
rocking chair

side table
sofa-bed
swivel chair
tea-trolley
three-piece suite
toilet table
truckle-bed
water bed
window-seat
writing desk
writing table

GAMES

Ball games
Card games and other games
Terms used in playing games
See also **SPORT**

BALL GAMES

4
golf
polo
pool

5
catch
fives
rugby

6
hockey
pelota
shinty
squash
tennis

7
cricket
croquet
hurling
netball
rackets
snooker

8
baseball
football
handball
hardball
lacrosse
rounders
softball

9
billiards

10
basketball
volleyball

CARD GAMES AND OTHER GAMES

2
go

3
gin
loo
nap
nim
pit
tag
taw
tig

4
brag
crib
dice
faro
keno
kino
ludo
ruff
skat
snap
solo

5
bingo
booby
cards
catch
cheat
chess
craps
darts
fives
house
jacks
keeno
lotto
monte

ombre
pairs
poker
quino
rummy
whist

6
beetle
boules
bridge
casino
chemmy
Cluedo®
crambo
donkey
ecarté
euchre
fantan
gammon
hazard
hearts
hoopla
kitcat
piquet
quoits
sevens
Tetris®
tipcat

7
auction
bezique
canasta
cassino
conkers
diabolo
hangman
marbles
pachisi
pinball
pontoon
primero
tombola

8
baccarat
charades

checkers
contract
cribbage
dominoes
draughts
forfeits
freecell
napoleon
patience
petanque
pinochle
roulette
rounders
Scrabble®
skittles
softball
Subbuteo®

9
bagatelle
blackjack
Monopoly®
newmarket
pelmanism
quadrille
solitaire
stoolball

10
backgammon
spillikins

11
shovelboard
tiddlywinks

12
consequences

2+ words
auction bridge
Aunt Sally
blindman's-buff
blow-football
catch-as-catch-can
chase-the-ace
chemin de fer
Chinese checkers

clock golf
contract bridge
crazy golf
Donkey Kong®
dumb crambo
fan-tan
gin rummy
housey-housey
hunt-the-slipper
hunt-the-thimble
I-spy
jack-straws
knockout whist
knuckle-bones
lucky dip
mah-jong
mah-jongg
musical chairs
old maid
pig(gy)-in-the-middle
postman's knock
seven-up
shove-halfpenny
Sim City®
snip-snap-snorp.
solo whist
Space Invaders®
strip poker
three-card brag
three-card monty
Tomb Raider®
Trivial Pursuit®
twenty-one
vingt-et-un

TERMS USED IN PLAYING GAMES

3
ace
bet
die
peg
toy

4
chip
club

crib
deal
deck
dice
draw
file
huff
jack
king
mate
odds
pack
pawn
play
pool
quiz
rank
rook
ruff
slam
suit
trey
turn
vint
vole

5
capot
check
clubs
deuce
dicer
dummy
heart
joker
knave
point
queen
score
spade
trick
trump
wheel

6
banker
bishop
casino

castle
cinque
dealer
domino
gambit
gamble
gammon
hearts
knight
rubber
scorer
spades
trumps

7
counter
discard
misdeal

8
chessman
chessmen
contract
counters

9
checkmate
stalemate

10
chessboard

2+ words
court card
face card
grand slam
yo-yo

GEOGRAPHY

See also **COUNTRY,
LAKE, MOUNTAIN,
RIVER, etc.**

GEOGRAPHICAL TERMS

3
alp
bay
ban
bog
cay
col
cwm
dam
fen
key
lea
map
sea
tor
voe

4
adit
arid
bank
beck
burn
cape
cave
city
cone
cove
crag
croy
dale
dell
dike
dune
dyke
east
eyot
ford
glen
gulf

hill
holm
holt
inch
isle
lake
land
loch
mere
mesa
morr
mull
naze
neap
ness
pass
peak
pole
pond
port
race
reef
rill
road
rock
spit
spur
tarn
tide
town
tump
vale
veld
wadi
weir
west
wold
wood
zone

5
abyss
atlas
atoll
basin
bayou
beach
bight

bluff
broad
brook
butte
cairn
canal
chasm
cliff
coast
combe
copse
creek
crest
delta
downs
drift
duchy
esker
fault
field
fiord
firth
fjord
glade
globe
gorge
grove
heath
hurst
inlet
islet
knoll
lande
llano
lough
marsh
monte
mound
mount
mouth
north
oasis
ocean
orient
plain
point
polar
range

ridge
river
sands
scale
scarp
shelf
shire
shoal
shore
sound
south
stack
state
swamp
sward
taiga
veldt

6
alpine
arctic
arroyo
bourne
canton
canyon
cirque
clough
common
corrie
county
crater
defile
desert
dingle
divide
domain
forest
geyser
hamlet
inland
island
jungle
lagoon
levant
maidan
meadow
morass
nullah

pampas
parish
polder
rapids
ravine
region
runnel
seaway
sierra
skerry
spinny
steppe
strait
strath
stream
summit
tropic
tundra
upland
valley
warren

7
bogland
caldera
channel
compass
contour
country
current
cutting
deltaic
deposit
eastern
equator
erosion
estuary
glacial
glacier
habitat
harbour
hillock
hilltop
hummock
iceberg
isthmus
lowland
montane

oceanic
oriental
plateau
prairie
rivulet
savanna
seaport
seaside
straits
thicket
torrent
tropics
village
volcano
western

8
affluent
alluvial
blowhole
cataract
crevasse
district
downland
easterly
eastward
environs
foothill
foreland
frontier
headland
highland
hillside
interior
isthmian
landmark
landslip
latitude
lowlands
mainland
meridian
moorland
mountain
northern
occident
quagmire
seaboard
seashore

snowline
southern
treeline
tropical
volcanic
westerly
westward
woodland

9
antarctic
antipodal
antipodes
avalanche
coastline
continent
foothills
heathlands
highlands
landslide
longitude
marshland
meltwater
northeast
northerly
northward
northwest
peninsula
precipice
shoreline
southeast
southerly
southward

southwest
tableland
tributary
waterfall
watershed

10
confluence
coordinate
demography
equatorial
escarpment
glaciation
hemisphere
landlocked
occidental
peninsular
plantation
population
projection
promontory
quicksands
rainforest
topography
wilderness

11
aggradation
archipelago
cartography
continental
conurbation
countryside

demographic
mountainous
subtropical
watercourse

12
northeastern
northwestern
principality
protectorate
southeastern
southwestern

13
Mediterranean
northeasterly
northeastward
northwesterly
northwestward
southeasterly
southeastward
southwesterly
southwestward

2+ words
bench mark
grid north
Gulf Stream
ice-floe
land mass
magnetic north
trig point
true north

GEOLOGY

GEOLOGICAL TERMS

2
aa

3
age
alp
eon
era
ore
puy
ria
vei

4
aeon
cone
core
culm
cusp
dune
kame
lava
Lias
lode
marl
oder
plug
rift
sial
sill
sima
spit
till
tuff
vent
zone

5
arête
chert
crust
delta
epoch
erode

esker
fault
flank
hexad
host
levee
loess
magma
nappe
phula
ridge
swarm
Trias

6
alpine
arkose
bourne
cirque
corrie
crater
diaper
durain
Eocene
facies
fossil
furrow
fusain
gangue
geyser
gneiss
graben
inlier
klippe
mantle
matrix
misfit
oolith
placer
podsol
schist
scoria
spring
striae
trough
valley

7
abyssal
aquifer
arcuate
barchan
bathyal
bedrock
breccia
caldera
corrode
crystal
cuvette
deltaic
drumlin
erosion
fissure
glacier
hardpan
horizon
igneous
lapilli
Miocene
molasse
moraine
Neogene
neritic
ophitic
outlier
paralic
Permian
procast
upthrow
vesicle
vitrain
weather

8
abrasion
alluvial
artesian
Bajocian
biserial
blowhole
Cambrian
Cenozoic
Charnian
cleavage
crevasse

Devonian
foliated
foreland
fracture
fumarole
ganister
granular
Holocene
isocline
isostasy
Jurassic
lopolith
Mesozoic
Orcadian
pavement
pinacoid
pisolith
Pliocene
porosity
sediment
Silurian
syncline
tectonic
Tertiary
trachyite
Triassic

9
amorphous
amygdales
anticline
attrition
batholith
Bathonian
clinodome
composite
coprolite
Corallian
corrosion
downthrow
dripstone
epicentre
evaporate
extrusion
flagstone
formation
freestone
hercynian

insequent
intercept
isoclinal
isoclinic
isostatic
isotropic
laccolith
laminated
macrodome
Oligocene
Oxfordain
peneplain
pericline
phacolith
rudaceous
saltation
striation
subhedral
tectonics
Uriconian

10
asymptotic
calcareous
caledonoid
Cenomanian
compaction
Cretaceous
depression
diagenetic
earthquake
epigenetic
ferugionous
flocculate
fluviatile
glaciation
Ordovician
orogenesis
overthrust
Palaeogene
Palaeozoic
Quaternary
stalactite
stalagmite
syngenetic
weathering

11
agglomerate
Archaeozoic
arenaceous
cementation
crystalline
degradation
exfoliation
geosyncline
groundwater
imbrication
isomorphous
leucocratic
Longmyndian
percolation
porphyritic
Portlandian
precipitate
Proterozoic
sedimentary
Torridonain
Tournasian
Westphalian

12
argillaceous
conglomerate
hydrothermal
interglacial
interstadial
metamorphism
permeability
petrogenesis
polymorphism

2+ words
artesian well
coal measure
ice age
Pre-cambrian
rift valley
tectonic plate
volcanic bomb
volcanic plug

GODS/GODDESSES

Gods
Goddesses
See also **MYTH/MYTHOLOGY**

GODS

EGYPTIAN

Amun	(chief god)
Anubis	(jackal-headed god of underworld)
Apis	(bull god of war)
Geb	(earth)
Hapi	(the Nile)
Horus	(hawk-headed sun god)
Osiris	(fertility, vegetation, and the dead)
Ptah	(creator god, arts and crafts)
Ra *or* Re	(sun)
Serapis	(death, underworld)
Set *or* Seth	(evil, brother and killer of Osiris)
Shu	(air)
Thoth	(baboon-headed god of wisdom)

GREEK

Aeolus	(winds)
Agathodaemon	(prosperity)
Alastor	(fate)
Apollo	(arts, beauty, healing, music and the sun)
Ares	(war)
Asclepius	(medicine)
Boreas	(north wind)
Cronos *or* Kronos	(early chief god, deposed by Zeus)
Dionysus	(wine and fertility)
Eros	(love)
Hades	(underworld)
Helios	(sun)
Hephaestus	(fire, the forge and craft)
Hermes	(messenger of the gods)
Hymen	(marriage)
Hypnos	(sleep)
Nereus	(the sea, 'the old man of the sea')
Oceanus	(the sea)
Pan	(flocks and herds)
Plutus	(riches)
Poseidon	(chief sea god)
Thanatos	(personification of death)
Triton	(sea god who blows through a conch shell)
Uranus	(first chief god deposed by Cronos)

Zeus	(supreme god)
Zephyrus	(west wind)

HINDU

Agni	(fire)
Brahma	(creator and chief god)
Ganesha	(elephant-headed god of wisdom)
Hanuman	(monkey god)
Indra	(rain)
Kama	(love)
Krishna	(earth, fertility, and love)
Shiva *or* Siva	(destroyer)
Vishnu	(preserver)
Yama	(lord of the dead)

MIDDLE EASTERN

Anu	(Babylonian chief god)
Ashur	(Assyrian national battle god)
Baal	(Phoenician fertility god)
Bel	= Baal
Dagon	(Philistine chief god)
Marduk	(Babylonian chief god)
Mithras	(Persian chief god and god of sun and light)
Moloch	(Ammonite fire and war god demanding human sacrifices)
Nabu *or* Nebo	(Babylonian god of wisdom)
Tammuz *or* Thammuz	(Babylonian fertility god, who died every winter and rose again every spring)

NATIVE AMERICAN

Inti	(Inca personification of the sun)
Huitzilopochtli	(Aztec god of war and the sun)
Kon-tiki	(Inca sun god)
Quetzacoatl	(Aztec chief god, a feathered serpent)
Tlaloc	(Aztec rain god)

NORSE

Aesir	(collective name for the chief gods)
Balder	(sun, the good god)
Bragi	(poetry and eloquence)
Frey *or* Freyr	(fertility)
Heimdal	(watchman, keeper of the rainbow bridge)
Loki	(fire and evil or mischief)
Njord *or* Njordhr	(sea and ships)
Odin	(chief god)
Thor	(thunder and war)
Woden	= Odin
Wotan	= Odin

ROMAN

Aesculapius	(medicine and healing)
Apollo	(arts, beauty, healing, music, and the sun)
Auster	(south wind, the Sirocco)
Bacchus	(wine and fertility)
Cupid	(love, son of Venus)
Dis	(underworld)
Faunus	(forest and field and prophecy)
Genius	(individual man's attendant spirit)
Iacchus	= Bacchus
Janus	(doorways and beginnings)
Jove	= Jupiter
Jupiter	(supreme god)
Lar(es)	(the household, family and ancestors)
Liber	= Bacchus
Lupercus	= Faunus or Pan
Mars	(war)
Mercury	messenger of the gods, god of science, commerce, travellers and thieves)
Morpheus	(dreams)
Neptune	(the sea)
Orcus	(underworld)
Penates	(protective gods of the household and storeroom)
Phoebus	(sun)
Pluto	(underworld)
Saturn(us)	(early chief god deposed by Jupiter)
Silvanus	(woods)
Somnus	(sleep)
Terminus	(boundaries)
Vulcan	(fire, the forge and crafts)

GODDESSES

EGYPTIAN

Bast *or* Bubastis	(cat goddess)
Hathor	(love and joy)
Isis	(chief goddess, sister of Osiris)
Ma *or* Maat	(justice)
Nut	(earth mother)
Tefnut	(sea)

GREEK

Amphitrite	(sea, wife of Poseidon)
Aphrodite	(love and beauty)
Artemis	(hunting and the moon)
Astraea	(justice)
Ate	(vengeance and mischief)

Athene	(wisdom)
Chloris	(flowers)
Cybele	(earth)
Cynthia	= Artemis
Demeter	(crops and harvest)
Enyo	(war)
Eos	(dawn)
Erinyes	= Furies
Eumenides	= Furies
Furies	(avengers of crimes)
Gaea *or* Ge	(earth)
Hebe	(goddess of youth and cup-bearer to the gods)
Hecate	(night, the underworld and witchcraft)
Hera	(queen of the gods, goddess of marriage and women, wife of Zeus)
Hestia	(the hearth and fire)
Hygiea	(health)
Irene	(peace)
Iris	(goddess of the rainbow and divine messenger)
Mnemosyne	(memory, mother of the Muses)
Moirai	(goddesses of fate)
Muses	(goddesses of the arts)
Nemesis	(retribution and vengeance)
Nike	(victory)
Nyx	(night)
Persephone	(underworld)
Rhea	(mother of the gods)
Selene	(moon)
Tyche	(destiny)

HINDU

Devi	(chief goddess)
Durga	= Kali
Kali	(destruction, wife of Shiva)
Lakshmi	(beauty and wealth, wife of Vishnu)

MIDDLE EASTERN

Astarte	(Phonecian goddess of love)
Ishtar	(Babylonian goddess of love and fertility)
Tiamit	(Babylonian dragon goddess)

NORSE

Freya	(god of love and fertility)
Frigg *or* Frigga	(chief goddess and wife of Odin)
Hel	(the underworld and the dead)
Valkyries	(warrior maidens who brought the souls of warriors slain in battle to Valhalla)

ROMAN

Aurora	(dawn)
Bellona	(war)
Ceres	(crops and harvest)
Diana	(moon and hunting)
Fauna	(country goddess, sister of Faunus)
Flora	(flowers)
Fortuna	(fortune, destiny)
Juno	(queen of heaven, goddess of marriage and women, and wife of Jupiter)
Juventas	(youth)
Libera	= Proserpina
Luna	(moon)
Minerva	(wisdom)
Nox	(night)
Ops	(wife of Saturn)
Parcae	(the Fates)
Pax	(peace)
Pomona	(orchards and gardens)
Proserpina	(the underworld, wife of Pluto)
Salus	(health)
Tellus *or* Terra	(earth)
Venus	(love and beauty)
Vesta	(fire and the hearth)
Victoria	(victory)

GOLF

Golf clubs
Golf courses
Famous golfers
Terms used in golf

GOLF CLUBS

4
iron
wood

5
cleek
spoon
wedge

6
driver
mashie
putter

7
brassie
niblick

9
sandwedge

GOLF COURSES

5
Troon

6
Belfry, the

7
Augusta
Hoylake

8
Sandwich

9
Muirfield
Prestwick

Turnberry
Wentworth

10
Carnoustie
Gleneagles

11
Blairgowrie
Sunningdale

2+ words
Lytham St Annes
Royal Birkdale
St Andrews

FAMOUS GOLFERS

4
Lyle (Sandy)
Rees (Dai)

5
Faldo (Nick)
Hogan (Ben)
Locke (Bobby)
Snead (Sam)
Woods (Tiger)

6
Alliss (Peter)
Cotton (Henry)
Langer (Bernhard)
Norman (Greg)
Palmer (Arnold)
Player (Gary)

7
Jacklin (Tony)
Trevino (Lee)
Woosnam (Ian)

8
Baiocchi (Hugh)
Nicklaus (Jack)
Olazabal (José)

11
Ballesteros (Seve)

GOLFING TERMS

3
cut
par
tee

4
club
fore
hole
putt

5
bogie
drive
eagle
green
rough
round
slice
swing

6
birdie
bunker

8
fairway

9
matchplay

2+ words
eighteen-hole
hole in one
nine-hole
stroke play
tee off

GRAMMAR

*GRAMMATICAL AND
LANGUAGE TERMS*

4
case
dash
mood
noun
past
root
stem
verb
weak

5
acute
affix
breve
caret
colon
comma
grave
idiom
parse
quote
Roman
slang
slash
spell
spelt
tense
tilde
usage
vowel

6
accent
active
adverb
aorist
braces
clause
cliché
dagger
dative
define

derive
ending
finite
formal
future
gender
gerund
govern
hyphen
italic
jargon
neuter
number
object
period
person
phonic
phrase
plural
prefix
prolix
simile
stress
strong
suffix
syntax
umlaut
verbal

7
antonym
apocope
article
bracket
cedilla
context
decline
diction
digraph
elision
homonym
inflect
italics
lexical
lexicon
litotes
parsing
passive

perfect
phoneme
phonics
present
pronoun
regular
subject
synonym
verbose

8
ablative
absolute
anaphora
archaism
asterisk
definite
ellipsis
euphuism
feminine
glossary
genitive
guttural
informal
misspell
morpheme
negative
optative
particle
phonetic
pleonasm
question
relative
sentence
singular
solecism
syllable
syntaxis
vocative

9
accidence
adjective
ampersand
Anglicism
conjugate
consonant
diacritic

diphthong
etymology
euphemism
Gallicism
gerundive
hyperbole
idiomatic
imperfect
indention
inflexion
inversion
irregular
masculine
neologism
objective
paragraph
parataxis
partitive
philology
platitude
predicate
preterite
privative
pronounce
punctuate
quotation
reflexive
semantics
semicolon
semivowel
syllabic
syntactic
tautology
underline

10
accusative
apostrophe

apposition
circumflex
colloquial
comparison
concessive
declension
definition
derivation
derivative
generative
grammarian
hyphenated
imperative
impersonal
indefinite
indicative
infinitive
inflection
intonation
morphology
nominative
palindrome
paraphrase
participle
pluperfect
possessive
pronominal
subjective
transitive
vernacular

11
anacoluthon
association
comparative
conditional
conjunction
conjunctive
declination

descriptive
disjunctive
dissyllabic
dissyllable
exclamation
grammatical
interrobang
linguistics
misspelling
parenthesis
preposition
proposition
punctuation
subjunctive
subordinate
substantive
superlative

12
alphabetical
etymological
indeclinable
intransitive

13
interrogative
pronunciation

2+ words
dangling participle
double negative
exclamation mark
full point
full stop
inverted comma
question mark
split infinitive

GROUPS

A group
Pop groups

A GROUP

3
bee
duo
lot
mob
pod
set

4
army
band
bevy
bloc
body
cell
clan
club
crew
fold
gang
herd
host
knot
pack
pool
ring
sect
sort
team
trio
unit

5
batch
bunch
cadre
caste
chain
class
clump
combo

covey
crowd
circle
drove
fleet
flock
genre
genus
guild
octet
panel
party
posse
shoal
squad
swarm
tribe
troop
truss

6
bundle
cartel
caucus
circle
clique
clutch
cohort
colony
convoy
family
gaggle
league
litter
parcel
phylum
school
septet
series
sextet
stable
string
troupe

7
cluster
commune
company

coterie
faction
platoon
quartet
quintet
society
trilogy

8
assembly
caboodle
category
ensemble
sorority
taxonomy

9
community
gathering
orchestra
syndicate

10
assemblage
collection
consortium
contingent
federation
fraternity
sisterhood

11
brotherhood
combination

12
congregation

POP GROUPS

3
ABC
Dio
Elo
Fox
Gun
Jam
Mud

PhD
Sky
UFO
Wah!
Who
XTC
Yes

4
Abba
AC/DC
Band
Beat
Bros
Cars
Chic
Cult
Cure
Devo
Firm
Free
Herd
Inxs
Jets
Linx
Move
News
Nice
Opus
Pips
Ruts
Slik
Styx
Tams
Them
Toto
Toys
Trio
Wham

5
Alarm
Avons
Bread
Byrds
Cameo
Clash
Cream

Darts
Doors
Exile
Faces
Falco
Focus
Goons
Hello
Japan
Kenny
Kinks
Mojos
O'Jays
Pilot
Queen
Racey
Rufus
Saxon
Skids
Slade
Space
Steam
Sweet
Truth
Tymes
Wings
Yazoo

6
Angels
Berlin
Comets
Damned
Dollar
Eagles
Equals
Europe
Family
Fureys
Gillan
Motors
Nolans
Pearls
Pigbag
Pogues
Police
Raydio
Rumour

Sailor
Smiths
Smokie
Sparks
Tweets
Vapors
Vipers
Visage

7
Amazulu
America
Animals
Archies
Arrival
Bangles
Bauhaus
Beatles
Blondie
Buggles
Casuals
Chicago
Dakotas
Delrons
Doolies
Dynasty
Erasure
Genesis
Goodies
Hollies
Jesters
Luvvers
Madness
Marbles
Marcels
Merseys
Moments
Monkees
Monsoon
Odyssey
Osmonds
Ottawan
Outlaws
Peppers
Piglets
Pinkies
Pirates
Rainbow

Ramones
Ramrods
Rattles
Redbone
Redding
Regents
Replays
Santana
Seekers
Shadows
Sherbet
Squeeze
Strawbs
Tavares
Tonight
Traffic
Trammps
Turtles
Wailers
Weavers
Whistle
Wizards
Wombles
Wurzels
Zodiacs
Zombies

8
Allisons
Banshees
Chiffons
Coasters
Crickets
Crystals
Diamonds
Dreamers
Drifters
Fentones
Floaters
Fortunes
Fourmost
Hawkwind
Heatwave
Honeybus
Hotshots
Jacksons
Miracles
Mixtures

Mudlarks
Nazareth
Newbeats
Olympics
Pedlers
Pharaohs
Pioneers
Piranhas
Platters
Pussycat
Ronettes
Scaffold
Shakatak
Shalamar
Specials
Spinners
Supremes
Surfaris
Survivor
Tornados
Tourists
Ultravox
Ventures
Whispers

9
Bachelors
Badfinger
Bluebells
Bluetones
Bluenotes
Buzzcocks
Crusaders
Cufflinks
Dubliners
Easybeats
Foreigner
Greyhound
Kraftwerk
Landscape
Marillion
Marmalade
Motorhead
Poni-tails
Scorpions
Searchers
Shirelles
Shondells

Spotnicks
Teenagers
Tremelodes
Upsetters
Vandellas
Yardbirds

10
Bananarama
Blancmange
Blockheads
Caravelles
Carpenters
Checkmates
Chordettes
Commodores
Communards
Eurythmics
Highwaymen
Honeycombs
Hurricanes
Kajagoogoo
Lambrettas
Pacemakers
Pretenders
Sandpipers
Stargazers
Stranglers
Stylistics
Supertramp
Undertones
Wavelength
Whitesnake

11
Foundations
Hilltoppers
Imagination
Jordonaires
Lindisfarne
Marvelettes
Merseybeats
Mindbenders
Modernaires
Overlanders
Steppenwolf
Temptations

12
Cryptkickers
Dreamweavers
Housemartins
Showstoppers
Springfields

13
Heartbreakers
Showaddywaddy

2+ words
Adam and The Ants
A-Ha
All-Stars
Altered Images
Althia and Donna
Amen Corner
Andrews Sisters
Arctic Monkeys
Art Of Noise
Atomic Rooster
Bad Manners
Barron Knights
Bay City Rollers
Beach Boys
Bee Gees
Bellamy Brothers
Belle Stars
Beverly Sisters
Big Ben Banjo Band
Big Brothers
Big Country
Big Roll Band
Big Three
Black Lace
Black Sabbath
Blue Minx
Bob And Earl
Bob And Marcia
Bon Jovi
Boney M
Boomtown Rats
Bow Wow Wow
Box Tops
Boystown Gang
Bronski Beat
Brook Brothers

Bucks Fizz
Canned Heat
Chas and Dave
Chicory Tip
Chi-lites
China Crisis
Classic Nouveaux
Cockney Rebel
Crew Cuts
Culture Club
Dave Clark Five
Dead or Alive
Deep Purple
Deep River Boys
Def Leppard
Delta Rhythm Boys
Depeche Mode
Detriot Emeralds
Detroit Spinners
Dire Straits
Dixie Cups
Doobie Brothers
Dorsey Brothers
Duran Duran
Everly Brothers
Fat Larry's Band
Fatback Band
Fiddlers Dram
Fifth Dimensions
First Edition
Five Star
Fleetwood Mac
Flowerpot Men
Flying Lizards
Flying Pickets
Four Aces
Four Freshmen
Four Pennies
Four Preps
Four Seasons
Four Tops
Fun Boy Three
Gap Band
Generation X
Gibson Brothers
Glitter Band
Go West
Godley and Creme

Grateful Dead
Guys and Dolls
Haysi Fantayzee
Hermans Hermits
Hot Butter
Hot Chocolate
Human League
Ink Spots
Iron Maiden
Isley Brothers
It Bites
Ivy League
Jackson Five
Jan and Dean
Jethro Tull
John Barry Seven
Jon and Vangelis
Judas Priest
Kalin Twins
Kaye Sisters
Killing Joke
King Brothers
Kingston Trio
Kool and the Gang
Lipps Inc
Liquid Gold
Loose Ends
Los Bravos
Lovin' Spoonful
Magic Lanterns
Mai Tai
Manfred Mann
Matt Bianco
McGuinness Flint
McGuire Sisters
Meat Loaf
Medicine Head
Mel And Kim
Men At Work
Middle of the Road
Midnight Star
Migil Five
Miki and Griff
Mills Brothers
Modern Lovers
Modern Romance
Modern Talking
Moody Blues

Motley Crue
Mott The Hoople
Mr Big
Mr Minster
Mungo Jerry
Musical Youth
Nashville Teens
New Edition
New Order
New Seekers
New World
Ohio Express
Ollie and Gerry
Orange Juice
Our Kid
Paper Lace
Partridge Family
Paul and Paula
Peaches and Herb
Pet Shop Boys
Peter and Gordon
Peters and Lee
Picketty Witch
Piltdown Men
Pink Floyd
Plastic Ono Band
Plastic Penny
Playboy Band
Pointer Sisters
Poppy Family
Power Station
Pretty Things
Procol Harum
Psychedelic Furs
Public Image Ltd
Quantum Jump

Racing Cars
Ram Jam Band
Real Thing
Red Box
Renée and Renato
Reo Speedwagon
Rockin' Berries
Rocksteady Crew
Rolling Stones
Rooftop Singers
Rose Royce
Roxy Music
Sad Café
Sam and Dave
Scritti Politti
Secret Affair
Sex Pistols
Shaky and Bonnie
Shangri-las
Shocking Blue
Simple Minds
Simply Red
Sister Sledge
Small Faces
Soft Cell
Sonny and Cher
SOS Band
Spandau Ballet
Spice Girls
St Louis Union
Status Quo
Stealers Wheel
Steeleye Span
Steely Dan
Stray Cats
Style Council

Sunshine Band
Sweet Sensation
Swing Out Sister
T Connection
Talk Talk
Talking Heads
Tears For Fears
Teddy Bears
Temperance Seven
The Young Ones
Thin Lizzy
Third World
Thompson Twins
Three Degrees
Three Dog Night
Tight Fit
Tom Tom Club
Trans-x
T-Rex
Twisted Sister
UK Subs
Union Gap
Unit Four Plus Two
Van Halen
Vanity Fare
Vernons Girls
Village People
Walker Brothers
Weather Girls
White Plains
Womack and Womack
Yellow Dog
Young Rascals
Zager and Evans.
Zz Top

HEALTH

Health
Healthy
Unhealthy
See also **DISEASE,**
MEDICINE

HEALTH

4
pink
tone
trim

5
bloom

6
energy
fettle
vigour

7
fitness

8
eupepsia
haleness
strength
vitality
wellness

9
condition
longevity
soundness

10
heartiness
robustness

12
constitution
recuperation

HEALTHY

3
fit

4
fine
hale
rosy
well

5
bonny
cured
fresh
great
hardy
lusty
ruddy
sound
tonic

6
healed
hearty
robust
strong
sturdy

7
bracing
glowing

8
blooming
bouncing
eupeptic
hygienic
salutary
sanitary
stalwart
thriving
vigorous

9
energetic
healthful
strapping
wholesome

10
beneficial
nourishing
nutritious
salubrious

11
flourishing

12
advantageous
convalescent
invigorating

2+ words
fighting fit
fit as a fiddle
fit as a flea
full of beans
hale and hearty
in fine fettle
in good shape
in the pink
on the mend
on the up (and up)
sound as a bell
strong as an ox

ILL OR UNHEALTHY

3
ill
wan

4
pale
sick
weak

5
frail
gouty
green
mangy
peaky
seedy

toxic
unfit
white

6
ailing
infirm
morbid
pallid
peaked
poorly
queasy
rotten
sallow
sickly
spotty
tender
unwell
yellow

7
anaemic
bilious
bulimic
febrile
fevered
harmful
leprous
painful
palsied
pyretic
sniffly
snuffly
swollen
throaty
unsound

8
affected
allergic
anorexic
decrepit
delicate
fatigued
feverish
infected
inflamed
morbific
polluted
purulent
stressed
stricken
ulcerous
underfed
venereal

9
bloodless
bronchial
cancerous
delirious
emaciated
exhausted
festering
injurious
jaundiced
leukaemic
liverish
paralysed
paralytic
phthisic
rheumatic
shivering
ulcerated
unhealthy
unnatural

10
bronchitic
contagious
indisposed
infectious
insanitary
oncogenous
pathogenic
rheumatoid
tubercular
unhygienic

11
consumptive
detrimental
distempered
rheumaticky
tuberculous
unwholesome

12
carcinogenic
contaminated
degenerative
insalubrious
malnourished
pathological

13
hypochondriac

2+ words
not oneself
off-colour
out of shape
out of sorts
run down
under the weather
white as a sheet

HERBS

See also **SPICES**

HERBS

3
bay
rue

4
balm
dill
mint
sage

5
basil
caper
chive
cress
orris
tansy
thyme

6
balsam
betony
borage

catnip
chives
cicely
fennel
garlic
hyssop
lovage
savory
sesame
sorrel

7
aconite
caraway
catmint
comfrey
chervil
dittany
gentian
juniper
mustard
oregano
parsley
pimento
saffron
salsify
verbena
vervain

8
angelica
camomile
feverfew
marjoram
plantain
purslain
rosemary
tarragon
turmeric
valerian

9
chamomile
coriander
fenugreek
liquorice
spearmint
woundwort

10
belladonna
peppermint

11
horseradish

2+ words
lemon-grass

HORSES

A horse
Famous horses
Terms connected with
horses and riding
See also
RACE/RACING

A HORSE

3
bay
cob
dun
gee
nag

4
Arab
barb
colt
foal
grey
hack
jade
mare
pony

roan
stud

5
filly
genet
mount
pinto
shire
steed

6
bronco
dapple
Dobbin
Exmoor
geegee
hogget
hunter

7
charger
courser
eventer
gelding
hackney
mustang
palfrey

piebald
trotter

8
chestnut
palomino
skewbald
stallion
yearling

9
Percheron

10
Clydesdale
Lippizaner

12
thoroughbred

13
steeplechaser

2+ words
Shetland pony
Suffolk Punch

FAMOUS HORSES

Arion	horse belonging to Neptune and Hercules that spoke with a human voice
Arkle	steeplechaser
Black Beauty	in book by Anna M. Sewell
Black Bess	ridden by Dick Turpin
Black Nell	ridden by Wild Bill Hickock
Boxer	character in George Orwell's *Animal Farm*
Bucephalus	horse ridden by Alexander the Great
Champion	the 'wonder horse' in 1950s TV series
Clover	character in George Orwell's *Animal Farm*
Copenhagen	the Duke of Wellington's horse, ridden by him at Waterloo
Desert Orchid	steeplechaser
Grane	Brunnhilda's horse in Wagner's *Ring Cycle*
Houyhnhm	civilised horse in Swift's *Gulliver's Travels*
Hercules	horse owned by Steptoe and son in TV series
Incitatus	the horse that the Roman emperor Caligula made a consul
Lamri	King Arthur's horse

Marengo	horse ridden by Napoleon at Waterloo
Marsala	Garibaldi's horse
Mollie	character in George Orwell's *Animal Farm*
Pegasus	winged horse ridden by Bellerophon and Perseus
Red Rum	Grand National winner
Ronald	horse ridden by Lord Cardigan at the Charge of the Light Brigade
Rosinante	Don Quixote's horse that was all skin and bone
Scout	Tonto's horse in *The Lone Ranger*
Shergar	kidnapped racehorse
Silver	horse ridden by the Lone Ranger
Sleipner	Odin's eight-legged horse in Norse myth
Sorrel	horse ridden by King William III, which tripped over a molehill, throwing off the king who eventually died from the fall
Trigger	horse ridden by Roy Rogers
Velvet	character in book by Enid Bagnold and films
Volonel	horse ridden by Lord Roberts
White Surrey	horse ridden by King Richard III at the battle of Bosworth

TERMS CONNECTED WITH HORSES AND RIDING

3
bit

4
curb
dock
frog
gear
hock
hoof
loin
mane
pace
poll
rein
shoe
spur
tack
tail
trot
walk
whip

5
cinch
crest
croup
ergot
girth
groom
trace

6
bridle
canter
gallop
livery
manège
Pelham
saddle

7
farrier
fetlock
pastern
snaffle
stirrup
withers

8
bareback

blinkers
dressage
eventing
farriery
feathers
grooming
gymkhana
noseband

9
currycomb
hackamore
headstall
neckstrap

10
martingale.

2+ words
hard hat
hind quarters
horse box
point-to-point
pony trekking
show jumping
side-saddle

INSECTS

TYPES OF INSECT

3
ant
bee
bot
bug
fly
lug
nit

4
cleg
flea
frit
gnat
lice
mite
moth
pupa
tick
wasp

5
aphid
aphis
borer
drone
egger
emmet
louse
midge
nymph

6
bedbug
beetle
botfly
caddis
chafer
chigoe
cicada
earwig
gadfly
hopper
hornet
jigger

locust
mantis
maybug
mayfly
sawfly
scarab
spider
stylops
thrips
tsetse
weevil

7
antlion
chigger
cricket
cutworm
firefly
gallfly
katydid
sandfly
skipper
termite

8
alderfly
blackfly
bookworm
geometer
greenfly
horsefly
itchmite
ladybird
lacewing
mosquito
scorpion
silkworm
stinkbug
wireworm
woodworm

9
anopheles
bloodworm
booklouse
butterfly
centipede
cochineal
cockroach

damselfly
dragonfly
ichneumon
millipede
tarantula

10
bluebottle
cockchafer
demoiselle
fritillary
froghopper
silverfish
webspinner

11
bristletail
caterpillar
grasshopper
greenbottle
lamellicorn

2+ words
ant-lion
black widow
boll-weevil
bumble-bee
cabbage-fly
caddis-fly
cheese-mite
daddy-long-legs
crane-fly
glow-worm
hook-worm
ichneumon fly
inch-worm
leaf-cutter
mealy-bug
pond-skater
praying mantis
puss-moth
shield-bug
stag-beetle
swallow-tail
tsetse-fly
warble-fly
water boatman

INVENTORS

4

Bell (*telephone*)
Benz (*car engine*)
Biró (*ball-point pen*)
Colt (*revolver*)
Davy (*miner's lamp*)
Holt (*combine harvester*)
Howe (*sewing machine*)
Hunt (*safety pin*)
Land (*Polaroid camera*)
Otis (*passenger lift*)
Otto (*four-stroke engine*)
Tull (*seed drill*)
Very (*flare signal*)
Watt (*steam engine*)
Yale (*cylinder lock*)

5

Aiken (*digital computer*)
Baird (*mechanical television*)
Booth (*vacuum cleaner*)
Carré (*refrigerator*)
Dewar (*vacuum flask*)
Dyson (*vacuum cleaner, etc.*)
Gabor (*holograph*)
Hyatt (*celluloid*)
Magee (*parking meter*)
Maxim (*machine gun*)
Morse (*telegraph*)
Smith (*ship's propeller*)
Volta (*electric battery*)

6

Bunsen (*bunsen burner*)
Cayley (*glider*)
Diesel (*diesel engine*)
Dunlop (*pneumatic tyre*)
Eckert (*phonograph*)
Fuller (*solar battery*)
Fulton (*torpedo*)
Geiger (*geiger counter*)
Hughes (*microphone*)
Judson (*zip-fastener*)
Lenior (*internal-combustion engine*)

McAdam (*tarmac*)
Pincus (*contraceptive pill*)
Sholes (*typewriter*)
Singer (*sewing machine*)
Sperry (*gyro-compass*)
Wallis (*bouncing bomb*)

7

Bardeen (*transistor*)
Braille (*reading system for the blind*)
Daimler (*car engine pioneer*)
Dickson (*terylene*)
Gatling (*rapid-fire gun*)
Glidden (*barbed wire*)
Lumière (*cinema*)
Mauchly (*electronic computer*)
Neilson (*blast furnace*)
Parsons (*turbine steam-ship*)
Pearson (*solar battery*)
Poulsen (*tape recorder*)
Stanley (*electric transformer*)
Whitney (*cotton gin*)
Whittle (*jet engine*)

8

Berliner (*gramophone*)
Bessemer (*steel converter*)
Birdseye (*frozen food process*)
Brattain (*transistor*)
Brewster (*kaleidoscope*)
Bushnell (*submarine*)
Crompton (*spinning mule*)
Daguerre (*daguerrotype photography*)
Foucault (*gyroscope*)
Franklin (*lightning conductor*)
Gillete (*safety razor*)
Goodyear (*vulcanized rubber*)
Harrison (*chronometer*)
Jacquard (*Jacquard loom*)
Mercator (*cylindrical world projection*)
Newcomen (*steam engine*)
Oughtred (*slide rule*)

Plantson (*dental plate*)
Shockley (*transistor*)
Shrapnel (*shrapnel shell*)
Sikorsky (*helicopter*)
Sturgeon (*electro-magnet*)
Waterman (*fountain pen*)
Zeppelin (*rigid airship*)
Zworykin (*standard television*)

9

Arkwright (*spinning frame*)
Baekeland (*bakelite*)
Blanchard (*parachute*)
Burroughs (*commercial adding machine*)
Cockerell (*hovercraft*)
Gutenberg (*printing press*)
Macintosh (*waterproof clothing*)
Poniatoff (*videotape recorder*)
Whinfield (*terylene*)

10

Fahrenheit (*mercury thermometer*)
Farnsworth (*electrical television*)
Hargreaves (*spinning jenny*)
Harrington (*water closet*)
Lanchester (*disc-brake*)
Lippershey (*telescope*)
Torricelli (*barometer*)
Trevithick (*steam carriage*)

11

Baskerville (*advanced printing type*)
Montgolfier (*hot-air balloon*)

2+ words

Fox-Talbot (*calotype photography*)
Mège-mouriés (*margarine*)

IRELAND/IRISH

Famous Irishmen and Irishwomen
Towns and cities in Ireland

FAMOUS IRISHMEN AND IRISHWOMEN

4
Best (George, footballer)
Bono (pop singer)
Shaw (George Bernard, dramatist)

5
Ahern (Bertie, prime minister)
Balfe (Michael, composer)
Behan (Brendan, playwright)
Binche (Maeve, novelist)
Boyle (Robert, scientist)
Burke (Edmund, writer and politician)
Colum (Padraic, poet)
Doyle (Roddy, novelist)
Field (John, composer)
Friel (Brian, playwright)
Joyce (James, novelist)
Keane (Robbie, Roy, footballers)
Moore (Thomas, poet)
Swift (Jonathan, satirist)
Synge (John, dramatist)
Wilde (Oscar, dramatist)
Wogan (Terry, TV personality)
Yeats (William Butler, poet)

6
Cusack (Cyril, Niamh, Sorcha, actors)
Galway (James, musician)
Geldof (Bob, pop singer, activist)
Harris (Richard, actor)

Heaney (Seamus, poet)
Jordan (Eddie, racing driver)
Neeson (Liam, actor)
O'Brien (Flann, novelist)
O'Brien (Edna, novelist)
O'Casey (Sean, dramatist)
O'Leary (Michael, businessman)
Pearse (Patrick, revolutionary)
Stoker (Bram, novelist)

7
Andrews (Eamonn, TV personality)
Beckett (Samuel, dramatist)
McBride (Willie John, rugby player)
McKenna (Siobhan, actress)
Parnell (Charles, politician)

8
Banville (John, novelist)
Berkeley (George, philosopher)
Casement (Roger, revolutionary)
Collins (Michael, statesman)
Congreve (William, dramatist)
Guinness (Arthur, brewer)
McGuigan (Barry, boxer)
Milligan (Spike, humorist)
Morrison (Van, singer, songwriter)
O'Connell (Daniel, politician)
Sheridan (Richard Brinsley, dramatist)

9
Goldsmith (Oliver, writer)
McCormack (John,

singer)
O'Flaherty (Liam, novelist)
Robinson (Mary, president)

10
Harrington (Padraig, golfer)

2+ words
Brian Boru (king)
De Burg (Chris, pop singer)
De Valera (Eamonn, president)

TOWNS AND CITIES IN IRELAND
(NI = Northern Ireland)

4
Bray
Cobh
Cork

5
Balla
Boyle
Derry (NI)
Doagh (NI)
Ennis
Glynn (NI)
Keady (NI)
Knock
Larne (NI)
Newry (NI)
Omagh (NI)
Sligo
Toome (NI)

6
Antrim (NI)
Arklow
Augher (NI)
Bangor (NI)
Bantry
Carlow

Cashel
Dublin
Galway
Lurgan (NI)

7
Athlone
Belfast
Blarney
Caledon
Carrick (NI)
Clonmel
Dundalk
Dundrum (NI)
Dunmore (NI)
Kildare
Lisburn (NI)
Wexford
Youghal

8
Clontarf
Drogheda
Dungiven (NI)
Kilkenny
Limerick

Listowel
Maynouth
Portrush (NI)
Rathdrum
Strabane (NI)

9
Ballymena (NI)
Banbridge (NI)
Bushmills (NI)
Coleraine (NI)
Dungannon (NI)
Killarney
Portadown (NI)
Roscommon
Rostrevor (NI)
Tipperary
Tobermore (NI)
Waterford

10
Ballyclare (NI)
Ballymoney (NI)
Castlederg (NI)
Glengariff
Shillelagh

Strangford (NI)
Tanderagee (NI)

11
Ballycastle (NI)
Ballygawley (NI)
Ballymurphy
Carrickmore (NI)
Crossmaglen (NI)
Downpatrick (NI)
Enniskillen (NI)
Londonderry (NI)
Portglenone (NI)
Randalstown (NI)
Castlewellan (NI)

12
Hillsborough (NI)
Inishtrahull (NI)
Stewartstown (NI)

13
Brookborough (NI)
Carrickfergus (NI)

ISLANDS

An island
Islands of the British Isles
Islands of Greece
Islands of the world

AN ISLAND

3
ait

4
eyot
inch
isle

5
atoll
islet

6
refuge

ISLANDS OF THE BRITISH ISLES
Not true islands

3
Hoy
Man
Rat
Rum

4
Aran
Bere
Bute
Eigg
Herm
High
Iona
Jura
Muck
Mull
Rhum
Sark
Skye
Tory
Uist

5
Annet
Arran
Barra
Barry
Caldy
Canna
Clare
Clear
Eagle
Ensay
Foula
Islay
Lewis
Lundy
Ronay
Tiree
Wight

6
Achill
Canvey
Dursey
Fetlar
Harris
Jersey
Lambay
Mersea
Oldany
Potton
Puffin
Raasay
Ramsey
Rousay
Sanday
Scarba
Skomer
Staffa
Stroma
Tresco
Walney

7
Bardsey
Cramond

Eriskay
Gometra
Hayling
Lismore
Orkneys
Oronsay
Portsea
Rathlin
Rockall
Sheppey
Thorney
Westray
Whalsey

8
Alderney
Anglesey
Brownsea
Colonsay
Foulness
Gruinard
Guernsey
Hebrides
Mainland
Mingulat
Portland
Scillies
Skokholm
Stronsay
Valentia
Vatersay
Wallasea

9
Arranmore
Benbecula
Havengore
Inchkeith
Inishmaan
Inishmore
Inishturk
Innisfree
Runnymede
Shetlands

10
Inishbofin
Inishshark

11
Lindisfarne

2+ words
Calf of Man
Fair Isle
Flat Holm
Holy Island
North Uist
South Uist
Steep Holm
St Kilda
Isle of Dogs*
Isle of Ely*
Isle of Purbeck*
Isle of Thanet*

ISLANDS OF GREECE

3
Cos
Zea

4
Ceos
Idra
Paxo
Scio
Simi
Syra

5
Chios
Corfu
Crete
Delos
Hydra
Leros
Melos
Milos
Naxos
Samos
Skyro
Thera
Zante

6
Aegina

Andros
Calamo
Ischia
Ithaca
Lemnos
Lesbos
Patmos
Rhodes
Skiros

7
Mikonos
Mykonos
Salamis
Serifos

8
Cyclades
Seriphos
Skiathos
Skopelos

9
Negropont
Santorini

10
Cephalonia
Dodecanese
Samothrace

ISLANDS OF THE WORLD

4
Bali
Cebu
Cook
Cuba
Elba
Fiji
Guam
Java
King
Line
Long
Oahu
Wake

5
Banks
Batan
Capri
Cocos
Coney
Devon
Ellis
Farne
Haiti
Ibiza
Kuril
Leyte
Luzon
Malta
Nauru
Nevis
Oland
Ormuz
Palau
Panay
Samoa
Samar
Sunda
Timor
Tonga
Upolu
Whale

6
Azores
Baffin
Barrow
Bikini
Borneo
Cyprus
Devil's
Djerba
Easter
Ellice
Faroes
Flores
Hawaii
Honshu
Hormuz
Kodiak
Kurile
Kyushu

Midway
Penang
Phuket
Quemoy
Robben
Sicily
Staten
Tahiti
Taiwan
Tobago
Tuvalu

7
Andaman
Antigua
Bahamas
Barbuda
Bermuda
Bonaire
Celebes
Chatham
Corsica
Curacao
Formosa
Frisian
Gambier
Gilbert
Gotland
Grenada
Hawaiki
Iceland
Jamaica
Keeling
Leeward
Liberty
Lofoten
Madeira
Majorca
Mariana
Menorca
Minorca
Nicobar
Norfolk
Okinawa
Palmyra
Reunion
Roanoke
Shikoku
Society

Solomon
Sumatra
Vanuatu

8
Alcatraz
Aleutian
Andamans
Anguilla
Antilles
Balearic
Barbados
Bathurst
Canaries
Caroline
Catalina
Dominica
Friendly
Gothland
Hokkaido
Kiribati
Krakatoa
Maldives
Mallorca
Marianas
Marshall
Mindanao
Miquelon
Moluccas
Mustique
Navarino
Pitcairn
Principe
Sakhalin
Sandwich
Sardinia
Tasmania
Tenerife
Trinidad
Windward
Zanzibar

9
Ascension
Christmas
Ellesmere
Falklands
Galapagos
Galveston

Greenland
Kerguelen
Lampedusa
Lanzarote
Manhattan
Marquesas
Mauritius
Melanesia
Nantucket
Polynesia
Rarotonga
Singapore
Stromboli
Vancouver
Walcheren

10
Cephalonia
Guadeloupe
Heligoland
Hispaniola
Madagascar
Martinique
Micronesia
Montserrat
Seychelles

11
Guadalcanal
Spitzbergen

12
Newfoundland
Seringapatam

2+ words
Belle Isle
Gran Canaria
Hong Kong
Key Largo
Iwo Jima
Long Island
New Guinea
Puerto Rico
Sri Lanka
South Georgia
St Helena
St Kitts
St Lucia

JEWELS/ JEWELLERY

Gemstones
Jewellery

GEMSTONES

3
jet

4
jade
onyx
opal
rock
ruby
sard

5
agate
amber
beryl
lapis
pearl
topaz

6
garnet
jasper
quartz
scarab

7
crystal
diamond
jacinth
peridot
smaragd

8
amethyst
baguette
cabochon
diamanté
hyacinth
sapphire
sardonyx

9
carbuncle
cornelian
girandole
marcasite
moonstone
solitaire
turquoise

10
aquamarine
bloodstone
chalcedony
chrysoberyl
chrysolite
rhinestone
serpentine
tourmaline

2+ words
cat's eye
fire-opal
lapis lazuli

JEWELLERY

3
gem
orb
pin

4
band
bead
clip
drop
gaud
ouch
ring
rope
stud
torc

5
aglet
badge
bezel
bijou

bugle
cameo
charm
clasp
crown
tiara

6
aigret
amulet
anklet
armlet
bangle
bauble
brooch
choker
collet
diadem
fibula
gorget
hatpin
locket
signet
tiepin
torque

7
annulet
circlet
chaplet
coronet
earcuff
eardrop
earring
necklet
pendant
regalia
rivière
sleeper
spangle
trinket

8
aigrette
baguette
bracelet
carcanet
claddagh

cufflink
intaglio
necklace
pectoral

9
breastpin
girandole
medallion
paillette

thumbring

10
chatelaine

2+ words
engagement ring
eternity ring
guard-ring

navel ring
navel stud
nose-ring
nose-stud
scarf-pin
slave band
wedding band
wedding ring

JOURNALISM

Journalist
Newspaper
Terms used in journalism

JOURNALIST

2
ed

3
cub
sub

4
hack

6
anchor
critic
editor
journo
writer

8
hackette
reporter
stringer

9
anchorman
columnist
muckraker
newshound
newswoman
subeditor

10
newscaster
newsreader

13
correspondent

2+ words
agony aunt
cub reporter

leader writer
gossip columnist

NEWSPAPER

2
FT

3
rag
Sun
TES
TLS

4
Mail
Post
Star

5
daily
extra
Times

6
Express
Sunday
review
weekly

7
gazette
journal
tabloid

8
giveaway
Guardian
Standard

9
freesheet
Telegraph

10
broadsheet
feuilleton
supplement

TERMS USED IN JOURNALISM

2
ad

3
ads
cub
cut
NUJ
run
rag
set
sub

4
copy
edit
lead
news
page
pull
type

5
daily
libel
paper
press
quote
scoop
sheet
spike
story

6
banner
byline
column
glossy
leader
notice
redtop
report
review
scribe
serial

spiked
splash
spread
weekly

7
article
caption
cartoon
edition
feature
gazette
journal
monthly
subedit
tabloid

8
Berliner
biweekly
coverage

dateline
deadline
headline
magazine
obituary
screamer
streamer

9
crossword
editorial
exclusive
journalese
newspaper
newsprint
newssheet
personals
quarterly
reportage
reporting

10
broadsheet
newsletter
periodical
supplement
syndicated

11
advertising
advertorial
circulation
fortnightly
syndication

2+ words
agony column
City editor
Fleet Street
fourth estate
Grub Street
gutter press
leader writer
sits vac

LAKES

A lake
Lakes of England and Wales
Lakes of the world
Irish loughs
Scottish lochs

A LAKE

4
llyn
loch
mere
pool
tarn

5
broad
lough
oxbow

LAKES OF ENGLAND AND WALES

4
Bala
Wast (Water)

5
Celyn
Ogwen
Rydal (Water)

6
Brenig
Devoke (Water)

7
Cwellyn
Derwent (Water)
Grafham (Water)
Rutland (Water)

8
Coniston (Water)
Crummock (Water)
Grasmere

Virginia (Water)

9
Ennerdale (Water)
Esthwaite (Water)
Llangorse
Thirlmere
Ullswater

10
Buttermere
Hayeswater
Loweswater
Serpentine
Windermere

2+ words
Malharm Tarn
Tal-y-lynn

LAKES OF THE WORLD

3
Tuz (Turkey)
Van (Turkey)

4
Bled (Slovenia)
Chad (Africa)
Como (Italy)
Erie (Canada, US)
Eyre (Australia)
Kivu (Congo, Rwanda)
Mead (US)
Nemi (Italy)
Ohau (New Zealand)
Tana (Ethiopia)
Thun (Switzerland)

5
Garda (Italy)
Gatun (Panama)
Huron (US, Canada)
Kioga (Uganda)
Kyoga (Uganda)
Leman (Switzerland, France)
Nyasa (Africa)

Onega (Russia)
Tahoe (US)
Taupo (New Zealand)

6
Albert (Congo, Uganda)
Averno (Italy)
Baikal (Russia)
Geneva (Switzerland, France)
Kariba (Zambia, Zimbabwe)
Ladoga (Russia)
Lugano (Italy)
Malawi (Africa)
Mobutu (Congo)
Nasser (Egypt)
Oneida (US)
Peipus (Estonia, Russia)
Placid (US)
Puyang (China)
Rudolf (Kenya, Ethiopia)
Saimaa (Finland)
Vanern (Sweden)
Wanaka (New Zealand)
Zurich (Switzerland)

7
Balaton (Hungary)
Bolsena (Italy)
Chapala (Mexico)
Francis (US)
Lucerne (Switzerland)
Oinghai (China)
Ontario (Canada, US)
Quesnel (Canada)
Torrens (Australia)

8
Attersee (Austria)
Bodensee (Germany, Switzerland)
Chiemsee (Germany)
Flathead (US)
Kentucky (US)
Maggiore (Italy)
Manitoba (Canada)
Michigan (US, Canada)

Seminole (US)
Superior (Canada, US)
Tiberias (Israel)
Titicaca (Peru, Bolivia)
Victoria (Uganda,
Kenya, Tanzania)
Wakatipu (New Zealand)
Winnipeg (Canada)

9
Champlain (Canada)
Constance (Germany,
Switzerland)
Maracaibo (Venezuela)
Neuchatel (Switzerland)
Nicaragua (Nicaragua)
Trasimeno (Italy)

10
Ijsselmeer (Netherlands)
Tanganyika (East Africa)

2+ words
Cabora Bassa (Africa)
Great Bear (Canada)
Great Salt (US)
Great Slave (Canada)

IRISH LOUGHS

3
Beg
Dan
Key
Ree

4
Conn
Derg
Hyne
Lene
Mask
Owel

5
Allen
Carra
Foyle

Neagh

6
Corrib
Ennell
Swilly

7
Belfast
Sheelin

SCOTTISH LOCHS

3
Ard
Awe
Dee
Eck
Eil
Ewe
Ken
Lee
Moy
Tay
Urr

4
Alsh
Buie
Doon
Earn
Fyne
Gare
Gilp
Goil
Gorm
Hope
Inch
Long
Lyon
Mhor
More
Ness
Ryan
Shin
Voil

5
Broom
Duich
Etive
Fitty
Garry
Hourn
Leven
Lochy
Loyal
Loyne
Lussa
Maree
Morar
Muick
Naver
Nevis
Orrin
Quien
Shiel
Sween
Treig
Tuath

6
Arkaig
Assynt
Calder
Ericht
Laggan
Linnhe
Lomond
Quoich
Riddon
Sunart
Tummel
Watten

7
Cluanie
Coruisk
Eishort
Eriboll
Fannich
Katrine
Melfort
Mochrum
Rannoch

Snizort
Striven

Torridon
Venachar

10
Mullardoch

8
Faskally
Scridain
Seaforth

9
Kirbister
Ochiltree
Vennachar

11
Glascarnoch

LANGUAGES

Language
Languages of the world
See also **GRAMMAR**

LANGUAGE

5
argot
idiom
lingo

6
jargon
patois
pidgin
speech
tongue

7
dialect

8
parlance

9
discourse

10
vernacular
vocabulary

11
terminology

LANGUAGES OF THE WORLD

2
Wu

3
Ibo
Ido
Kwa
Twi

4
Ainu
Akan
Erse
Igbo
Manx
Norn
Pali
Thai
Tupi
Urdu
Zulu

5
Aleut
Aztec
Bantu
Carib
Czech
Doric
Dutch
Fante
Fanti
Farsi
Greek
Hindi
Iraqi
Irish
Karen
Khmer
Latin
Malay
Maori
Norse
Oriya
Oscan
Saxon
Scots
Shona
Tamil
Tatar
Ugric
Uzbek
Welsh
Xhosa
Yakut

6
Arabic
Basque
Basuto
Berber
Bihari
Breton
Creole
Danish
French
Gaelic
German
Gothic
Gullah
Hebrew
Herero
Ionian
Kalmyk
Ladino
Magyar
Micmac
Mongol
Pahari
Pashto
Polish
Pushtu
Romaic
Romany
Shelta
Slovak
Syriac
Telugu
Tswana
Turkic
Ugrian
Yoruba

7
Amharic
Aramaic
Avestan
Bengali
Burmese
Catalan
Chinese
Chinook
Choctaw
Cornish

English
Finnish
Flemish
Frisian
Guarani
Iranian
Kalmuck
Kurdish
Lallans
Lettish
Maltese
Marathi
Nahuatl
Nynorsk
Persian
Punjabi
Quechua
Russian
Semitic
Sesotho
Slovene
Spanish
Swahili
Swedish

Tagalog
Turkish
Yiddish

8
Albanian
Assamese
Bulgaric
Cherokee
Cushitic
Estonian
Etruscan
Gujarati
Japanese
Mandarin
Nepalese
Romansch
Romanian
Sanskrit
Slavonic

9
Afrikaans
Bulgarian

Cantonese
Castilian
Esperanto
Franglais
Hungarian
Icelandic
Mongolian
Norwegian
Provencal
Sinhalese
Ukrainian

10
Hindustani
Portuguese
Rajasthani
Vietnamese

2+ words
Anglo-Saxon
Serbo-Croat

LAW/LEGAL

A law
Lawyer
Legal
Legal terms
See also **CRIME**

A LAW

3
act

4
code
rule

5
axiom
bylaw
canon
edict
order
tenet

6
decree
dictat
dictum

7
precept
premise
statute
theorem

9
directive
ordinance
principle

10
regulation

LAWYER

2
DA

KC
QC

3
bar

4
silk

5
brief

6
junior
jurist
notary

7
counsel
shyster

8
advocate
attorney
defender
recorder

9
barrister
solicitor

10
magistrate
procurator
prosecutor

LEGAL

4
just

5
legit
licit
right
valid

6
honest
lawful
proper

7
allowed

8
official
rightful

9
allowable

10
authorized (authorised)
legitimate
sanctioned

11
legitimized (legitimised)
permissible

14
constitutional

2+ words
above-board

LEGAL TERMS

3
aka
DPP
fee
rob
sue

4
abet
bail
bars
case
dock
fine
gaol
jail

jury
lien
oath
plea
seal
stay
suit
will
writ

5
alias
alibi
alien
award
bench
brief
cause
chose
clerk
costs
court
guilt
judge
juror
order
penal
plead
police
proof
quash
right
steal
swear
trial
trust
usher
valid

6
action
affirm
appeal
arrest
bailee
bailor
breach
charge

commit
disbar
domain
duress
entail
equity
escrow
estate
fiscal
guilty
Hilary
legacy
malice
master
pardon
parole
police
prison
puisne
remand
repeal
seisin
surety
tenure

7
accused
alimony
assizes
bailiff
bequest
Borstal
capital
caution
circuit
codicil
consent
control
coroner
custody
damages
defence
demesne
divorce
garnish
hearsay
impeach
inquest

justice
lawsuit
licence
neglect
querent
release
reserve
servant
sevice
sheriff
statute
summary
summons
suspect
trustee
verdict
warrant
witness

8
absolute
abstract
chancery
contract
covenant
dominium
estoppel
eviction
evidence
executor
forensic
guardian
indecent
jointure
judgment
judicial
licensee
litigant
majority
mandamus
messuage
mortmain
movables
novation
petition
pleading
preamble
reprieve

sentence
subpoena
tenement
testator
tribunal
unlawful
validity

9
acquittal
ademption
agreement
allotment
annulment
attainder
champerty
committal
copyright
defendant
discharge
dismissal
distraint
endowment
equitable
execution
executory
extenuate
guarantee
guarantor
indemnity
innocence
intestacy
intestate
judiciary
licensing
litigious
mandatory
plaintiff
precatory
precedent
privilege
probation
procedure
refresher
registrar
remainder
remission
restraint

reversion
servitude
statutory
surrender
testament
testimony

10
adjudicate
alienation
assessment
assignment
attachment
attornment
bankruptcy
confession
connivance
conveyance
disclaimer
executrix
forfeiture
fraudulent
immovables
impediment
indictment
injunction
judicature
legitimacy
legitimacy
limitation
litigation
personalty
respondent
revocation
separation
tortfeasor

11
adjudicator
advancement
affiliation
appointment
arbitration
arrangement
association
attestation
composition
deportation

dissolution
disturbance
enforcement
engrossment
extenuating
extradition
foreclosure
hereditament
impeachment
maintenance
prerogative
prescription
proceedings
prosecution
questioning
requisition
restitution
stipendiary

12
adjudication
compensation
constabulary
conveyancing
guardianship
imprisonment
ratification
testamentary

2+ words
co-respondent
cross-examine
cross-examination
de facto
de jure
fee simple
fee tail
good faith
Habeas Corpus
high court
in camera
law lords
legal aid
not guilty
not proven
Old Bailey
sine die
summing-up

LITERATURE/ LITERARY

See also **NOVEL, POEM/POET/ POETRY/ THEATRE**

LITERARY TERMS

3
lay
ode
pun

4
agon
bard
copy
Edda
epic
epos
foot
form
glee
hymn
iamb
play
plot
poem
poet
rime
rune
saga
scan
song

5
blurb
canto
carol
dirge
ditty
drama
elegy
epode
essay
fable
farce

folio
genre
haiku
idyll
Iliad
image
irony
lyric
maxim
metre
motif
novel
poesy
prose
psalm
quote
rhyme
rondo
scald
scene
style
theme
triad
verse

6
Aeneid
alcaic
anthem
ballad
chanty
chorus
climax
comedy
crisis
dactyl
ending
genius
heroic
humour
iambic
iambus
legend
lyrist
memoir
parody
pathos
poetic

poetry
review
rhythm
satire
simile
sketch
sonnet
stanza
symbol

7
anapaest
apology
article
ballade
bucolic
cadence
caesura
chanson
content
context
couplet
eclogue
edition
elegiac
epigram
episode
epistle
epitaph
fantasy
fiction
Georgic
Homeric
idyllic
imagery
journal
lampoon
leonine
lyrical
mimesis
novella
Odyssey
persona
poetics
polemic
prosody
proverb
refrain

Sapphic
skaldic
spondee
strophe
tragedy
trilogy
triplet
trochee
villain
virelay
western

8
allusion
anapaest
antihero
balladry
choliamb
choriamb
clerihew
critique
dialogue
doggerel
dramatic
epigraph
epilogue
euphuism
laureate
libretto
limerick
lyricism
madrigal
metaphor
metrical
pastoral
Pindaric
poetical
prologue
quatrain
rhapsody
rhetoric
romantic

scanning
scansion
scenario
suspense
threnody
thriller
tribrach
trimester
unpoetic
versicle
vignette
whodunit

9
anapaestic
anonymous
anthology
archetype
biography
broadside
burlesque
catharsis
classical
criticism
decastich
dithyramb
flashback
hemistich
hexameter
hyperbole
leitmotiv
phillipic
poetaster
prosodist
roundelay
soliloquy
symbolism
symposium
Virgilian

10
amphibrach

amphimacer
anapaestic
antagonist
antiphonal
bestseller
bowdlerize (bowdlerise)
caricature
choliambic
choriambic
denouement
manuscript
picaresque
plagiarism
plagiarist
tetrameter
unpoetical

11
alexandrine
antistrophe
catastrophe
dithyrambic
hudibrastic
tragicomedy

12
alliteration
alliterative
bibliography
epigrammatic
epithalamium
metaphorical
onomatopoeia
prothalamium

2+ words
avant-garde
blank verse
free verse
nom de plume
pot boiler
terza rima

LONDON

Areas and boroughs of London
Famous places and streets in London
London Underground Lines

AREAS AND BOROUGHS OF LONDON

2
EC

3
Bow
Kew

4
City
Oval
Soho

5
Acton
Brent
Cheam
Penge

6
Balham
Barnes
Barnet
Camden
Ealing
Eltham
Fulham
Hendon
Hoxton
Leyton
Merton
Morden
Newham
Poplar
Putney

7
Aldgate

Archway
Barking
Borough
Brixton
Catford
Chelsea
Clapham
Clapton
Croydon
Dulwich
Edgware
Enfield
Hackney
Holborn
Kilburn
Lambeth
Mayfair
Neasden
Norwood
Peckham
Stepney
Tooting
Wembley

8
Barbican
Charlton
Chiswick
Deptford
Edmonton
Finchley
Finsbury
Haringey
Highbury
Highgate
Holloway
Hounslow
Lewisham
Moorgate
Richmond
Southall
Woolwich

9
Battersea
Bayswater
Belgravia
Brentford

Docklands
Fitzrovia
Greenwich
Hampstead
Islington
Plumstead
Southwark
Stockwell
Stratford
Streatham
Tottenham
Wimbledon

10
Bermondsey
Blackheath
Bloomsbury
Camberwell
Earlsfield
Kennington
Kensington
Marylebone
Paddington
Shoreditch
Twickenham
Wandsworth

11
Clerkenwell
Cricklewood
Hammersmith
Leytonstone
Southfields
Walthamstow
Westminster
Whitechapel

13
Knightsbridge

2+ words
Bethnal Green
Canary Wharf
Canning Town
Chalk Farm
Covent Garden
Crouch End
Crystal Palace

Earl's Court
East End
East Ham
Golders Green
Herne Hill
Holland Park
King's Cross
Maida Vale
Manor Park
Marble Arch
Muswell Hill
Notting Hill
Palmer's Green
Shepherd's Bush
St John's Wood
Stoke Newington
Swiss Cottage
Threadneedle Street
Tower Hamlets
West End
West Ham
Wood Green

FAMOUS PLACES AND STREETS IN LONDON

4
Bank
Mall (the)

5
Tower (of London)

6
Strand (the)

7
Aldwych

8
Monument (the)
Victoria (station)
Waterloo (station)

9
Cheapside
Guildhall
Haymarket
Whitehall

10
Embankment (the)
Piccadilly
Smithfield

12
Billingsgate

2+ words
Buckingham Palace
Charing Cross (Station)
Covent Garden
Downing Street
Elephant and Castle
Fleet Street
Green Park
Hampstead Heath
Hyde Park
Law Courts (the)
London Eye (the)
Mansion House
Mile End Road

Old Bailey (the)
Old Kent Road
Oxford Street
Pall Mall
Petticoat Lane
Portobello Road
Primrose Hill
Regent's Street
Sloane Square
South Bank
St James's Park
St Pancras
St Paul's
Tate Modern
Tower Bridge
Trafalgar Square

LONDON UNDERGROUND LINES

6
Circle

7
Central
Jubilee

8
Bakerloo
District
Northern
Victoria

10
Piccadilly

12
Metropolitan

MACHINES/ MACHINERY

See also **TOOL**

TYPES OF MACHINE

3
car
fan
fax
gin

4
grab
jack
lift
loom
mill
mule
pump
till
tool
unit

5
adder
baler
borer
churn
crane
drier
dryer
hoist
jenny
lathe
lever
mixer
motor
mower
plant
press
punch
robot
telex
video
winch
Xerox®

6
binder
blower
bowser
copier
cutter
device
digger
dredge
dynamo
engine
harrow
jogger
linter
mangle
milker
mincer
packer
peeler
picker
plough
pulper
reaper
scales
seeder
shears
washer
winder

7
automat
balance
capstan
crusher
cyclone
dredger
grinder
ejector
exciter
printer
riveter
spinner
stapler
starter
steamer
tumbler
turbine
wringer

8
aircraft
apparatus
appliance
calender
clockwork
computer
conveyor
elevator
espresso
mechanism
motorbike
pulsator
purifier
recorder
shredder
teletype
vibrator
windmill

9
automaton
bulldozer
dispenser
escalator
excavator
extractor
generator
harvester
headphone
incubator
lawnmower
macerator
motorcycle
photostat
polygraph
projector
radiogram
separator
sigmatron
simulator
telephone
tomograph
totalizer (totaliser)
treadmill

10
calculator

centrifuge
compressor
cyclostyle
Dictaphone®
dishwasher
duplicator
exsiccator
galvanizer (galvaniser)
gramophone
guillotine
mimeograph
passimeter
phonograph
sterilizer (steriliser)
travelator
travolator
typewriter
ventilator

11

comptometer
contraption
contrivance
epidiascope
nickelodeon
pasteurizer (pasteuriser)
paternoster
photocopier

teleprinter
totalizator (totalisator)
weighbridge

13

decompressor

2+ words

beam-engine
block and tackle
cash register
coal-cutter
coffee-mill
concrete mixer
conveyor belt
donkey engine
drop-hammer
dumb-waiter
extractor fan
feed-pump
foot-pump
fruit machine
hand-loom
hand-mill
heat-pump
iron lung
jacquard loom
jig-borer

letter-press
motor-mower
paper feeder
paper-cutter
pile-driver
power-lathe
power-loom
power-press
printing press
pulp-mill
record player
spin-drier
spinning jenny
steam-hammer
stirrup-pump
stone-mill
sugar-mill
tape recorder
tilt-hammer
trip-hammer
tumble-drier
vacuum cleaner
vacuum-pump
video recorder
water-mill
water-wheel
wine-press

MATHEMATICS

Mathematical terms (including terms used in geometry)

2
pi

3
add
arc
cos
log
set
sin
sum
tan

4
area
axes
axis
base
cone
cube
edge
face
line
loci
mean
plus
ring
root
sine
tens
term
unit
zero

5
acute
angle
carry
chord
conic
cosec
cubic

curve
digit
equal
field
focal
focus
graph
group
helix
index
lemma
limit
locus
maths
minus
plane
point
power
probe
proof
radii
range
ratio
slope
solid
table
times
total

6
amount
answer
binary
bisect
braces
centre
circle
conoid
convex
cosine
cuboid
degree
divide
domain
equals
equate
factor
figure

finite
height
matrix
maxima
median
minima
minute
modulo
moment
normal
number
oblate
oblong
obtuse
radial
radian
radius
random
reckon
result
scalar
secant
sector
series
sphere
square
subset
vector
vertex
volume

7
algebra
average
Boolean
cissoid
commute
compute
complex
concave
conical
cycloid
decagon
digital
divisor
ellipse
evolute
hexagon

indices
integer
inverse
mapping
maximum
minimum
modulus
numeral
oblique
octagon
ordinal
percent
polygon
produce
product
problem
pyramid
rhombic
rhombus
scalene
section
segment
subtend
surface
tangent
theorem
trapeze
unitary
unknown

8
abscissa
addition
analysis
binomial
bisector
calculus
cardinal
centroid
circular
constant
converse
cosecant
cuboidal
cylinder
diagonal
diameter
dihedral

distance
dividend
division
elliptic
equation
estimate
friction
frustrum
function
geometer
geometry
gradient
helicoid
heptagon
identity
infinite
infinity
integral
involute
matrices
meridian
momentum
multiply
negative
numeracy
numerate
operator
ordinate
osculate
parabola
parallel
pentagon
positive
quadrant
quantify
quantity
quartile
quotient
rational
rhomboid
rotation
sequence
spheroid
subtract
symmetry
triangle
trigonal
variable

velocity

9
algorithm
amplitude
symptote
calculate
Cartesian
corollary
cotangent
directrix
dodecagon
ellipsoid
expansion
factorize (factorise)
frequency
geometric
hexagonal
hyperbola
identical
imaginary
increment
induction
inflection
intersect
iscosceles
logarithm
Napierian
numerator
numerical
octagonal
parabolic
parameter
perimeter
polygonal
polyhedra
primitive
quadratic
reckoning
rectangle
reduction
remainder
resultant
spherical
trapezium
trapezoid

10
arithmetic
concentric
continuity
coordinate
decahedron
derivative
dimensions
epicycloids
equivalent
expression
hemisphere
heptagonal
hyperbolic
hypotenuse
hypothesis
irrational
kinematics
multiplier
octahedron
orthogonal
osculation
paraboloid
pentagonal
percentage
polyhedral
polyhedron
polymomial
proportion
regression
semicircle
statistics
stochastic
tangential

11
approximate
associative
calculation
calculative
coefficient
combination
computation
coordinates
denominator
determinant
eigenvector
enumeration
equilateral
equilibrium
equivalence
exponential
geometrical
hyperboloid
icosahedron
isomorphism
orthocentre
permutation
probability
progression
rectangular
rectilinear
subtraction
symmetrical
tetrahedron
translation

12
acceleration
asymmetrical
differential
dodecahedron
eccentricity
intersection
semicircular
trigonometry

13
approximation
circumference
extrapolation
hemispherical
parallelogram
perpendicular
quadrilateral

14
multiplication

2 words
chi-square
cube root
right angle
right-angled
square root

MEASUREMENT

Area
Capacity
Length
Paper
Time
Weight
Other terms used in
measurement

AREA

3
are

4
acre
rood

5
verst

6
morgen

7
hectare

2 words
square inch
square foot
square metre
square mile

CAPACITY

2
cc

3
tot
tun

4
butt
dram
gill

peck
pint

5
litre
quart
stoup
terce

6
barrel
bushel
firkin
gallon

8
hogshead

9
decalitre
decilitre

10
centilitre
hectolitre
millilitre

2 words
cubic centimetre
cubic foot
cubic inch
cubic metre
cubic yard

LENGTH

2
cm
en
em
ft
km
mm
yd

3
ell
rod

4
foot
inch
mile
nail
pace
pole
yard

5
cable
cubit
chain
metre
perch

6
fathom
league
micron
parsec

7
furlong

9
decametre
decimetre
kilometre

10
centimetre
millimetre

2 words
light year

PAPER

4
bale
copy
demy
post
pott
ream

5
atlas
brief
crown
draft
quire
royal

6
bundle
casing
medium
octavo

7
emperor

8
elephant
foolscap
imperial

9
cartridge
colombier

TIME

2
hr
mo

3
age
day
min
sec

4
hour
week
year

6
decade
minute
second

7
century

10
millennium
nanosecond

WEIGHT

2
lb
oz

3
cwt
ton

4
dram
gram
kilo

5
carat
grain
ounce
pound
stone
tonne

6
drachm
gramme

7
kiloton
megaton
quarter
quintal
scruple

8
kilogram
nanogram

9
milligram

13
hundredweight

OTHER TERMS USED IN MEASUREMENT

3
amp
bar
bel
bit
BTU
erg
kph
lux
mph
nit
ohm
rad

4
bolt
byte
cord
cran
dyne
hand
hank
keel
knot
lakh
line
mole
phon
pica
pipe
pood
reel
rule
sack
size
slug
tape
tare
troy
volt

5
brace
cable
count
crore
curie
cusec
cycle
farad
Fermi
gauge
gauss
gross
henry
hertz
joule
lumen
meter
point
quota
range
ruler
scale
scope
skein
stade
tesla
therm
toise

truss
weber

6
amount
ampere
assess
barrel
calory
degree
denier
extent
kelvin
megohm
metric
newton
pascal
survey

7
calorie
candela
Celsius
coulomb
decibel
Faraday
Gilbert
kilobar
Maxwell

modicum
Oersted
outsize
Röntgen
Siemens

8
angstrom
chaudron
evaluate
kilowatt
quantify
standard

9
calculate
criterion
kilocycle
kilohertz
yardstick

10
barleycorn
Fahrenheit
horsepower

11
avoirdupois

MEDICINE/ MEDICAL

Medical fields
Medical practitioners
Terms used in medicine and surgery
See also **BODY, DISEASE, DRUG, HEALTH**

MEDICAL FIELDS

3
ENT

7
anatomy
mycology
otology
shiatsu
urology

8
cytology
eugenics
nosology
oncology
serology

9
aetiology
andrology
audiology
chiropody
dentistry
histology
necrology
neurology
orthotics
osteology
pathology
pleoptics
radiology
rhinology

10
cardiology

embryology
geriatrics
homeopathy
immunology
iridology
morphology
nephrology
obstetrics
orthoptics
osteopathy
proctology
psychology
semeiology
teratology

11
acupressure
acupuncture
anaesthesia
dermatology
gerontology
gynaecology
haematology
laryngology
logopaedics
paediatrics
radiography
reflexology
stomatology

12
aromatherapy
chiropractic
cytogenetics
epidemiology
orthopaedics
pharmacology
radiobiology
therapeutics
traumatology

13
balneotherapy
endocrinology
ophthalmology
psychometrics
psychotherapy

MEDICAL PRACTITIONERS

2
Dr
GP
MO

3
doc
vet

5
leech
medic
nurse
quack

6
doctor
healer
matron
medico
shaman
sister

7
dentist
masseur
oculist
surgeon

8
alienist
masseuse
optician
sawbones

9
clinician
dietician
herbalist
homeopath
hypnotist
osteopath
otologist
paramedic
physician

registrar
therapist
urologist

10
bonesetter
consultant
eugenicist
homoeopath
natruropath
nosologist
pedicurist
oncologist
pedicurist
pharmacist

11
aetiologist
chiropodist
histologist
neurologist
orthopedist
osteologist
pathologist
radiologist
rhinologist

12
anaesthetist
cardiologist
chiropractor
craniologist
embryologist
geriatrician
immunologist
neurosurgeon
nutritionist
obstetrician
psychiatrist
psychologist
radiographer

13
dermatologist
diagnostician
gerontologist
gynaecologist
paediatrician

reflexologist

2 words
district nurse
practice manager
staff nurse

***TERMS USED IN
MEDICINE AND SURGERY***

2
op

3
jab

4
cast
dose
drip
lint
pill
scan
shot
swab
tent
ward

5
bolus
clamp
enema
gauze
graft
lance
nurse
probe
sling
tonic

6
balsam
bedpan
clinic
elixir
excise
iatric
induce

lancet
matron
physic
potion
powder
premed
remedy
sedate
sister
splint
suture
tampon
trauma
trepan

7
bandage
bedbath
capsule
cardiac
dialyse
draught
keyhole
linctus
lozenge
mixture
operate
perfuse
pessary
placebo
plaster
scalpel
section
surgery
vaccine

8
amputate
clinical
compress
curative
diagnose
dialysis
dressing
immunity
incision
infusion
lobotomy

pastille
pedicure
poultice
practice
syndrome
tenotomy

9
ambulance
Caesarean
cataplasm
colostomy
diagnosis
injection
inoculate
maternity
operation
transfuse

traumatic
treatment
vasectomy

10
amputation
laparotomy
mastectomy
medicament
medication
palliative
phlebotomy
prosthesis
tourniquet
transplant
ultrasound

11
fingerstall
inoculation
suppository
transfusion
venesection

12
anaesthetize
(anaesthetise)
appendectomy
auscultation
hysterectomy

2+ words
intensive care unit
keyhole surgery
out-patient
X-ray

METALS

Metals
Metal alloys

METALS

3
tin (Sn)

4
gold (Au)
iron (Fe)
lead (Pb)
zinc (Zn)

6
barium (Ba)
chrome (Cr)
cobalt (Co)
copper(Cu)
nickel (Ni)
osmium (Os)
radium (Ra)
silver (Ag)
sodium (Na)

7
argento (Ag)
bismuth (Bi)
cadmium (Cd)
calcium (Ca)

gallium (Ga)
iridium (Ir)
lithium (Li)
mercury (Hg)
thorium (th)
uranium (U)
wolfram (W)

8
antimony (Sb)
chromium (Cr)
platinum (Pt)
thallium (Tl)
titanium (Ti)
tungsten (W)
vanadium (V)

9
aluminium (Al)
beryllium (Al)
magnesium (Mg)
manganese (Mn)
palladium (Pd)
potassium (K)
strontium (Sr)
ytterbium (Yb)
zirconium(Zr)

10
molybdenum (Mo)
phosphorus (P)

METAL ALLOYS

5
brass
steel

6
babbit
bronze
ormolu
pewter
tombac

8
gunmetal

9
britannia
pinchbeck

11
cupronickel

MILITARY

Armour
A soldier
Famous admirals
Famous generals
Fortifications
Military ranks
Military terms

ARMOUR

4
helm (head)
jack (upper body)
mail (body)

5
armet (head)
visor (face)

6
beaver (face)
casque (head)
cuisse (thigh)
gorget (neck)
greave (leg)
gusset
helmet
morian (head)
morion (head)
shield
tasset (hip)

7
baldric
buckler (shield)
cuirass (front)
hauberk (body)
sabaton (foot)

8
baldrick
corselet (body)
gauntlet (hand)
pauldron (shoulder)
vambrace (forearm)

9
habergeon (body)

11
breastplate

A SOLDIER

2
GI
OR

3
NCO
vet

5
brave
cadet
guard
sepoy
tommy

6
askari
cornet
gunner
gurkha
hussar
lancer
marine
ranker
sapper
yeoman

7
chasseur
chindit
Cossack
dragoon
fighter
hoplite
officer
private
redcoat
regular
squaddy
terrier

trooper
veteran
warrior

8
commando
doughboy
engineer
fusilier
guerrilla
ironside
rifleman
squaddie

9
centurion
guardsman
irregular
janissary
legionary
mercenary
minuteman
musketeer
reservist
signaller

10
bombardier
cuirassier
militiaman
serviceman

11
infantryman
legionnaire
paratrooper
Territorial

12
servicewoman

FAMOUS ADMIRALS

4
Byng (*British*)
Howe (*British*)
Spee (*German*)
Togo (*Japanese*)

5
Anson (*British*)
Blake (*British*)
Hawke (*British*)
Rooke (*British*)
Tromp (*Dutch*)

5
Beatty (*British*)
Benbow (*British*)
Dönitz (*German*)
Fisher (*British*)
Nelson (*British*)
Nimitz (*US*)
Rodney (*British*)
Ruyter (*Dutch*)
Scheer (*German*)

6
Canaris (*German*)
Decatur (*US*)
Doenitz (*German*)
Tirpitz (*German*)

8
Boscawen (*British*)
Jellicoe (*British*)
Yamamoto (*Japanese*)

10
Villeneuve (*French*)

11
Collingwood (*British*)

2 words
St Vincent (*British*)
van Tromp (*Dutch*)

FAMOUS GENERALS

3
Lee (Robert E., *US*)
Ney (Marshal *French*)

4
Foch (Marshal, *French*)
Haig (*British*)

Slim (*British*)

5
Dayan (Moshe, *Israel*)
Grant (Ulysses S., *US*)
Wolfe (*British*)

6
Custer (*US*)
Gordon (*British*)
Joffre (*French*)
Patton (*US*)
Rommel (*German*)
Zhukov (Marshal, *USSR*)

7
Allenby (*British*)
Blücher (*German*)
Jackson (Stonewall, *US*)
Roberts (Lord, *British*)
Sherman (*US*)

8
Burnside (*US*)
Montcalm (*French*)
Pershing (*US*)
Wolseley (*British*)

9
Bonaparte (*French*)
Lafayette (*French*)
Kitchener (*British*)
Macarthur (*US*)

10
Clausewitz (*German*)
Eisenhower (*US*)
Hindenburg (*German*)
Kesselring (*German*)
Ludendorff (*German*)
Montgomery (*British*)
Wellington (Duke of, *British*)

11
Marlborough (Duke of, *British*)

2 words
de Gaulle (*French*)

FORTIFICATIONS

3
dun
sap

4
berm
dike
dyke
fort
keep
moat
wall

5
fosse
motte
redan
scarp
talus

6
abatis
bailey
donjon
escarp
gabion
glacis
merlon
trench
turret
vallum

7
barrier
bastion
bulwark
citadel
curtain
flanker
foxhole
mirador
outwork
parados

parapet
pillbox
rampart
ravelin
redoubt

8
abutment
barbette
barbican
bartisan
casemate
defilade
fortress
loophole
martello
parallel
platform
stockade

9
banquette
barricade
earthwork
embrasure
fortalice
gabionade
pontlevis
revetment

10
battlement
blockhouse
breastwork
drawbridge
epaulement
portcullis
stronghold

11
strongpoint

12
counterscarp

13
machicolation

2 words
cheval-de-frise
martello tower

MILITARY RANKS

BRITISH ARMY
Private
Bombadier
Lance Corporal
Corporal
Sergeant
Colour/Staff Sergeant
Warrant Officer
Second Lieutenant
Lieutenant
Captain
Major
Lieutenant Colonel
Colonel
Brigadier
Major General
Lieutenant general
General
Field Marshal

ROYAL NAVY
Junior Seaman
Ordinary Seaman
Able Seaman
Leading Seaman
Petty Officer
Chief Petty Officer
Warrant Officer
Midshipman
Sublieutenant
Lieutenant
Lieutenant Commander
Commander
Captain
Commodore
Rear Admiral
Vice Admiral
Admiral
Admiral of the Fleet

RAF
Aircraftman

Leading Aircraftman
Senior Aircraftman
Junior Technician
Corporal
Sergeant
Chief Technician
Flight Sergeant
Warrant Officer
Pilot Officer
Flying Officer
Flight Lieutenant
Squadron Leader
Wing Commander
Group Captain
Air Commodore
Air Vice Marshal
Air Marshal
Air Chief Marshal
Marshal of the Royal
Air Force

MILITARY TERMS

2
AB
CO
MP
RE
RN
SS
TA

3
arm
DMZ
dud
gas
gun
HMS
kit
man
NCO
RAF
sap
SAS
USA
USN
USS

van
war

4
ally
arms
army
AWOL
base
camp
duty
file
fire
flag
flak
foot
halt
jeep
kepi
levy
line
loot
MASH
mess
mine
NATO
navy
plan
post
push
raid
rake
rank
rear
rout
shot
sink
take
tank
taps
unit
USAF
wing
yomp
zero
zone

5
abort
alert
armed
baton
beret
blast
blitz
booty
busby
corps
cover
craft
demob
depot
ditch
draft
drill
enemy
enrol
equip
feint
field
fight
flank
flare
fleet
foray
front
group
guard
harry
Jerry
jihad
khaki
leave
lines
march
medal
melee
mufti
naval
order
parry
peace
power
prime
radar

rally
range
ranks
recce
repel
rifle
round
sally
salvo
scale
scout
seize
shako
shell
shoot
siege
snipe
sonar
squad
staff
stand
storm
strap
troop
truce
wound

6
action
ambush
armada
armour
attack
bailey
banner
battle
billet
breech
bunker
castle
charge
cohort
colour
column
combat
convoy
cordon
curfew

decamp	signal	conquer
defeat	sniper	counter
defend	sortie	courage
deploy	spoils	cruiser
desert	square	crusade
detach	stores	debouch
detail	strafe	defence
disarm	strike	degrade
dugout	stripe	destroy
engage	supply	détente
enlist	target	disband
ensign	tattoo	dismiss
escape	thrust	dungeon
escarp	treaty	echelon
escort	trench	epaulet
firing	valour	evacuee
flight	victor	fallout
forces	volley	fanfare
guards		fatigue
helmet	**7**	fighter
invade	advance	flanker
invest	airdrop	fortify
kitbag	airlift	forward
legion	archery	foxhole
maquis	armoury	frigate
marine	arsenal	gunboat
marker	assault	gunfire
mining	baldric	gunnery
muster	baggage	gunship
mutiny	barrage	gunshot
occupy	battery	holster
parade	besiege	hostage
parley	bivouac	hostile
parole	bombard	invader
patrol	bombing	jankers
puttee	bomblet	lookout
raider	brigade	martial
ransom	bulwark	megaton
recoil	canteen	militia
redcap	cashier	missing
relief	cavalry	mission
report	charger	neutral
resist	chevron	nuclear
retake	citadel	outpost
retire	colours	parapet
review	command	pennant
salute	company	phalanx
sensor	conchie	pillbox

platoon
quarter
rampart
rations
redoubt
refugee
regular
repulse
reserve
retreat
reverse
salient
sandbag
section
service
sinking
sniping
tactics
theatre
unarmed
uniform
valiant
warfare
warlord
warpath
wounded

8
advanced
airborne
alliance
armament
armoured
attacker
baldrick
barracks
bearskin
blockade
campaign
casualty
chivalry
civilian
conflict
conquest
decimate
defender
despatch
detonate

dispatch
division
dogfight
drumfire
enfilade
entrench
escalate
evacuate
fighting
flagpole
flotilla
fortress
furlough
garrison
infantry
invasion
janizary
jingoism
kamikaze
knapsack
massacre
mobilize (mobilise)
Mulberry
musketry
mutineer
mutinous
ordnance
outflank
overkill
pacifist
palisade
paradrop
partisan
password
prisoner
quarters
quisling
regiment
reprisal
reveille
ricochet
sabotage
saboteur
scramble
security
shelling
shooting
skirmish

squadron
standard
stockade
straddle
strafing
strategy
supplies
support
surround
tactical
training
traverse
turncoat
warhorse
weaponry
yeomanry

9
aggressor
armistice
artillery
assailant
attrition
ballistic
banderole
bandolier
barricade
battalion
beachhead
beleaguer
bloodshed
bombproof
bombshell
bombsight
cannonade
ceasefire
colonelcy
combatant
combative
conqueror
conscript
crossfire
defensive
desertion
discharge
earthwork
encounter
epaulette

equipment
espionage
firepower
fortified
fusillade
gallantry
guardroom
guerrilla
incursion
insurgent
invalided
irregular
janissary
legionary
lifeguard
manoeuvre
mercenary
minefield
objective
offensive
onslaught
operation
packdrill
parachute
patriotic
pressgang
rearguard
rebellion
reconquer
reinforce
semaphore
shellfire
strategic
surrender
terrorism
terrorist
trainband
troopship
uniformed
unopposed

10
amphibious
annihilate
ballistics
blitzkrieg
blockhouse
breastwork

bridgehead
camouflage
campaigner
cantonment
capitulate
chauvinism
checkpoint
commandeer
commission
defensible
demobilize
deployment
despatches
detachment
divisional
encampment
engagement
enlistment
escalation
evacuation
glasshouse
guardhouse
heliograph
inspection
insurgency
jingoistic
manoeuvres
militiaman
militarism
occupation
propaganda
recruiting
regimental
rendezvous
resistance
stronghold
superpower
surrounded
victorious
watchtower

11
battledress
battlefield
battlegroup
bombardment
bulletproof
collaborate

countermine
defenceless
disarmament
hostilities
impregnable
peacekeeper
rangefinder
reconnoitre
recruitment
requisition
searchlight
smokescreen
underground

12
battleground
capitulation
collaborator
commissariat
commissioned
conscription
decommission
headquarters
militaristic
mobilization
(mobilisation)
outmanoeuvre
paramilitary
peacekeeping
surveillance

2+ words
ack-ack
active service
advance guard
air raid
air raid shelter
at the double
barbed wire
battle line
body bag
body count
bomb bay
bomb shelter
bomb squad
civil war
cold war
court-martial

dog tag
draft dodger
fire power
firing squad
forage cap
forced march
friendly fire
gas mask
germ warfare
gun carriage
gun turret
hand-to-hand
home front
last post
mark time
martello tower
no man's land

non-combatant
over the top
peace treaty
point blank
present arms
prison camp
red ensign
rifle range
roll call
route march
sentry box
sentry duty
sentry-go
shell shock
shell-shocked
shoulder arms

slit trench
slope arms
stand guard
task force
total war
under fire
under siege
war crime
war criminal
war cry
war dance
war grave
war memorial
white ensign
white flag
world war

MOUNTAINS

Mountains
Ranges of mountains and hills
See also **Scotland**

MOUNTAINS

3
Aso (Japan)
Ida (Turkey)

4
Cook (New Zealand)
Dore (France)
Ebal (Israel, Palestine)
Etna (Sicily)
Fuji (Japan)
Jaya (Indonesia)
Joma (Norway)
Meru (Tanzania)
Ossa (Greece)
Rigi (Switzerland)
Roan (USA)
Rosa (Italy)
Viso (Italy)

5
Adams (USA)
Athos (Greece)
Baker (USA)
Binga (Mozambique)
Blanc (France)
Cenis (Alps)
Cinto (Corsica)
Corno (Italy)
Dendi (Ethiopia)
Djaja (Indonesia)
Eiger (Switzerland)
Elgon (Uganda, Kenya)
Hekla (Iceland)
Huila (Colombia)
Kamet (India)
Kenya (Kenya)
Lenin (Russia)
Logan (Canada)
Lyell (USA)

Maipu (Argentina)
Marcy (USA)
Misti (USA)
Mönch (Switzerland)
Pelee (Martinique)
Perdu (France)
Sinai (Egypt)
Table (South Africa)
Tabor (Israel)
Vinta (USA)

6
Ararat (Turkey)
Bogong (Australia)
Carmel (Israel)
Duarte (Dominican Republic)
Egmont (New Zealand)
Elbert (USA)
Elbrus (Georgia)
Erebus (Antarctica)
Hayden (USA)
Hermon (Syria, Lebanon)
Hotaka (Japan)
Kailas (Tibet)
Kazbek (Georgia)
Lelija (Bosnia)
Makalu (Nepal, Tibet)
Musala (Bulgaria)
Muztag (China)
Ortles (Italy)
Pissis (Argentina)
Powell (USA)
Rungwe (Tanzania)
Sajama (Bolivia)
Sangay (Ecuador)
Tasman (New Zealand)
Tolima (Colombia)
Wilson (USA)
Yeguas (USA)
Zirkel (USA)

7
Belukha (Russia)
Bernina (Switzerland)
Bolivar (Colombia)
Brocken (Germany)
Darling (Australia)

Everest (Nepal)
Foraker (USA)
Harvard (USA)
Hoffman (USA)
Illampu (Bolivia)
Jezerce (Croatia)
Kailash (Tibet)
Kerinci (Indonesia)
Lookout (USA)
Markham (USA)
Ohakune (New Zealand)
Olympus (Greece)
Palomar (USA)
Pelvoux (France)
Peteroa (Chile)
Pilatus (Switzerland)
Pollino (Italy)
Rainier (USA)
Rhodope (Turkey)
Roraima (S. America)
Ruahine (New Zealand)
Sanford (USA)
Simplon (Switzerland)
Skiddaw (England)
Snowdon (Wales)
Thabana (Lesotho)
Toubkal (Morocco)
Triglav (Slovenia)
Whitney (USA)

8
Columbia (SA)
Cotopaxi (Ecuador)
Demavend (Iran)
Durmitor (Montenegro)
Fujiyama (Japan)
Hymettus (Greece)
Illimani (Bolivia)
Jungfrau (Switzerland)
Kinabalu (Malaysia)
Klinovec (Czech Rep.)
Krakatoa (Indonesia)
McKinley (USA)
Mitchell (USA)
Mulhacén (Spain)
Murallón (Argentina)
Olivares (Chile)
Rushmore (USA)

Sarameti (Burma)
Smólikas (Greece)
Snaefell (Isle of Man)
Snöhetta (Norway)
Sokhondo (Russia)
Tarawera (New Zealand)
Vesuvius (Italy)
Victoria (Canada, Hong Kong)
Wrangell (USA)

9
Aconcagua (Argentina)
Annapurna (Nepal)
Breithorn (Switzerland)
Communism (Tajikistan)
Dachstein (Austria)
Helvellyn (England)
Huascarán (Peru)
Jotunheim (Norway)
Karisimbe (Rwanda)
Kosciusko (Australia)
Lafayette (USA)
Maladetta (Spain)
Marmolada (Italy)
Muztagata (China)
Parnassus (Greece)
Pietrosul (Romania)
Pinlimmon (Wales)
Rakaposhi (Pakistan)
Stromboli (Italy)
Tocorpuri (Chile)
Tongariro (New Zealand)
Tupungato (Chile)
Zugspitze (Germany)

10
Chimborazo (Ecuador)
Dhaulagiri (Nepal)
Diablerets (Switzerland)
Kebnekaise (Sweden)
Matterhorn (Switzerland, Italy)
Mercedario (Argentina)
Washington (USA)
Wetterhorn (Switzerland)
Wildspitze (Austria)

11
Assiniboine (Canada)
Descapezado (Chile)
Drachenfels (Germany)
Fairweather (Canada)
Hochstetter (New Zealand)
Jotunheimen (Norway)
Kilimanjaro (Tanzania)
Kirkpatrick (Antarctica)
Loolmalasin (Tanzania)
Schreckhorn (Switzerland)
Vatnajokull (Iceland)

12
Citlaltepetl (Mexico)
Galdhöpiggen (Norway)
Llullaillaco (Chile)
Popocatepetl (Mexico)
Tinguiririca (Chile)

13
Grossglockner (Austria)
Kangchenjunga (Nepal)

2+ words
Adam's Peak (Sri Lanka)
Anai Mudi (India)
Cader Idris (Wales)
Champagne Castle (South Africa)
Dent du Midi (France)
Giant's Castle (South Africa)
Godwin Austen (Nepal)
Gran Paradiso (Italy)
Gran Sasso (Italy)
Grand Teton (USA)
Grassy Knob (USA)
Mauna Kea (New Zealand)
Mont Aux Sources (Lesotho)
Mont Blanc (France)
Mont Cenis (France)
Mont Dore (France)
Mont Perdu (France)

Monte Cinto (Corsica)
Monte Corno (Italy)
Monte Pollino (Italy)
Monte Rosa (Italy)
Monte Viso (Italy)
Mount of Olives (Israel)
Nanda Devi (India)
Nanga Parbat (Pakistan)
Pic du Midi (France)
Pike's Peak (USA)
Ras Dashan (Ethiopia)
Robson Peak (Canada)
Spruce Knob (USA)
St Elias (Greece)
St Helens (USA)
Sugar Loaf (Brazil)
Table Mountain (South Africa)
Tabun Bogdo (Asia)
Vatna Jökull (Iceland)
Wheeler Peak (USA)

RANGES OF MOUNTAINS AND HILLS

4
Alps (Europe)
Blue (Mts, Australia)
Harz (Mts, Germany)
Jura (France)
Naga (Hills, India)

5
Altai (Mts, Asia)
Andes (South America)
Asahi (Range, Japan)
Atlas (Mts, Algeria, Morocco)
Black (Mts, Wales)
Downs (England)
Ghats (India)
Ochil (Hills, Scotland)
Sayan (Mts, Russia)
Tatra (Mts, Europe)
Urals (Russia)
Wolds (England)

6
Balkan (Mts, Europe)
Lennox (Hills, Scotland)
Mendip (Hills, England)
Ochils (Scotland)
Pindus (Mts, Greece)
Rocky (Mts, USA)
Tatras (Europe)
Taunus (Germany)
Taurus (Mts, Turkey)
Vosges (France)
Zagros (Mts, Iran)

7
Ahaggar (Mts, Algeria)
Balkans (Europe)
Cascade (Mts, N. America)
Cheviot (Hills, England)
Cuillin (Hills, Scotland)
Malvern (Hills, England)
Mendips (England)
Nilgiri (Hills, India)
Pennine (Hills, Chain, England)
Pentland (Hills, Scotland)
Preseli (Hills, Wales)
Rockies (USA)
Sierras (USA)
Wicklow (Mts, Ireland)

8
Apennine (Mts, Italy)
Ardennes (Hills, Belgium, France)
Cambrian (Mts, Wales)

Cascades (N. America)
Catskill (Mts, USA)
Caucasus (Mts, Georgia, Armenia)
Cheviots (England)
Chiltern (Hills,England)
Cotswold (Hills, England)
Cuillins (Scotland)
Malverns (England)
Nilgiris (India)
Pennines (England)
Pyrenees (France, Spain)
Quantock (Hills, England)

9
Allegheny (Mts, USA)
Apennines (Italy)
Cairngorm (Mts, Scotland)
Catskills (USA)
Chilterns (England)
Cotswolds (England)
Dolomites (Italy)
Grampians (Scotland)
Hamersley (Range, Australia)
Himalayas (Asia)
Karakoram (Range, Asia)
Quantocks (England)
Yablonovy (Russia)

10
Adirondack (Mts, USA)
Cairngorms (Scotland)
Cantabrian (Mts, Spain)
Carpathian (Mts, Europe)
Erzgebirge (Germany)
Lammermuir (Hills, Scotland)

11
Adirondacks (USA)
Alleghenies (USA)
Appalachian (Mts, USA)
Cantabrians (Spain)
Carpathians (Europe)
Drakensberg (Mts, South Africa)

12
Appalachians (USA)

2+ words
Blue Ridge (Mts, USA)
Hindu Kush (Asia)
Mountains of Mourne (N Ireland)
North Downs (England)
Peak District (England)
Sierra Madre (Mexico)
Sierra Morena (Spain)
Sierra Nevada (Spain, USA)
South Downs (England)
Tien Shan (Asia)

MOVES

Move
Move fast
Move slowly
Move backwards
Move downwards
Move forwards
Move upwards
Movement

MOVE

2
go

3
act
ebb
tug

4
back
dive
draw
flip
flow
haul
hike
hoik
jerk
jolt
pass
pull
push
rise
send
sink
soar
spin
step
stir
sway
tack
toss
turn
yank

5
budge
carry
climb
drift
drive
flick
glide
hitch
impel
lurch
mount
nudge
shake
shift
shove
shunt
slide
start
steer
surge
swing
throw
tweak

6
ascend
convey
depart
gather
jiggle
joggle
plunge
propel
quiver
rotate
return
revert
scroll
shiver
spiral
spread
stream
switch
travel
twitch

7
advance
descend
deviate
flounce
journey
migrate
proceed
regress
retreat
scatter

8
dislodge
dispatch
disperse
displace
mobilize (mobilise)
progress
redeploy
relocate
scramble
transfer

9
fluctuate
freewheel
gravitate
manoeuvre
oscillate
rearrange
transport
transpose

10
transplant

MOVE FAST

3
cut
fly
nip
run
zip

4
belt

bolt
dart
dash
flee
flit
hare
leap
race
rush
scud
skip
tear
whiz
zoom

5
bound
chase
flash
haste
hurry
scoot
scour
scram
shoot
speed
split
spurt
whirl
whisk
whizz

6
bustle
careen
career
hasten
hurtle
hustle
rocket
scurry
sprint
streak

7
scamper
scuttle

10
accelerate

MOVE SLOWLY

3
jog

4
chug
drip
ease
edge
idle
inch
limp
lope
ooze
plod
trog

5
amble
coast
crawl
creep
drift
mince
mooch
mosey
sidle
skulk
sneak
steal

6
hobble
stroll
tiptoe
toddle
totter
trudge

7
dogtrot
saunter
shamble
shuffle

slither
stagger
traipse
trickle
trundle

MOVE BACKWARDS

4
back

6
recede
recoil
retire
return
revert

7
regress
retract
retreat
reverse

8
withdraw

9
backslide
backtrack

10
retrogress

2+ words
do an about turn
do a U turn
pull back
row back

MOVE DOWNWARDS

3
ebb

4
dive
drop

fall
sink

5
crash
slope
slump
stoop

6
abseil
alight
derive
plunge
rappel

7
decline
subside

8
decrease
dismount

9
gravitate

MOVE FORWARDS

4
gain

5
forge

6
charge
proceed
process

7
advance
progress

MOVE UPWARDS

4
lift

rise
shin
soar

5
arise
clear
climb
mount
scale

6
ascend
breast
hurdle
rocket

8
escalate
increase
levitate
scramble
surmount

MOVEMENT

3
nod

4
dive
drop
fall
gait
jerk
jump
leap
rise
rush
step
stir
tide
turn
wave
wink

5
drift

feint
lurch
shake
shift
start
swing
taxis
trend

6
action
ascent
motion
quiver
return
shiver
travel

7
advance
decline
descent
gesture
kinesis
progress
retreat

8
activity
campaign
increase
rotation
transfer

9
manoeuvre
migration

10
escalation
relocation

11
fluctuation

MUSIC/MUSICAL

Musical instruments
Musical notes
Musical terms
Musical terms from Italian
Pieces of music
Famous musicals

MUSICAL INSTRUMENTS

3
sax
uke

4
bell
drum
fife
gong
harp
horn
lute
lyre
Moog®
oboe
pipe
tuba
viol

5
banjo
bones
brass
bugle
cello
flute
gamba
grand
kazoo
organ
piano
pipes
rebec
regal
shawm
sitar
tabor

vibes
viola

6
cornet
cymbal
fiddle
guitar
spinet
spoons
syrinx
violin
zither

7
baryton
bassoon
bombard
celesta
celeste
cembalo
cithara
cittern
clarion
gamelan
maracas
marimba
ocarina
pianola
piccolo
sackbut
saxhorn
serpent
strings
tambour
theorbo
timbrel
timpani
trumpet
ukelele
ukulele
upright
whistle

8
bagpipes
bouzouki
clappers

clarinet
dulcimer
handbell
keyboard
mandolin
melodeon
oliphant
psaltery
recorder
triangle
trombone
virginal
waldhorn
woodwind

9
accordion
alpenhorn
balalaika
castanets
euphonium
flageolet
harmonica
harmonium
krummhorn
saxophone
washboard
xylophone

10
clavichord
concertina
didgeridoo
flügelhorn
fortepiano
ophicleide
percussion
pianoforte
sousaphone
tambourine

11
harpsichord
violoncello

12
glockenspiel

2+ words

aeolian harp
barrel-organ
bass drum
basset horn
cor anglais
double-bass
French horn
grand piano
hurdy-gurdy
jew's-harp
kettle-drum
mouth-organ
nose-flute
post-horn
snare-drum
tam-tam
theatre organ
tom-tom
viola da gamba
wobble-board

MUSICAL NOTES

2
do
fa
la
mi
re
so
te
ti

3
doh
lah
ray
soh

5
breve
minim

6
quaver

8
crotchet

9
semibreve

10
accidental
semiquaver

MUSICAL TERMS

3
bar
bow
cue
hum
key
lay
pop
run
tie

4
alto
band
bass
beat
clef
echo
flat
fret
glee
high
hold
jazz
lilt
mode
mute
note
peal
pean
reed
rest
root
sing
slur
solo

stop
time
toll
tone
tune
vamp

5
baton
bebop
chant
chime
choir
chord
crook
croon
dirge
ditty
drone
duple
fugal
gamut
knell
kyrie
lyric
major
minor
motif
paean
pause
pedal
pitch
resin
rosin
scale
score
shake
sharp
sixth
slide
stave
strad
strum
swell
swing
tempo
tenor
theme

third
thrum
tonic
triad
trill
vocal
yodel

6
accent
atonal
bridge
cantor
catgut
chorus
damper
dulcet
encore
figure
finale
intone
lyrist
melody
monody
octave
phrase
rhythm
serial
timbre
treble
tuning
unison
volume

7
arrange
baroque
cadence
chanter
concert
conduct
descant
discord
harmony
jukebox
karaoke
keynote
maestro

melisma
melodic
natural
offbeat
recital
reprise
skiffle
soloist
soprano
subject
tuneful

8
arranger
baritone
composer
diapason
diatonic
dominant
drumbeat
ensemble
exercise
falsetto
interval
libretto
ligature
mistrel
movement
notation
plectrum
semitone
subtonic
tonality
virtuosi
virtuoso
vocalist

9
accompany
acoustics
atonality
augmented
cacophony
chromatic
conductor
contralto
dissonant
extempore

harmonize (harmonise)
improvise
inversion
leitmotif
melodious
metronome
orchestra
plainsong
polyphony
signature
transpose
variation
voluntary

10
coloratura
diminished
dissonance
embouchure
gramophone
instrument
intonation
modulation
mouthpiece
musicology
orchestral
polyphonic
recitative
suspension
syncopated

11
accompanist
arrangement
composition
discordance
extemporize
(extemporise)
fiddlestick
fingerboard
nickelodeon
orchestrate
polyphonist
progression
syncopation

12
chromaticism

counterpoint
instrumental
musicologist
orchestrator
philharmonic

2 words
signature tune
tuning fork
twelve tone

MUSICAL TERMS FROM ITALIAN

1
f (forte - loudly)
p (piano - softly)

2
ff (fortissimo - very loudly)
fz (sforzando - with sudden emphasis)
mf (mezzo forte – quite loudly)
mp (mezzo piano – quite softly)
pp (pianissimo – very softly)

3
bis (repeat)
piu (more)
rit (ritardando – slowing down)

4
arco (bow)
coda (end piece)
meno (less)

5
assai (very)
dolce (sweetly)
forte (loudly)
largo (slowly)
lento (slowly)
mezzo (moderately)

mosso (rapidly)
piano (quietly)
senza (without)
tacet (is silent)
tutti (all)

6
adagio (slowly)
legato (smoothly)
presto (very fast)
rubato (in flexible tempo)
vivace (briskly)

7
agitato (agitatedly)
allegro (quite fast)
amoroso (lovingly)
andante (quite slowly)
animato (animatedly)
tremolo (with a shake)
vibrato (decorative fluctuation in pitch)

8
arpeggio (split chord)
maestoso (majestically)
ritenuto (held back)
staccato (jerkily)

9
adagietto (slowly)
cantabile (in a singing tone)
crescendo (getting louder)
glissando (sliding run)
obbligato (obligatory accompaniment)
pizzicato (with plucked strings)
sforzando (sf – with sudden emphasis)
sostenuto (sustained)

10
allegretto (quite lively)
diminuendo (getting softer)
fortissimo

(ff – very loudly)
pianissimo (pp – very softly)

11
decrescendo (getting softer)
prestissimo (very fast)
rallentando (slowing down)

2 words
da capo (repeat)
con brio (with spirit)
a capella (unaccompanied singing)

PIECES OF MUSIC

3
air
duo
rag

4
aria
coda
duet
hymn
lied
mass
opus
song
trio

5
blues
canon
carol
dumka
étude
fugue
galop
gigue
march
motet
nonet
octet

opera
polka
rondo
round
suite
waltz

6
anthem
aubade
ballad
bolero
chorus
medley
minuet
septet
sextet
shanty
sonata

7
arietta
ballade
cadenza
cantata
chorale
fanfare
gavotte
lullaby
mazurka
partita
quartet
quintet
scherzo
toccata

8
canticle
cavatina
chaconne
concerto
fantasia
madrigal
nocturne
operetta
oratorio
overture
rhapsody

ricercar
serenade
sonatina
symphony

9
allemande
bagatelle
barcarole
cantilena
capriccio
cassation
impromptu
pastorale
polonaise

2 words
tone poem

FAMOUS MUSICALS

4
Cats
Fame
Gigi
Hair
Mame

5
Annie
Evita
Gypsy
Tommy

6
Grease
Jeeves
Kismet
Oliver
Xanadu

7
Cabaret
Chicago
Camelot
Rosalie
Scrooge

8
Carousel
Godspell
Oklahoma
Showboat

9
Brigadoon
Evergreen

2+ words
A Chorus Line
Annie Get Your Gun
Anything Goes
April In Paris
Blood Brothers
Blue Hawaii
Broadway Melody
Call Me Madam
Carmen Jones
Chu Chin Chow
Daddy Long Legs
Easter Parade
Finian's Rainbow
Flower Drum Song
Flying Down to Rio
Follow The Fleet
GI Blues
Guys And Dolls
Half A Sixpence
Hello Dolly
High Society
Jailhouse Rock
Kiss Me Kate
Lady Be Good
Les Miserables
Love Me Tender
Mamma Mia
Mary Poppins
Me And My Girl
Meet Me In St Louis
My Fair Lady
No No Nanette
Paint Your Wagon
Pal Joey
Phantom of the Opera
Silk Stockings
Singin' In The Rain

South Pacific	The Gay Divorce	The Vagabond King
Summer Holiday	The King And I	The Wiz
Sweet Charity	The Music Man	The Wizard Of Oz
The Boy Friend	The Pajama Game	Top Hat
The Desert Song	The Sound Of Music	Viva Las Vegas

MUSICIANS

A musician
Famous classical musicians
Famous jazz, popular and
rock musicians
See also **COMPOSER,
GROUP, SINGER**

A MUSICIAN

4
alto
bass

5
mezzo
tenor

6
bugler
busker
leader
oboist
player
singer

7
artiste
bassist
cellist
drummer
fiddler
flautist
harpist
jazzman
maestro
pianist
soloist

8
arranger
bandsman
bluesman
composer
flautist
lyricist
minstrel

organist
psalmist
songster
virtuoso
vocalist

9
balladeer
conductor
guitarist
performer
timpanist
trumpeter
violinist

10
bandleader
bandmaster
bassoonist
repetiteur
songwriter
trombonist
troubadour

11
accompanist
saxophonist

12
clarinettist
orchestrator

*FAMOUS CLASSICAL
MUSICIANS*

4
Hess (Myra, pianist)
Lind (Jenny, singer)
Wood (Henry, conductor)

5
Arrau (Claudio, pianist)
Baker (Janet, singer)
Boult (Adrian, conductor)
Brain (Dennis, horn
player)
Bream (Julian, singer)
Church (Charlotte,

singer)
Davis (Colin, conductor)
Evans (Geriant, singer)
Gedda (Nicolai, singer)
Gigli (Beniamino, singer)
Gobbi (Tito, singer)
Jones (Aled, singer)
Lanza (Mario, singer)
Melba (Nellie, singer)
Munch (Charles,
conductor)
Ogden (John, pianist)
Patti (Adelina, singer)
Pears (Peter, singer)
Sharp (Cecil, folk music
collector)
Sills (Beverly, singer)
Solti (George, conductor)
Stern (Isaac, violinist)
Szell (George, conductor)

6
Callas (Maria, singer)
Caruso (Enrico, singer)
Casals (Pablo, cellist)
Cortot (Alfred, pianist)
Curzon (Clifford, pianist)
Galway (James, flautist)
Gilels (Emil, pianist)
Gould (Glenn, pianist)
Groves (Charles,
conductor)
Jochum (Eugen,
conductor)
Maazel (Lorin,
conductor)
Previn (André, pianist,
conductor, composer)
Rattle (Simon, conductor)
Tauber (Richard, singer)
Watson (Russell, singer)

7
Beecham (Thomas,
conductor)
Boccelli (Andrea, singer)
Brendel (Alfred, pianist)
Caballé (Montserrat,

singer)
Domingo (Placido, singer)
Ferrier (Kathleen, singer)
Giulini (Carlo Maria, conductor)
Hammond (Joan, singer)
Jenkins (Catherine, singer)
Karajan (Herbert von, conductor)
Kennedy (Nigel, violinist)
Lehmann (Lotte, singer)
Menuhin (Yehudi, violinist)
Monteux (Pierre, conductor)
Nilsson (Birgit, singer)
Ormandy (Eugene, conductor)
Perlman (Itzhak, violinist)
Richter (Sviatislov, pianist)
Tebaldi (Renate, singer)
Wallace (Ian, singer)

8
Björling (Jussi, singer)
Carreras (José, singer)
Flagstad (Kirsten, singer)
Hoffnung (Gerard, humourist)
Horowitz (Vladimir, pianist)
Isserlis (Stephen, cellist)
Kreisler (Fritz, violinist)
Milstein (Nathan, violinist)
Oistrakh (David, violinist)
Schnabel (Arthur, pianist)

9
Ashkenazy (Vladimir, pianist and conductor)
Barenboim (Daniel, pianist and conductor)
Bernstein (Leonard, conductor)
Brannigan (Owen, singer)

Chaliapin (Feodor, singer)
Klemperer (Otto, conductor)
McCormack (John, singer)
Pavarotti (Luciano, singer)
Stokowski (Leopold, conductor)
Tortelier (Paul, cellist)
Toscanini (Arturo, conductor)

10
Barbirolli (John, conductor)
Rubinstein (Artur, pianist)
Soderstrom (Elizabeth, singer)
Sutherland (Joan, singer)

11
Furtwängler (Wilhelm, conductor)
Schwarzkopf (Elizabeth, singer)

2 words
du Pré (Jacqueline, cellist)
Lloyd Webber (Julian, cellist)
Te Kanawa (Kiri, singer)

FAMOUS JAZZ, POPULAR AND ROCK MUSICIANS

3
Ant (Adam)
Day (Doris)
Lee (Peggy)
Ono (Yoko)
Ray (Johnnie)
Vee (Bobby)

4
Anka (Paul)
Baez (Joan)
Bart (Lionel)

Bilk (Acker)
Bono
Bush (Kate)
Byrd (Charlie)
Cash (Johnny)
Cher
Cole (Nat King)
Como (Perry)
Dion (Celine)
Dury (Ian)
Eddy (Duane)
Fame (Georgie)
Ford (Tennessee Ernie)
Fury (Billy)
Gaye (Marvin)
Getz (Stan)
Idol (Billy)
Ives (Burl)
Joel (Billy)
John (Elton)
Keel (Howard)
Kidd (Johnny)
King (B.B./Carole)
Kitt (Eartha)
Lulu
Lynn (Vera)
Monk (Thelonius)
Piaf (Edith)
Reed (Lou)
Ross (Diana)
Shaw (Artie/Sandie)

5
Adams (Bryan)
Adler (Larry/Lou)
Autry (Gene)
Basie (Count)
Berry (Chuck)
Black (Cilla)
Bolan (Marc)
Boone (Pat)
Bowie (David)
Brown (James)
Clark (Dave/Petula)
Cohen (Leonard)
Darin (Bobby)
Davis (Miles/Sammy)
Dylan (Bob)

Essex (David)
Faith (Adam)
Ferry (Brian)
Harry (Debbie)
Haley (Bill)
Hines (Earl)
Holly (Buddy)
Jarre (Jean-Michel)
Jones (Quincy/Tom)
Laine (Frankie)
Lewis (Huey/Jerry Lee)
Moyet (Alison)
Ocean (Billy)
Paige (Elaine)
Price (Alan)
Proby (P.J.)
Sayer (Leo)
Seger (Bob)
Simon (Carly/Paul)
Smith (Bessy)
Starr (Ringo)
Sting
Tatum (Art)
Tormé (Mel)
Wyman (Bill)
Young (Neil/Paul)
Zappa (Frank)

6

Alpert (Herb)
Atwell (Winifred)
Avalon (Frankie)
Baldry (Long John)
Barber (Chris)
Bassey (Shirley)
Bechet (Sidney)
Berlin (Irving)
Burdon (Eric)
Cocker (Joe)
Cooper (Alice)
Coward (Noel)
Crosby (Bing)
Dekker (Desmond)
Denver (John)
Domino (Fats)
Easton (Sheena)
Fields (Gracie)
Fisher (Eddie)

Formby (George)
Geldof (Bob)
Gentry (Bobby)
Hooker (John Lee)
Jagger (Mick)
Jolson (Al)
Joplin (Janis/Scott)
Kramer (Billy J.)
Lauper (Cindie)
Lennon (John)
Lennox (Annie)
Lerner (Alan Jay)
Marley (Bob)
Martin (Dean/George)
Mathis (Johnny)
Miller (Glenn)
Mingus (Charlie)
Morton (Jelly Roll)
Nelson (Ricky/Willie)
Osmond (Donny)
Parker (Charlie)
Parton (Dolly)
Pitney (Gene)
Porter (Cole)
Prince
Reeves (Jim)
Ritchie (Lionel)
Rogers (Kenny)
Sedaka (Neil)
Seeger (Pete)
Simone (Nina)
Sledge (Percy)
Steele (Tommy)
Stills (Stephen)
Summer (Donna)
Taupin (Bernie)
Trenet (Charles)
Turner (Tina)
Twitty (Conway)
Valens (Ritchie)
Waller (Fats)
Waters (Muddy)
Webber (Andrew Lloyd)
Weller (Paul)
Womack (Bobby)
Wonder (Stevie)

7

Andrews (Julie)
Bennett (Tony)
Brubeck (Dave)
Calvert (Eddy)
Cassidy (David)
Charles (Ray)
Checker (Chubby)
Clapton (Eric)
Clooney (Rosemary)
Cochran (Eddy)
Collins (Judy/Phil)
Diamond (Neil)
Diddley (Bo)
Donegan (Lonnie)
Donovan
Francis (Connie)
Gabriel (Peter)
Garland (Judy)
Guthrie (Woody)
Hendrix (Jimi)
Holiday (Billie)
Houston (Whitney)
Jackson (Janet/Michael)
Madonna
Manilow (Barry)
Mercury (Freddie)
Michael (George)
Minogue (Kylie)
Orbison (Roy)
Perkins (Carl)
Pickett (Wilson)
Presley (Elvis)
Preston (Billy)
Redding (Otis)
Richard (Cliff/Keith)
Robeson (Paul)
Rodgers (Richard)
Shankar (Ravi)
Shannon (Del)
Shapiro (Helen)
Sinatra (Frank)
Stevens (Cat)
Stewart (Rod)
Vaughan (Frankie/Sarah)
Vincent (Gene)
Wakeman (Rick)
Warwick (Dionne)

Wynette (Tammy)

8

Aznavour (Charles)
Bygraves (Max)
Campbell (Glen)
Coltrane (John)
Costello (Elvis)
Flanders (Michael)
Franklin (Aretha)
Hamlisch (Marvin)
Harrison (George)
Iglesias (Julio)
Liberace
Marsalis (Winton)
Minnelli (Liza)
Mitchell (Joni)
Morrison (Van)
Oldfield (Mike)
Osbourne (Ozzy)
Peterson (Oscar)
Rafferty (Gerry)
Ronstadt (Linda)

Sondheim (Stephen)
Vandross (Luther)
Williams (Andy/Robbie)

9

Armstrong (Louis)
Bacharach (Burt)
Belafonte (Harry)
Chevalier (Maurice)
Echobelly
Ellington (Duke)
Faithfull (Marianne)
Garfunkel (Art)
Gillespie (Dizzy)
Grappelli (Stephane)
Leadbelly
Lyttelton (Humphry)
McCartney (Paul)
O'Sullivan (Gilbert)
Reinhardt (Django)
Streisand (Barbara)
Townshend (Pete)

10

Carmichael (Hoagy)
Fitzgerald (Ella)
Washington (Dinah)

11

Armatrading (Joan)
Beiderbecke (Bix)
Hammerstein (Oscar)
Springfield (Dusty)
Springsteen (Bruce)

2 words

Boy George
De Burgh (Chris)
Little Eva
Meat Loaf
Newton-John (Olivia)

MYTH/ MYTHOLOGY

*Greek and Roman
mythology
Mythical beings
The Muses*
See also
GODS/GODDESSES

GREEK AND ROMAN MYTHOLOGY

4
Ajax (hero)
Argo (ship)
Dido (queen)
Echo (nymph)
Leda (beloved of Zeus)
Leto (mother of Apollo
and Artemis)
moly (magic herb)
muse (goddess, inspirer
of artists)
Styx (river of the
underworld)
Troy (city)

5
Argos (city)
Argus (giant with
hundred eyes)
Atlas (giant who
supported the world on
his shoulders)
Attis (beautiful youth)
Circe (enchantress)
Creon (king of Thebes)
Danae (beloved of Zeus)
Doris (nymph)
dryad (wood nymph)
Fates (goddesses ruling
human destiny)
Hades (underworld)
Harpy (monster)
Helen (beautiful wife of
Menelaus abducted to
Troy)

Hydra (serpent killed by
Hercules)
Ilium (Troy)
Ixion (king tortured in
the underworld)
Jason (hero, who found
the golden fleece)
Lethe (river of
forgetfulness in the
underworld)
Medea (witch and
beloved of Jason)
Midas (king of Phrygia
with golden touch)
Minos (king of Crete)
naiad (water nymph)
Niobe (weeping mother)
nymph (female nature
spirit)
oread (mountain nymph)
Orion (hunter)
Paris (Trojan prince who
abducted Helen)
Priam (king of Troy)
Remus (founder of Rome)
satyr (goat-like male
spirit following Dionysus)
sibyl (prophetess)
siren (creature luring
sailors onto the rocks)
Titan (one of family of
early gods)

6
Adonis (beautiful youth)
Aegeus (Athenian king,
father of Theseus)
Aeneas (Trojan prince,
founder of Rome)
amazon (female warrior)
Boreas (north wind)
Castor (one of the
heavenly twins)
Charon (boatman in the
underworld)
Chiron (centaur)
Clotho (one of the Fates)
Daphne (nymph turned

into a laurel tree)
Delphi (sacred site with
oracle)
Europa (beloved of Zeus)
Furies (avenging spirits)
Gorgon (female monster)
Hector (Trojan hero)
Hecuba (queen of Troy)
Icarus (son of Daedalus,
who flew too near the
sun)
Ithaca (island, home of
Odysseus)
maenad (female follower
of Dionysus)
Medusa (gorgon)
Mentor (wise counsellor)
nereid (sea nymph)
oracle (message from the
gods or priest(ess)
transmitting this)
Pollux (heavenly twin)
Psyche (girl loved by
Eros/Cupid)
Pythia (priestess at
Delphi)
Python (monster slain by
Apollo)
Scylla (monster)
Stheno (a gorgon)
Thebes (city)
Thetis (nereid, mother
of Achilles)
Thisbe (lover of Pyramus)
Triton (minor sea god)
Trojan ([person] from
Troy)
Zephyr (west wind)

7
Acheron (river of the
underworld)
Actaeon (youth killed by
his own hounds)
Arachne (expert weaver,
turned into a spider)
Ariadne (Cretan princess
who helped Theseus)

Atropos (one of the Fates)
centaur (creature with body of a horse and chest and head of a man)
Cyclops (one-eyed monster)
Electra (daughter of Agamemnon)
Elysium (heaven)
Jocasta (mother and wife of Oedipus)
Laertes (father of Odysseus)
Oedipus (king of Thebes, fated to kill his father and marry his mother)
Olympus (mountain where the gods lived)
Orestes (son of Agamemnon)
Orpheus (wonderful musician)
Pandora (first woman)
Pegasus (winged horse)
Perseus (hero who killed Medusa and rescued Andromeda)
Proteus (minor god, able to change his shape)
Pyramus (lover of Thisbe)
Romulus (Remus's twin, founder of Rome)
Theseus (hero who killed the Minotaur)
Ulysses (Roman name of Odysseus)

8
Achilles (greatest Greek warrior in the Trojan war)
Cerberus (three-headed dog, guarding the underworld)
Daedalus (great inventor, who escaped from Crete by making wings)
Ganymede (youth taken to Olympus by Zeus)

Heracles (Greek name for Hercules)
Hercules (hero with great strength who performed twelve labours)
Lachesis (one of the Fates)
Maeander (winding river)
Menelaus (Grecian king, husband of Helen of Troy)
Minotaur (bull-headed monster, killed in Crete by Theseus)
Odysseus (hero of the Trojan war, who had an epic journey home)
Penelope (wife of Odysseus)
Phaethon (youth who drove the chariot of the sun)
Sisyphus (king, tortured in the underworld)
Tantalus (king, tortured in the underworld)
Tartarus (hell)
Tiresias (blind prophet who changed sex)

9
Agamemnon (king, leader of the Greeks in the Trojan War)
Andromeda (princess saved from a monster by Perseus)
Cassandra (Trojan princess, who forecast disaster but was not believed)
Charybdis (whirlpool, near Sicily)
Iphigenia (daughter of Agamemnon, sacrificed at the start of the Trojan War)
Mnemosyne (minor

goddess, mother of the muses)
Narcissus (beautiful youth, turned into a flower)
Parnassus (mountain home of the muses)
Pygmalion (king who fell in love with a statue, which was brought to life)

10
Persephone (daughter of Demeter, taken to be queen of the underworld)
Polyphemus (Cyclops who imprisoned Odysseus)
Prometheus (stole fire from the gods and gave it to humans)
Proserpina (Roman name of Persephone)

MYTHICAL BEINGS

3
elf
fay
imp
lar
orc
roc

4
bogy
boyg
faun
jinn
ogre
peri
pixy
puck
yeti

5
bogle
demon

djinn
drake
dryad
dwarf
fairy
genie
ghost
ghoul
giant
gnome
golem
harpy
jinni
jotun
lamia
naiad
nymph
oread
pisky
pixie
satyr
shade
siren
snark
spook
sylph
troll
zombie

6
boojum
bunyip
daemon
dragon
dybbuk
goblin
kelpie
kobold
kraken
merman

nereid
ogress
sphinx
undine
wivern
wyvern
zombie

7
banshee
Bigfoot
brownie
bugaboo
centaur
chimera
Cyclops
gremlin
Grendel
griffin
griffon
gryphon
incubus
lakshmi
Lorelei
mermaid
phantom
phoenix
sandman
spectre
unicorn
vampire
warlock

8
basilisk
behemoth
giantess
isengrim
minotaur
phantasm

succubus
sylphide
werewolf

9
cacodemon
firedrake
hamadryad
hobgoblin
leviathan
manticore
Sasquatch

10
cockatrice
hippogriff
leprechaun
salamander

11
hippocampus
poltergeist

12
bandersnatch
doppelgänger
hippocentaur

THE MUSES
Calliope (epic poetry)
Clio (history)
Erato (love songs)
Euterpe (lyric poetry)
Melpomene (tragedy)
Polyhymnia (singing)
Terpsichore (dancing)
Thalia (comedy)
Urania (astronomy)

NAMES

A name
Boys' names
Girls' names

NAME

1
N

3
dub

4
call
term

5
label
style
title

6
handle

7
appoint
baptize (baptise)
moniker
surname

8
christen
cognomen
forename
nominate

9
designate
pseudonym
sobriquet

10
matronymic
patronymic

11
appellation
designation

BOYS' NAMES

2
Al
Cy
Ed
Jo
Oz
Si

3
Abe
Aby
Alf
Ali
Art
Asa
Baz
Ben
Bob
Bud
Col
Dai
Dan
Dec
Dee
Del
Den
Don
Eli
Ern
Gil
Gus
Guy
Hal
Hew
Huw
Ian
Ike
Ira
Ivo
Jan
Jay
Jed
Jem
Jim
Job
Joe
Jon
Ken
Kev
Kim
Kit
Lal
Lee
Len
Leo
Lev
Lex
Lew
Lou
Mat
Max
Mel
Nat
Ned
Nye
Odo
Pat
Pip
Ray
Red
Reg
Rex
Rod
Rog
Roy
Sam
Seb
Sid
Sly
Tam
Ted
Tim
Tom
Val
Van
Vic
Viv
Wat
Wes
Wyn

4

Abel	Ewan	Mort
Adam	Ezra	Muir
Alan	Finn	Neil
Alec	Fred	Nero
Aled	Fulk	Nick
Algy	Gary	Niki
Alun	Gene	Noah
Alva	Glen	Noël
Alyn	Glyn	Olaf
Amos	Greg	Olav
Andy	Hank	Omar
Axel	Hans	Otho
Bart	Hope	Otis
Bert	Huey	Otto
Bill	Hugh	Owen
Boyd	Hugo	Paul
Bram	Iain	Pepe
Bryn	Igor	Pete
Buck	Ivan	Phil
Burt	Jack	René
Cain	Jake	Rhys
Carl	Jean	Rick
Cary	Jeff	Rolf
Chad	Jess	Rory
Chas	Jock	Ross
Chay	Jody	Russ
Chip	Joel	Ryan
Clem	Joey	Saul
Dale	John	Sean
Dave	Josh	Seth
Davy	Joss	Stan
Dean	Juan	Sven
Dick	Jude	Theo
Dirk	Karl	Thor
Dion	Keir	Toby
Drew	Kent	Todd
Duff	King	Tony
Duke	Kirk	Trev
Earl	Kurt	Vere
Eddy	Kyle	Walt
Egon	Lars	Wilf
Emil	Leon	Will
Eric	Liam	Wynn
Erle	Luke	Yves
Eryl	Marc	Zeke
Esau	Mark	
Evan	Matt	**5**
	Mick	Aaron

Abdul	Cliff	Ferdy
Abner	Clint	Flann
Abram	Clive	Floyd
Adolf	Clyde	Frank
Aidan	Colin	Frans
Airey	Conan	Franz
Alain	Cosmo	Fritz
Alban	Craig	Garry
Alfie	Cyril	Garth
Alick	Cyrus	Gavin
Allan	Dacre	Geoff
Allen	Damon	Gerry
Alvin	Danny	Giles
Alwin	Darcy	Glenn
Alwyn	Daryl	Grant
Amyan	David	Griff
André	Davie	Guido
Angel	Denis	Harry
Angus	Denny	Heinz
Anton	Denys	Henri
Archy	Derek	Henry
Artie	Dicky	Hiram
Aubyn	Donal	Homer
Barry	Duane	Horst
Basil	Dwane	Humph
Benny	Dylan	Hyram
Bevis	Eamon	Hywel
Billy	Earle	Inigo
Blake	Eddie	Innes
Bobby	Edgar	Isaac
Booth	Edwin	Izaak
Boris	Eldon	Jabez
Brett	Elias	Jacky
Brian	Ellis	Jacob
Bruce	Elmer	Jaime
Bruno	Elton	James
Bryan	Elvis	Jamie
Buddy	Elwyn	Jared
Bunny	Emery	Jason
Busby	Emile	Jerry
Caius	Emlyn	Jesse
Caleb	Emrys	Jimmy
Carlo	Enoch	Jonah
Carol	Ernie	Jonas
Cecil	Ernst	Jules
Chris	Errol	Keith
Chuck	Ewart	Kelly
Claud	Felix	Kenny

Kevin	Romeo	Archie
Lance	Rowan	Armand
Larry	Rubin	Arnold
Leigh	Rufus	Arthur
Lenny	Sacha	Ashley
Leroy	Sandy	Ashoka
Lewin	Scott	Aubrey
Lewis	Serge	Austin
Lloyd	Shane	Aylmer
Louie	Silas	Aylwin
Louis	Simon	Barney
Lucas	Solly	Benito
Luigi	Sonny	Benjie
Major	Spiro	Bennie
Micah	Steve	Bernie
Micky	Taffy	Bertie
Miles	Teddy	Brutus
Monty	Terry	Bulwer
Moses	Tibor	Buster
Mungo	Titus	Caesar
Murdo	Tommy	Calvin
Nahum	Ulick	Carlos
Neddy	Ulric	Caspar
Nevil	Ultan	Cedric
Niall	Urban	Claude
Nigel	Uriah	Colley
Nolan	Vince	Connor
Oscar	Wahab	Conrad
Osman	Wally	Cuddie
Osric	Wayne	Damian
Oswin	Willy	Daniel
Paddy	Wolfe	Darian
Pedro	Woody	Darren
Percy	Wyatt	Darryl
Perry		Declan
Peter	**6**	Delroy
Piers	Adolph	Dennis
Ralph	Adrian	Denzil
Ramon	Aeneas	Dermot
Raoul	Alaric	Deryck
Rhett	Albert	Dickie
Ricky	Aldred	Donald
Rider	Alexis	Donnie
Roald	Alfred	Dougal
Robin	Andrew	Dougie
Roddy	Angelo	Dugald
Roger	Anselm	Duggie
Rollo	Antony	Duncan

Dundas	Hubert	Milton
Dwight	Hughie	Morgan
Eamonn	Ignace	Morris
Edmond	Ingram	Mostyn
Edmund	Irvine	Murphy
Eduard	Isaiah	Murray
Edward	Isodor	Nathan
Egbert	Israel	Neddie
Eldred	Jackie	Nelson
Elliot	Jarvis	Nichol
Ernest	Jasper	Ninian
Esmond	Jeremy	Norman
Eugene	Jerome	Norris
Evelyn	Jervis	Oliver
Fabian	Jethro	Onslow
Fergus	Johann	Osbert
Finlay	Johnny	Osmond
Forbes	Joseph	Osmund
Gareth	Joshua	Oswald
Gaston	Josiah	Pascal
Gawain	Julian	Pascoe
George	Julius	Paulus
Gerald	Justin	Pearce
Gerard	Justus	Pelham
Gideon	Kelvin	Perkin
Godwin	Kieran	Philip
Gordon	Konrad	Pierce
Graeme	Laurie	Pierre
Graham	Lawrie	Ramsay
Grogan	Lemuel	Randal
Gunter	Leslie	Rastus
Gwilym	Lester	Rayner
Hamish	Lionel	Reggie
Hamlet	Lorcan	Rhodes
Hansel	Lucius	Richie
Harold	Ludwig	Robbie
Harris	Luther	Robert
Harvey	Magnus	Rodger
Haydon	Manuel	Rodney
Hector	Marcel	Roland
Hedley	Marcus	Ronald
Helmut	Marius	Rowley
Herman	Martin	Rudolf
Hilary	Martyn	Rupert
Hilton	Melvin	Samson
Horace	Melvyn	Samuel
Howard	Merlin	Sancho
Howell	Mickie	Seamas

Seamus
Sefton
Selwyn
Sexton
Sidney
Simeon
Simkin
Soames
Stefan
Steven
Stevie
Stuart
Sydney
Thomas
Tobias
Trevor
Tybalt
Tyrone
Vernon
Victor
Virgil
Vivian
Vyvian
Wallis
Walter
Warren
Wesley
Wilbur
Willie
Xavier
Yehudi

7

Abraham
Absalom
Ainsley
Alfonso
Alister
Almeric
Amadeus
Ambrose
Anatole
Aneurin
Anthony
Antoine
Antonio
Artemus
Auberon

Auguste
Baldwin
Baptist
Barclay
Barnaby
Bernard
Bertram
Brandon
Brendan
Brynmor
Cameron
Caradoc
Casimir
Charles
Charley
Charlie
Chester
Clayton
Clement
Clinton
Compton
Connell
Crispin
Cyprian
Delbert
Derrick
Desmond
Diggory
Dominic
Donovan
Douglas
Eleazer
Ephraim
Erasmus
Eustace
Everard
Ezekiel
Feargal
Findlay
Francis
Frankie
Freddie
Gabriel
Georgie
Geraint
Gervase
Gilbert
Godfrey

Gregory
Gustave
Hadrian
Hartley
Herbert
Hercule
Hermann
Hilaire
Horatio
Humbert
Ingleby
Isidore
Jackson
Jacques
Jeffrey
Joachim
Jocelyn
Johnnie
Kenneth
Kimball
Lachlan
Lambert
Lazarus
Leonard
Leopold
Lindsay
Lorenzo
Ludovic
Malachi
Malcolm
Matthew
Maurice
Maxwell
Maynard
Merrick
Michael
Montagu
Myrddin
Neville
Nicolas
Obadiah
Orlando
Orpheus
Orville
Osborne
Patrick
Perseus
Phileas

Phineas	**8**	Hercules
Quentin	Achilles	Hereward
Quintin	Adolphus	Hezekiah
Ranulph	Alasdair	Horatius
Raphael	Alastair	Humphrey
Raymond	Algernon	Ignatius
Raymund	Alistair	Immanuel
Redvers	Aloysius	Jedediah
Reynard	Alphonso	Jeremiah
Reynold	Antonius	Jonathan
Richard	Augustus	Kimberly
Royston	Aurelius	Kingsley
Rudolph	Bardolph	Lancelot
Rudyard	Barnabas	Laurence
Russell	Bartleby	Lawrence
Sampson	Benedict	Leonidas
Seymour	Benjamin	Llewelyn
Sheldon	Bertrand	Ludovick
Shelley	Beverley	Lutwidge
Sigmund	Campbell	Marshall
Solomon	Christie	Meredith
Spencer	Clarence	Mohammed
Stanley	Claudius	Montague
Stavros	Clifford	Mordecai
Stephen	Constant	Mortimer
Stewart	Courtney	Nehemiah
Tarquin	Crawford	Nicholas
Terence	Crispian	Octavius
Timothy	Cuthbert	Oliphant
Torquil	Dinsdale	Oughtred
Tristan	Dominick	Paulinus
Uchtred	Ebenezer	Perceval
Ughtred	Emmanuel	Percival
Ulysses	Ethelred	Peterkin
Umberto	Eusebius	Philemon
Vaughan	Farquhar	Randolph
Vincent	Francois	Randulph
Wallace	Franklin	Reginald
Wilfred	Frederic	Robinson
Wilfrid	Geoffrey	Roderick
Wilhelm	Giovanni	Ruairidh
William	Giuseppe	Salvador
Winston	Greville	Secundus
Wyndham	Griffith	Septimus
Wynford	Gustavus	Sherlock
Zachary	Hamilton	Siegmund
Zebedee	Harrison	Sinclair
	Havelock	Stafford

Sylvanus
Terrance
Thaddeus
Theobald
Theodore
Tristram
Vladimir

9
Alexander
Alexandre
Alphonsus
Archibald
Aristotle
Athelstan
Augustine
Balthazar
Bartimeus
Christian
Cornelius
Courtenay
Courteney
Demetrius
Dionysius
Engelbert
Ethelbert
Ferdinand
Frederick
Gillespie
Granville
Grenville
Jefferson
Justinian
Kimberley
Launcelot
Llewellyn
Lucretius
Mackenzie
Marmaduke
Nathaniel
Nicodemus
Peregrine
Rodriguez
Sebastian
Siegfried
Sigismund
Stanislas
Sylvester

Thaddaeus
Theodoric
Valentine
Zachariah
Zechariah

10
Alessandro
Athanasius
Athelstane
Barrington
Caractacus
Desederius
Hildebrand
Maximilian
Pierrepont
Stanislaus
Theodosius
Theophilus
Washington
Willoughby

11
Bartholomew
Christopher
Constantine
Desideratus
Sacheverell.

GIRLS' NAMES

2
Bo
Di
Jo
Mo
Vi

3
Ada
Amy
Ann
Ava
Bea
Bet
Cyd
Dee
Dot

Ena
Eva
Eve
Fay
Flo
Gay
Ida
Ina
Ivy
Jan
Jen
Joy
Kay
Kim
Kit
Lea
Lee
Liz
Lou
Lyn
Mai
May
Meg
Mia
Nan
Pam
Pat
Ray
Sal
Sue
Una
Val
Viv
Win
Zoe

4
Ally
Alma
Alys
Anna
Anne
Babs
Bebe
Bess
Beth
Cass
Cath

Ceri	June	Zena
Cher	Kate	Zola
Cleo	Katy	
Cora	Kaye	**5**
Dale	Kiki	Abbie
Dana	Lara	Adela
Dawn	Leah	Adele
Dora	Lena	Aggie
Edie	Lily	Agnes
Edna	Lisa	Ailsa
Ella	Liza	Alexa
Elsa	Lois	Alice
Else	Lola	Angie
Emma	Lucy	Anita
Emmy	Lulu	Annie
Enid	Lynn	Anona
Esme	Mary	Aphra
Etta	Maud	April
Evie	Mimi	Avril
Faye	Mina	Beate
Fern	Moll	Becky
Fifi	Mona	Bella
Fran	Myra	Belle
Gaby	Nell	Beryl
Gaye	Nina	Betsy
Gert	Noel	Bette
Gigi	Nola	Betty
Gill	Nora	Biddy
Gina	Olga	Bobby
Gwen	Oona	Bunny
Hope	Prue	Bunty
Ines	Rene	Candy
Inga	Rita	Carla
Inge	Rosa	Carly
Iona	Rose	Carol
Iris	Ruby	Casey
Irma	Ruth	Cathy
Isla	Sara	Celia
Jade	Sian	Chloe
Jane	Sita	Chris
Jean	Suky	Cilla
Jess	Susy	Cindy
Jill	Tara	Circe
Joan	Tess	Cissy
Jodi	Thea	Clair
Joni	Tina	Clara
Jude	Vera	Coral
Judy	Zara	Daisy

Debby	Jodie	Nelly
Delia	Joyce	Nessa
Della	Julia	Nesta
Diana	Julie	Netta
Diane	Karen	Niobe
Dilys	Katie	Norah
Dinah	Katya	Norma
Donna	Kelly	Olive
Doris	Kerry	Olwen
Edele	Kitty	Pansy
Edith	Kylie	Patsy
Effie	Laura	Patty
Elise	Leigh	Paula
Eliza	Leila	Pearl
Ellen	Letty	Peggy
Ellie	Liana	Penny
Elsie	Libby	Pippa
Emily	Lilly	Polly
Erica	Linda	Poppy
Ethel	Lindy	Renée
Faith	Lorna	Rhian
Fanny	Lotty	Rhoda
Fiona	Lucia	Robin
Fleur	Lydia	Robyn
Flora	Lynda	Rosie
Freda	Lynne	Sadie
Gemma	Mabel	Sally
Gerda	Madge	Sandy
Ginny	Maeve	Sarah
Grace	Magda	Sibyl
Greer	Mamie	Sindy
Greta	Mandy	Sissy
Gussy	Maria	Sonia
Haley	Marie	Sonja
Hazel	Maude	Stacy
Heidi	Mavis	Susan
Helen	Megan	Susie
Helga	Mercy	Sybil
Hilda	Merle	Tammy
Holly	Meryl	Tania
Honor	Milly	Tanya
Ilana	Minna	Terry
Irene	Mitzi	Tessa
Isold	Moira	Thora
Janet	Molly	Tilly
Janie	Morag	Tracy
Jenny	Nancy	Trixy
Jilly	Naomi	Trudy

Venus
Vesta
Vicky
Viola
Wanda
Wendy
Wilma
Xenia
Zelda

6
Adella
Agatha
Aileen
Alexis
Alicia
Alison
Althea
Alyssa
Amanda
Amelia
Andrea
Angela
Anneka
Anthea
Arleen
Arlene
Astrid
Audrey
Aurora
Averil
Barbie
Beatty
Benita
Bertha
Bessie
Biddie
Billie
Bobbie
Bonita
Bonnie
Brenda
Brigid
Briony
Bryony
Bunnie
Carmel
Carmen

Carole
Carrie
Cecile
Cecily
Cherry
Cissy
Claire
Connie
Daphne
Davina
Deanna
Debbie
Denise
Dianne
Dionne
Dorcas
Doreen
Dulcie
Edwina
Eileen
Elaine
Elinor
Eloisa
Eloise
Elvira
Emilia
Esther
Eunice
Evelyn
Fatima
Felice
Flavia
Frieda
Gaynor
Gertie
Ginger
Gladys
Glenda
Glenys
Gloria
Glynis
Gracie
Gretel
Gudrun
Gussie
Gwenda
Hannah
Hattie

Hayley
Hedwig
Helena
Hester
Hilary
Ianthe
Imelda
Imogen
Ingrid
Isabel
Isobel
Isolda
Isolde
Jackie
Janice
Jemima
Jennie
Jessie
Joanna
Joanne
Joleen
Jolene
Judith
Juliet
Kirsty
Lalage
Lallie
Lauren
Leonie
Lesley
Lettie
Lilian
Lillie
Linsay
Linsey
Lizzie
Lottie
Louisa
Louise
Lynsey
Maggie
Maisie
Marcia
Margie
Margot
Marina
Marion
Marnie

Marsha
Martha
Mattie
Maxine
Melody
Millie
Minnie
Miriam
Molly
Monica
Morven
Muriel
Myrtle
Nadine
Nellie
Nessie
Nettie
Nicola
Nicole
Odette
Olivia
Oonagh
Pamela
Pattie
Petula
Phoebe
Portia
Rachel
Ramona
Regina
Renata
Robina
Rosina
Rowena
Roxana
Sabina
Sabine
Salome
Sandie
Sandra
Sappho
Saskia
Selina
Serena
Sharon
Sheena
Sheila
Sherry

Sigrid
Silvia
Simone
Sinead
Sophia
Sophie
Sorcha
Stella
Stevie
Sylvia
Sylvie
Tamara
Tamsin
Teresa
Tessie
Thalia
Thecla
Thelma
Tracey
Trixie
Ulrica
Ursula
Valery
Verity
Violet
Vyvyen
Winnie
Yasmin
Yvette
Yvonne

7
Abigail
Adelina
Adeline
Adriana
Annabel
Annette
Antonia
Ariadne
Aurelia
Augusta
Babette
Barbara
Beatrix
Belinda
Bernice
Bettina

Blanche
Blodwen
Blossom
Bridget
Bronwen
Camilla
Candice
Candida
Carolyn
Cecilia
Celeste
Charity
Chloris
Clarice
Claudia
Clodagh
Colette
Coralie
Corinna
Corinne
Crystal
Cynthia
Deborah
Deidre
Désirée
Dolores
Dorinda
Dorothy
Eleanor
Elspeth
Estella
Eugenia
Eugenie
Eulalia
Evelina
Eveline
Fenecia
Fenella
Florrie
Flossie
Frances
Georgia
Gillian
Gwyneth
Harriet
Heather
Heloise
Horatia

Hypatia	Monique	**8**
Isadora	Morgana	Adelaide
Isidora	Morwena	Adrianne
Jacinta	Myfanwy	Adrienne
Jacquie	Nanette	Angelica
Janetta	Natalia	Angelina
Janette	Natasha	Angharad
Jasmine	Natalie	Arabella
Jeannie	Ninette	Atalanta
Jessica	Octavia	Beatrice
Jillian	Olympia	Berenice
Jocelyn	Ophelia	Beverley
Johanna	Ottilie	Brigitta
Josepha	Pandora	Brigitte
Juanita	Paulina	Carlotta
Juliana	Pauline	Carolina
Juliane	Perdita	Caroline
Justina	Phyllis	Catriona
Kathryn	Queenie	Charlene
Katrina	Rebecca	Charmian
Katrine	Ricarda	Chrissie
Lavinia	Roberta	Chrystal
Leonora	Rosalia	Clarinda
Letitia	Rosalie	Clarissa
Lettice	Rosanna	Clotilda
Lillian	Rosetta	Consuela
Lisbeth	Rosheen	Cordelia
Lisette	Sabrina	Cornelia
Loretta	Shelley	Daniella
Lorinda	Shirley	Danielle
Lucilla	Sidonia	Dorothea
Lucille	Siobhan	Drusilla
Lucinda	Susanna	Eleanora
Lucrece	Susanne	Emmeline
Lynette	Suzanne	Euphemia
Madonna	Sybilla	Faustina
Margery	Tabitha	Felicity
Marilyn	Tatiana	Florence
Marjory	Theresa	Francine
Marlene	Therese	Georgina
Martina	Tiffany	Germaine
Matilda	Vanessa	Gertrude
Maureen	Venetia	Gretchen
Melanie	Yolanda	Griselda
Melissa	Yolande	Hermione
Michele	Zenobia	Hortense
Mildred		Hyacinth
Miranda		Ingeborg

Isabella
Jacintha
Jeanette
Jennifer
Joceline
Julietta
Katerina
Kathleen
Kimberly
Kirsteen
Laetitia
Lauretta
Lavender
Lorraine
Lucretia
Madeline
Marcelle
Margaret
Marianne
Marietta
Marigold
Marjorie
Michaela
Michelle
Nathalie
Patience
Patricia
Penelope
Philippa
Phyllida
Primrose
Prudence
Prunella
Rhiannon
Rosalind
Rosaline
Rosamond
Rosamund
Roseanna
Rosemary
Samantha
Sapphire
Sheelagh

Susannah
Tallulah
Theodora
Theresia
Veronica
Victoria
Violetta
Virginia
Vivienne
Winifred

9
Albertine
Alexandra
Anastasia
Annabella
Annabelle
Cassandra
Catharine
Catherine
Celestine
Charlotte
Charmaine
Christina
Christine
Cleopatra
Clothilda
Clothilde
Columbine
Constance
Desdemona
Elisabeth
Elizabeth
Ernestine
Esmeralda
Francesca
Francoise
Frederica
Gabriella
Gabrielle
Genevieve
Georgette
Georgiana

Geraldine
Guinevere
Gwendolen
Henrietta
Hephzibah
Hildegard
Hortensia
Iphigenia
Jacquelyn
Jacquetta
Jessamine
Josephine
Katharine
Katherine
Kimberley
Madeleine
Margareta
Millicent
Philomena
Priscilla
Stephanie
Thomasina
Valentina

10
Antoinette
Bernadette
Christabel
Clementina
Clementine
Ermintrude
Evangelina
Evangeline
Gwendoline
Jacqueline
Margherita
Marguerite
Petronella
Wilhelmina

12
Alexandrina

NAUTICAL TERMS

See also **SHIP/BOAT**

WORDS USED IN CONNECTION WITH SHIPS, SAILING AND THE SEA

2
AB
MV
SS
RN

3
aft
bow
cox
FOB
guy
HMS
hog
jib
lee
log
MFV
oar
rig
rum
sag
set
SOS
tar
way
yaw

4
ahoy
back
bale
beam
bend
bitt
boom
bows
brig

bunk
bunt
buoy
calk
calm
cott
crew
deck
eddy
fore
foul
furl
gaff
gale
grog
hank
haul
haze
helm
hold
hove
hulk
hull
jury
keel
knot
last
lead
leak
line
list
load
loof
luff
lute
mast
mess
mole
moor
neap
oars
peak
pair
pier
poop
port
prow
quay

rail
rake
RNLI
roll
rope
RORO
rove
sail
scud
seam
sink
skeg
slip
spar
stay
stem
swab
tack
taut
tide
trim
veer
wake
warp
wave
wind
yard
yarn

5
aback
abaft
abeam
about
afore
afoul
after
ahull
aloft
apeak
aport
avast
baler
beach
belay
below
berth
bilge

block
board
bosun
botel
bouse
bower
bowse
brace
brail
cabin
cable
cadet
cargo
casco
caulk
chain
chart
chock
clamp
cleat
cuddy
davit
douse
dowse
drift
fleet
float
fluke
hands
hatch
haven
hawse
hitch
hoist
jetty
kedge
kevel
leach
leaky
leech
naval
oakum
oiler
orlop
pitch
refit
roads
rower

royal
sally
screw
sheer
sheet
shoal
shore
siren
sound
steer
stern
surge
swell
thole
tidal
truck
truss
waist
watch
wharf
wheel
winch
wreck

6

aboard
adrift
afloat
anchor
ashore
astern
aweigh
awning
batten
beacon
bridge
bunker
canvas
careen
comber
convoy
cooper
course
cruise
debark
embark
engine
ensign

escort
fathom
fender
fo'c'sle
for'ard
fother
furled
galley
gasket
gunnel
hawser
jetsam
kelson
lading
lateen
leewat
Lloyd's
locker
marina
marine
maroon
mayday
mizzen
moored
mutiny
offing
paddle
pennon
pintle
piracy
pirate
rating
ratlin
reefed
reefer
rigged
rigger
rocket
rudder
sailor
saloon
sculls
seaman
seaway
sheets
shroud
splice
squall

stocks
strake
strand
tackle
thwart
tiller
timber
toggle
towage
trough
unfurl
inlade
unship
vessel

7

aground
athwart
backing
ballast
bearing
boarder
bobstay
bollard
bowline
bulwark
bunkers
caboose
calking
capsize
capstan
captain
carline
channel
charter
clipper
coaming
cockpit
cordage
corsair
counter
cyclone
deadeye
degauss
dismast
dockage
draught
dunnage

embargo
fairway
flotsam
fogbank
foghorn
foretop
forward
founder
freight
freshen
freshet
frogman
futtock
gangway
gimbals
grapnel
grating
grommet
gudgeon
gunwale
harbour
harpoon
headway
horizon
iceberg
inboard
inshore
jibstay
keelage
keelson
landing
lanyard
lashing
listing
loading
logbook
lookout
luffing
lugsail
maintop
marine
mariner
marline
matelot
moorage
mooring
oarsman
oceanic

painter
pennant
pontoon
rations
ratline
reefing
rigging
rolling
rowlock
sailing
salvage
scupper
scuttle
seamark
seasick
seaward
sextant
shipper
shipway
shrouds
sickbay
sinking
skipper
skysail
slipway
spanker
squally
steward
stowage
tonnage
topmast
topsail
topside
towline
towrope
transom
trysail
unladen
waftage
warping
wrecked
wrecker
yardarm

8

anchored
backstay
backwash

barnacle	magazine	wreckage
bearings	mainmast	
becalmed	mainsail	**9**
bearthage	mainstay	admiralty
berthing	mainyard	afterdeck
binnacle	maritime	alongside
boathook	masthead	amidships
bowsprit	mastless	anchorage
bulkhead	messmate	bargepole
bulwarks	midships	broadside
buntline	moorings	bunkering
castaway	mutineer	chartered
caulking	mutinous	chartroom
chandler	navigate	companion
coasting	outboard	container
crossing	pilotage	corposant
cruising	plimsoll	crosstree
cutwater	porthole	crosswind
deckhand	portside	deadlight
dockyard	quarters	demurrage
dogwatch	salvable	discharge
doldrums	salvager	disembark
floating	sandbank	doggerman
flotilla	seafarer	driftwood
fogbound	seagoing	foreshore
forefoot	shallows	gangplank
foremast	shipmate	holystone
forepeak	shipment	kentledge
foresail	shipping	lobscouse
forestay	smuggler	maelstrom
gaffsail	sounding	mainbrace
halliard	spyglass	mainsheet
hatchway	staysail	midstream
headfast	steerage	mizzenmast
headsail	sternway	mizzentop
helmsman	stowaway	navigable
hornpipe	stranded	navigator
jackstay	stunsail	overboard
keelhaul	submerge	periscope
landfall	taffrail	promenade
landmark	tranship	revictual
landsman	unfurled	roadstead
landward	upstream	sailcloth
larboard	wardroom	seafaring
leeboard	waterman	seaworthy
lifebelt	waterway	semaphore
lifeboat	windlass	shipboard
lifeline	windward	shipowner

shipshape
shipwreck
shoreward
sidelight
spindrift
spinnaker
spritsail
stanchion
starboard
stateroom
steersman
sternmost
sternpost
stormsail
stormstay
stretcher
tarpaulin
telescope
uncharted
waterline

10

alongshore
astarboard
bilgewater
bluejacket
breakwater
charthouse
crosstrees
degaussing
downstream
embarkment
figurehead
forecastle
frightage
freshwater
inflatable
landlocked
landlubber
lifejacket

lighthouse
martingale
midshipman
mizzenmast
mizzensail
navigation
pilothouse
quarantine
reshipment
rudderless
seamanlike
seamanship
shipmaster
shipwright
topgallant
upperworks
victualler
watertight
waterspout
watertight
wheelhouse

11

beachcomber
centreboard
debarkation
embarkation
lifeboatman
maintopmast
maintopsail
marlinspike
quarterdeck
searchlight
seasickness
shipbreaker
sternsheets
submersible
unnavigable
waterlogged
weatherdeck

12

companionway
displacement
longshoreman
marlinespike
navigability
recommission
transhipment
undercurrent
weatherboard
weatherbound
weatherglass
weatherproof

2+ words

air-sea rescue
bale out
beam ends
blue peter
boat drill
cast off
compass rose
Davy Jones
dead reckoning
deck cargo
dry dock
go about
heave to
hove to
red ensign
riding light
sea lane
sea legs
set sail
sheer hulk
under way
weigh anchor
white ensign

NEW ZEALAND

Famous New Zealanders
New Zealand's native birds
New Zealand's towns and regions

4
Lomu (Jonah, rugby player)

5
Blake (Peter, yachtsman)
Clark (Helen, politician)
Crowe (Russell, actor)
Marsh (Ngaio, writer)
Meads (Colin, rugby player)
Snell (Peter, athlete)

6
Batten (Jean, aviator)
Cairns (Chris, cricketer)
Going (Sid, rugby player)
Hadlee (Richard, cricketer)
Kanawa (Kiri Te, singer)
Pearse (Richard, aviation pioneer)

7
Campion (Jane, film director)
Hammond (Joan, singer)
Hillary (Edmund, mountaineer)
Holyoak (Keith, politician)
Jackson (Peter, film director)

Lawless (Lucy, actress)
McLaren (Bruce, racing driver)

9
Mansfield (Katherine, writer)

10
Rutherford (Ernest, scientist)

NEW ZEALAND'S NATIVE BIRDS

3
kea
tui

4
hihi
kaka
kaki
kiwi
weka
whio

5
hoiho
mohua
taiko
tieke

6
kakapo
kawana
kereru
kokako
pateke
takahe

2 words
black robin
fairy tern

NEW ZEALAND TOWNS AND REGIONS

5
Otago (region)

6
Napier (town)
Nelson (town and region)

7
Dunedin (town)
Rotorua (town)

8
Auckland (town and region)
Hamilton (town)
Taranaki (region)
Westland (region)

9
Canterbury (region)
Southland (region)

12
Christchurch (town and region)

2 words
Hawke's Bay (region)

NOVELS

Novel titles
Novelists
See also **DICKENS**

NOVEL TITLES

3
Kim (Kipling)
She (Haggard)

4
Clea (Durrell)
Emma (Austen)
Gigi (Colette)
Nana (Zola)
Watt (Beckett)

5
Chéri (Colette)
Crash (Ballard)
Hotel (Hailey)
Kipps (Wells)
Money (Martin Amis)
Scoop (Waugh)
Sybil (Disraeli)
Zadig (Voltaire)

6
Amelia (Fielding)
Chocky (Wyndham)
Lolita (Nabokov)
Molloy (Beckett)
Nausea (Sartre)
Pamela (Richardson)
Romola (Eliot)

7
Camilla (Burney)
Candide (Voltaire)
Cecilia (Burney)
Dracula (Stoker)
Evelina (Burney)
Erewhon (Butler)
Ivanhoe (Scott)
Justine (Durrell)
Maurice (Forster)

Orlando (Woolf)
Rebecca (Du Maurier)
Shirley (Charlotte Bronte)
Ulysses (Joyce)

8
Clarissa (Richardson)
Cranford (Gaskell)
Flashman (Fraser)
Germinal (Zola)
Saturday (McEwan)
Villette (Charlotte Bronte)
Waverley (Scott)

9
Amsterdam (McEwan)
Atonement (McEwan)
Balthazar (Durrell)
Coningsby (Disraeli)
Dubliners (Joyce)
Hawksmoor (Ackroyd)
Kidnapped (Stevenson)
Waterland (Graham Swift)

10
Clayhanger (Bennett)
Goldfinger (Fleming)
Kenilworth (Scott)
Mountolive (Durrell)
Persuasion (Austen)
Possession (Byatt)

11
Gormenghast (Peake)
Middlemarch (Eliot)

12
Frankenstein (Shelley)
Resurrection (Tolstoy)

2+ words
Adam Bede (Eliot)
Agnes Grey (Anne Bronte)
Animal Farm (Orwell)
Anna Karenina (Tolstoy)

Antic Hay (Huxley)
Ben Hur (Wallace)
Black Beauty (Sewell)
Brideshead Revisited (Waugh)
Brighton Rock (Greene)
Cancer Ward (Solzhenitsyn)
Crime and Punishment (Dostoievski)
Dead Souls (Gogol)
Don Quixote (Cervantes)
Dr No (Fleming)
Fanny Hill (Cleland)
Gulliver's Travels (Jonathan Swift)
Hotel du Lac (Brookner)
I, Claudius (Graves)
Jane Eyre (Charlotte Bronte)
Jo's Boys (Alcott)
Jude the Obscure (Hardy)
Lord Jim (Conrad)
Lord of the Flies (Golding)
Lucky Jim (Kingsley Amis)
Madame Bovary (Flaubert)
Moby Dick (Melville)
Moll Flanders (Defoe)
Moon Tiger (Lively)
Mrs Dalloway (Woolf)
Northanger Abbey (Austen)
Portrait of a Lady (James)
Pride and Prejudice (Austen)
Rob Roy (Scott)
Room at the Top (Braine)
Sense and Sensibility (Austen)
Sons and Lovers (Lawrence)
Tess of the Durbervilles (Hardy)
The Ambassadors (James)
The Bell (Murdoch)

The Bostonians (James)
The Castle (Kafka)
The Devils (Dostoievski)
The Fall (Camus)
The Hobbit (Tolkien)
The Idiot (Dostoievski)
The Magus (Fowles)
The Mayor of
Casterbridge (Hardy)
The Millstone (Drabble)
The Plague (Kafka)
The Rainbow (Lawrence)
The Secret Agent
(Conrad)
The Spire (Golding)
The Trial (Kafka)
The Waves (Woolf)
The Woodlanders
(Hardy)
The Years (Woolf)
Titus Groan (Peake)
Tom Jones (Fielding)
To the Lighthouse
(Woolf)
Tristram Shandy (Sterne)
Vanity Fair (Thackeray)
War and Peace (Tolstoy)
Women in Love
(Lawrence)

NOVELISTS

3
Eco (Umberto, Italian)
Sue (Eugène, French)

4
Agee (James, US)
Amis (Kingsley/Martin,
UK)
Baum (L. Frank, US)
Böll (Heinrich, German)
Buck (Pearl S., US)
Cary (Joyce, UK)
Ford (Ford Madox, UK)
Gide (André, French)
Hope (Anthony, UK)
Hugo (Victor, French)

King (Stephen, US)
Loti (Pierre, French)
Mann (Thomas, German)
Rhys (Jean, UK)
Roth (Philip, US)
Sade (Marquis de,
French)
Sand (Georges, French)
Seth (Vikram, Indian)
Snow (C. P., UK)
Wain (John, UK)
Webb (Mary, UK)
West (Rebecca, UK)
Wren (P. C., UK)
Zola (Emile, French)

5
Adams (Richard, UK)
Barth (John, US)
Bates (H.E., UK)
Benét (Stephen, US)
Bowen (Elizabeth, UK)
Butor (Michel, French)
Byatt (A.S., UK)
Camus (Albert, French)
Carey (Peter, Australian)
Crane (Stephen, US)
Defoe (Daniel, UK)
Dumas (Alexandre,
French)
Doyle (Roddy, Irish)
Duras (Marguerite,
French)
Eliot (George, Mary
Anne Evans, UK)
Gogol (Nikolai, Russian)
Gorki (Maxim, Russian)
Grass (Günther, German)
Hardy (Thomas, UK)
Harte (Brett, US short-
story writer)
Hesse (Hermann,
German)
James (Henry, US/UK/
P.D., UK)
Joyce (James, Irish)
Kafka (Franz, Czech)
Kesey (Ken, US)

Lewis (Sinclair, US/
Wyndham, UK)
Lively (Penelope, UK)
Lodge (David, UK)
Lowry (Malcolm, UK)
Marsh (Ngaio, NZ)
Musil (Robert, Austrian)
Orczy (Baroness, UK)
Paton (Alan, SA)
Peake (Mervyn, UK)
Powys (John Cowper,
UK)
Sagan (Françoise, French)
Scott (Walter, UK)
Shute (Neville, Australian)
Spark (Muriel, UK)
Storm (Theodor,
German)
Stowe (Harriet Beecher,
US)
Smith (Zadie, UK)
Swift (Graham, UK/
Jonathan, Irish)
Twain (Mark, US)
Verne (Jules, French)
Vidal (Gore, US)
Waugh (Evelyn, UK)
Wells (H.G., UK)
White (Patrick, Australian)
Wolfe (Thomas, US)
Woolf (Virginia, UK)
Yonge (Charlotte, UK)

6
Alcott (Luisa M., US)
Aldiss (Brian, UK)
Asimov (Isaac, US)
Atwood (Margaret,
Canadian)
Austen (Jane, UK)
Balzac (Honoré de,
French)
Bellow (Saul, US)
Binchy (Maeve, Irish)
Borges (Jorge, Argentine)
Braine (John, UK)
Bronte (Ann, Charlotte,
Emily, UK)

Buchan (John, UK)
Burney (Fanny, UK)
Butler (Samuel, UK)
Capote (Truman, US)
Conrad (Joseph, UK)
Cooper (James Fenimore, US)
Cronin (A.J., UK)
Daudet (Alphonse, French)
Fowles (John, UK)
France (Anatole, French)
Fraser (George Macdonald, UK)
Graves (Robert, UK)
Greene (Graham, UK)
Hailey (Arthur, US)
Hamsun (Knut, Norwegian)
Harris (Joel Chandler, US)
Heller (Joseph, US)
Hughes (Richard, UK)
Huxley (Aldous, UK)
Irving (Washington, US)
Laclos (Pierre Choderlos de, French)
London (Jack, US)
Mailer (Norman, US)
McEwan (Ian, UK)
Miller (Henry, US)
O'Brien (Edna/Flann, Irish)
Orwell (George, UK)
Porter (Katherine Anne, US)
Powell (Anthony, UK)
Proust (Marcel, French)
Sartre (Jean-Paul, French)
Sewell (Anna, UK)
Singer (Isaac Bashevis, US)
Sterne (Laurence, UK)
Stoker (Bram, Irish)
Updike (John, US)
Wilson (Angus, UK)
Wright (Richard, US)

7

Ackroyd (Peter, UK)
Allende (Isabel, Chilean)
Balchin (Nigel, UK)
Baldwin (James, US)
Beckett (Samuel, Irish)
Bennett (Arnold, UK)
Burgess (Anthony, UK)
Cleland (John, UK)
Coetzee (J.M., SA)
Colette (French)
Collins (Wilkie, UK)
Dickens (Charles, UK)
Drabble (Margaret, UK)
Dreiser (Theodore, US)
Duhamel (Georges, French)
Durrell (Lawrence, UK)
Fleming (Ian, UK)
Forster (E.M., UK)
Gaskell (Elizabeth, UK)
Gissing (George, UK)
Golding (William, UK)
Grisham (John, US)
Haggard (Rider, UK)
Hammett (Dashiell, US)
Hartley (L.P., UK)
Kerouac (Jack, US)
Lessing (Doris, UK)
Malraux (André, French)
Manzoni (Alessandro, Italian)
Maugham (Somerset, UK)
Mauriac (François, French)
Merimée (Prosper, French)
Moravia (Alberto, Italian)
Murdoch (Iris, UK)
Nabokov (Vladimir, US)
Naipaul (V.S., West Indian)
Peacock (Thomas Love, UK)
Prévert (Jacques, French)
Pynchon (Thomas, US)
Queneau (Raymond, French)
Rolland (Romain, French)
Romains (Jules, French)
Roussel (Raymond, French)
Rushdie (Salman, UK)
Shelley (Mary, UK)
Simenon (Georges, Belgian)
Surtees (Robert, UK)
Tolkien (J.R.R., UK)
Tolstoy (Leo, Russian)
Wallace (Edgar, UK/Lew US)
Wharton (Edith, US)
Wyndham (John, UK)

8

Barbusse (Henri, French)
Beauvoir (Simone de, French)
Bernanos (Georges, French)
Bradbury (Ray, US)
Brookner (Anita, UK)
Chandler (Raymond, US)
Christie (Agatha, UK)
Constant (Benjamin, French)
Disraeli (Benjamin, UK)
Faulkner (William, US)
Fielding (Henry, UK)
Flaubert (Gustave, French)
Forester (C.S., UK)
Goncourt (Edmond/Jules de, French)
Huysmans (Joris Karl, French)
Keneally (Thomas, Aus)
Kingsley (Charles, UK)
Lawrence (D. H., UK)
Marquand (J.P., US)
McCarthy (Mary, US)
Melville (Herman, US)
Meredith (George, UK)
Mitchell (Margaret, US)
Ondaatje (Micheal,

Canadian)
Salinger (J.D., US)
Sillitoe (Alan, UK)
Sinclair (Upton, US)
Smollett (Tobias, UK)
Spillane (Mickey, US)
Stendhal (Henri Beyle, French)
Trollope (Anthony/ Joanna, UK)
Turgenev (Ivan, Russian)
Voltaire (François-Marie Arouet, French)
Vonnegut (Kurt, US)

9
Allingham (Marjorie, UK)
Blackmore (R.D., UK)
Burroughs (Edgar Rice/William, US)
Cervantes (Miguel de, Spanish)
Hawthorne (Nathaniel, US)
Hemingway (Ernest, US)

Highsmith (Patricia, US)
Isherwood (Christopher, UK)
Lampedusa (Giuseppe di, Italian)
Linklater (Eric, UK)
Llewellyn (Richard, UK)
McCullers (Carson, US)
Monsarrat (Nicholas, UK)
O'Flaherty (Liam, Irish)
Pasternak (Boris, Russian)
Pratchett (Terry, UK)
Priestley (J.B., UK)
Pritchett (V.S., UK)
Steinbeck (John, US)
Stevenson (Robert Louis, UK)
Thackeray (William Makepeace, UK)
Wodehouse (P.G., UK)

10
Bainbridge (Beryl, UK)
Chesterton (G.K., UK)
Fitzgerald (Scott, US)
Galsworthy (John, UK)
Richardson (Samuel, UK)

11
Dostoievski (Fyodor, Russian)
Montherlant (Henry de, French)

12
Solzhenitsyn (Aleksandr, Russian)

2 words
Conan Doyle (Arthur, UK)
Du Maurier (Daphne, UK)
Le Carré (John, UK)
Saint-Exupery (Antoine de, French)

NUMBERS

A number
Numbers in different
languages

A NUMBER

1
C
D
E
I
K
L
M
N
V
X

2
no
pi

3
one
par
PIN
six
sum
ten
two

4
five
four

hash
host
lots
many
nine
raft
sign
slew
some
unit

5
count
digit
dozen
eight
fifty
forty
gross
group
prime
seven
sixty
tally
three
total

6
amount
binary
cipher
eighty
factor
googol
figure
lepton

myriad
ninety
symbol
thirty
twelve
twenty

7
billion
decimal
divisor
handful
hundred
fifteen
integer
million
numeral
ordinal
seventy
sixteen
zillion

8
abscissa
cardinal
constant
fourteen
fraction
quantity
thirteen
thousand

9
aggregate
multitude
numerator

NUMBERS IN DIFFERENT LANGUAGES

	Roman	French	German	Italian	Spanish
1	I	un	ein	uno	uno
2	II	deux	zwei	due	dos
3	III	trois	drei	tre	tres
4	IV	quatre	vier	quattro	cuatro
5	V	cinq	fünf	cinque	cinco
6	VI	six	sechs	sei	seis
7	VII	sept	sieben	sette	siete

8	VIII	huit	acht	otto	ocho
9	IX	neuf	neun	nove	nueve
10	X	dix	zehn	dieci	diez
11	XI	onze	elf	undici	undécimo
12	XII	douze	zwölf	dodici	doce
20	XX	vingt	zwanzig	venti	veinte
30	XXX	trente	dreissig	trenta	treinta
40	XL	quarante	vierzig	quaranta	cuaranta
50	L	cinquante	fünfzig	cinquanta	cincuenta
60	LX	soixante	sechzig	sessenta	sesenta
70	LXX	soixante-dix	siebzig	settanta	setenta
80	LXXX	quatre-vingt	achtzig	ottanta	ochenta
90	XC	quatre-vingt-dix	neunzig	novanta	noventa
100	C	cent	hundert	cento	cien(to)
500	D	conq cents	fünfhundert	cinquecento	quinientos
1000	M	mille	tausend	mille	mil

OCCUPATIONS

An occupation
Occupations

AN OCCUPATION

3
job

4
duty
line
post
role
task
work

5
chore
craft
field
place
skill
trade

6
career
living
metier
office

7
calling
pastime
project
pursuit

8
activity
business
capacity
function
position
sinecure
vocation

9
avocation
diversion
situation

10
assignment
commission
employment
livelihood

11
appointment

OCCUPATIONS

2
GP
MO
PA
PM

3
doc
don
gyp
pro
rep
spy
vet

4
amah
ayah
bard
boss
char
chef
cook
diva
dyer
grip
hack
hand
head
herd
lead
maid

mate
mime
page
peon
poet
seer
serf
syce
temp
tout
ward
whip

5
actor
agent
baker
boots
bosun
caddy
clerk
clown
coach
comic
crier
daily
envoy
extra
fakir
fence
filer
flier
gluer
groom
guard
guide
hirer
leech
mason
medic
miner
navvy
nurse
oiler
pilot
piper
quack
rabbi

rater	casual	gunman
reeve	censor	gunner
scout	cleric	hacker
sewer	coiner	harper
shoer	comber	hatter
slave	coolie	hawker
smith	cooper	healer
sower	copper	heaver
staff	cowboy	hodman
sweep	cowman	hooper
tamer	critic	horner
tiler	cutler	hosier
tuner	cutter	hunter
tutor	dancer	intern
usher	dealer	issuer
valet	digger	jailer
	docker	jobber
6	doctor	jockey
airman	dowser	joiner
archer	draper	jurist
artist	drawer	keeper
aurist	driver	lackey
author	drover	lascar
bagman	editor	lawyer
bailer	factor	lector
balker	farmer	lender
banker	feller	loader
barber	fisher	logman
bargee	fitter	marker
barker	flayer	master
barman	forger	matron
batman	fowler	medico
bearer	framer	mender
binder	fuller	menial
boffin	gaffer	mentor
bookie	ganger	mercer
bowman	gaoler	milker
brewer	gaucho	miller
broker	gauger	minter
bugler	geisha	monger
bursar	gigolo	mummer
busker	gilder	mystic
butler	gillie	nailer
cabbie	glazer	notary
cabman	glover	oboist
canner	graver	oilman
carter	grocer	orator
carver	guider	ostler

packer	singer	**7**
parson	skivvy	acolyte
pastor	slater	acrobat
pavier	slaver	actress
pedant	sleuth	actuary
pedlar	snarer	almoner
penman	sorter	analyst
picker	souter	Arabist
pieman	spicer	arbiter
pirate	squire	artisan
pitman	stager	artiste
plater	stoker	assayer
player	storer	assizer
porter	tailor	assurer
potboy	tanner	auditor
potter	taster	aviator
priest	teller	awarder
pruner	tester	bailiff
purser	tiller	barmaid
ragman	tinker	bellboy
ranger	tinner	bellhop
ratter	toller	birdman
reader	touter	blaster
reaper	tracer	blender
reaver	trader	boatman
rector	tubman	bookman
regent	turner	bottler
relief	tycoon	bouncer
renter	typist	breeder
rigger	usurer	brigand
ringer	valuer	builder
roadie	vassal	butcher
robber	vendor	callboy
roofer	verger	cambist
sacker	viewer	carrier
sailor	waiter	caseman
salter	walker	cashier
sapper	waller	caterer
sawyer	warden	caulker
scribe	washer	cellist
sealer	weaver	chanter
seaman	weeder	chapman
seizor	welder	chemist
seller	whaler	cleaner
server	worker	clippie
setter	wright	coalman
sexton	writer	cobbler
signer		cockler

collier	grantee	peddler
copyist	grantor	pianist
coroner	grazier	picador
corsair	grinder	planner
counsel	gymnast	planter
courier	hackler	pleader
cowherd	harpist	plumber
cowpoke	haulier	poacher
crofter	herbist	poolman
cropper	herdman	postboy
curator	heritor	postman
currier	hogherd	presser
danseur	hostler	printer
dentist	indexer	puddler
dietist	inlayer	rancher
ditcher	ironist	realtor
diviner	janitor	refiner
dominie	juggler	riveter
doorman	junkman	roadman
drapier	juryman	roaster
drayman	keelman	rustler
dredger	knacker	sacrist
dresser	knitter	saddler
drogman	laceman	sampler
drummer	linkboy	samurai
dustman	linkman	scourer
farrier	lombard	scraper
fiddler	mailman	servant
fireman	maltman	sharper
flesher	manager	shearer
florist	mangler	shipper
flunkey	marbler	showman
flutist	marcher	shunter
footboy	mariner	silkman
footman	marshall	simpler
foreman	masseur	skinner
founder	matador	skipper
friseur	midwife	slipper
frogman	milkman	smelter
furrier	monitor	socager
gateman	newsboy	soldier
girdler	oculist	soloist
glazier	officer	spencer
gleaner	orderly	spinner
gleeman	packman	spotter
glosser	pageboy	stainer
grafter	painter	stamper
granger	palmist	stapler

steward
surgeon
swabber
sweeper
taborer
tallier
tapster
teacher
tipster
tracker
trainer
trapper
trawler
trimmer
trucker
trustee
tumbler
turnkey
vintner
violist
wagoner
warrior
webster
weigher
wheeler
whetter
wireman
woodman
woolman
workman
wrapper

8

aeronaut
analyser
aphorist
apiarist
arborist
armourer
armorist
assessor
attorney
bagpiper
bandsman
bargeman
bearherd
bedesman
bedmaker

bleacher
boatsman
bondmaid
bondsman
botanist
bowmaker
boxmaker
brewster
broacher
cellarer
ceramist
chandler
choirboy
clothier
coachman
codifier
collator
comedian
compiler
composer
conjurer
conveyor
courtier
coxswain
croupier
cutpurse
dairyman
danseuse
deckhand
defender
designer
director
domestic
doughboy
dragoman
druggist
educator
embalmer
emissary
engineer
engraver
enroller
essayist
examiner
exorcist
explorer
exporter
factotum

falconer
farmhand
ferryman
figurant
finisher
flautist
fletcher
fodderer
forester
forgeman
fugleman
gangster
gardener
gavelman
glassman
goatherd
governor
guardian
gunsmith
hammerer
handmaid
handyman
hatmaker
haymaker
headsman
helmsman
henchman
herdsman
hireling
histrion
hotelier
houseboy
huckster
huntsman
importer
improver
inventor
japanner
jeweller
jongleur
labourer
landgirl
landlady
landlord
lapidary
larcener
larderer
leadsman

lecturer	raftsman	thespian
linesman	ranchero	thresher
magician	rapperee	tinsmith
maltster	receiver	torturer
masseuse	recorder	toymaker
measurer	relessor	truckman
mechanic	repairer	turncock
melodist	reporter	turnspit
merchant	resetter	tutoress
milkmaid	restorer	unionist
millhand	retailer	valuator
milliner	retainer	vintager
minister	reviewer	virtuoso
minstrel	romancer	vocalist
modeller	rugmaker	waitress
muleteer	salesman	wardress
muralist	satirist	warrener
musician	sawbones	watchman
novelist	scullion	waterman
operator	sculptor	whaleman
optician	seamster	wigmaker
ordinand	seedsman	winnower
organist	sempster	wrestler
outrider	servitor	
overseer	shearman	**9**
pargeter	shepherd	alchemist
penmaker	shipmate	anatomist
perfumer	shopgirl	annotator
peterman	showgirl	announcer
pewterer	sidesman	architect
picaroon	sketcher	archivist
pinmaker	smuggler	artificer
plougher	spearman	astronaut
polisher	spurrier	attendant
portress	starcher	authoress
potmaker	stitcher	auxiliary
preacher	stockman	balladeer
prefacer	storeman	ballerina
pressman	stripper	barrister
procurer	strummer	beefeater
promoter	stuntman	beekeeper
prompter	supplier	biologist
provider	surveyor	boatswain
psalmist	swindler	bodyguard
publican	tallyman	boilerman
pugilist	taverner	bondslave
purveyor	teamster	bondwoman
quarrier	thatcher	bookmaker

bootblack	ecologist	inspector
bootmaker	enameller	intendant
buccaneer	engineman	ironsmith
burnisher	engrosser	itinerant
cameraman	estimator	lacemaker
caretaker	excavator	lacquerer
carpenter	excerptor	lampooner
casemaker	exchanger	larcenist
catechist	exciseman	launderer
cellarman	executive	laundress
chanteuse	fabricant	legionary
charwoman	fashioner	librarian
chauffeur	figurante	linotyper
cheapjack	financier	liveryman
chorister	fisherman	locksmith
clarifier	freelance	lumberman
clergyman	freighter	machinist
clinician	fruiterer	magnetist
clogmaker	furbisher	majordomo
coalminer	furnisher	mannequin
collector	galvanist	mechanist
colourist	gazetteer	memoirist
columnist	geologist	mercenary
companion	gluemaker	mesmerist
comprador	goldsmith	messenger
concierge	gondolier	metallist
conductor	gospeller	middleman
conserver	governess	mortician
cosmonaut	guardsman	musketeer
costumier	guitarist	myologist
courtesan	harlequin	navigator
couturier	harmonist	newsagent
cowfeeder	harpooner	nursemaid
cowkeeper	harvester	operative
cracksman	Hellenist	ordinator
craftsman	herbalist	osteopath
crayonist	herbarian	otologist
cymbalist	herborist	outfitter
dairymaid	Hispanist	paralegal
decorator	historian	paramedic
detective	homeopath	paymaster
dietitian	hosteller	pedagogue
dispenser	housemaid	performer
dissector	housewife	physician
distiller	hygienist	physicist
draftsman	hypnotist	pitsawyer
dramatist	innkeeper	planisher
drysalter	inscriber	plasterer

ploughboy
ploughman
pluralist
poetaster
pointsman
policeman
portrayer
portreeve
postilion
postwoman
poulterer
precentor
preceptor
predicant
prelector
priestess
privateer
professor
profilist
publicist
publisher
puppeteer
qualifier
quarryman
racketeer
railmaker
recruiter
reformist
rehearser
ribbonman
roadmaker
ropemaker
roundsman
sacristan
safemaker
sailmaker
schoolman
scientist
scrivener
secretary
shoeblack
shoemaker
signalman
sinologue
soapmaker
solicitor
sonneteer
stableboy

stableman
stagehand
stationer
steersman
stevedore
subeditor
succentor
swineherd
switchman
swordsman
tablemaid
tactician
tentmaker
therapist
theurgist
timberman
toolsmith
tradesman
tragedian
treasurer
trepanner
tributary
trumpeter
tympanist
usherette
varnisher
versifier
vexillary
violinist
volcanist
wadsetter
warranter
washerman
waxworker
webmaster
whitester
winemaker
workwoman
zookeeper
zoologist
zootomist

10

accoucheur
accountant
advertiser
aerologist
agronomist

amanuensis
apothecaty
apprentice
arbitrator
astrologer
astronomer
auctioneer
balloonist
bandmaster
bassoonist
beautician
billposter
biochemist
biographer
blacksmith
bladesmith
blockmaker
bombardier
bondswoman
bonesetter
bookbinder
bookkeeper
bookseller
bootlegger
bricklayer
brickmaker
brushmaker
bureaucrat
cartoonist
cartwright
ceramicist
chairmaker
charioteer
classicist
clockmaker
coalheaver
coastguard
colporteur
comedienne
compositor
consultant
contractor
controller
copyholder
copywriter
cordwainer
counsellor
cultivator

cytologist
directress
discounter
dishwasher
dispatcher
doorkeeper
dramaturge
dressmaker
enamellist
epitaphist
evangelist
fishmonger
flowergirl
forecaster
freebooter
fundraiser
gamekeeper
geneticist
geographer
glossarist
governante
grammarian
handmaiden
harvestman
hatcheller
homoeopath
horologist
huckstress
husbandman
instructor
ironmonger
ironworker
journalist
journeyman
keyboarder
laundryman
legislator
librettist
lighterman
linotypist
liquidator
lobsterman
lumberjack
magistrate
manageress
manicurist
manservant
matchmaker

militiaman
millwright
mineralist
missionary
naturalist
negotiator
newscaster
newsreader
newsvendor
nosologist
nurseryman
obituarist
orchardist
overlocker
panegyrist
pathfinder
pawnbroker
pedicurist
penologist
perruquier
pharmacist
philologer
platelayer
playwright
politician
postillion
postmaster
procurator
programmer
proprietor
prospector
pyrologist
quizmaster
railwayman
recitalist
researcher
ringmaster
roadmender
ropedancer
roughrider
saleswoman
scrutineer
sculptress
seamstress
seminarist
shipmaster
shipwright
shopfitter

shopkeeper
signwriter
sinologist
specialist
stewardess
strategist
supervisor
symphonist
technician
technocrat
theologian
timekeeper
translator
trawlerman
troubadour
typesetter
veterinary
victualler
vivandiere
wainwright
watchmaker
wharfinger
wholesaler
winegrower
wireworker
woodcarver
woodcutter
woodworker
yardmaster

11
accompanist
acoustician
adjudicator
antiquarian
audiologist
audiotypist
bargemaster
basketmaker
beachcomber
boatbuilder
boilermaker
broadcaster
bullfighter
businessman
candlemaker
chambermaid
chiropodist

choirmaster
chronologer
conductress
congressman
conveyancer
coordinator
coppersmith
cosmologist
demographer
draftswoman
draughtsman
electrician
embroiderer
entertainer
ethnologist
etymologist
executioner
facilitator
firefighter
genealogist
gravedigger
greengrocer
haberdasher
hairdresser
hairstylist
histologist
housefather
housekeeper
housemaster
housemother
hymnologist
illuminator
illusionisy
illustrator
infantryman
interpreter
interviewer
kennelmaid
kitchenmaid
laundrymaid
lifeboatman
maidservant
miniaturist
nurologist
nuerotomist
nightworker
numismatist
orientalist

osteologist
pamphleteer
paperhanger
parlourmaid
pathologist
pearlfisher
petrologist
philologist
philosopher
phytologist
phonologist
polyphonist
portraitist
probationer
proofreader
proprietrix
radiologist
rhetorician
roadsweeper
saxophonist
scoutmaster
scrapdealer
sharebroker
shepherdess
shipbreaker
shipbuilder
silversmith
slaughterer
smallholder
sociologist
stakeholder
steeplejack
stockbroker
stockholder
stockjobber
stonecutter
storekeeper
taxidermist
telegrapher
telephonist
toastmaster
tobacconist
topographer
typographer
underwriter
upholsterer
washerwoman
wheelwright

witchdoctor
woolstapler
xylophonist

12

accordionist
ambulanceman
anaesthetist
artilleryman
calligrapher
caricaturist
cardiologist
cartographer
cheesemonger
chiropractor
chronologist
churchwarden
clarinettist
commissioner
confectioner
cosmographer
costermonger
craniologist
demonstrator
dendrologist
ecclesiastic
Egyptologist
elocutionist
entomologist
entrepreneur
escapologist
ethnographer
footplateman
geometrician
geriatrician
greasemokey
hagiographer
hydrographer
immunologist
instructress
jurisconsult
longshoreman
manufacturer
metallurgist
mineralogist
newspaperman
nutritionist
obstetrician

orchestrator
orthodontist
orthographer
paediatrician
photographer
phrenologist
physiologist
postmistress
practitioner
professional
propagandist
proprietress
psychiatrist
psychologist
radiographer
receptionist
restaurateur
schoolmaster
screenwriter
scriptwriter
seismologist
sharecropper
sharpshooter
slaughterman
sportscaster
sportwriter
statistician
stenographer
stonebreaker
stonedresser
technologist
telegraphist
toxicologist
veterinarian
warehouseman

13
administrator
agriculturist
archaeologist
bibliographer
campanologist
choreographer
contortionist
cryptographer
dermatologist
draughtswoman
gynaecologist

industrialist
lexicographer
mathematician
meteorologist
ornithologist
paediatrician
schoolteacher
subcontractor
ventriloquist

2+ words
able seaman
ad-man
air hostess
air steward
antique dealer
army officer
art critic
art dealer
art master
art mistress
audit clerk
ballet dancer
ballet master
bank clerk
bank manager
barrow boy
bell founder
bell ringer
bill-sticker
bird-watcher
booking clerk
bus conductor
bus driver
cab driver
cabin boy
cabinet maker
café owner
car salesman
carpet fitter
civil servant
claim agent
clapper boy
clog dancer
cloth worker
co-pilot
corn chandler
co-star

crane driver
daily help
delivery man
desk clerk
disc jockey
dog breeder
dog trainer
dress designer
drum major
dry-cleaner
engine driver
errand boy
eye doctor
faith healer
farm labourer
field worker
film actor
film critic
film director
film extra
film maker
film producer
film star
fish curer
fortune teller
fruit picker
gas fitter
gem cutter
ghost writer
glass blower
glass cutter
glue boiler
harbour master
harness maker
hired hand
hired help
home help
hop picker
ink maker
invoice clerk
iron founder
jet pilot
kennel maid
kennel man
lady's maid
land agent
lion tamer
loan agent

loan shark
lock keeper
log roller
lorry driver
loss adjuster
maid-of-all-work
maitre d'hotel
male model
man-at-arms
manual worker
metal worker
mill owner
nautch girl
night porter
night sister
odd job man
office boy
office worker
onion seller
onion-man
opera singer
organ builder
organ grinder
panel beater
park keeper
park ranger

pastry cook
pearl diver
piano tuner
pop singer
press officer
prima donna
prison warder
private eye
prize fighter
racing driver
rat catcher
sales manager
scene painter
scene shifter
scullery maid
seed merchant
servant girl
serving maid
serving man
sheep farmer
ship owner
shop assistant
shop steward
special agent
speed cop
station master

street sweeper
sugar refiner
systems analyst
tally clerk
tax collector
tax inspector
tea blender
tea planter
theatre critic
tin miner
town planner
traffic cop
tram driver
travel agent
tree surgeon
wet nurse
weather man
window cleaner
window dresser
wine merchant
wine waiter
wool carder
wool sorter
wool trader
works manager

OPERA

Famous operas
Gilbert and Sullivan
Opera terminology

FAMOUS OPERAS

4
Aida (Verdi)
Lulu (Berg)

5
Faust (Gounod)
Norma (Bellini)
Orfeo (Monteverdi)
Tosca (Puccini)

6
Carmen (Bizet)
Ernani (Verdi)
Figaro (*The Marriage of*,
Mozart)
Oberon (Weber)
Onegin (*Eugene*,
Tchaikovsky)
Otello (Verdi)
Rienzi (Wagner)

7
Fidelio (Beethoven)
Macbeth (Verdi)
Nabucco (Verdi)
Tristan (*and*
Isolde,Wagner)
Wozzeck (Berg)

8
Falstaff (Verdi)
Idomineo (Mozart)
Parsifal (Wagner)
Traviata (*La*, Verdi)
Turandot (Puccini)

9
Lohengrin (Wagner)
Pagliacci (*I*, Leoncavallo)
Trovatore (*Il*, Verdi)

2+ words
Cavalleria Rusticana
(Mascagni)
Cosi Fan Tutte (Mozart)
Don Giovanni (Mozart)
Hansel and Gretel
(Humperdinck)
La Bohème (Puccini)
Peter Grimes (Britten)
The Ring (Wagner)

GILBERT AND SULLIVAN

OPERAS
Gondoliers, The (*or* The
King of Barataria)
Grand Duke, The (*or*
The Statutory Duel)
HMS Pinafore (*or* The
Lass that Loved a Sailor)
Iolanthe (*or* The Peer
and the Peri)
Mikado, The (*or* The
Town of Titipu)
Patience (*or* Bunthorne's
Bride)
Pirates of Penzance (*or*
The Slave of Duty)
Princess Ida (*or* Castle
Adamant)
Ruddigore (*or* The
Witch's Curse)
Sorcerer, The
Trial by Jury
Utopia Limited
Yeomen of the Guard,
The (*or* The Merryman
and his Maid)

CHARACTERS
Angelina (plaintiff, *Trial*)
Bunthorne (caricature of
Oscar Wilde and
aesthetes, *Patience*)
Duke of Plaza Toro
('celebrated underrated
nobleman', *Gondoliers*)
Edwin (defendant, *Trial*)

Ko-Ko (Lord High
Executioner, *Mikado*)
Little Buttercup (bum-
boat woman, *Pinafore*)
Lord Chancellor ('such a
susceptible Chancellor',
Iolanthe)
Major General ('the very
model of a modern
major general', *Pirates*)
Nanki-Poo (prince
disguised as a wandering
minstrel, *Mikado*)
Pirate King (*Pirates*)
Point, Jack (sad jester,
Yeomen)
Pooh-Bah (Lord High
Everything Else, *Mikado*)
Porter, Sir Joseph ('ruler
of the Queen's navy',
Pinafore)
Ruth (pirate maid of all
work, *Pirates*)
Yum-Yum (delicious
heroine, *Mikado*)

OPERA TERMINOLOGY

3
ENO
Met
ROH

4
aria

5
buffa (comic)
seria (serious)

6
chorus

7
verismo (realism)

8
libretto

operetta
overture

9
singspiel (opera with
spoken dialogue)

10
intermezzo
recitative

12
sprechgesang (speech-
song)

2+ words
bel canto (smooth and
sweet tone)
prima donna

PAINT/PAINTING

Paint
Painting
See also **ART**

PAINT

3
dye
oil

4
coat
daub
draw
limn
matt
oils
tint
tone
wash

5
glaze
gloss
shade
shape
trace

6
colour
enamel
medium
pastel
primer
raddle
sketch

7
acrylic
gouache
lacquer
outline
portray
scumble

tempera
varnish

8
describe
eggshell
emulsion

9
distemper
undercoat
whitewash

10
illuminate
illustrate
underpaint

11
watercolour

PAINTING

3
oil

4
bust
daub
head
icon
nude
view

5
mural
pietà
tondo

6
canvas
fresco

7
diptych
gouache

profile
reredos
retable

8
exterior
interior
nativity
nocturne
panorama
pastoral
portrait
prospect
seascape
skyscape
triptych

9
aquarelle
grisaille
landscape
miniature
townscape

10
altarpiece
cloudscape
monochrome
nightpiece
polychrome
riverscape

11
composition
crucifixion
watercolour

12
annunciation
illumination

2+ words
still life

PAINTERS

FAMOUS PAINTERS

3

Cox (David, UK)
Dix (Otto, German)
Dou (Gerard, Dutch)
Fry (Roger, UK)

4

Bell (Robert Anning, UK)
Bone (Muirhead, UK)
Cuyp (Albert, Dutch)
Dali (Salvador, Spanish)
Doré (Gustave, French)
Dufy (Raoul, French)
Etty (William, UK)
Gill (Eric, UK)
Goya (Francisco, Spanish)
Gris (Juan, Spanish)
Gros (Antoine, French)
Hals (Frans, Dutch)
Hunt (William Holman, UK)
John (Augustus/Gwen UK)
Kent (William, UK)
Klee (Paul, Swiss)
Lely (Peter, UK)
Maes (Nicolaes, Dutch)
Marc (Franz, German)
Miro (Joan, Spanish)
Nash (Paul, UK)
Opie (John, UK)
Reni (Guido, Italian)
Rosa (Salvator, Italian)
West (Benjamin, US/UK)

5

Bacon (Francis, Irish/UK)
Bakst (Leon, Russian)
Blake (Peter/William, UK)
Bosch (Hieronymus, Dutch)
Bouts (Dirk, Dutch)
Brown (Ford Madox, UK)

Corot (Camille, French)
Crome (John, UK)
Danby (Francis, Irish)
David (Jacques Louis, French)
Degas (Edgar, French)
Dürer (Albrecht, German)
Ensor (James, Belgian)
Ernst (Max, German)
Frith (William, UK)
Grosz (George, German)
Hirst (Damien, UK)
Homer (Winslow, US)
Klimt (Gustav, Austrian)
Johns (Jasper, US)
Léger (Fernand, French)
Lewis (Wyndham, UK)
Lippi (Fra Filippo, Italian)
Lowry (L. S., UK)
Manet (Eduard, French)
Mengs (Anton, German)
Metsu (Gabriel, Dutch)
Monet (Claude, French)
Moses (Grandma, US)
Munch (Edvard, Norwegian)
Nolde (Emil, German)
Orpen (William, Irish)
Piper (John, UK)
Redon (Odilon, French)
Ricci (Sebastiano, Italian)
Riley (Bridget, UK)
Rossi (Giovanni, Italian)
Scott (Peter, UK)
Spear (Ruskin, UK)
Steen (Jan, Dutch)
Watts (George Frederick, UK)

6

Boudin (Eugène, French)
Braque (Georges, French)
Buffet (Bernard, French)
Claude (*Claude Lorrain*, French)
Cooper (Samuel, UK)

Copley (John, US)
Cosway (Richard, UK)
Cotman (John Sell, UK)
Derain (André, French)
Duccio (di Bouninsegna, Italian)
Fuseli (Henry Swiss/UK)
Giotto (di Bondoni, Italian)
Girtin (Thomas, UK)
Greuze (Jean-Baptiste, French)
Guardi (Francesco, Italian)
Haydon (Benjamin Robert, UK)
Ingres (Jean, French)
Knight (Laura, UK)
Laszlo (Philip, Hungarian)
Lurçat (Jean, French)
Mabuse (Jan, Dutch)
Martin (John, UK)
Matsys (Quentin, Dutch)
Millet (Jean, French)
Morris (William, UK)
Palmer (Samuel, UK)
Pisano (Nicola, Italian)
Renoir (Pierre, French)
Ribera (José de, Spanish)
Rivera (Diego, Mexican)
Romney (George, UK)
Rothko (Mark, US)
Rubens (Peter-Paul, Flemish)
Seurat (Georges, French)
Signac (Paul, French)
Sisley (Alfred, UK)
Stubbs (George, UK)
Titian (*Tiziano Vecellio*, Italian)
Turner (J.W.M., UK)
Verrio (Antonio, Italian)
Warhol (Andy, US)
Wilkie (David, UK)
Zeuxis (ancient Greece)

7

Apelles (ancient Greece)
Audubon (John, US)
Bellini (Gentile/Giovanni, Italian)
Bonnard (Pierre, French)
Cézanne (Paul, French)
Chagall (Marc, Russian/French)
Chardin (Jean-Baptiste, French)
Cimabue (Italian)
Courbet (Gustave, French)
Cranach (Lukas, German)
Daumier (Honoré, French)
Gauguin (Paul, French)
Hobbema (Meindert, Dutch)
Hockney (David, UK)
Hogarth (William, UK)
Hokusai (Japanese)
Holbein (Hans, German)
Hoppner (John, UK)
Kneller (Godfrey, UK)
Lancret (Nicolas, French)
Lochner (Stefan, German)
Lorrain (Claude, French)
Martini (Simone, Italian)
Matisse (Henri, French)
Memlinc/Memling (Hans, Dutch)
Millais (John, UK)
Morisot (Berthe, French)
Morland (George, UK)
Murillo (Bartolome, Spanish)
O'Keeffe (Georgia, US)
Picasso (Pablo, Spanish)
Pollock (Jackson, US)
Poussin (Nicolas, French)
Rackham (Arthur, UK)
Raeburn (Henry, UK)
Raphael (*Raffaello Sanzio*, Italian)
Rouault (Georges, French)

Sargent (John Singer, US/UK)
Schiele (Egon, Austrian)
Sickert (Walter, UK)
Soutine (Chaim, French)
Spencer (Stanley, UK)
Teniers (David, Dutch)
Tiepolo (Giovanni, Italian)
Uccello (Paolo, Italian)
Utrillo (Maurice, French)
Vermeer (Jan, Dutch)
Watteau (Antoine, French)
Wootton (Frank, UK)

8

Angelico (Fra, Italian)
Annigoni (Pietro, Italian)
Beckmann (Max, German)
Bronzino (*Agnolo di Cosimo*, Italian)
Brueghel (Jan/Pieter, Flemish)
Carraci (Annibale, Italian)
Crivelli (Carlo, Italian)
Hilliard (Nicholas, UK)
Jordaens (Jakob, Dutch)
Kirchner (Ludwig, German)
Kollwitz (Käthe, German)
Landseer (Edwin, UK)
Lawrence (Thomas, UK)
Leonardo (da Vinci, Italian)
Magritte (René, Belgian)
Mantegna (Andrea, Italian)
Masaccio (Tommaso, Italian)
Mondrian (Piet, Dutch)
Munnings (Alfred, UK)
Perugino (Pietro, Italian)
Piarensi (Giambattista, Italian)
Pissarro (Camille, French)
Reynolds (Joshua, UK)

Rossetti (Dante Gabriel, UK)
Rousseau (Henri 'douanier', French)
Ruysdael/Ruisdael (Jakob, Dutch)
Veronese (Paolo, Italian)
Vlaminck (Maurice, French)
Whistler (James, US/Rex, UK)

9

Altdorfer (Albrecht, German)
Beardsley (Aubrey, UK)
Bonington (Richard, UK)
Canaletto (*Antonio Canal*, Italian)
Carpaccio (Vittore, Italian)
Constable (John, UK)
Correggio (Antonio, Italian)
Delacroix (Eugene, French)
Feininger (Lyonel, US)
Fragonard (Jean, French)
Friedrich (Caspar David, German)
Giorgione (Giorgio Italian)
Greenaway (Kate, UK)
Grünewald (Matthias, German)
Hiroshige (Japanese)
Honthorst (Gerrit, Dutch)
Kandinsky (Wassily, Russian)
Kokoschka (Oscar Austrain)
Nicholson (Ben, UK)
Rembrandt (van Rijn, Dutch)
Velasquez/Velazquez (Diego, Spanish)

10
Botticelli (Sandro, Italian)
Caravaggio (Michelangelo, Italian)
Modigliani (Amedeo, Italian)
Rowlandson (Thomas, UK)
Sutherland (Graham, UK)
Tintoretto (*Jacopo Robusti*, Italian)
Verrochio (Andrea, Italian)

10
Gentileschi (Orazio, Italian)
Ghirlandaio (Domenico, Italian)

11
Gainsborough (Thomas UK)
Lichtenstein (Roy US)
Michelangelo (Buonarrotti, Italian)

2+ words
Alma-Tadema (Lawrence, UK)
Burne-Jones (Edward, UK)
Da Vinci (Leonardo, Italian)
de Hooch (Pieter, Dutch)
Della Robbia (Luca, Italian)
Del Sarto (Andrea, Italian)

El Greco (*Domenikos Theotokopoulos*, Greek/Spanish)
Fantin-Latour (Henri, French)
Holman Hunt (William, UK)
Toulouse-Lautrec (Henri de, French)
Van Dyck (Anthony, Dutch/English)
Van Eyck (Jan, Flemish)
Van Gogh (Vincent, Dutch)

PHILOSOPHERS

4

Ayer (Alfred, UK)
Cato (Roman)
Hume (David, UK)
Kant (Immanuel,
German)
Marx (Karl, German)
Mill (John Stuart, UK)
Ryle (Gilbert, UK)
Vico (Giambattista,
Italian)
Weil (Simone, French)
Zeno (Greek)

5

Bacon (Francis, UK)
Comte (Auguste,
French)
Hegel (Goerg Wilhelm
Friedrich, German)
Locke (John, UK)
Moore (G.E., UK)
Plato (Greek)

6

Adorno (Theodor,
German)
Berlin (Isaiah, UK)
Fichte (Johann Gottlieb,
German)
Herzen (Aleksandr,
Russian)
Hobbes (Thomas,
English)
Pascal (Blaise, France)

Popper (Karl, UK)
Sartre (Jean-Paul,
French)
Scotus (Duns *or* John,
Scottish)
Seneca (Roman)
Tagore (Rabindrath,
Indian)
Thales (Greek)

7

Abelard (Peter, French)
Aquinas (St Thomas,
Italian)
Bentham (Jeremy, UK)
Bergson (Henri, French)
Derrida (Jacques,
French)
Diderot (Denis, French)
Erasmus (Desiderius,
Dutch)
Jaspers (Karl, German)
Russell (Bertrand, UK)
Scruton (Roger, UK)
Spinoza (Benedict,
Dutch)

8

Diogenes (Greek)
Epicurus (Greek)
Leibnitz (Gottfried,
German)
Rousseau (Jean-Jacques,
Swiss)
Socrates (Greek)
Voltaire (*François-Marie
Arouet*, French)

9

Aristotle (Greek)
Confucius (Chinese)
Descartes (René,
French)
Epictetus (Greek)
Heidegger (Martin,
German)
Lucretius (Roman)
Montaigne (Michel de,
French)
Nietzsche (Friedrich,
German)
Whitehead (Alfred
North, UK)

10

Democritus (Greek)
Empedocles (Greek)
Heraclitus (Greek)
Pythagoras (Greek)
Xenocrates (Greek)

11

Kierkegaard (Søren,
Danish)
Montesquieu (Charles,
French)

12

Schopenhauer (Arthur,
German)
Wittgenstein (Ludwig,
Austrian)

PLANTS

A plant
Parts of a plant
Plant species

A PLANT
.

4
bush
herb
tree
vine
reed
weed
wort

5
cycad
grass
liana
shrub

6
alpine
annual
cactus
cereal
exotic
flower

7
climber
creeper
potherb
sapling

8
biennial
epiphyte
parasite
seedling

9
evergreen
perennial
succulent
vegetable

xerophyte

PARTS OF A PLANT

3
bud
pod

4
bark
bulb
burr
corm
leaf
pith
root
seed
stem
wood

5
berry
blade
bract
calyx
float
frond
petal
sepal
spore
stalk
stipe
theca
tuber
whorl
xylem

6
anther
branch
carpel
lamina
lignin
pistil
pollen
runner
stamen
stigma

sucker

7
eyespot
petiole
radicle
rhizoid
rhizome

8
holdfast
perianth

PLANT SPECIES

3
box
bur
dal
ers
fog
hop
ivy
rue
rye
udo
urd
yam

4
aira
alga
aloe
anil
arum
bene
bent
blue
coca
coix
deme
diss
dock
doob
dura
fern
flag
gill

hebe
hemp
herb
iris
kans
kava
ling
lyme
moss
rape
reed
rice
rusa
rush
sago
sunn
tare
teff
tore
tutu
vine
weld
whin
woad
wort
yarr

5
abaca
anise
anona
arold
bhang
bluet
bohea
briar
brier
briza
broom
buchu
bugle
bunch
calla
canna
caper
carex
chive
couch

cress
cumin
cutch
durra
dwale
erica
furze
gorse
guaco
halfa
haulm
henna
jalap
kemps
liana
lotus
lupin
medic
morel
naiad
orach
orris
oryza
oshac
panax
panic
rhyne
sedge
sisal
spear
spink
sumac
thorn
vetch
viola

6
acacia
allium
alpine
alsike
arnica
arrach
arundo
bajree
barley
bedder
bejuco

betony
biblus
blinks
bocage
borage
briony
bryony
burnet
cactus
cassia
catnip
cereal
cereus
cicely
cicuta
cissus
citrus
cockle
coffee
comfry
conium
cotton
cowage
cowpea
crocus
croton
darnel
datura
derris
desmid
dodder
fescue
filago
fimble
fiorin
frutex
fungus
garlic
gervas
ginger
gnetum
gromel
hedera
hypnum
iberis
kalmia
knawel
kousso

lolium
lupine
madder
mallow
marram
matico
medick
myrtle
nardus
nettle
orache
orchil
orpine
paigle
pampas
pepper
phleum
privet
protea
pteris
quitch
radish
ramson
rattan
redtop
riccia
ruppia
salvia
sesame
silene
smilax
spurge
squill
sumach
teasel
teazel
thrift
twitch
uniola
urtica
yarrow
zinnia

7

aconite
alfalfa
alkanet
allseed

alyssum
amellus
atropin
begonia
blawort
bracken
bramble
bugloss
bulrush
burdock
calumba
campion
caraway
cardoon
carduus
carline
cassava
catmint
clivers
comfrey
cowbane
cowslip
cudweed
dioecia
dittany
dogbane
dogwood
esparto
eulelia
festuca
foggage
foxtail
genista
ginseng
heather
hemlock
henbane
hogweed
honesty
kingcup
jasmine
lucerne
malacca
manihot
milfoil
mugwort
mullein
mustard

navette
nigella
opuntia
oregano
papyrus
petunia
ragwort
rhubarb
saffron
skirret
sorghum
spignel
spurrey
squitch
statice
syringa
thistle
timothy
tobacco
trefoil
verbena
vervain
vetiver
whangee
zizania

8

absinthe
acanthus
agrimony
angelica
arenaria
asphodel
banewort
barberry
bedstraw
bindweed
camomile
cannabis
capsicum
cinqfoil
cleavers
costmary
cowberry
cyclamen
dogberry
eleusine
feverfew

fleabane
fleawort
foxglove
fumitory
geranium
gromwell
goutweed
henequen
hibiscus
larkspur
lavender
lungwort
mandrake
marigold
mariposa
milkweed
milkwort
oleander
plantain
plumbago
pondweed
puffball
ratsbane
reedmace
sainfoin
saltwort
samphire
shamrock
sparaxis
tuberose
turmeric
valerian
veronica
virginia
wormwood
xanthium

9

anthurium
aquilegia
arrowroot
artemisia
aubrietia
baldmoney
blueberry
celandine
chickweed
columbine

coriander
cranberry
crosswort
dandelion
edelweiss
eglantine
eyebright
fenugreek
forsythia
germander
gladiolus
glasswort
goldenrod
groundsel
hellebore
hollyhock
horehound
horsetail
liverwort
marijuana
moneywort
monkshood
narcissus
penstemon
pimpernel
portulaca
pyrethrum
raspberry
sagebrush
saxifrage
snakewort
spearmint
spearwort
speedwell
spikenard
stinkweed
sunflower
tormentil
witchweed
woundwort

10

agapanthus
angiosperm
aspidistra
astragalus
belladonna
blackberry

blackthorn
butterwort
chokeberry
corncockle
cornflower
cuckoopint
dragonroot
fritillary
goatsbeard
goosegrass
gooseberry
granadilla
heliotrope
jimsonweed
loganberry
marguerite
mignonette
montbretia
nasturtium
pennyroyal
pentstemon
peppermint
polyanthus
potentilla
spiderwort
spleenwort
stitchwort
tumbleweed
watercress
willowherb

11

bittersweet
bladderwort
calceolaria
convolvulus
cotoneaster
gillyflower
honeysuckle
huckleberry
meadowsweet
pelargonium
wintergreen

2+ words
ale-hoop
all-good
ash-wort

awl-wort
bog-bean
bog-rush
bug-wort
cow parsley
dog-grass
dog-wheat

dyer's broom
flax-wort
lady's smock
moss pink
old man's beard
ox-heel
pop-weed

puss-tail
pussy willow
rubber plant
sea-pink
self-heal
star-wort
sweet pea

POEMS/POETRY

A poem
Parts of a poem
Poetic feet and metres
Poets

A POEM

3
lay
ode

4
epic
epos
hymn
saga
song

5
dirge
elegy
epode
haiku
idyll
lines
lyric
psalm
rhyme
tanka
verse

6
aubade
ballad
rondel
sonnet

7
ballade
eclogue
epigram
georgic
rondeau
sestina
triolet
virelay

8
clerihew
encomium
limerick
madrigal
palinode
threnody

9
complaint
dithyramb
roundelay
villanelle

12
epithalamium
prothalamium

PART OF A POEM

3
fit

4
book
foot
line

5
canto
envoi
epode
octet
stave
verse

6
burden
chorus
octave
sestet
stanza
tercet

7
couplet
distich
measure

refrain
strophe

8
quatrain

POETIC FEET AND METRES

4
iamb

6
dactyl
iambic
iambus

7
anapest
spondee
trochee

8
choriamb
dactylic
spondaic
tribrach
trochaic

9
hexameter

10
amphibrach
choriambic
choriambus
heptameter
pentameter
tetrameter
tribrachic

11
alexandrine

12
amphibrachic

POETS

3

Poe (Edgar Allen, US)
Pye (Henry, UK)

4

Benn (Gottfried, German)
Cruz (Juana, Mexican)
Gray (Thomas, UK)
Gunn (Thom, UK/US)
Hill (Geoffrey, UK)
Hogg (James, Scottish)
Hood (Thomas, UK)
Hugo (Victor, French)
Hunt (Leigh, UK)
Lear (Edward, UK)
Muir (Edwin, Scottish)
Ovid (Roman)
Owen (Wilfred, UK)
Pope (Alexander, UK)
Sadi (Persian)
Tate (Allen, US/Nahum, English)
Wain (John, UK)

5

Auden (W. H., UK)
Blake (William, UK)
Burns (Robert, Scottish)
Byron (Lord George Gordon, UK)
Carew (Thomas, English)
Clare (John, UK)
Colum (Padraic, Irish)
Crane (Hart, US)
Dante (Alighieri, Italian)
Donne (John, English)
Eliot (T. S., US/UK)
Frost (Robert, US)
Gower (John, English)
Hafiz (Persian)
Hardy (Thomas, UK)
Heine (Heinrich, German)
Homer (Greek)
Keats (John, UK)

Keyes (Sidney, UK)
Lorca (Federico Garcia, Spanish)
Lucan (Roman)
Marot (Clément, French)
Moore (Marianne, US/Thomas, Irish)
Noyes (Alfred, UK)
Péguy (Charles, French)
Perse (St Jean, French)
Plath (Sylvia, US)
Pound (Ezra, US)
Prior (Matthew, UK)
Rilke (Rainer Maria, Austrian)
Sachs (Hans, German)
Scott (Sir Walter, Scottish)
Smith (Stevie, UK)
Tasso (Torquato, Italian)
Varro (Marcus Terentius, Roman)
Vigny (Alfred de, French)
Watts (Isaac, UK)
Wyatt (Thomas, English)
Yeats (W.B., Irish)

6

Austin (Alfred, UK)
Belloc (Hilaire, UK)
Binyon (Robert, UK)
Bishop (Elizabeth, US)
Brooke (Rupert, UK)
Bryant (William Cullens, US)
Camoes (Luis de, Portuguese)
Céline (Louis, French)
Cowley (Abraham, English)
Cowper (William, UK)
Crabbe (George, UK)
Dobson (Henry, UK)
Dowson (Ernest, UK)
Dryden (John, English)
Dunbar (William, Scottish)
Eluard (Paul, French)
Eusden (Laurence, UK)

Fuller (Roy, UK)
George (Stefan, German)
Gibran (Kahlil, Lebanese)
Goethe (J.W. von, German)
Graves (Robert, UK)
Heaney (Seamus, Irish)
Hesiod (Greek)
Horace (Roman)
Hughes (Ted, UK)
Jonson (Ben, English)
Landor (Walter Savage, UK)
Larkin (Philip, UK)
Lowell (Amy/James Russell, Robert, US)
Millay (Edna St Vincent, US)
Milton (John, English)
Motion (Andrew, UK)
Musset (Alfred de, French)
Neruda (Pablo, Chilean)
Nerval (Gérard de, French)
Pindar (Greek)
Ransom (John Crowe, US)
Sappho (Greek)
Sidney (Sir Philip, English)
Thomas (Dylan, Welsh/Edward, English)
Valéry (Paul, French)
Villon (François, French)
Virgil (Roman)
Warton (Thomas, UK)

7

Addison (Joseph, UK)
Alcaeus (Greek)
Ariosto (Ludovico, Italian)
Bentley (Edmund Clerihew, UK)
Blunden (Edmund, UK)
Boileau (Nicolas, French)
Bridges (Robert, UK)

Caedmon (Old English)
Chapman (George, English)
Chaucer (Geoffrey, English)
Chénier (André, French)
Collins (William, UK)
Crashaw (Richard, English)
Douglas (Keith, UK)
Drayton (Michael, English)
Emerson (Ralph Waldo, US)
Flecker (James Elroy, UK)
Gautier (Théophile, French)
Herbert (George, English)
Herrick (Robert, English)
Hopkins (Gerard Manley, UK)
Housman (A.E., UK)
Jeffers (Robinson, US)
Johnson (Lionel/Dr Samuel, UK)
Juvenal (Roman)
Khayyam (Omar, Persian)
Kipling (Rudyard, UK)
Lindsay (Vachel, US)
Martial (Roman)
Marvell (Andrew, English)
McGough (Roger, UK)
Mistral (Frédéric, Provencal French)
Newbolt (Sir Henry, UK)
Pushkin (Alexander, Russian)
Rimbaud (Arthur, French)
Ronsard (Pierre de, French)
Sassoon (Siegfried, UK)
Shelley (Percy Bysshe, UK)
Sitwell (Dame Edith, UK)
Skelton (John, English)

Southey (Robert, UK)
Spender (Stephen, UK)
Stevens (Wallace, US)
Vaughan (Henry, English)
Whitman (Walt, US)

8
Anacreon (Greek)
Berryman (John, US)
Betjeman (John, UK)
Browning (Robert, UK)
Campbell (Roy, South African)
Catullus (Roman)
Claudian (Roman)
cummings (e.e., US)
Davenant (Sir William, English)
Ginsberg (Allen, US)
Henryson (Robert, Scottish)
Lawrence (D.H., UK)
Macleish (Archibald, US)
Malherbe (François de, French)
Mallarmé (Stéphane, French)
Petrarch (Francesco, Italian)
Philemon (Greek)
Rossetti (Dante Gabriel/Christina, UK)
Sandburg (Carl, US)
Suckling (John, English)
Tennyson (Alfred Lord, UK)
Traherne (Thomas, English)
Verlaine (Paul, French)
Williams (William Carlos, US)

9
Akhmatova (Anna, Russian)
Coleridge (Samuel Taylor, UK)

D'Annunzio (Gabriele, Italian)
Dickinson (Emily, US)
Goldsmith (Oliver, Irish)
Hölderlin (Friedrich, German)
Lamartine (Alphonse de, French)
Lermontov (Mikhail, Russian)
Lucretius (Roman)
Masefield (John, UK)
Rochester (John Wilmot, English)
Swinburne (Algernon Charles, UK)

10
Baudelaire (Charles, French)
Chesterton (G.K., UK)
Fitzgerald (Edward, UK)
Longfellow (Henry Wadsworth, US)
Mandelstam (Osip, Russian)
Propertius (Sextus, Roman)
Theocritus (Greek)
Wordsworth (William, UK)

11
Apollinaire (Guillaume, French)
Shakespeare (William, English)
Yevtushenko (Yevgeny, Russian)

2+ words
Day Lewis (Cecil, UK)
de la Mare (Walter, UK)
La Fontaine (Jean de, French)

POLITICIANS

A politician
Famous politicians
Presidents of the USA
Prime ministers of Great
Britain

A POLITICIAN

2
MP
PM

3
dry
MEP
MSP
MWA
PPS
red
wet

4
Nazi
peer
Tory
Trot
whip

5
lefty

6
commie
leftie
Maoist
member

7
comrade
Fabian
fascist
leftist
liberal
Marxist
radical
senator

activist
Blairite
centrist
Democrat
minister
moderate
politico
populist
rightist
royalist
unionist

9
anarchist
canvasser
communist
secretary
sectarian
socialist
Stalinist
Taioseach

10
chancellor
monarchist
Republican

11
backbencher
Congressman
imperialist
independent
nationalist
reactionary

2+ words
chief whip
first minister
foreign secretary
hard-liner
home secretary
junior minister
left-winger
Lib Dem
life peer
neo-con
prime minister
right-winger

party member

FAMOUS POLITICIANS
AND POLITICAL FIGURES
(excluding British prime
ministers and US
presidents)

3
Fox (Charles James, UK
Whig leader)
Kun (Bela, Hungarian
Communist)
Mao (Zedong/Tse Tung,
Communist Chinese
leader)

4
Amin (Idi, Ugandan
president)
Benn (Tony, UK Labour
politician)
Biko (Steve, South
African activist)
Blum (Léon, French
socialist)
Chou (En-Lai,
Communist Chinese
statesman)
Foot (Michael, Labour
Party leader)
Gore (Al, US vice-
president)
Hess (Rudolf, German
Nazi leader)
Holt (Harold, Australian
PM)
Howe (Geoffrey, UK
Conservative politician)
King (Martin Luther,
US civil rights leader)
Kohl (Helmut, German
chancellor)
Meir (Golda, Israeli PM)
Owen (David, UK
Labour and SDP
politician)

Rhee (Singman, South Korean statesman)

Rusk (Dean, US statesman)

Tito (Marshal, Yugoslavian Communist leader)

Tutu (Desmond, South African church leader)

5

Agnew (Spiro T., US vice-president)

Ahern (Bertie, Irish PM)

Annan (Kofi, UN secretary general)

Astor (Nancy, UK politician)

Banda (Hastings, Malawian statesman)

Begin (Menachem, Israeli PM)

Beria (Lavrenti, USSR politician)

Bevan (Aneurin, UK politician, founder of the NHS)

Bevin (Ernest, UK politician)

Botha (Louis/ P.W. South African PMs)

Brown (Gordon, UK Labour politician)

Burke (Edmund, UK politician and writer)

Clark (Helen, NZ PM)

Dewar (Donald, Scottish First Minister)

Hague (William, UK Conservative Party leader)

Laval (Pierre, French PM)

Lenin (*Vladimir Ilyich Ulyanov*, USSR leader)

Mbeki (Thabo, South African president)

Nehru (Jawaharlal, Indian PM)

Peròn (Juan, Argentinian leader)

Putin (Vladimir, Russian president)

Rabin (Yitzhak, Israeli PM)

Sadat (Anwar, Egyptian president)

Smith (Ian, Rhodesian PM)

Smith (John, UK Labour Party leader)

Smuts (Jan, South African general and PM)

Solon (Athenian lawgiver)

Steel (David, UK Liberal Party leader)

Villa (Pancho, Mexican revolutionary)

6

Aquino (Cory, Philippine president)

Arafat (Yasser, Palestinian leader)

Bhutto (Benazir (Pakistani politician)

Brandt (Willi, West German chancellor)

Caesar (Julius, Roman general and dictator)

Castro (Fidel, Cuban president)

Cavour (Camillo, Italian statesman)

Chirac (Jacques, French president)

Danton (Georges, French revolutionary leader)

Dubcek (Alexander, Czech leader)

Dulles (John Foster, US statesman)

Engels (Friedrich, German political writer)

Erhard (Ludwig, West German chancellor)

Franco (Francisco, Spanish Fascist leader)

Gandhi (Indira, Indian PM)

Gandhi (Mohandas, Indian leader)

Healey (Denis, UK Labour politician)

Hitler (Adolf, German Nazi leader, the Führer)

Howard (John, Australian PM)

Howard (Michael, UK Conservative leader)

Kaunda (Kenneth, Zambian president)

Kruger (Paul, president of Transvaal)

Marcos (Ferdinand, Indonesian president)

Merkel (Angela, German chancellor)

Mobutu (Sese Seko, Zairean president)

Morgan (Rhodri, Welsh First Minister)

Mosley (Oswald, UK Fascist)

Nasser (GamalAbdel, Egyptian president)

Pétain (Henri, French general and Vichy leader)

Powell (Enoch, UK politician)

Quayle (Dan, US vice-president)

Revere (Paul, US revolutionary)

Rhodes (Cecil, South African financier and PM)

Saddam (Hussein, Iraqi dictator)

Stalin (Joseph, USSR leader)

Wilkes (John, UK radical)

Zapata (Emiliano, Mexican revolutionary)

7
Acheson (Dean,
US statesman)
Allende (Salvador,
Chilean president)
Ataturk (Kemal, Turkish
leader)
Bolivar (Simon, South
American liberator)
Bormann (Martin,
German Nazi leader)
Gaddafi (Colonel
Muammar, Libyan leader)
Goering (Herman,
German Nazi leader)
Guevara (Che, Latin
American guerrilla)
Himmler (Heinrich,
Nazi leader)
Jenkins (Roy, UK Labour
and Lib Dem politician)
Kinnock (Neil, Labour
Party leader)
Kosygin (Aleksei, USSR
statesman)
Lumumba (Patrice,
Congolese leader)
Mandela (Nelson, South
African president)
Menzies (Robert,
Australian PM)
Mintoff (Dom, Maltese
leader)
Molotov (Vyacheslav,
USSR statesman)
Nkrumah (Kwame,
Ghanaian president)
Nyerere (Julius,
Tanzanian president)
Paisley (Rev. Ian, Ulster
politician)
Parnell (Charles, Irish
nationalist)
Pearson (Lester,
Canadian PM)
Raffles (Thomas,
founder of Singapore)
Salazar (Antonio,

Portuguese dictator)
Salmond (Alex, Scottish
SNP leader)
Sukarno (Ahmed,
Indonesian president)
Trotsky (Leon, USSR
leader)
Trudeau (Pierre,
Canadian PM)
Vorster (Johannes, South
African PM)
Wallace (William,
Scottish nationalist hero)
Whitlam (Gough,
Australian PM)
Yeltsin (Boris, Russian
president)

8
Adenauer (Konrad,
German chancellor)
Bismarck (Otto, Prussian
statesman)
Brezhnev (Leonid,
USSR leader)
Bulganin (Marshal
Nicolai, USSR leader)
Goebbels (Joseph,
German Nazi
propagandist)
Kenyatta (Jomo, Kenyan
president)
Khomeini (Ayatollah
Ruholla, Iranian leader)
Napoleon (Bonaparte,
French general and
emperor)
Pinochet (Augusto,
Chilean president)
Podgorny (Nikolai,
USSR statesman)
Poincaré (Raymond,
French president)
Pompidou (Georges,
French president)
Verwoerd (Hendrik,
South African PM)
Waldheim (Kurt, UN

secretary general)
Williams (Shirley, UK
Labour and Lib Dem
politician)

9
Berlusconi (Silvio, Italian
PM)
Gaitskell (Hugh, UK
Labour Party leader)
Garibaldi (Guiseppe,
Italian revolutionary)
Gorbachev (Mikhail,
USSR leader)
Milosevic (Slobodan,
Serbian president)
Mussolini (Benito,
Italian Fascist leader)
Pankhurst (Mrs
Emmeline, UK
suffragette leader)
Spartacus (leader of
Roman slave revolt)

10
Clemenceau (Georges,
French PM)
Hindenburg (Paul,
German general and
president)
Khrushchev (Nikita,
USSR leader)
Metternich (Klemens,
Austrian statesman)
Mitterand (François,
French president)
Ribbentrop (Joachim
von, German Nazi
leader)

11
Chamberlain (Austen,
UK statesman)
Diefenbaker (John,
Canadian PM)
Mountbatten (Lord
Louis, UK admiral and
administrator)

Robespierre (Maximilien, French revolutionary leader)
Shaftesbury (Earl of, UK social reformer)
Wilberforce (William, UK anti-slavery campaigner)

12
Banderanaike (Solomon, Sri Lankan statesman)
Hammarskjold (Dag, UN secretary general)

2+ words
Ben Gurion (David, Israeli PM)
Chiang Kai-shek (nationalist Chinese leader)
De Gaulle (Charles, French general and president)
De Valera (Eamon, Irish president)
Giscard d'Estaing (Valéry, French president)
Ho Chi Minh (Vietnamese revolutionary and leader)
Lee Kuan-yew (Singaporean president)

PRESIDENTS OF THE USA

4
Bush (George/George W.)
Ford (Gerald)
Polk (James K.)
Taft (William Howard)

5
Adams (John/John Quincey)
Grant (Ulysses S.)
Hayes (Rutherford B.)

Nixon (Richard M.)
Tyler (John)

6
Arthur (Chester A.)
Carter (Jimmy)
Hoover (Herbert C.)
Monroe (James)
Pierce (Franklin)
Reagan (Ronald)
Taylor (Zachary)
Truman (Harry S.)
Wilson (Woodrow)

7
Clinton (Bill [William Jefferson])
Harding (Warren Gamaliel)
Jackson (Andrew)
Johnson (Andrew/Lyndon B.)
Kennedy (John F.)
Lincoln (Abraham)
Madison (John)

8
Buchanan (James)
Coolidge (Calvin)
Fillmore (Millard)
Garfield (James A.)
Harrison (Benjamin/William)
McKinley (William)

9
Cleveland (Grover)
Jefferson (Thomas)
Roosevelt (Franklin Delano/Theodore)

10
Eisenhower (Dwight D.)
Washington (George)

2+ words
Van Buren (Martin)

PRIME MINISTERS OF GREAT BRITAIN

4
Bute (Lord/Earl of)
Eden (Sir Anthony)
Grey (Earl)
Peel (Sir Robert)
Pitt (William)

5
Blair (Tony)
Derby (Earl of)
Heath (Edward)
Major (John)
North (Lord)

6
Attlee (Clement)
Pelham (Henry)
Wilson (Harold)

7
Asquith (Herbert Henry)
Baldwin (Stanley)
Balfour (Arthur)
Canning (George)
Chatham (Earl of)
Grafton (Duke of)
Russell (Lord John)
Walpole (Sir Robert)

8
Aberdeen (Earl of)
Disraeli (Benjamin)
Goderich (Viscount)
Perceval (Spencer)
Portland (Duke of)
Rosebery (Earl of)
Thatcher (Margaret)

9
Addington (Henry)
Callaghan (James)
Churchill (Winston Spencer)
Gladstone (William Ewart)

Grenville (George)
Liverpool (Earl of)
Macdonald (James
Ramsay)
Macmillan (Harold)
Melbourne
(Lord/Viscount)
Newcastle (Duke of)
Salisbury (Marquess of)
Shelburne (Earl of)

10
Devonshire (Duke of)
Palmerston (Viscount)
Rockingham (Marquess
of)
Wellington (Duke of)
Wilmington (Earl of)

11
Chamberlain (Neville)

2+ words
Bonar Law (Andrew)
Douglas-Hume (Sir Alec)
Lloyd George (David)

POLITICS/ PARLIAMENT

Parliaments
Political parties
Terms used in parliament and politics

PARLIAMENTS

Country	Single Chamber	Lower House	Upper House
Australia		House of Representatives	Senate
Austria		Nationalrat	Bundesrat
Canada		House of Commons	Senate
China	National People's Congress		
Denmark	Folketing		
Finland	Eduskunta		
France		National Assembly	Senate
Germany		Bundestag	Bundesrat
Iceland	Althing		
India		Lok Sabha	Rajya Sabha
Iran	Majlis		
Ireland		Dáil (Eireann)	Seanad
Isle of Man	House of Keys		
Israel	Knesset		
Italy		Chamber of Deputies	Senate
Japan	Diet		
Netherlands	Staaten-Generaal (States General)		
Norway	Storting		
Poland	Sejm		
Portugal	Cortes		
Russia	Duma		
Spain	Cortes		
Sweden	Riksdag		
Turkey	Porte		
USA	Congress	House of Representatives	Senate

POLITICAL PARTIES

	Con	**4**
	DUP	bloc
2	GOP	
NF	Lab	**5**
	Lib	Whigs
3	SDP	
BNP	SNP	

6
Greens
Labour
Tories

7
Zionist

8
Fascists
Jacobins
Liberals
Marxists
Radicals

9
Democrats
Unionists

10
Bolsheviks
Communists
Falangists
Girondists
Mensheviks
Socialists

11
Blackshirts
Brownshirts
Republicans
Trotskyists

12
Nationalists

13
Conservatives

2+ words
Al Fatah
Fianna Fáil
Fine Gael
Lib Dems
New Labour
Plaid Cymru
Sinn Fein

***TERMS USED IN
PARLIAMENT AND
POLITICS***

2
EU
PR
UN

3
act
CBI
CIA
EEC
FBI
FCO
gag
IRA
law
PFI
PLO
red
sit
tax
TUC

4
ayes
bill
chad
coup
gain
left
lord
mace
NATO
noes
oath
OPEC
pact
pair
pass
peer
poll
rump
seat
spin
veto

vote
whip
writ

5
agent
amend
bench
bylaw
cadre
chair
clerk
count
draft
edict
elect
enact
forum
house
issue
junta
lobby
Lords
order
paper
party
purge
rally
right
SEATO
state
valid
voter

6
agenda
assent
backer
ballot
budget
caucus
clause
decree
divide
govern
heckle
leader
motion

oppose
picket
policy
putsch
quorum
recess
reform
report
ruling
satrap
secede
second
senate
speech
strike
summit
summon
teller
tyrant

7
adjourn
anarchy
barrack
boycott
cabinet
canvass
censure
chamber
closure
Commons
council
deficit
détente
devolve
dissent
elector
fascism
federal
finance
gallery
Hansard
heckler
impeach
mandate
Marxism
neutral
opening

outvote
pairing
passage
premier
primary
propose
radical
reading
recount
session
speaker
statute
toryism
tribune
tyrany
vacancy
Zionism

8
apartheid
assembly
autarchy
autocrat
autonomy
blockade
caudillo
chairman
commissar
commoner
democrat
dictator
dissolve
division
dominion
election
elective
feminism
feminist
hardline
hustings
lobbyist
majority
marginal
ministry
minority
monopoly
national
official

oligarch
petition
prorogue
republic
rollback
suffrage
Treasury
triumvir
unionism
woolsack

9
amendment
anarchism
autocracy
bicameral
coalition
Comintern
Cominform
democracy
deterrent
electoral
exchequer
legislate
oligarchy
ombudsman
politburo
president
sanctions
secretary
socialism
Stalinism
terrorism
Watergate
Whitehall

10
aristocrat
capitalism
collective
conference
federation
filibuster
government
guillotine
honourable
opposition
parliament

plebiscite
psephology
radicalism
referendum
republican
resolution
revolution
scrutineer
Troskyism
unicameral

11
adjournment
aristocracy
coexistence
confederacy
confederate
constituent
demarcation
dissolution
enfranchise
impeachment
imperialism
legislation
legislative
legislature
McCarthyism
nationalist
prerogative
reactionary
revisionism
revisionist

suffragette
syndicalism
syndicalist
Westminster
Witenagemot

12
commissioner
Commonwealth
conservatism
conservative
constituency
constitution
dictatorship

13
demonstration
international

2+ words
ballot box
Black Rod
corn law

division bell
Downing Street
free vote
green paper
home rule
House of Commons
House of Lords
lower house
left wing
number ten
order paper
poll tax
poor law
privy council
right wing
upper house
sit-in
welfare state
White House
white paper

PORTS

4
Acre (Israel)
Aden (Yemen)
Bari (Italy)
Cobh (Ireland)
Cork (Ireland)
Hull (UK)
Kiel (Germany)
Kobe (Japan)
Oban (UK)
Oran (Algeria)
Oslo (Norway)
Riga (Latvia)
Suez (Egypt)
Tyre (Lebanon)
Wick (UK)

5
Accra (Ghana)
Basra (Iraq)
Beira (Mozambique)
Belem (Brazil)
Brest (France)
Cadiz (Spain)
Dover (UK)
Eilat (Israel)
Emden (Germany)
Genoa (Italy)
Goole (UK)
Haifa (Israel)
Jaffa (Israel)
Lagos (Nigeria)
Larne (N. Ireland)
Malmo (Sweden)
Osaka (Japan)
Ostia (Italy)
Palma (Spain)
Perth (Australia)
Poole (UK)
Pusan (S. Korea)
Rabat (Morocco)
Sidon (Lebanon)
Tunis (Tunisia)
Vaasa (Sweden)

Yalta (Ukraine)

6
Abadan (Iran)
Albany (USA)
Ancona (Italy)
Barrow (UK)
Belize (Belize)
Bergen (Norway)
Bilbao (Spain)
Bombay (India)
Bootle (UK)
Boston (USA)
Bremen (Germany)
Calais (France)
Canton (China)
Cochin (India)
Danzig (Poland)
Darwin (Australia)
Dieppe (France)
Dublin (Ireland)
Durban (South Africa)
Gdansk (Poland)
Havana (Cuba)
Jarrow (UK)
Jeddah (Saudi Arabia)
Kuwait (Kuwait)
Lisbon (Portugal)
London (UK)
Luanda (Angola)
Lübeck (Germany)
Madras (India)
Manila (Philippines)
Mumbai (India)
Muscat (Oman)
Naples (Italy)
Narvik (Norway)
Odense (Denmark)
Odessa (Ukraine)
Oporto (Portugal)
Ostend (Belgium)
Panama (Panama)
Penang (Malaysia)
Recife (Brazil)
Sydney (Australia)
Tobruk (Libya)
Toulon (France)
Tromso (Norway)

Venice (Italy)
Whitby (UK)

7
Aalborg (Denmark)
Abidjan (Ivory Coast)
Ajaccio (Corsica)
Antwerp (Belgium)
Bangkok (Thailand)
Belfast (N. Ireland)
Bristol (UK)
Chatham (UK)
Colombo (Sri Lanka)
Conakry (Guinea)
Corunna (Spain)
Dunedin (New Zealand)
Dunkirk (France)
Foochow (China)
Geelong (Australia)
Grimsby (UK)
Hamburg (Germany)
Harwich (UK)
Karachi (Pakistan)
Leghorn (Italy)
Livorno (Italy)
Mombasa (Kenya)
Newport (UK)
Palermo (Italy)
Piraeus (Greece)
Rangoon (Burma)
Roscoff (France)
Rostock (Germany)
Swansea (UK)
Tallinn (Estonia)
Trieste (Italy)
Tripoli (Libya)

8
Auckland (New Zealand)
Benghazi (Libya)
Bordeaux (France)
Boulogne (France)
Brindisi (Italy)
Brisbane (Australia)
Calcutta (India)
Djibouti (Djibouti)
Haiphong (Vietnam)
Helsinki (Finland)

Holyhead (UK)
Honolulu (Hawaii)
Istanbul (Turkey)
Kingston (Jamaica)
Limassol (Cyprus)
Murmansk (Russia)
Nagasaki (Japan)
Newhaven (UK)
Rosslare (Ireland)
Shanghai (China)
Tientsin (China)
Valencia (Spain)
Valletta (Malta)

9
Algericas (Spain)
Archangel (Russia)
Baltimore (US)
Barcelona (Spain)
Fremantle (Australia)
Liverpool (UK)
Lowestoft (UK)
Newcastle (UK)
Peterhead (UK)
Santander (Spain)
Sheerness (UK)
Stavanger (Norway)
Stockholm (Sweden)
Trondheim (Norway)
Vancouver (Canada)
Zeebrugge (Belgium)

10
Alexandria (Egypt)
Casablanca (Morocco)
Charleston (US)
Copenhagen (Denmark)
Folkestone (UK)
Gothenburg (Sweden)
Hartlepool (UK)
Marseilles (France)
Montevideo (Uruguay)
Portsmouth (UK)
Sunderland (UK)
Wellington (NZ)
Wollongong (Australia)

11
Southampton (UK)
Trincomalee (Sri Lanka)

12
Kristiansund (Norway)
Thessaloniki (Greece)

2+ words
Cape Town (South
Africa)
Hong Kong (China)
Le Havre (France)
San Francisco (USA)
St Malo (France)
St Nazaire (France)

PUBLISHING AND PRINTING

*Terms used in publishing
and printing
Typefaces*

**TERMS USED IN
PUBLISHING AND
PRINTING**

2
en
em
pi

3
bed
box
cut
die
dtp
imp
mat
out
pie
pot
run
set
web

4
back
body
bold
book
caps
case
copy
cyan
dash
demy
edit
face
film
flap
font
grid

page
pica
pull
quad
ream
ruby
rule
sewn
sink

5
beard
black
bleed
block
blurb
cameo
canon
caret
chase
cloth
crown
draft
dummy
folio
fount
gloss
index
leads
linen
litho
metal
pearl
plate
point
proof
punch
quire
recto
reset
Roman
rough
royal
serif
solid
sorts
spine
tilde

title
verso

6
boards
cliché
delete
editor
flimsy
footer
format
galley
gutter
header
indent
italic
jacket
layout
linage
makeup
matrix
minion
morgue
offset
ozalid
punch
revise
rotary
screen

7
artwork
binding
brevier
bromide
capital
caption
cedilla
clicker
compile
diamond
display
edition
endnote
engrave
gravure
gripper
imprint

justify
leading
literal
masking
measure
overrun
overset
preface
prelims
printer
publish
release
reprint
rewrite
typeset
woodcut

8
ascender
bleeding
boldface
colophon
designer
endpaper
footnote
hairline
halftone
hardback
headband
imperial
keyboard
linotype
monotype
offprint
paginate
photoset
slipcase
streamer
tailband
turnover
vignette
woodpulp

9
bookplate
brilliant
casebound
collating

copyright
duplicate
facsimile
furniture
justified
laminate
lineblock
nonpareil
overprint
pageproof
paperback
paragraph
photocopy
photostat
proofread
watermark
woodblock

10
annotation
blockmaker
compositor
copytaster
copywriter
imposition
impression
imprimatur
interleave
keyboarder
lamination
lithograph
monochrome
overmatter
pagination
paraphrase
plagiarism
remainder
separation
stereotype
typesetter
typography
xerography

11
copyfitting
letterpress
lithography
platemaking

proofreader
unjustified

12
illustration
photogravure

13
justification

2+ words
art board
body text
front matter
galley proof
lower case
running head(s)
special sorts
upper case

Typefaces

3
dow
gem

4
bell
bold
gill
ruby
zapf

5
agate
arial
aster
bembo
canon
doric
elite
erbar
folio
goudy
ionic
kabel
lotus

mitra
pearl
point
roman
ronde
sabon
Times

6
aachen
adroit
caslon
Cicero
cochin
cooper
corona
fenice
future
glypha
gothic
italic
janson
lucian
melior
minion
modern
oliver
ondine
optima
romana
uncial

7
antique
basilica
Bauhaus
Bernard
bookman

brevier
candida
century
coronet
cursive
diamond
electra
elzevir
english
floreal
fraktur
futura
korinna
lubalin
madison
neuzeit
paragon
plantin
raleigh
spartan
stempel
tiffany
univers
wexford
windsor

8
benguiat
berkeley
breughel
cloister
concorde
egyptian
fournier
franklin
galliard
garamond
kennerly

novarese
olympian
palatino
perpetual
rockwell
sanserif
souvenir

9
americana
athenaeum
barcelona
bourgeois
brilliant
britannic
caledonia
clarendon
clearface
columbian
criterion
dominante
excelsior
fairfield
grotesque
helvetica
nonpareil
worcester

10
cheltenham
churchward
devanagari
egyptienne
leamington

11
baskerville
copperplate

RACE/RACING

A race
Racecourses
Racing circuits (motor-racing)
Terms used in racing

A RACE

2
TT

4
dash
heat
mile
Oaks

5
chase
Derby
event
rally
relay

6
gallop
medley
slalom
sprint
stakes

7
classic
contest

8
handicap
marathon
scramble
speedway

11
Cesarewitch
competition

12
steeplechase

2+ words
egg and spoon race
fun run
Grand National
grand prix
obstacle race
point-to-point
sack race
St Leger

RACECOURSES

3
Ayr

4
Bath
Evry (France)
Naas (Ireland)
York

5
Ascot
Epsom
Perth
Ripon

6
Bangor
Craven (Ireland)
Galway (Ireland)
Laurel (USA)
Ludlow
Redcar
Thirsk

7
Aintree
Auteuil (France)
Cartmel
Chester
Curragh, the (Ireland)
Lincoln
Newbury
Taunton

Warwick
Windsor

8
Beverley
Brighton
Camptown (USA)
Carlisle
Chepstow
Goodwood
Hereford
Wetherby
Yarmouth

9
Catterick
Chantilly (France)
Deauville (France)
Doncaster
Edinburgh
Leicester
Longchamp (France)
Newcastle
Newmarket
Stratford
Uttoxeter
Worcester

10
Cheltenham
Folkestone
Huntingdon
Nottingham
Pontefract

2+ words
Churchill Downs (USA)
Haydock Park
Kempton Park
Market Rasen
Newton Abbot
Sandown Park

RACING CIRCUITS (MOTOR-RACING)

3
Pau (France)

Rio (Brazil)
Spa (Belgium)

5
Imola (Italy)
Monza (Italy)

6
Monaco

7
Daytona (USA)
Detroit (USA)
Kyalami (South Africa)

8
Adelaide (Australia)
Goodwood
Montreal (Canada)
Thruxton

9
Montlhéry (France)
Zandvoort (Netherlands)

10
Brooklands
Hockenheim (Germany)

11
Nurburgring (Germany)
Silverstone

12
Indianapolis

2+ words
Brand's Hatch
Castle Combe
Le Mans (France)

TERMS USED IN RACING

2
FI
GP

3
bet
gun
lap
pit

4
bell
bend
cert
flat
form
grid
jump
odds
pits
post
tape
tote
turf

5
evens
fence
going
place
price
silks
rails
start
track

6
double
faller
finish
inside

maiden
runner
stayer
sticks

7
chicane
furlong
hairpin
marshal
outside
paddock
pitstop
scratch
stagger
starter
steward

8
handicap
outsider
overtake
straight

9
certainty
favourite
objection
pacemaker

11
totalisator

2+ words
chequered flag
dead heat
false start
flying start
national hunt
non-starter
photo-finish
starting block
starting gate
starting pistol

RELIGION/ RELIGIOUS

Religions and religious
believers
Clergy
Patron saints
Religious terms

RELIGIONS AND RELIGIOUS BELIEVERS

3
Jew
Zen

4
Copt
Jain
Shia
Sufi
Sikh

5
Amish
Arian
Baha'i
deism
deist
druid
Hindu
Islam
pagan
Parsi
Sunna
Sunni
Wicca
witch

6
Mormon
Moslem
Muslim
Parsee
Quaker
Shaker
Shiite
Shinto

Sufism
Taoism
Taoist
voodoo
Wahabi
Wiccan

7
animism
animist
atheism
atheist
Baha'ism
Baptist
Gnostic
Jainism
Judaism
Lamaism
Sikhism
Wahhabi
warlock

8
agnostic
Anglican
Arianism
Arminian
Buddhism
Buddhist
Catholic
Donatism
Donatist
druidess
druidism
Erastian
Hasidism
Hinduism
Humanism
humanist
idolater
idolatry
Lutheran
Mahayana
Mazdaism
Mazdaist
Moravian
Orthodox
Paganism

Satanism
Satanist
Tantrism
Wahabism
Wesleyan

9
Adventism
Adventist
Calvinism
Christian
Huguenot
Jansenism
Jansenist
Methodism
Methodist
Mormonism
Nestorian
pantheism
pantheist
Parseeism
Quakerism
shamanism
Shintoism
theosophy
Theraveda
Unitarian
Waldenses

10
Anabaptism
Anabaptist
Brahmanism
evangelism
Gnosticism
gymnosophy
Manichaean
Mohammedan
monotheism
monotheist
polytheism
polytheist
Protestant
theosopher
Waldensian

11
agnosticism

Albigensian
Anglicanism
Arminianism
Catholicism
creationism
creationist
Erastianism
Lutheranism
Rastafarian
Scientology
spiritualism
spiritualist
Wesleyanism
Zoroastrian

12
Christianity
Confucianism
nestorianism
Presbyterian
Salvationism
Salvationist
theosophist
Trinitarian
Unitarianism

13
Episcopalian
Manichaeanism
Nonconformism
Nonconformist
Protestantism
Scientologist

14
Evangelicalism
fundamentalism
fundamentalist
Pentecostalism
Pentecostalist
Rastafarianism
Trintarianism
Zoroastrianism

2+ words
Anglo-Catholic
Christian Science

Christian Scientist
Church of England
Church of Scotland
Greek Orthodox
high church
Jehovah's witness
low church
Russian Orthodox
Society of Friends

***CLERGY AND RELIGIOUS
PEOPLE***

3
nun

4
abbé
curé
dean
guru
imam
lama
monk
pope
yogi

5
abbot
bonze
canon
druid
elder
fakir
friar
hadji
mufti
padre
prior
rabbi
vicar

6
abbess
bishop
curate
deacon

mullah
nuncio
parson
pastor
rector
sexton
sister
verger

7
acolyte
brahmin
brother
muezzin
pontiff
prelate
primate

8
cardinal
chaplain
minister
ordinand
prioress
sidesman

9
ayatollah
deaconess
moderator
monsignor
patriarch
presbyter
sacristan
suffragan

10
archbishop
archdeacon
missionary
prebendary

12
churchwarden
ecclesiastic
metropolitan

PATRON SAINTS

Patron saint of:

Accountants	St Matthew
Actors	St Genesius
Animals	St Francis of Assisi
Archers	St Sebastian
Artists	St Luke
Athletes	St Sebastian
Bakers	St Elizabeth of Hungary, St Nicholas
Bellfounders	St Agatha
Blacksmiths	St Dunstan
Booksellers	St John of God
Brewers	St Augustine
Bricklayers	St Stephen
Carpenters	St Joseph
Children	St Nicholas
Comedians	St Vitus
Cooks	St Lawrence
Czech Republic	St Wenceslas
Dentists	St Apollonia
Doctors	St Luke, St Pantaleon
England	St George
Farmers	St George
Firefighters	St Florian
France	St Denis (Denys), St Joan
Gardeners	St Dorothea
Grocers	St Michael
Housewives	St Anne
Hunters	St Hubert
Innkeepers	St Amand
Ireland	St Patrick
Jewellers	St Eloi
Librarians	St Jerome
Lost causes	St Jude
Music and musicians	St Cecilia
Scotland	St Andrew
Shoemakers	St Crispin, St Crispinian
Travellers	St Christopher
Wales	St David
Wine growers	St Vincent
Workers	St Joseph

RELIGIOUS TERMS

3
alb
ark
ave
BVM
God
haj
Jah
law
lay
pew
pix
pyx
RIP
see
sin
vow
yin

4
alms
amen
bell
Cana
cant
cell
cope
cowl
cult
cure
Ebor
evil
ewer
Fall (the)
fast
font
guni
hadj
hajj
halo
harp
hell
holy
hood
host
hymn

icon
idol
ikon
INRI
ka'ba
kara
kesh
kirk
lama
Lent
Mass
monk
oath
pall
pope
pray
puja
rite
rood
sect
sext
soul
Sura
text
veil
vows
Word (the)
Xmas
yang
yoga
zend
Zion

5
abbey
abyss
agape
aisle
Allah
Alpha
altar
amice
angel
banns
beads
Bible
bless
bodhi

canon
carol
chant
chela
choir
cotta
credo
creed
cross
culpa
curia
deity
demon
devil
dirge
dogma
elder
ephod
exalt
faith
fakir
flock
friar
glory
godly
grace
habit
hafiz
halal
hijab
Hijra
image
Jesus
jihad
Kaaba
Koran
laity
lauds
limbo
logos
manse
matin
Mazda
Mecca
mercy
mitre
mohel
myrrh

nones
Omega
pahul
papal
Pasch
piety
pious
prior
psalm
Purim
rabbi
relic
saint
salat
Sarum
Satan
selah
stole
Sudra
synod
taboo
terce
Torah
tract
vedic
vigil
zakat
zazen
Zohar

6
abbacy
Advent
amulet
anoint
anthem
ascend
ascent
ashram
armlet
Assisi
beadle
Belial
bishop
Brahma
Buddha
burial
candle

cantor
censer
chapel
cherub
chrism
Christ
church
clergy
cleric
collar
curacy
decade
decani
devout
dharma
divine
dossal
Easter
Elohim
Essene
father
Fatima
ferial
friary
gloria
Gospel
gradin
grotto
guimpe
hallow
heaven
Hebrew
Hegira
Hejira
heresy
hermit
homily
hymnal
intone
Jahweh
Jesuit
Jewish
Judaic
kachha
kakkar
kangha
kirpan
kosher

latria
lavabo
layman
lector
lesson
Levite
litany
living
manger
mantle
mantra
Marian
martyr
matins
Maundy
Medina
missal
mortal
mosaic
mosque
mystic
nimbus
novena
novice
oblate
occult
office
ordain
orders
orison
pagoda
palmer
papacy
papist
parish
popery
praise
prayer
preach
primus
priory
proper
psalms
pulpit
rector
repent
reveal
ritual

rochet
Romish
rosary
rubric
sacred
Saddhu
santon
schism
scribe
seraph
sermon
server
sexton
shaman
sharia
shrine
shrive
sinful
sinner
sister
spirit
stalls
Sunday
suttee
tablet
Talmud
temple
tierce
tippet
Tophet
trance
triune
unholy
venial
verger
vestry
virgin
vision
votive
wimple
Yahweh

7

acolyte
Ahriman
Alcoran
Alkoran
ampulla

angelic
angelus
apostle
baptism
baptist
baptize (baptise)
beatify
believe
bigotry
biretta
blessed
brother
Calvary
cassock
chalice
chancel
chaplet
chapter
charity
chrisom
cloister
Cluniac
collect
confirm
convent
Creator
crosier
crozier
crucify
crusade
deanery
decanal
defrock
dervish
diocese
diptych
Elohist
epistle
epitaph
eternal
exegete
fanatic
fasting
frontal
funeral
Galilee
gaudete
Gehenna

gentile
Gideons
glorify
goddess
godhead
godless
godlike
gradine
hassock
heathen
heretic
hosanna
hymnary
hymnody
impiety
incense
infidel
introit
Jehovah
Judaize (Judaise)
justify
kenosis
Lateran
lectern
liturgy
Lourdes
Lucifer
madonna
mandala
mastaba
mattins
menorah
Messiah
mezuzah
minaret
minster
miracle
mission
muezzin
narthex
nirvana
nocturn
nunnery
oratory
ordinal
orphrey
paschal
passion

penance
pilgrim
piscina
pontiff
poverty
prayers
prebend
prelate
primacy
primate
profane
prophet
psalter
raiment
Ramadan
rebirth
recluse
rectory
rejoice
requiem
reredos
retable
retreat
Sabbath
sainted
saintly
sanctum
sanctus
satanic
saviour
secular
service
Shabbat
shahada
shariah
shariat
Shaitan
Shastra
soutane
steeple
stipend
synodal
tantric
tempter
tonsure
Trinity
unction
Vatican

vespers
Vulgate
worship
Yahwist

8
ablution
affinity
alleluia
almighty
anathema
anointed
antiphon
antipope
apostasy
apostate
basilica
beatific
believer
benifice
berretta
biblical
blessing
brethren
breviary
canonize (canonise)
canticle
Capuchin
cardinal
catacomb
celibacy
celibate
cemetery
cenobite
cenotaph
ceremony
chastity
chasuble
cherubic
cherubim
choirboy
chrismal
christen
ciborium
clerical
compline
conclave
covenant

creation
credence
crucifer
crucifix
crusader
dalmatic
deaconry
devilish
devotion
diaconal
diocesan
disciple
divinity
doctrine
doxology
Emmanuel
enthrone
epiphany
episcopy
eternity
ethereal
Eusebian
evensong
evildoer
exegesis
exegetic
exequies
exorcism
exorcist
exorcize (exorcise)
faithful
frontlet
Golgotha
gurdwara
hallowed
heavenly
hecatomb
hierarch
hieratic
hinayana
holiness
Immanuel
immortal
infernal
Jubilate
Kabbalah
Lazarist
libation

meditate
minister
ministry
minorite
miserere
Mohammed
monachal
monastic
mozzetta
mujtahid
nativity
Nazarene
Nazareth
neophyte
obituary
oblation
offering
orthodox
pantheon
pardoner
Passover
pastoral
pericope
Peshitta
pharisee
pontifex
preacher
predella
priestly
prioress
prophecy
prophesy
psalmist
psalmody
psaltery
quietism
quietist
rabbinic
Ramadhan
redeemer
religion
response
revealed
reverend
reverent
rogation
sacristy
Sadducee

sanctify
sanctity
scapular
Sephardi
seraphic
seraphim
sidesman
skullcap
summoner
superior
surplice
swastika
Tenebrae
theodicy
theology
theogony
thurible
thurifer
transept
triptych
unbelief
venerate
versicle
vestment
viaticum
vicarage
vocation
ziggurat

9
ablutions
adoration
alleluiah
allelujah
Amaterasu
anchorite
anointing
antiphony
Apocrypha
apostolic
archangel
archfiend
Ascension
Ashkenazi
atonement
baptismal
baptistry
beatitude

Beelzebub
Bethlehem
bishopric
bismillah
blasphemy
Candlemas
canonical
Carmelite
catechism
catechist
catechize (catechise)
cathedral
celebrant
celebrate
celestial
chorister
Christmas
churching
churchman
clergyman
cloistered
coenobite
communion
confessor
converted
Cordelier
cremation
dalmatica
damnation
deaconess
Decalogue
dedicated
desecrate
devotions
diaconate
dissenter
doctrinal
Dominican
encyclical
episcopal
Eucharist
firmament
genuflect
godliness
gospeller
graveyard
Gregorian
hagiology

Halloween
hereafter
hermitage
heterodox
Hexateuch
hierogram
hierology
hymnodist
hymnology
incumbent
induction
interdict
interment
Jerusalem
justified
laudation
layperson
Lazarists
Mariology
martyrdom
moderator
monastery
mysticism
novitiate
obedience
obeisance
obsequies
offertory
officiant
officiate
orthodoxy
Paraclete
patriarch
Pentecost
plainsong
postulant
preaching
precentor
presbyter
priestess
profanity
prothesis
purgatory
Quicunque
reliquary
religious
repentant
reverence

righteous
sacrament
sacrarium
sacrifice
sacrilege
sacristan
salvation
sanctuary
Sanhedrin
scripture
sepulchre
solemnize (solemnise)
spiritual
synagogue
synodical
synoptics
synoptist
teleology
Testament
theocracy
theomachy
theophany
unworldly
venerable
vestments
visionary

10
absolution
abstinence
altarpiece
antichrist
apocalypse
Armageddon
assumption
baptistery
Beatitudes
benedicite
Barnardine
Buddhistic
canonicals
Carthusian
catechumen
ceremonial
churchgoer
churchyard
circumcise
Cistercian

confession
consecrate
consistory
dedication
devotional
Eastertide
ecumenical
episcopacy
episcopate
evangelism
evangelist
evangelize (evangelise)
exaltation
fellowship
Gethsemane
hallelujah
heptateuch
heterodoxy
hierocracy
hierophant
iconoclasm
iconoclast
immaculate
impanation
indulgence
infallible
invocation
irreverent
magnificat
mariolatry
meditation
ministrant
misericord
missionary
mujtahidun
monstrance
omnipotent
omniscient
ophiolatry
ordination
Pentateuch
pharisaism
possession
pilgrimage
prebendary
presbytery
priesthood
prophetess

rabbinical
rectorship
redemption
repentance
revelation
sacerdotal
sacrosanct
sanctified
sanctifier
schismatic
scriptural
Scriptures
secularism
secularist
septuagint
Sexagesima
Shrovetide
shibboleth
soothsayer
tabernacle
temptation
theologian
Tridentine
unbeliever
veneration
visitation
worshipper

11
antiphonary
archdiocese
Benedictine
benediction
benedictory
blasphemous
bodhisattva
chrismation
Christendom
christening
churchwoman
commination
communicant
contemplate
convocation
crematorium
crucifixion
deification
desecration

doxological
ecclesiarch
ecclesiology
eschatology
established
evangelical
everlasting
freethinker
genuflection
hagiography
hierography
hymnography
hymnologist
iconography
immortality
incarnation
inquisition
intercessor
irreligious
irreverence
omnipotence
omnipresent
omniscience
parishioner
paternoster
pharisaical
pontificate
priestcraft
procession
proselytism
proselytize (proselytise)
Reformation
religionist
religiosity
reservation
ritualistic
sacramental
unchristian
unrighteous
Whitsuntide

12
Annunciation
archdeaconry
canonization
(canonisation)
churchwarden
circumcision

confessional
confirmation
congregation
consecration
consistorial
disestablish
dispensation
ecclesiastic
ecclesiology
enthronement
episcopalian
frankincense
hymnographer
intercession
interdiction
omnipresence
purification
Quadragesima
reconsecrate
Resurrection
Septuagesima
thanksgiving
transmigrate

2+ words
Ahura Mazda
All Hallows
All Saints
All Saints' Day
All Souls' Day
altar cloth
altar frontal
altar rail
Ascension Day
Ash Wednesday
auto-da-fe
bar mitzvah
bat mitzvah
Bible Belt
Bible Society
bible study
black friar
Black Mass
born-again
chapel of ease
Christmas Day
Christmas Eve
Church Army

church bell
church parade
church school
closed order
Curia Romana
Dalai Lama
deadly sin
Dei Gratia
Diet of Worms
divine light
divine right
dog collar
Easter day
Easter Sunday
Ember Day
eternal life
evil spirit
false prophet
general synod
Geneva Bible
God's acre
god-fearing
Good Friday
Good Shepherd
graven image
Hail Mary
hell fire
high altar
High Mass
high priest
holy city
holy day
Holy Family
Holy Father
Holy Ghost
Holy Land
holy of holies

Holy Orders
holy roller
Holy See
Holy Spirit
Holy Trinity
holy war
holy water
Holy Week
Holy Writ
Holy Year
hot gospeller
house of God
hymn book
inner light
inner sanctum
joss stick
Judgement Day
Kingdom of God
Lady Day
Lamb of God
Lammas Day
Last Judgment
last rites
Last Supper
lay brother
lay clerk
lay preacher
lay reader
Lion of Judah
Lord's Day
Lord's prayer
Lord's Supper
Lord's Table
Low Mass
Low Sunday
lych gate
mea culpa

mortal sin
Mosaic law
New Testament
Nicene Creed
nunc dimittis
Old Testament
Opus Dei
original sin
Our Lady
Palm Sunday
papal bull
passing bell
passion play
Passion Week
patron saint
Pearly Gates
prayer beads
prayer book
prayer mat
prayer rug
prayer wheel
psalm book
red letter day
Rogation Days
Rogation Week
Sabbath day
Sacred Heart
Second Coming
Sunday School
Te Deum
Tower of Babel
venial sin
vicar general
wee free
white friar
Xmas day
Zend-Avesta

REPTILES

Reptiles and amphibians
See also **SNAKE**

3
eft
olm

4
frog
newt
toad

5
agama
gecko
siren

skink
snake
tokay

6
cayman
gavial
iguana
lizard
moloch
mugger
turtle

7
axolotl
gharial
monitor
tuatara

8
basilisk
bullfrog
dinosaur
matamata
mudpuppy
terrapin
tortoise

9
alligator
chameleon
crocodile

10
natterjack
salamander

RIVERS

A river
Rivers of the world

A RIVER

4
beck
burn
rill

5
brook
canal
creek
flood

6
arroyo
rillet
runnel
stream

7
channel
freshet
rivulet

8
affluent
waterway

9
tributary

11
watercourse

RIVERS OF THE WORLD

2
Aa (France)
Ii (Finland)
Ob (Russia)
Po (Italy)

3
Aar (Switzerland)
Ain (France)
Aln (England)
Axe (England)
Ayr (Scotland)
Bug (Ukraine, Poland)
Cam (England)
Dee (England, Scotland, Wales)
Don (England, Russia, Scotland)
Ems (Germany, Netherlands)
Esk (Australia)
Fal (England)
Han (China)
His (China)
Inn (Austria, Germany)
Lea (England)
Lee (England, Ireland)
Lot (France)
Lys (France)
Rib (England)
Rye (England)
Sid (England)
Sow (England)
Taw (England)
Tay (Scotland)
Ure (England)
Usk (England, Wales)
Wey (England)
Wye (England, Wales)
Yeo (England)

4
Adda (Italy)
Adur (England)
Aire (England)
Amur (China, Russia)
Arno (Italy)
Arun (England)
Aube (France)
Aude (France)
Avon (England)
Bann (Ireland)
Bure (England)
Char (England)

Cher (France)
Chew (England)
Cole (England)
Coln (England)
Dart (England)
Doon (Scotland)
Dove (England)
Earn (Scotland)
East (USA)
Ebro (Spain)
Eden (England, Scotland)
Elbe (Germany)
Isar (Germany)
Isis (England)
Kama (Russia)
Kwai (Thailand)
Lahn (Germany)
Lech (Germany)
Loir (France)
Lune (England)
Maas (Netherlands)
Main (Germany, Ireland)
Mole (England)
Naze (England)
Neath (Wales)
Nene (England)
Nidd (England)
Nile (Africa, Egypt)
Nith (Scotland)
Oder Czech R.,
Germany, Poland)
Ohio (USA)
Oise (France)
Orne (France)
Ouse (England)
Peel (Australia, USA)
Rede (England)
Ruhr (Germany)
Saar (France, Germany)
Spey (Scotland)
Swan (Australia)
Taff (Wales)
Tajo (Spain)
Tarn (France)
Tawe (Wales)
Tees (England)
Test (England)
Thur (Switzerland)

Towy (Wales)
Tyne (England, Scotland)
Ural (Russia)
Vaal (South Africa)
Vire (France)
Waal (Netherlands)
Wear (England)
Yare (England)

5
Adige (Italy)
Aisne (France)
Alice (Australia)
Allan (Scotland)
Allen (Scotland)
Annan (Scotland)
Avoca (Australia)
Blood (South Africa)
Bogie (Scotland)
Boyne (Ireland)
Brent (England)
Camel (England)
Clyde (Scotland)
Colne (England)
Congo (Africa)
Conwy (Wales)
Deben (England)
Devon (Scotland)
Dnepr (Russia)
Doubs (France)
Douro (Portugal, Spain)
Dovey (Wales)
Drava (Austria, Hungary, Italy)
Dvina (Russia)
Etive (Scotland)
Fleet (England)
Forth (Scotland)
Foyle (Ireland)
Frome (Australia, England)
Huang (China)
Indus (India, Pakistan)
James (USA)
Katun (Russia)
Lagan (Ireland)
Leven (Scotland)
Loire (France)

Marne (France)
Memel (Germany)
Meuse (France)
Moose (Canada)
Mosel (Germany)
Nairn (Scotland)
Niger (Africa, Nigeria)
Oglio (Italy)
Otter (England)
Peace (Canada, USA)
Pearl (China, USA)
Pecos (USA) ·
Piave (Italy)
Plate (South America)
Rhine (Germany)
Rhone (France)
Saale (Germany)
Saone (France)
Seine (France)
Sheaf (England)
Shiel (Scotland)
Somme (France)
Spree (Germany)
Stort (England)
Stour (England)
Swale (England)
Tagus (Portugal, Spain)
Tamar (England)
Tarim (China)
Teign (England)
Tiber (Italy)
Trent (England, Canada)
Tweed (England, Scotland)
Volga (Russia)
Volta (W. Africa)
Weser (Germany)
Yarra (Australia)
Yukon (Canada, USA)
Zaire (Congo)

6
Albany (Canada)
Allier (France)
Amazon (Brazil)
Barrow (Ireland)
Calder (England)
Charles (USA)

Coquet (England)
Crouch (England)
Danube (Austria, SE Europe)
Dnestr (Ukraine)
Elster (Germany)
Fraser (Canada)
Gambia (W Africa)
Ganges (India)
Hamble (England)
Hudson (USA)
Humber (England)
Hunter (Australia)
Irwell (England)
Itchen (England)
Japura (Brazil)
Jordan (Israel, Jordan)
Kennet (England)
Kolyma (Russia)
Liffey (Ireland)
Loddon (England)
Medway (England)
Mekong (Vietnam)
Mersey (England)
Mobile (USA)
Mohawk (USA)
Moldau (Czech R.)
Monnow (England, Wales)
Moskva (Russia)
Murray (Australia)
Neckar (Germany)
Neisse (Germany, Poland)
Nelson (Canada)
Oneida (USA)
Orange (South Africa)
Orwell (England)
Ottawa (Canada)
Parana (Brazil)
Parima (Brazil)
Parrot (England)
Platte (USA)
Ribble (England)
Rother (England)
Sambre (France)
Sarthe (France)
Severn (England, Canada)
Swanee (USA)

Swilly (Ireland)
Teviot (Scotland)
Thames (England)
Tigris (Iraq)
Ticino (Italy)
Tugela (South Africa)
Tummel (Scotland)
Ussuri (China, Russia)
Vienne (France)
Vltava (Czech R.)
Wabash (USA)
Weaver (England)
Wensum (England)
Yarrow (Scotland)
Yellow (China, USA)

7
Abitibi (Canada)
Alabama (USA)
Catawba (USA)
Chelmer (England)
Darling (Australia)
Derwent (England)
Deveron (Scotland)
Dnieper (Russia)
Durance (France)
Ettrick (Scotland)
Gamtoos (South Africa)
Garonne (France)
Gironde (France)
Hooghli (India)
Lachlan (Australia)
Limpopo (South Africa)
Mattawa (Canada)
Moselle (Germany)
Niagara (Canada, USA)

Olifant (South Africa)
Orinoco (Venezuela)
Orontes (Syria)
Potomac (USA)
Scheldt (Belgium)
Shannon (Ireland)
Spokane (USA)
Uruguay (Uruguay)
Vistula (Poland)
Waveney (England)
Welland (England)
Yangtse (China)
Zambezi (Zimbabwe,
Africa)

8
Arkansas (USA)
Beaulieu (England)
Canadian (USA)
Cherwell (England)
Chindwin (Buma)
Colorado (USA)
Columbia (USA)
Delaware (USA)
Demerara (Guyana)
Dordogne (France)
Evenlode (England)
Gatineau (Canada)
Kankakee (USA)
Kennebec (USA)
Missouri (USA)
Paraguay (Paraguay)
Savannah (USA)
Suwannee (USA)
Torridge (England)
Wansbeck (England)

Windrush (England)

9
Churchill (Canada)
Euphrates (Iraq)
Irrawaddy
(Burma/Myanmar)
Mackenzie (Canada)
Macquarie (Australia)
Mallagama (Canada)
Mirimichi (Canada)
Tennessee (USA)

10
Blackwater (England,
Ireland)
Hawkesbury (Canada)
Sacramento (USA)
Shenandoah (USA)

11
Brahmaputra (India)
Mississippi (USA)
Susquehanna (USA)
Yellowstone (USA)

12
Guadalquivir (Spain)
Murrumbidgee
(Australia)
Saskatchewan (Canada)

2+ words
Rio Grande (South
America, USA)
St Lawrence (Canada)

ROAD AND RAIL

Roads
Terms associated with the railway

ROADS
See also CAR

1
A
B
M

2
AI
MI
Rd
St

3
Ave
row
way

4
drag
exit
kerb
lane
mall
mews
pavé
pike
ride

5
alley
byway
close
court
drive
route
track

6
artery

avenue
bypass
camber
feeder
filter
street
tarmac

7
asphalt
beltway
bollard
chicane
cobbles
flyover
freeway
highway
orbital
parkway
terrace

8
alleyway
arterial
autobahn
causeway
clearway
corniche
crescent
junction
motorway
overpass
pavement
ringroad
sidewalk
turnpike

9
autopista
autoroute
boulevard
crossroad
underpass

10
autostrada
cloverleaf
crossroads

expressway
interstate
roundabout
throughway

11
carriageway
interchange

12
intersection
superhighway
thoroughfare

2+ words
bus-lane
cul de sac
dead end
dual carriageway
fast lane
hard shoulder
major road
median strip
minor road
one-way
rat run
slip road
slow lane
through road
T junction
trunk road

TERMS ASSOCIATED WITH THE RAILWAY

2
BR
RY
SR

3
cab
GWR
LMS
TGV
van

4
halt
LNER
line
loco
loop

5
bogey
bogie
coach
gauge
goods
guard
shunt
steam
track
train
truck
wagon

6
Amtrak
banker
boiler
couple
driver
engine
funnel
points
porter
return
Rocket
season
siding
signal

single
stoker
subway
tender
tunnel

7
caboose
cutting
express
fireman
Pacific
Pullman
railbus
railcar
roadbed
shunter
sleeper
station
viaduct
whistle

8
brakevan
carriage
corridor
coupling
engineer
gradient
junction
monorail
railroad
terminus
Victoria
Waterloo

9
conductor
couchette
fishplate
footplate
funicular
intercity
signalman
turntable

10
embankment
locomotive
Paddington
platelayer
switchback

11
compartment
underground

2+ words
boat train
cattle truck
Charing Cross
dining car
guard's van
King's Cross
light engine
Liverpool Street
marshalling yard
milk train
observation car
Orient Express
signal box
station master
tank engine
wagon-lit

ROCKS AND MINERALS

3
jet
ore

4
alum
bort
calx
clay
coal
coke
gold
grit
jade
lava
lime
marl
mica
salt
sand
spar
talc
tufa

5
agate
beryl
borax
boron
chalk
emery
flint
fluor
glass
ochre
pitch
scree
shale
silex
slate
topaz
trona

6
albite

arkose
barite
baryte
basalt
carbon
clunch
dunite
gabbro
galena
garnet
gneiss
gravel
gypsum
halite
iolite
kaolin
marble
norite
oolite
pumice
pyrite
pyrope
quartz
schist
silica
silver
sinter
sphene
spinel
zircon

7
alumina
alunite
anatase
apatita
azurite
barytes
bauxite
bismuth
bitumen
breccia
calcite
calomel
cuprite
cyanite
diamond
diorite

emerald
felspar
granite
jacinth
kainite
kernite
kyanite
leucite
lignite
moraine
olivine
peridot
perlite
pyrites
realgar
silicon
sparite
thorite
tripoli
uralite
zeolite

8
allanite
analcite
ankerite
antimony
asbestos
calamine
chromite
cinnabar
corundum
cryolite
diopside
dioptase
dolomite
dolerite
feldspar
fluorite
graphite
hematite
laterite
lazurite
obsidian
platinum
peridote
plumbago
porphyry

pyroxene
rocksalt
sapphire
siderite
silicate
steatite
sunstone
tinstone
titanite

9
acanthite
alabaster
almandine
aluminite
anhydrite
atacamite
brimstone
fluorspar
hornstone
ironstone
limestone
lodestone

magnesite
magnetite
malachite
marcasite
nepheline
periclase
saltpetre
sandstone
soapstone
turquoise
wulfenite

10
actinolite
aventurine
chalcedony
chrysolite
hornblende
meerschaum
peridotite
phosphorus
serpentine
sphalerite

11
cassiterite
chalcydonyx
chrysoberyl
molybdenite
pitchblende
vesuvianite

12
puddingstone

2+ words
fool's gold
iron pyrites
lapis lazuli
milky quartz
rock crystal
smoky quartz

ROYALTY

Emperors and empresses
Kings of England/Britain
Kings of Scotland
Kings in the Bible
Other kings
Queens
Royal dynasties
Royal titles

EMPERORS AND EMPRESSES

3
Leo (Byzantium)

4
Anna (Russia)
Geta (Rome)
Ivan (Russia)
Nero (Rome)
Otho (Rome)
Zeno (Rome)

5
Carus (Rome)
Darius (Persia)
Galba (Rome)
Irene (Byzantium)
Nerva (Rome)
Niger (Rome)
Titus (Rome)

6
Decius (Rome)
Gallus (Rome)
Jovian (Rome)
Julian (Rome)
Philip (Rome)
Probus (Rome)
Trajan (Rome)
Xerxes (Persia)

7
Bokassa (Central African Empire)
Carinus (Rome)

Charles (Holy Roman)
Eugenie (France)
Florian (Rome)
Gordian (Rome)
Gratian (Rome)
Hadrian (Rome)
Maximus (Rome)
Tacitus (Rome)

8
Arcadius (Rome)
Augustus (Rome)
Aurelian (Rome)
Balbinus (Rome)
Caligula (Rome)
Claudius (Rome)
Commodus (Rome)
Domitian (Rome)
Floranus (Rome)
Galerius (Rome)
Hirohito (Japan)
Macrinus (Rome)
Maximian (Rome)
Napoleon (France)
Nicholas (Russia)
Pertinax (Rome)
Pupienus (Rome)
Tiberius (Rome)
Valerian (Rome)
Victoria (Britain)

9
Alexander (Macedon, Russia)
Atahualpa (Inca)
Caracalla (Rome)
Catherine (Russia)
Elizabeth (Russia)
Gallienus (Rome)
Hostilian (Rome)
Josephine (France)
Justinian (Byzantium)
Montezuma (Aztec)
Procopius (Rome)
Vespasian (Rome)
Vitellius (Rome)

10
Barbarossa, Frederick (Holy Roman)
Charlemagne (Holy Roman)
Diocletian (Rome)
Elagabalus (Rome)
Quintillus (Rome)

11
Constantine (Rome)

2+ words
Antoninus Pius (Rome)
Ci-Xi (China)
Franz Josef (Austria)
Genghis Khan (Mongol)
Haile Selassie (Ethiopia)
Ivan the Terrible (Russia)
Kublai Khan (Mongol)
Marcus Aurelius (Rome)
Maria Theresa (Austria)
Peter the Great (Russia)
Septimius Severus (Rome)

KINGS OF ENGLAND/BRITAIN

4
Cnut
Edwy
John
Knut

5
Edgar
Edwin
James (I – II)
Henry (I – VIII)
Sweyn

6
Canute
Eadred
Eadwig
Edward (I – VIII)

George (I – VI)
Harold (I – II)

7
Charles (I – II)
Richard (I – III)
William (I – IV)
Stephen

8
Ethelred (I – II)

9
Aethelred

2+ words
Edmund Ironside
Edward the Confessor
Edward the Martyr
Harold Harefoot
Richard the Lionheart
William the Conqueror
William Rufus

KINGS OF SCOTLAND

4
Aedh
Duff

5
Colin
David (I – II)
Edgar
Eocha
Girac
James (I – VI)

6
Donald (I – III)
Duncan (I – II)
Robert (I – III)

7
Kenneth (I – III)
Macbeth
Malcolm (I – IV)

9
Alexander (I – III)
Indulphus

12
Constantine (I- III)

2+ words
Donald Bane
John Balliol
Kenneth MacAlpine
Robert (the) Bruce
William the Lion

KINGS IN THE BIBLE

3
Asa
Evi
Hur

4
Ahab
Ahaz
Amon
Bera
Elah
Jehu
Omri
Saul

5
Balak
Cyrus
David
Eglon
Hadad
Herod
Hiram
Hoham
Hosea
Jabin
Joash
Joram
Judah
Nabat
Nadab
Pekah

Piram
Rezin
Zebar
Zimri

6
Baasha
Darius
Hoshea
Japhia
Josiah
Jotham
Lemuel
Sargon
Uzziah
Xerxes

7
Ahaziah
Amaziah
Azariah
Jehoash
Jehoram
Menahem
Shallum
Solomon
Tryphon

8
Hezekiah
Jehoahaz
Jeroboam
Manasseh
Pekahiah
Rehoboam
Zedekiah

9
Jehoiakim
Zechariah

10
Artaxerxes
Belshazzar
Jehoiachin
Salmanazar

11
Jehoshaphat
Melchizedek
Sennacherib

14
Nebuchadnezzar

OTHER KINGS

3
Zog (Albania)

4
Fahd (Saudi Arabia)
Lear (Britain)
Offa (Mercia)

5
Louis (France)
Midas (myth)
Priam (Troy)

6
Alfred (Wessex)
Arthur (Britain, myth)
Clovis (France)
Farouk (Egypt)
Haakon (Norway)
Harald (Norway)

7
Hussein (Jordan)
Ptolemy (Egypt)
Rameses (Egypt)
Tarquin (Rome)

8
Athelstan (Wessex)
Baudouin (Belgium)
Leonidas (Sparta)
Menelaus (Gk myth)

9
Agamemnon (Gk myth)
Wenceslas (Bohemia)

QUEENS

4
Anne (England)
Bess (Elizabeth I)
Dido (Carthage)
Mary (England)
Maud (England)

5
Vasht (Bible)

6
Candace (Bible)
Hecuba (Troy)
Michal (Bible)

7
Eleanor (England)
Jezebel (Bible)
Juliana (Netherlands)
Matilda (England)

8
Adelaide (England)
Beatrix (Netherlands)
Boadicea (Iceni)
Boudicca (Iceni)
Caroline (England)
Margaret (Scotland)
Victoria (England)

9
Alexandra (England)
Catherine (England)
Charlotte (England)
Cleopatra (Egypt)
Elizabeth (England)
Guinevere (myth)
Hephzibah (Bible)
Nefertiti (Egypt)
Semiramis (Assyria)

10
Wilhelmina (Netherlands)

2+ words
Jane Grey (England)
Marie Antoinette (France)
Mary Tudor (England)
Mary Stuart (Scotland)
Queen of Sheba (Bible)

WIVES OF KING HENRY VIII
Catherine of Aragon
Anne Boleyn
Jane Seymour
Anne of Cleves
Catherine Howard
Catherine Parr

ROYAL DYNASTIES

Country	Dynasty
Austria	Hapsburg
Bavaria	Wittelsbach
Belgium	Coburg
Britain	Plantagenet, Tudor, Stuart, Hanover, Windsor
China	Hwan, Tang, Ming, Manchu
Denmark	Oldenburg
France	Capet, Valois, Bourbon
Germany	Hohenzollern
Greece	Schleswig-Holstein

Country	Dynasty
Italy	Savoy
Monaco	Grimaldi
Morocco	Alaouite
Netherlands	Orange
Poland	Jagellon
Portugal	Braganza
Romania	Hohenzollern
Russia	Romanoff
Spain	Hapsburg, Bourbon
Sweden	Vasa, Bernadotte

ROYAL TITLES

3
Rex

4
Czar
Khan
King
Raja
Rana
Rani
Shah
Tsar

5
Queen
Rajah
Ranee

6
Kaiser
Mikado
Prince
Regent
Regina
Sultan

7
Consort
Czarina
Dauphin
Emperor
Empress
Infanta
Infante
monarch
Pharaoh
Tsarina

8
Dauphine
Maharaja
Maharani
Padishah
Princess
Tsaritsa

9
Maharajah
Maharanee

10
Tsarevitch

2+ words
Crown prince
Prince-consort
Princess Royal
Queen-consort
Queen-mother

SAY/SPEAK/TALK

3
coo
cry
gab
gas
rap
yak

4
aver
bark
bawl
blab
boom
chat
cite
crow
lisp
pant
pipe
roar
sigh
snap
tell
wail
yell
yelp

5
claim
drawl
growl
imply
opine
orate
quote
reply
shout
snarl
speak

state
utter
voice
whine

6
affirm
allege
answer
assert
babble
betray
confer
convey
debate
gabble
gossip
impart
inform
jabber
mumble
murmur
mutter
natter
parley
preach
recite
relate
remark
repeat
report
reveal
scream
shriek
squeal

7
address
blabber
blather
chatter
comment
confess

declaim
declare
deliver
discuss
divulge
exclaim
express
lecture
mention
observe
recount
respond
suggest
thunder
whisper

8
announce
converse
disclose
indicate
intimate
maintain
proclaim
vocalize (vocalise)

9
discourse
ejaculate
enunciate
formulate
interject
interrupt
negotiate
pronounce
verbalize (verbalise)

10
articulate
vociferate

11
communicate

SCIENCE/
SCIENTIFIC

Sciences
Scientific terms

SCIENCES

5
ology

6
botany
optics

7
alchemy
algebra
anatomy
biology
ecology
geodesy
geogony
geology
hygiene
myology
orology
otology
phonics
physics
zoology
zootomy

8
agronomy
atmology
biometry
ethology
etiology
eugenics
genetics
geometry
medicine
mycology
nosology
ontology
penology
pharmacy

sitology
taxonomy
topology
typology
virology
zymology

9
acoustics
aerometry
aetiology
allopathy
astronomy
barometry
cartology
chemistry
chorology
cosmology
dentistry
dietetics
ethnology
geography
harmonics
histology
horometry
hydrology
hygrology
ichnology
lithology
mechanics
neurology
osteology
pathology
petrology
philology
phonetics
phonology
phytology
radiology
sociology
tectonics
telephony
uranology

10
aesthetics
apiculture
archeology

arithmetic
ballistics
bathymetry
biophysics
cardiology
conchology
craniology
demography
dendrology
Egyptology
embryology
geophysics
hydraulics
hydrometry
hydropathy
immunology
lexicology
metallurgy
microscopy
morphology
nematology
nosography
nucleonics
obstetrics
pedagogics
photometry
phrenology
physiology
planimetry
pneumatics
psychiatry
psychology
seismology
somatology
statistics
technology
telegraphy
teratology
topography
toxicology
volcanology
vulcanology

11
aeronautics
aerostatics
agriculture
arachnology

archaeology
arteriology
campanology
carcinology
cartography
chronometry
climatology
cosmography
criminology
cybernetics
dermatology
electronics
engineering
ethnography
gynaecology
haematology
ichthyology
linguistics
mathematics
meteorology
methodology
ornithology
paediatrics
palaeography
radiography
sericulture
thanatology

12
aerodynamics
anthropology
architecture
astrophysics
biochemistry
econometrics
epidemiology
horticulture
hydrostatics
lexicography
microbiology
neurobiology
palaeography
pharmacology
pisciculture
pneumatology
sylviculture
trigonometry

14
parapsychology
thermodynamics

SCIENTIFIC TERMS

2
AC
DC

3
bar
bel
DNA
EMF
erg
gas
ion
lux
ohm
ore
ray
RNA

4
acid
apex
atom
base
bond
cell
dyne
heat
lens
mach
mass
mole
pile
pole
salt
soda
volt
watt

5
anion
anode
azote

basic
curie
cycle
diode
earth
ester
ether
ethyl
farad
focus
force
Freon
genus
group
joule
laser
lever
light
lipid
lumen
maser
meson
metal
model
monad
phase
power
prism
shell
solid
sonic
stable
valve
weber

6
acetic
acidic
adduct
aerate
aerobe
albino
alkali
allele
ampere
atomic
baryon
biotic

buffer
charge
dipole
energy
enzyme
ethane
ferric
fusion
gangue
genome
halide
hybrid
Kelvin
lepton
liquid
litmus
mutant
neuron
oocyte
photon
phylum
plasma
raceme
reduce
refine
retort
solute
torque
triode
vacuum
vector
weight

7

acetate
acetone
acidity
aerobic
aerosol
ammeter
aneroid
antigen
asexual
battery
calorie
candela
cathode
Celsius

circuit
coulomb
crystal
culture
current
density
element
entropy
ferrate
ferrous
fission
gaseous
gravity
habitat
hormone
impulse
inertia
kinetic
Maxwell
meiosis
mitosis
mineral
neutral
neutron
nitrate
nitride
nuclear
nucleon
optical
orbital
organic
osmosis
quantum
reactor
soluble
solvent
species
thermal
titrate
torsion
valence
valency
voltage
voltaic

8

adhesion
aeration

afferent
antinode
Brownian
cellular
cohesion
dominant
dynamics
efferent
electric
electron
emission
enthalpy
feedback
friction
heredity
isogonic
kilowatt
klystron
magnetic
membrane
molecule
momentum
mutation
negative
neutrino
particle
pendulum
periodic
polarity
polaroid
positive
reactant
reaction
roentgen
saturate
solenoid
solution
spectrum
unstable
velocity

9

amplifier
amplitude
anaerobic
antimeson
autonomic
barometer

capacitor
catabolic
catalysis
coherence
commensal
condenser
conductor
corpuscle
cyclotron
digestion
ecosystem
electrode
evolution
excretion
fertilize (fertilise)
frequency
galvanize (galvanise)
generator
germinate
gyroscope
hydration
impedance
induction
inorganic
insoluble
insulator
isoclinic
magnetism
magnetron
manometer
potential
radiation
recessive
rectifier
resonance
stability
substrate
symbiosis
titration
tricuspid
vibration
viscosity

10

aberration
absorption
achromatic

adsorption
analytical
catabolism
catenation
conduction
convection
copulation
dehiscence
dielectric
dispersion
generation
hereditary
incubation
inductance
inhibition
ionization (ionisation)
laboratory
locomotion
microscope
neutralize (neutralise)
oscillator
parasitism
phototaxis
population
protoplasm
reflection
refraction
relativity
scattering
solubility
supersonic
thermionic
thermopile
vertebrate
wavelength

11

accelerator
aestivation
capacitance
capillarity
centrifugal
centripetal
compression
conductance
declination
diffraction

electricity
environment
exoskeleton
germination
gravitation
hibernation
inheritance
oscillation
parturition
pollination
radioactive
resistivity
respiration
temperature
transformer
transuranic

12

acceleration
condensation
conductivity
diamagnetism
displacement
dissociation
eccentricity
electrolysis
endoskeleton
fermentation
interference
invertebrate
polarization (polarisation)
reproduction

2+ words

atomic number
atomic weight
Bunsen burner
centre of gravity
centre of mass
half-life
infra-red
Leyden jar
latent heat
specific gravity
test tube

SCIENTISTS

A scientist
Famous scientists

A SCIENTIST

6
boffin
expert

7
chemist

8
botanist

9
alchemist
anatomist
biologist
ecologist
geologist
physicist
zoologist

10
astronomer
biochemist
geneticist
researcher
taxonomist
virologist

11
cosmologist
ethnologist
naturalist
philologist
phonetician
phonologist
sociologist

12
archaeologist
biophysicist
geophysicist
metallurgist

physiologist
psychologist
seismologist
statistician
technologist
toxicologist

FAMOUS SCIENTISTS

3
Ohm (Georg, physicist)
Ray (John, naturalist)

4
Bell (Alexander Graham, scientist and inventor)
Bohr (Niels, physicist)
Born (Max, physicist)
Bose (Jagadis Chandra, physicist)
Davy (Humphry, chemist)
Hahn (Otto, chemist and physicist)
Hess (Victor, physicist)
Koch (Robert, bacteriologist)
Jung (Carl, psychologist)
Mach (Ernst, physicist)
Ryle (Martin, astronomer)
Salk (Jonas, virologist)
Swan (Joseph, physicist)
Watt (James, engineer)

5
Aston (Francis, chemist)
Bacon (Roger, scientist)
Banks (Joseph, botanist)
Boole (George, mathematician)
Boyle (Robert, physicist and chemist)
Brahe (Tycho, astronomer)
Chain (Ernst, biochemist)
Crick (Francis, biochemist)
Curie (Marie, chemist)
Curie (Pierre, physicist)

Fermi (Enrico, physicist)
Gauss (Karl, mathematician)
Hertz (Heinrich Rudolf, physicist)
Hooke (Robert, physicist)
Hoyle (Fred, astronomer)
Joule (James, physicist)
Krebs (Hans, biochemist)
Nobel (Alfred, chemist)
Pauli (Wolfgang, physicist)
Volta (Alessandro, physicist)
White (Gilbert, naturalist)

6
Ampère (André, physicist)
Buffon (George, naturalist)
Bunsen (Robert, chemist)
Dalton (John, chemist)
Darwin (Charles, naturalist)
Euclid (mathematician)
Fermat (Pierre de, mathematician)
Florey (Howard, biochemist)
Geiger (Hans, physicist)
Halley (Edmund, astronomer)
Hubble (Edwin, astronomer)
Huxley (Thomas, biologist)
Joliot (Frédéric, physicist)
Kelvin (Lord, physicist)
Kepler (Johannes, astronomer)
Liebig (Justus, chemist)
Mendel (Gregor, botanist)
Napier (John, mathematician)
Newton (Isaac, physicist)
Pascal (Blaise, mathematician)

Planck (Max, physicist)
Teller (Edward, physicist)
Turing (Alan, mathematician)
Watson (James, biochemist)

7
Audubon (John, naturalist)
Babbage (Charles, mathematician)
Candela (Felix, physicist)
Coulomb (Charles, physicist)
Doppler (Christian, physicist)
Faraday (Michael, chemist and physicist)
Fleming (Alexander, biologist)
Galileo (*Galileo Galilei*, astronomer)
Galvani (Luigi, physician)
Gilbert (William, physicist)
Haldane (J.B.S., biochemist)
Hawking (Stephen, physicist)
Huygens (Christiaan, astronomer)
Lamarck (Jean-Baptiste, naturalist)
Leibniz (Gottfried, mathematician)
Maxwell (James Clark, physicist)
Pasteur (Louis, chemist and microbiologist)

Pauling (Linus, chemist)
Reaumur (René-Antoine, physicist)
Wallace (Alfred Russell, naturalist)

8
Angstrom (Anders, physicist)
Avogadro (Amedeo, physicist)
Einstein (Albert, physicist)
Foucault (Jean Bernard, physicist)
Herschel (William, astronomer)
Humboldt (Alexander von, scientist)
Linnaeus (*Carl Linné*, botanist)
Rayleigh (John, physicist)
Roentgen (Wilhelm, physicist)
Sakharov (Andrei, physicist)
Stirling (James, mathematician)

9
Aristotle (scientist and philosopher)
Becquerel (Henri, physicist)
Bernoulli (Daniel, mathematician and physicist)
Boltzmann (Ludwig, physicist)

Bronowski (Jacob, mathematician)
Cavendish (Henry, physicist)
Davenport (Charles, zoologist)
Descartes (René, mathematician)
Fibonacci (Leonardo, mathematician)
Flamsteed (John, astronomer)
Lavoisier (Anton, chemist)
Priestley (Joseph, chemist)

10
Archimedes (mathematician)
Copernicus (Nicolaus, astronomer)
Heisenberg (Werner, physicist)
Hipparchus (astronomer)
Mendeleyev (Dimitri, chemist)
Pythagoras (mathematician)
Rutherford (Ernest, physicist)
Torricelli (Evangelista, physicist)
Wheatstone (Charles, physicist)

11
Oppenheimer (Robert, physicist)

SCOTLAND/ SCOTTISH

Famous Scots
Scottish mountains
Scottish towns and cities

FAMOUS SCOTS

4
Adam (Robert, architect)
Home (Alexander
Douglas, prime minister)
Hume (David,
philosopher)
Knox (John, church
reformer)
Lulu (pop singer)
Owen (Robert, social
reformer)
Park (Mungo, explorer)
Watt (James, inventor)

5
Baird (John Logie,
inventor)
Black (Joseph, chemist)
Bruce (Robert (the), king)
Burns (Robert, poet)
Clark (Jim, racing driver)
Conti (Tom, actor)
Dewar (Donald, first
minister)
Niven (David, actor)
Scott (Walter, novelist)
Smith (Adam, economist)
Spark (Muriel, novelist)

6
Barrie (James, dramatist)
Buchan (John, novelist)
Carson (Willie, jockey)
Dunlop (John Boyd,
entrepreneur)
Fleming (Alexander,
scientist)
Lauder (Harry,
entertainer)

Lipton (Thomas,
entrepreneur)
Lister (Joseph, medical
pioneer)
McAdam (John, engineer)
Napier (John,
mathematician)
Ramsay (Allan, painter)

7
Balfour (Arthur, prime
minister)
Boswell (James,
biographer)
Carlyle (Thomas, writer
and historian)
Connery (Sean, actor)
Dowding (Hugh, World
War II air marshal)
Glennie (Evelyn,
musician)
Grahame (Kenneth,
author)
Liddell (Eric Henry,
athlete)
Raeburn (Henry, painter)
Stewart (Andy,
entertainer)
Stewart (Jackie, racing
driver)
Telford (Thomas,
engineer)
Wallace (William,
national hero)

8
Carnegie (Andrew,
industrialist)
Connolly (Billy,
comedian)
Dalglish (Kenny,
footballer)
Smollett (Tobias, novelist)

9
Stevenson (Robert
Louis, author)

11
Livingstone (David,
explorer)
McGonagall (William,
bad poet)

2+ words
Bonar-Law (Andrew,
prime minister)
Conan Doyle (Arthur,
author)
Kier Hardie (James,
founder of the Labour
Party)
Mary Queen of Scots
(last Catholic queen)
Ramsay Macdonald
(James, prime minister)
Rennie Mackintosh
(Charles, designer)
Rob Roy (Macgregor,
cattle thief and Jacobite)

SCOTTISH MOUNTAINS
(*all preceded by the word*
Ben)

4
More

5
Nevis
Venue
Wyvis

6
Lawers
Lomond

SCOTTISH TOWNS AND CITIES

3
Ayr
Uig

4
Alva

Barr
Duns
Elie
Kirn
Luss
Nigg
Oban
Reay
Rona
Stow
Wick

5
Alloa
Angus
Annan
Appin
Avoch
Ayton
Banff
Beith
Brora
Bunaw
Busby
Ceres
Clova
Clune
Crail
Cupar
Denny
Downe
Elgin
Ellon
Errol
Fyvie
Govan
Insch
Keiss
Keith
Kelso
Lairg
Largs
Leith
Nairn
Perth
Salen
Troon

6
Aboyne
Alford
Barvas
Beauly
Biggar
Buckie
Carron
Cawdor
Comrie
Cullen
Colter
Dollar
Drymen
Dunbar
Dundee
Dunlop
Dunnet
Dunoon
Dysart
Edzell
Findon
Forfar
Forres
Girvan
Glamis
Gretna
Hawick
Huntdy
Irvine
Killin
Lanark
Lauder
Leslie
Kilmun
Linton
Lochee
Meigle
Moffat
Pladda
Reston
Rhynie
Rosyth
Rothes
Shotts
Thurso
Tongue
Wishaw

Yarrow

7
Airdrie
Balfron
Balloch
Banavie
Bowmore
Braemar
Brechin
Brodick
Canobie
Cantyre
Carbost
Cargill
Carluke
Crathie
Culross
Cumnock
Denholm
Douglas
Dunkeld
Dunning
Evanton
Fairlie
Falkirk
Galston
Gifford
Glasgow
Glencoe
Golspie
Gourock
Granton
Guthrie
Halkirk
Kenmore
Kessock
Kilmory
Kilmuir
Kilsyth
Kinross
Kintore
Lamlash
Larbert
Lybster
Macduff
Mallaig
Maybole

Meldrum
Melrose
Melvich
Methven
Monikie
Muthill
Paisley
Peebles
Polmont
Portree
Portsoy
Renfrew
Saddell
Sarclet
Scourie
Selkirk
Stanley
Strathy
Tarbet
Tarland
Tranent
Turriff
Tundrum
Ullster
Wigtown
Yetholm
Zetland

8
Aberdeen
Aberlady
Abington
Annadale
Arbroath
Arrochar
Auldearn
Ballater
Banchory
Barrhill
Beattock
Blantyre
Burghead
Canisbay
Carnwath
Creetown
Cromarty
Dalkeith
Dalmally

Dingwall
Dirleton
Dufftown
Dumfries
Dunbeath
Dunblane
Dunscore
Earlston
Eyemouth
Findhorn
Fortrose
Glenluce
Greenlaw
Greenock
Hamilton
Inverary
Inverury
Jeantown
Jedburgh
Kilbride
Kilniver
Kilrenny
Kinghorn
Kirkwall
Langhorn
Latheron
Leuchars
Loanhead
Markinch
Marykirk
Moniaive
Montrose
Monymusk
Muirkirk
Neilston
Newburgh
Newmilns
Penicuik
Pitsligo
Pooltiel
Quiraing
Rothesay
Roxburgh
Stirling
Stichen
Talikan
Taransay
Traquair

Whithorn
Ullapool
Woodside

9
Aberfeldy
Aberfoyle
Ardrossan
Berridale
Bettyhill
Blacklarg
Bracadale
Braeriach
Broadford
Broughton
Buckhaven
Cairntoul
Callander
Carstairs
Dumbarton
Edinburgh
Ferintosh
Fochabers
Inchkeith
Inveraray
Inverness
Johnstone
Kildrummy
Kingussie
Kirkcaldy
Leadhills
Lochgelly
Lochinvar
Lochnagar
Lockerbie
Logierait
Muachline
Milngavie
Peterhead
Pitlochry
Prestwick
Riccerton
Rothiemay
Saltcoats
Shieldaig
Slamannan
Stewarton
Stranraer

Strathdon
Strontian
Tobermory
Thornhill
Tomintoul

10
Abbotsford
Achnasheen
Anstruther
Applecross
Ardrishaig
Auchinleck
Ballantrae
Blackadder
Carnoustie
Carsphairn
Castletown
Coatbridge
Coldstream
Coldingham
Dalbeattie
Drumlithie
Galashiels
Glenrothes
Johnshaven
Kilcreggan
Killenaule
Kilmainham
Kilmalcolm
Kilmarnock
Kilwinning

Kincardine
Kingsbarns
Kirkmaiden
Kirkoswald
Kirriemuir
Lennoxtown
Lesmahagow
Linlithgow
Livingston
Milnathort
Motherwell
Portobello
Ronaldsay
Rutherglen
Stonehaven
Stonehouse
Stoneykirk
Strathaven
Strathearn
Strathmore
Tweedmouth
Wilsontown

11
Aberchirder
Balquhidder
Bannockburn
Blairgowrie
Campbeltown
Cumbernauld
Drummelzier
Dunfermline

Ecclefechan
Fettercairn
Fraserburgh
Helensburgh
Invergordon
Kirkmichael
Lossiemouth
Maxwelltown
Musselburgh
Prestonpans
Pultneytown
Strathblane

12
Auchterarder
Ballachulish
Garelochhead
Innerleithen
Lawrencekirk
Portmahomack
Strathpeffer
Tillicoultry

13
Inverkeithing
Kircudbright

2+ words
Fort William
St Andrews

SCULPTOR/ SCULPTURE

Sculptors
Sculpture

SCULPTORS

3
Arp (Hans, French)

4
Caro (Anthony, UK)
Gabo (Naum, Russian)
Gill (Eric, UK)

5
Moore (Henry, UK)
Rodin (Auguste, French)

6
Calder (Alexander, US)
Canova (Antonio, Italian)
Houdon (Jean, French)
Pisano (Andrea, Italian)

7
Bernini (Giovanni, Italian)
Duchamp (Marcel, French)
Epstein (Jacob, UK)
Gibbons (Grinling, English)
Gormley (Anthony, UK)
Phidias (Greek)

8
Brancusi (Constantine, Italian)
Ghiberti (Lorenzo, Italian)
Hepworth (Barbara, UK)
Landseer (Edwin, UK)

9
Donatello (Italian)

10
Giacometti (Alberto, Swiss)
Praxiteles (Greek)

12
Michelangelo (*Michelangelo Buonarroti*, Italian)

SCULPTURE

4
bust
cast
head
herm

5
cameo
group
medal
model
torso

6
bronze
effigy
figure
marble
mobile
relief
statue

7
carving
casting
stabile
telemon
waxwork

8
atlantes
caryatid
figurine
intaglio
maquette
monument
moulding
statuary

9
embossing
medallion
modelling
scrimshaw
statuette
whittling

10
assemblage
petroglyph
terracotta

11
woodcarving

12
installation

2+ words
objet trouvé
plaster cast

SEAS

The sea
Seas of the world
Sea creatures
Sea mammals
See also **FISH**,
NAUTICAL TERMS

THE SEA

4
deep
foam
main
mare
tide
wave

5
briny
ocean

SEAS OF THE WORLD

3
Med
Red

4
Aral
Azov
Dead
Java
Kara
Sulu

5
Banda
Black
Ceram
Coral
Crete
Irish
Japan
North
Timor
White

6
Aegean
Baltic
Bering
Celtic
Flores
Ionian
Laptev
Tasman
Wadden

7
Andaman
Arabian
Arafura
Barents
Caspian
Celebes
Galilee
Marmara
Molucca
Okhotsk
Solomon

8
Adriatic
Amundsen
Beaufort
Bismarck
Hebrides
Ligurian
Sargasso

9
Caribbean
Norwegian

10
Tyrrhenian

13
Mediterranean

2+ words
East China
South China

SEA CREATURES

4
clam
crab

5
conch
coral
gaper
murex
naiad
ormer
polyp
prawn
sepia
squid
whelk

6
cockle
cowrie
medusa
mussel
oyster
quahog
scampi
shrimp
sponge
triton
winkle

7
abalone
actinia
anemone
bivalve
eschara
lobster
mollusc
octopus
scallop
trepang

8
argonaut
barnacle
crawfish

crayfish
nautilus
sandworm
shipworm

9
bluepoint
jellyfish
kingprawn
langouste
shellfish

10
crustacean

11
langoustine

SEA MAMMALS

4
orca
seal

5
whale

6
dugong
walrus

7
dolphin
grampus
manatee

narwhal
rorqual
sealion

8
porpoise

2+ words
blue whale
elephant seal
killer whale
right whale
sea cow
sperm whale

SHAKESPEARE

Shakespeare's plays
Shakespearean characters

SHAKESPEARE'S PLAYS

All's Well That Ends Well (comedy – *abbrev. All's Well*)
Main characters: *Helena*, a physician's daughter; *Countess of Rousillon*; *Bertram*, her son; *King of France*; *Lafeu*, a lord; *Paroles*, a boastful soldier; *Diana*, a young Florentine woman.

Antony and Cleopatra (tragedy – *abbrev. Ant & Cleo*)
Main characters: *Mark Antony*, member of the ruling triumvirate of Rome; *Cleopatra*, Queen of Egypt; *Octavius Caesar*, *Aemilius Lepidus*, the other triumvirs; *Enobarbus*, a friend and follower of Antony; *Charmian* and *Iras*, women attending Cleopatra.

As You Like It (comedy – *abbrev. AYLI*)
Main characters: *Duke Senior*, the rightful ruler living in exile; *Duke Frederick*, his usurping brother; *Rosalind*, Duke Senior's daughter; *Celia*, Duke Frederick's daughter; *Orlando*, younger son of Sir Rowland de Bois; *Oliver*, his elder brother; *Touchstone*, a jester; *Corin*, an old shepherd; *Silvius*, a young shepherd; *Phoebe*, a shepherdess; *Audrey*, a goatherd.

Comedy of Errors, The (comedy – *abbrev. Com Err*)
Main characters: *Aegeon*, a merchant of Syracuse; *Antipholus of Ephesus* and *Antipholus of Syracuse*, his twin sons; *Dromio of Ephesus* and *Dromio of Syracuse*, their twin servants; *Adriana*, Antipholus of Ephesus's wife; *Luciana*, her sister; *Aemilia*, an abbess, revealed as Egeon's wife.

Coriolanus (tragedy – *abbrev. Corio*)
Main characters: *Caius Marcus Coriolanus*, a Roman aristocrat and soldier; *Volumnia*, his mother, *Virgilia*, his wife; *Menenius Agrippa*, an elderly Roman aristocrat; *Sicinius Velutus*, *Junius Brutus*, tribunes of the people; *Tullus Aufidius*, the leader of the Volscians.

Cymbeline (romance – *abbrev. Cymb*)
Main characters: *Cymbeline*, King of Britain; his wife, *Queen*; *Imogen*; his daughters, *Guiderius* and *Arviragus*; his sons (living under the names of *Polydore* and *Cadwal*); *Cloten*, the Queen's son; *Posthumus Leonatus*, Imogen's husband; *Iachimo*, an Italian gentleman; *Belisarius*, a nobleman.

Hamlet, Prince of Denmark (tragedy)
Main characters: *Hamlet*; *Claudius*, King of Denmark (Hamlet's uncle); *Gertude* (Hamlet's mother and Claudius' wife); *Polonius*, a royal counsellor; *Ophelia* (Polonius' daughter); *Laertes* (his son); *Horatio* (Hamlet's friend); the *Ghost* of Hamlet's father.

Henry IV Part 1 (history – *abbrev. Hen IV 1*)
Main characters: *King Henry IV*; *Prince Hal* (his son); *Earl of Northumberland*; *Earl of Worcester* (his brother); *Hotspur* (Henry Percy, Northumberland's son); *Owen Glendower*; *Sir John Falstaff* (Prince Hal's boon companion); *Bardolph*, Peto, Poins (associates of Falstaff and Hal); *Mistress Quickly* (landlady of the Boar's Head tavern).

Henry IV Part II (history – *abbrev. Hen IV 2*)
Main characters: *King Henry*; *Prince Hal*; *Prince John of Lancaster*; *Falstaff* and companions; *Mistress Quickly*; *Doll Tearsheet*; *Justice Shallow*; *Justice Silence*.

Henry V (history – *abbrev. Hen V*)
Main characters: *King Henry V of England*; *King Charles VI of France*; *The Dauphin* (his son); *Princess Catherine* (his daughter); Captains *Gower*, *Fluellen*, *Macmorris* and *Jamy* (of Henry's army); *Pistol*, *Nym* and *Bardolph* (former

companions of Falstaff); *Chorus*.

Henry VI Part 1 (history – *abbrev. Hen VI 1*)
Main characters: *King Henry VI*; *Humphrey, Duke of Gloucester*, his uncle; *Richard, Duke of York*; *Lord Talbot*; *Earl of Suffolk*; *Earl of Somerset*; *Margaret of Anjou*; *Joan La Pucelle*.

Henry VI Part 2 (history – *abbrev. Hen VI 2*)
Main characters: *King Henry VI*; *Queen Margaret*; *Humphrey, Duke of Gloucester*, his uncle; *Richard, Duke of York*; *Duke of Suffolk*; *Jack Cade*.

Henry VI Part 3 (history – *abbrev. Hen VI 3*)
Main characters: *King Henry VI*; *Queen Margaret*; *Edward, Prince of Wales*; *Richard, Duke of York*; *Edward, Earl of March*, *Richard, Duke of Gloucester*, *George, Duke of Clarence* and the *Earl of Rutland*, York's sons; *Lord Clifford*, a supporter of the king; *Earl of Warwick*, a Yorkist who changes sides.

Henry VIII (history – *abbrev. Hen VIII*)
Main characters: *King Henry VIII*; *Queen Katherine of Aragon*, *Anne Boleyn*; *Duke of Buckingham*; *Cardinal Wolsey*; *Archbishop Thomas Cranmer*.

Julius Caesar (tragedy – *abbrev. JC*)
Main characters: *Julius Caesar*; *Calpurnia*, his wife; *Brutus*, a friend of Caesar's who joins the conspiracy against him; *Cassius*, the main conspirator; *Casca*, the conspirator who stabs Caesar first; *Mark Antony*, a friend of Caesar's; *Octavius*, Caesar's nephew; *Portia*, Brutus' wife.

King John (history – *abbrev. K John*)
Main characters: *King John*; *Queen Eleanor*, his mother; *King Philip* of France; *Arthur*, Duke of Brittany, John's young nephew and a rival claimant to the throne; *Constance*, Arthur's mother; *Bastard*, Philip Falconbridge, an illegitimate son of King Richard Coeur-de-lion.

King Lear (tragedy – *abbrev. Lear*)
Main characters: *King Lear*; his daughters *Goneril, Regan, Cordelia*; *Earl of Gloucester*; *Edgar*, his legitimate son; *Edmund*, his illegitimate son; *Earl of Kent*, Lear's faithful follower; the *Fool*; *Duke of Albany*, Goneril's husband; *Duke of Cornwall*, Regan's husband.

Love's Labours Lost (comedy – *abbrev. LLL*)
Main characters: *King of Navarre*; *Berowne, Longueville, Dumaine*, the King's companions; *Princess of France*; *Rosaline, Catherine, Maria*, her ladies; *Boyet*, the Princess's

attendant; *Don Armado*, a Spanish braggart; *Costard*, a country bumpkin.

Macbeth (tragedy)
Main characters: *Macbeth*; *Lady Macbeth*; *Duncan*, king of Scotland; *Malcolm* and *Donalbain*, Duncan's sons; *Banquo*, a lord and friend of Macbeth; *Fleance*, his son; *Macduff*, a lord, and an opponent of Macbeth; *Lady Macduff*; the *Three Witches*.

Measure for Measure (dark comedy – *abbrev. M for M*)
Main characters: *Duke of Vienna*; *Angelo*, his deputy; *Isabella*, a novice in a convent; *Claudio*, her brother; *Mariana*, previously engaged to Angelo; *Mistress Overdone*, a bawd; *Pompey*, her servant.

Merchant of Venice, The (comedy – *abbrev. Merchant*)
Main characters: *Antonio*, a merchant of Venice; *Bassanio*, his friend; *Shylock*, a Jewish moneylender; *Portia*, an heiress; *Nerissa*, Portia's waiting gentlewoman; *Graziano, Salerio, Solanio, Lorenzo*, Venetian gentlemen; *Jessica*, Shylock's daughter.

Merry Wives of Windsor, The (comedy – *M Wives*)
Main characters: *Mistress Page, Mistress Ford*, the merry wives; *Master Page, Master Ford*, their husbands; *Anne Page*, the

Pages' daughter; *Sir John Falstaff*; *Bardolph*, *Pistol*, *Nym*, his companions; *Dr Caius*, a French doctor; *Sir Hugh Evans*, a Welsh parson; *Slender*, a foolish young man; *Fenton*, an eligible young man.

Midsummer Night's Dream, A (comedy – *abbrev. MND*)

Main characters: *Hermia* and *Lysander*, *Helena* and *Demetrius*, two pairs of lovers; *Oberon*, the fairy king; *Titania*, the fairy queen; *Puck*, a mischievous fairy servant to Oberon; the *Mechanicals*: Nick *Bottom*, a weaver; Peter *Quince*, a carpenter; Francis *Flute*, a bellows-mender; Tom *Snout*, a tinker; *Snug*, a joiner; Robin *Starveling*, a tailor; *Duke Theseus* and *Queen Hippolyta*.

Much Ado about Nothing (comedy – *abbrev. Much Ado*)

Main characters: *Beatrice* and *Benedict*, enemies who become lovers; *Hero*, Beatrice's cousin, daughter of Leonato; *Leonato*, governor of Messina; *Don Pedro*, Prince of Aragon; *Don John*, his villainous bastard brother; *Claudio*, a friend of Don Pedro and Benedict; *Dogberry* and *Verges*, comic watchmen.

Othello (tragedy)

Main characters: *Othello*, a Moor in the service of the state of Venice; *Desdemona*, his wife; *Iago*, his 'ancient'; *Emilia*, Iago's wife; *Cassio*, Othello's lieutenant; *Roderigo*, a Venetian gentleman in love with Desdemona.

Pericles, Prince of Tyre (romance – *abbrev. Peric*)

Main characters: *Pericles*, Prince of Tyre; *Thaisa*, his wife; *Marina*, his daughter; *Gower*, prologue and chorus; *Antiochus*, King of Antioch; *Simonides*, King of Pentapolis; *Cleon*, governor of Tarsus; *Dionyza*, Cleon's wife.

Richard II (history – *abbrev. Rich II*)

Main characters: *King Richard II*; *John of Gaunt*, Duke of Lancaster, and *Edmund Duke of York*, his uncles; Henry *Bolingbroke*, John of Gaunt's son; *Earl of Northumberland*, a supporter of Bolingbroke; *Bushy*, *Bagot*, *Green*, favourites of King Richard; Thomas *Mowbray*, Duke of Norfolk.

Richard III (history – *abbrev. Rich III*)

Main characters: *King Richard III* (Duke of Gloucester at start of play); *King Edward IV*, *George Duke of Clarence*, his brothers; *Duchess of York*, their mother; *Queen Elizabeth*, wife of Edward IV; *Queen Margaret*, widow of Henry VI; *Lady Anne*, widow of the former Prince of Wales and later Richard's wife;

Lord Hastings; *Duke of Buckingham*.

Romeo and Juliet (tragedy – *abbrev. R & J*)

Main characters: *Romeo*, heir of the house of Montague; *Juliet*, daughter of the head of the house of Capulet; *Tybalt*, Juliet's cousin; *Benvolio*, *Mercutio*, friends of Romeo; *Friar Lawrence*; *Juliet's nurse*; *Old Capulet*; *Lady Capulet*.

Taming of the Shrew, The (comedy – *abbrev. Shrew*)

Main characters: *Petruchio*, a gentleman of Verona; *Baptista Minola*, a gentleman of Padua; *Katherina*, his elder, bad-tempered daughter; *Bianca*, his younger daughter; *Grumio*, Petruchio's servant.

Tempest, The

Main characters: *Prospero*, deposed Duke of Milan; *Miranda*, his daughter; *Ariel*, an airy spirit attending Propsero; *Caliban*, a savage and deformed creature forced into Prospero's service; *Antonio*, Prospero's brother, the usurping Duke of Milan; *Alonso*, King of Naples; *Ferdinand*, his son; *Sebastian*, Alonso's brother; *Gonzalo*, an honest Neapolitan lord.

Timon of Athens (tragedy – *abbrev. Timon*)

Main characters: *Timon*, a rich Athenian; *Alcibiades*, an Athenian soldier;

Apemantus, a cynical philosopher; *Flavius*, Timon's faithful steward.

Titus Andronicus (tragedy – *abbrev. Titus*) Main characters: *Titus Andronicus*, a Roman general; *Lavinia*, his daughter; *Tamora*, Queen of the Goths; *Saturninus*, Roman emperor, her husband; *Aaron*, a Moor, Tamora's lover; *Chiron* and *Demetrius*, her sons.

Troilus and Cressida (tragicomedy – *abbrev. Tr. & Cres.*) Main characters: *Troilus*, a Trojan prince; *Cressida*, daughter of Calchas, a priest who has joined the Greeks; *Pandarus*, her uncle; *Agamemnon*, *Menelaus*, *Achilles*, *Ajax*, *Patroclus*, *Ulysses*, *Nestor*, Greeks; *Hector*, *Paris*, Trojan princes; *Helen* of Troy; *Thersites*, a scurrilous Greek.

Twelfth Night (comedy – *abbrev. T Night*) Main characters: *Orsino*, Duke of Illyria; *Viola*, a shipwrecked lady; *Sebastian*, her brother; *Olivia*, an Illyrian lady; *Malvolio*, her steward; *Maria*, her waiting gentlewoman; *Feste*, her jester; *Sir Toby Belch*, her cousin; *Sir Andrew Aguecheek*, Sir Toby's companion.

Two Gentlemen of Verona, The (comedy – *abbrev. Two Gents*) Main characters: *Valentine* and *Proteus*, two gentlemen of Verona; *Silvia*, daughter of the Duke of Milan; *Julia*, Proteus' sweetheart; *Lance*, Proteus' servant; *Speed*, Valentine's servant; *Crab*, Lance's dog.

Winter's Tale, The (romance – *abbrev. W Tale*) Main characters: *Leontes*, King of Sicily; *Hermione*, his wife; *Perdita*, his daughter; *Polixenes*, King of Bohemia; *Florizel*, his son; *Antigonus*, a Sicilian lord; *Paulina*, his wife; *Old Shepherd*, Perdita's foster father; *Autolycus*, a pedlar and rogue.

SHAKESPEAREAN CHARACTERS (*see above for abbreviations*)

3
Nym (*Hen V, M Wives*)
Say (Lord, *Hen VI 2*)
Sly (Christopher, *Shrew*)

4
Adam (*AYLI*)
Ajax (*Tr & Cres*)
Anne (Lady, *Rich III*)
Bona (*Hen VI 3*)
Cade (Jack *Hen VI 2*)
Cato (*JC*)
Davy (*Hen VI 2*)
Dick (*Hen VI 2*)
Dion (*W Tale*)
Dull (*LLL*)
Eros (*Ant & Cle*)
Fang (*Hen IV 2*)
Ford (*M Wives*)
Grey (*Hen V, Rich III*)
Hero (*Much Ado*)
Hume (*Hen VI 2*)
Iago (*Othello*)

Iden (*Hen VI 2*)
Iras (*Ant & Cle*)
Jamy (*Hen V*)
John (*K John, Rom & Jul, Hen IV 1&2*)
Juno (*Tempest*)
Kent (Earl, of Lear)
Lear (*Lear*)
Luce (*Com Err*)
Lucy (*Hen VI 1*)
Moth (*LLL, MND*)
Page (*M Wives*)
Peto (*Hen IV 1 & 2*)
Puck (*MND*)
Ross (*Macbeth, Rich III*)
Snug (*MND*)
Vaux (*Hen VIII, Hen VI 2*)
Wart (*Hen IV 2*)

5
Aaron (*Titus*)
Alice (*Hen V*)
Angus (*Macbeth*)
Ariel (*Tempest*)
Bagot (*Rich II*)
Bates (*Hen V*)
Belch (Sir Toby, *T Night*)
Bevis (*Hen VI 2*)
Bigot (*K John*)
Blunt (Sir Walter, *Hen IV 1*)
Boult (*Peric*)
Boyet (*LLL*)
Bushy (*Rich II*)
Butts (*Hen VIII*)
Caius (*Titus M Wives*)
Casca (*JC*)
Celia (*AYLI*)
Ceres (*Tempest*)
Cinna (*JC*)
Cleon (*Peric*)
Corin (*AYLI*)
Court (*Hen V*)
Cupid (*Timon*)
Curan (*Lear*)
Curio (*T Night*)
Denny (*Hen VIII*)
Diana (*All's Well, Peric*)

Edgar (*Lear*)
Egeus (*MND*)
Elbow (*M for M*)
Evans (Sir Hugh, *M Wives*)
Exton (Sir Piers of, *Rich II*)
Feste (*T Night*)
Flute (*MND*)
Froth (*M for M*)
Gobbo (*Merchant*)
Goffe (*Hen VI 2*)
Gower (*Hen IV 2, Henry V, Peric*)
Green (*Rich II*)
Helen (*Cymb, Tr & Cres*)
Henry (*K John, Hen V, Hen VI 3, Hen IV 1 & 2, Hen VIII, Rich III*)
Julia (*Two Gents*)
Lafeu (*All's Well*)
Lewis (*Henry V, K John*)
Louis (*Hen VI 3*)
Lovel (*Rich III*)
Lucio (*M for M*)
Maria (*LLL, T Night*)
Melun (*K John*)
Menas (*Ant & Cleo*)
Mopsa (*W Tale*)
Osric (*Hamlet*)
Paris (*Rom & Jul, Tr & Cres*)
Percy (*Hen IV 1 & 2, Rich II*)
Peter (*Hen VI 2, K John, M for M, Rom & Jul*)
Philo (*Ant & Cleo*)
Pinch (*Com Err*)
Poins (*Hen IV 1 & 2*)
Priam (*Tr & Cres*)
Regan (*Lear*)
Robin (*M Wives*)
Romeo (*Rom & Jul*)
Rugby (*M Wives*)
Smith (*Hen VI 2*)
Snare (*Hen IV 2*)
Snout (*MND*)
Speed (*Two Gents*)

Timon (*Timon*)
Titus (*Timon*)
Tubal (*Merchant*)
Varro (*JC*)
Viola (*T Night*)

6

Adrian (*Corio*)
Aegeon (*Com Err*)
Aeneas (*Tr & Cres*)
Alexas (*Ant & Cleo*)
Alonso (*Tempest*)
Amiens (*AYLI*)
Angelo (*Com Err, M for M*)
Antony (*Ant & Cleo*)
Arthur (*K John*)
Audrey (*AYLI*)
Banquo (*Macbeth*)
Basset (*Hen VI 1*)
Bianca (*Othello, Shrew*)
Blount (*Rich III*)
Bottom *MND*)
Brutus (*JC, Corio*)
Bullen (*Hen VIII*)
Ceasar (*Ant & Cle, JC*)
Caphis (*Timon*)
Cassio (*Othello*)
Chiron (*Titus*)
Cicero (*JC*)
Cimber (*JC*)
Clitus (*JC*)
Cloten (*Cymb*)
Cobweb (*MND*)
Curtis (*Shrew*)
Dennis (*AYLI*)
Dorcas (*W Tale*)
Dromio (*Com Err*)
Dumain (*LLL*)
Duncan (*Macbeth*)
Edmund (*Hen VI 3, Lear*)
Edward (*Hen VI 2 & 3, Rich III*)
Elinor (*KJ*)
Emilia (*Othello, W Tale*)
Fabian (*T Night*)
Feeble (*Henry IV 2*)
Fenton (*M Wives*)

Gallus (*Ant & Cleo*)
George (*Hen VI 3, Rich III*)
Gremio (*Shrew*)
Grumio (*Shrew*)
Gurney (*K John*)
Hamlet (*Hamlet*)
Hecate (*Macbeth*)
Hector (*Tr & Cres*)
Helena (*All's Well, MND*)
Hermia (*MND*)
Horner (*Hen VI 2*)
Hubert (*K John*)
Imogen (*Cymb*)
Isabel (*Hen V*)
Jaques (*AYLI*)
Juliet (*M for M, Rom & Jul*)
Launce (*Two Gents*)
Le Beau (*AYLI*)
Lennox (*Macbeth*)
Lovell (*Hen VIII*)
Lucius (*JC, Timon. Cymbel, Titus*)
Marina (*Peric*)
Minola (*Shrew*)
Morton (*Hen IV 2, Rich III*)
Mouldy (*Hen IV 2*)
Mutius (*Titus*)
Nestor (*Tr & Cres*)
Oliver (*AYLI*)
Olivia (*T Night*)
Orsino (*T Night*)
Oswald (*Lear*)
Phoebe (*AYLI*)
Pistol (*Hen IV, 2 Hen V, M Wives*)
Pompey (*M for M*)
Portia (*JC, Merchant*)
Quince (Peter, *MND*)
Rivers (Lord, *Rich III, Hen VI 3*)
Rumour (*Hen IV 2*)
Sandys (*Hen VIII*)
Scales (*Hen VI 2*)
Scarus (*Ant & Cleo*)
Scroop (*Hen IV 1 & 2,*

Rich II, Hen V)
Seyton (*Macbeth*)
Shadow (*Hen IV 2*)
Silius (*Ant & Cleo*)
Silvia (*Two Gents*)
Simple (*M Wives*)
Siward (*Macbeth*)
Strato (*JC*)
Talbot (*Hen VI 1*)
Tamora (*Titus*)
Taurus (*Ant & Cleo*)
Thaisa (*Peric*)
Thomas (*Hen IV 2, M for M*)
Thurio (*Two Gents*)
Tranio (*Shrew*)
Tybalt (*Rom & Jul*)
Tyrrel (*Rich III*)
Ursula (*Much Ado*)
Verges (*Much Ado*)
Vernon (*Hen IV 1, Hen VI 1*)
Wolsey (*Hen VIII*)

7
Abraham (*Rom & Jul*)
Adriana (*Com Err*)
Aemilia (*Com Err*)
Agrippa (*Ant & Cle, Corio*)
Alarbus (*Titus*)
Amazons (*Timon*)
Antenor (*Tr & Cres*)
Antonio (*Merchant, Much Ado, Tempest, T Night, Two Gents*)
Berowne (*LLL*)
Bertram (*All's Well*)
Blanche (*K John*)
Brandon (*Hen VIII, Rich II*)
Calchas (*Tr & Cres*)
Caliban (*Tempest*)
Camillo (*W Tale*)
Capulet (*Rom & Jul*)
Cassius (*JC*)
Catesby (*Rich III*)
Cerimon (*Peric*)
Charles (*AYLI, Hen VI 1,*

Hen V)
Claudio (*M for M, Much Ado*)
Conrade (*Much Ado*)
Costard (*LLL*)
Cranmer (*Hen VIII*)
Dionyza (*Peric*)
Douglas (Earl of *Hen IV 1*)
Eleanor (*Hen VI 2*)
Escalus (*M for M Rom & Jul*)
Escanes (*Peric*)
Flavius (*JC, Timon*)
Fleance (*Macbeth*)
Francis (*Hen IV 1, Much Ado*)
Goneril (*Lear*)
Gonzalo (*Tempest*)
Gregory (*Rom & Jul*)
Helenus (*Tr & Cres*)
Herbert (*Rich III*)
Holland (*Hen VI 2*)
Horatio (*Hamlet*)
Hotspur (*Hen IV 1*)
Iachimo (*Cymb*)
Jessica (*Merchant*)
Laertes (*Hamlet*)
Lartius (*Corio*)
Lavache (*All's Well*)
Lavinia (*Titus*)
Leonato (*Much Ado*)
Leonine (*Peric*)
Leontes (*W Tale*)
Lepidus (*Ant & Cleo JC*)
Lorenzo (*Merchant*)
Lucetta (*Two Gents*)
Luciana (*Com Err*)
Lymoges (*K John*)
Macbeth (*Macbeth*)
Macduff (*Macbeth*)
Malcolm (*Macbeth*)
Marcade (*LLL*)
Marcius (*Corio*)
Mardian (*Ant & Cleo*)
Mariana (*All's Well M for M*)
Martext (Sir Oliver, *AYLI*)

Martius (*Titus*)
Messala (*JC*)
Michael (*Hen VI 2, Hen IV 1*)
Miranda (*Tempest*)
Montano (*Othello*)
Montjoy (*Hen V*)
Mowbray (*Hen IV 2, Rich II*)
Nerissa (*Merchant*)
Nicanor (*Corio*)
Octavia (*Ant & Cleo*)
Ophelia (*Hamlet*)
Orlando (*AYLI*)
Othello (*Othello*)
Paroles (*All's Well*)
Paulina (*W Tale*)
Perdita (*W Tale*)
Phyrnia (*Timon*)
Pisanio (*Cymb*)
Proteus (*Two Gents*)
Provost (*M for M*)
Publius (*JC, Titus*)
Quickly (Mistress, *Hen IV 1 & 2, M Wives*)
Quintus (*Titus*)
Richard (*Hen VI 2 & 3, Rich II, Rich III*)
Salerio (*Merchant*)
Sampson (*Rom & Jul*)
Shallow (*M Wives, Hen I 2*)
Shylock (*Merchant*)
Silence (*Hen IV 2*)
Silvius (*AYLI*)
Simcox (*Hen VI 2*)
Slender (*M Wives*)
Solanio (*Merchant*)
Solinus (*Com Err*)
Stanley (*Hen VI 3, Rich III, Hen VI 2*)
Stefano (*Merchant*)
Theseus (*MND*)
Thyreus (*Ant & Cleo*)
Titania (*MND*)
Travers (*Henry IV 2*)
Tressel (*Rich III*)
Troilus (*Tr & Cres*)

Ulysses (*Tr & Cress*)
Urswick (*Rich III*)
Valeria (*Corio*)
Varrius (*Ant & Cleo*)
Vaughan (*Rich III*)
Velutus (*Corio*)
William (*AYLI*)
Witches (*Macbeth*)

8

Abhorson (*M for M*)
Achilles (*Tr & Cress*)
Aemilius (*Titus*)
Aufidius (*Corio*)
Bardolph (*Hen IV 1 & 2, Hen V, M Wives, Henry VI*)
Bassanio (*Merchant*)
Beatrice (*Much Ado*)
Beaufort (*Hen VI 1, 2& 3*)
Belarius (*Cymb*)
Benedick (*Much Ado*)
Benvolio (*Rom & Jul*)
Berkeley (*Rich II, Rich III*)
Bernardo (*Hamlet*)
Borachio (*Much Ado*)
Bullcalf (*Hen IV 2*)
Campeius (*Hen VIII*)
Canidius (*Ant & Cleo*)
Capucius (*Hen VIII*)
Charmian (*Ant & Cleo*)
Claudius (*Hamlet*)
Clifford (*Hen VI 2 & 3*)
Colville (*Hen IV 2*)
Cominius (*Corio*)
Cordelia (*Lear*)
Cressida (*Tr & Cress*)
Cromwell (*Hen VIII*)
Dercetas (*Ant & Cleo*)
Diomedes (*Ant & Cleo*)
Dogberry (*Much Ado*)
Eglamour (*Two Gents*)
Falstaff (Sir John *M Wives, Hen IV 1& 2*)
Fastolfe (*Hen VI 1*)
Florizel (*W Tale*)
Fluellen (*Hen V*)
Gadshill (*Hen IV 1*)

Gardiner (*Hen VIII*)
Gargrave (*Hen VI 1*)
Gertrude (*Hamlet*)
Grandpré (*Hen V*)
Gratiano (*Merchant, Othello*)
Griffith (*Hen VIII*)
Harcourt (*Hen IV 2*)
Hastings (*Hen IV 2, Hen VI 3, Rich III*)
Hermione (*W Tale*)
Humphrey (*Henry IV 2*)
Isabella (*M for M*)
Jourdain (*Hen VI 2*)
Lawrence (Friar, *Rom & Jul*)
Leonardo (*Merchant*)
Leonatus (*Cymb*)
Ligarius (*JC*)
Lodovico (*Othello*)
Lucentio (*Shrew*)
Lucilius (*JC, Timon*)
Lucullus (*Timon*)
Lysander (*MND*)
Maecenas (*Ant & Cleo*)
Malvolio (*T Night*)
Margaret (*Much Ado, Hen VI 1 2 & 3, Rich III*)
Marullus (*JC*)
Menelaus (*Tr & Cres*)
Menteith (*Macbeth*)
Mercutio (*Rom & Jul*)
Montague (*Rom & Jul*)
Mortimer (*Com IV 1, Hen VI 1, Hen VI 3*)
Overdone (Mistress, *M for M*)
Pandarus (*Tr & Cres*)
Pandulph (*K John*)
Panthino (*Two Gents*)
Patience (*Hen VIII*)
Pericles (*Peric*)
Philario (*Cymbel*)
Philemon (*Peric*)
Philotus (*Timon*)
Pindarus (*JC*)
Polonius (*Hamlet*)
Pompeius (*Ant & Cleo*)

Prospero (*Tempest*)
Rambures (*Hen V*)
Ratcliff (*Rich III*)
Reignier (*Hen VI 1*)
Reynaldo (*Hamlet*)
Roderigo (*Othello*)
Rosalind (*AYLI*)
Rosaline (*LLL*)
Seleucus (*Ant & Cleo*)
Stafford (*Hen VI 2 & 3*)
Stephano (*Tempest*)
Thaliard (*Peric*)
Timandra (*Timon*)
Titinius (*JC*)
Trinculo (*Tempest*)
Violenta (*All's Well*)
Virgilia (*Corio*)
Volumnia (*Corio*)
Whitmore (*Hen VI 2*)
Williams (*Hen V*)

9

Agamemnon (*Tr & Cres*)
Aguecheek (Sir Andrew, *T Night*)
Alexander (*Tr & Cres*)
Antigonus (*W Tale*)
Antiochus (*Peric*)
Apemantus (*Timon*)
Arviragus (*Cymbel*)
Autolycus (*W Tale*)
Balthasar (*Merchant, Much Ado, Rom & Jul*)
Balthazar (*Com Err*)
Bassianus (*Titus*)
Biondello (*Shrew*)
Brabantio (*Othello*)
Caithness (*Macbeth*)
Calpurnia (*JC*)
Cassandra (*Tr & Cres*)
Chatillon (*K John*)
Cleomenes (*W Tale*)
Cleopatra (*Ant & Cleo*)
Constance (*K John*)
Cornelius (*Cymb, Hamlet*)
Cymbeline (*Cymbel*)
Dardanius (*JC*)
Deiphobus (*Tr & Cres*)

Demetrius (*Ant & Cleo, MND, Titus*)
Desdemona (*Othello*)
Dolabella (*Ant & Cleo*)
Donalbain (*Macbeth*)
Elizabeth (*Rich III*)
Enobarbus (*Ant & Cleo*)
Erpingham (*Hen V*)
Ferdinand (*LLL, Tempest*)
Fitzwater (*Rich II*)
Flaminius (*Timon*)
Francisca (*M for M*)
Francisco (*Hamlet, Tempest*)
Frederick (*AYLI*)
Glansdale (*Hen VI 1*)
Glendower (*Hen IV 1*)
Guiderius (*Cymbel*)
Guildford (*Hen VIII*)
Helicanus (*Peric*)
Hippolyta (*MND*)
Hortensio (*Shrew*)
Katherina (*Shrew*)
Katharine (*LLL Hen VIII*)
Katherine (*Hen V*)
Lychorida (*Peric*)
Macmorris (*Hen V*)
Mamillius (*W Tale*)
Marcellus (*Hamlet*)
Nathaniel (*LLL*)
Patroclus (*Tr & Cres*)

Petruchio (*Shrew*)
Polixenes (*W Tale*)
Sebastian (*Tempest, T Night*)
Servilius (*Timon*)
Simonides (*Peric*)
Southwell (*Hen VI 2*)
Tearsheet (Doll, *Hen IV 2*)
Thersites (*Tr & Cres*)
Trebonius (*JC*)
Valentine (*Titus, T Night, Two Gents*)
Ventidius (*Ant & Cleo, Timon*)
Vincentio (*M for M, Shrew*)
Voltemand (*Hamlet*)
Volumnius (*JC*)
Woodville (*Hen VI 1*)

10

Alcibiades (*Timon*)
Andromache (*Tr & Cres*)
Andronicus (*Titus*)
Antipholus (*Com Err*)
Archidamus (*W Tale*)
Barnardine (*M for M*)
Brakenbury (*Rich III*)
Coriolanus (*Corio*)
Euphronius (*Ant & Cleo*)

Fortinbras (*Hamlet*)
Holofernes (*LLL*)
Jaquenetta (*LLL*)
Longaville (*LLL*)
Lysimachus (*Peric*)
Margareton (*Tr & Cres*)
Menecrates (*Ant & Cleo*)
Montgomery (*Hen VI 3*)
Proculeius (*Ant & Cleo*)
Saturninus (*Titus*)
Sempronius (*Timon Titus*)
Somerville (*Hen VI 3*)
Starveling (*MND*)
Touchstone (*AYLI*)

11

Abergavenny (*Henry VIII*)
Artemidorus (*JC*)
Bolingbroke (*Rich II*)
Longueville (*LLL*)
Mustardseed (*MND*)
Philostrate (*MND*)
Rosencrantz (*Hamlet*)

12

Guildenstern (*Hamlet*)
Peaseblossom (*MND*)

13

Faulconbridge (*K John*)

SHIPS AND BOATS

Ships and boats
Parts of a ship or boat

SHIPS AND BOATS

2
MV
SS

3
ark
cat
gig
HMS
hoy
MTB
sub
tug
USS

4
bark
brig
dhow
dory
duck
DUKW
junk
pair
pram
prau
proa
punt
raft
Roro
scow
trow
yawl

5
barge
canoe
coble
craft
dandy
eight
ferry
kayak
ketch
liner
praam
scull
shell
skiff
sloop
smack
tramp
xebec
yacht
zebec

6
barque
bireme
caique
carvel
cutter
dinghy
dugout
galiot
galley
launch
lugger
pedalo
randan
sampan
tanker
tender
whaler
wherry
zebeck

7
bumboat
caravel
carrack
carrier
catboat
clipper
coaster
collier
coracle
cruiser
currach
dredger
drifter
felucca
frigate
galleon
galliot
gondola
gunboat
jetfoil
lighter
monitor
pinnace
pirogue
polacca
polacre
rowboat
sculler
shallop
steamer
trawler
trireme
tugboat
vedette
warship

8
cockboat
corvette
flagship
galleass
indiaman
ironclad
lifeboat
longboat
longship
sailboat
schooner
showboat
trimaran

9
amphibian
catamaran
destroyer
ferryboat
freighter

houseboat
hydrofoil
jollyboat
lightship
minelayer
motorboat
multihull
outrigger
powerboat
privateer
speedboat
steamboat
steamship
submarine
troopship
vaporetto

10
barkentine
battleship
brigantine
cockleboat
hovercraft
hydroplane
icebreaker
narrowboat
paddleboat
quadrireme
windjammer

11
barquentine
cockleshell
dreadnought
merchantman
minesweeper
quinquereme
submersible
supertanker

13
battlecruiser

2+ words
aircraft carrier
bulk-carrier
cabin cruiser
landing craft

man-of-war
motor launch
motor torpedo boat
motor-vessel
pleasure boat
rowing boat
square-rigger
stern-wheeler
torpedo boat
U-boat

*PARTS OF A SHIP
OR BOAT*

3
aft
bow
guy
jib
oar
rib
rig

4
beam
bitt
boom
bows
bunk
deck
helm
hold
hull
keel
mast
poop
port
prow
rake
sail
skeg
spar
stay
stem
yard

5
berth

bilge
bower
brace
brail
cabin
cable
davit
hatch
kevel
orlop
stern
waist
wheel
winch

6
anchor
awning
bilges
bridge
engine
fender
fo'c'sle
for'ard
galley
gunnel
hawser
kelson
locker
mizzen
rudder
saloon
sheets
shroud
strake
tackle
thwart
tiller

7
bobstay
bollard
bulwark
caboose
capstan
coaming
cockpit
foghorn

futtock
gangway
gudgeon
gunwale
jibstay
keelson
lugsail
maintop
painter
ratline
rigging
rowlock
shrouds
sickbay
skysail
spanker
topmast
topsail
trysail
yardarm

8
backstay
binnacle
bowsprit
bulkhead
bulwarks
cutwater
forefoot
foremast
forepeak
foresail
forestay
gaffsail
hatchway

headfast
headsail
magazine
mainmast
mainsail
mainstay
mainyard
porthole
portside
staysail
steerage
stunsail
taffrail
wardroom

9
afterdeck
chartroom
crosstree
gangplank
mainbrace
mainsheet
mizzenmast
mizzentop
spinnaker
spritsail
stanchion
starboard
stateroom
stokehold
stormsail
stormstay

waterline

10
charthouse
figurehead
forecastle
mizzenmast
mizzensail
pilothouse
topgallant
upperworks
wheelhouse

11
centreboard
maintopmast
maintopsail
quarterdeck
sternsheets
weatherdeck

12
companionway

13
superstructure

2+ words
beam ends
conning tower
crow's nest
well deck

SINGERS

A singer
Famous classical singers
Famous popular singers

4
alto
bass
diva
wait

5
tenor

6
belter
canary
cantor
treble

7
chanter
crooner
soloist
soprano
warbler

8
baritone
castrato
choirboy
falsetto
minstrel
songster
vocalist

9
balladeer
chorister
choirgirl
contralto
precentor

10
troubadour

FAMOUS CLASSICAL SINGERS

4
Lind (Jenny)

5
Baker (Janet)
Church (Charlotte)
Evans (Geriant)
Gedda (Nicolai)
Gigli (Beniamino)
Gobbi (Tito)
Jones (Aled)
Lanza (Mario)
Melba (Nellie)
Patti (Adelina)
Pears (Peter)
Sills (Beverly)

6
Callas (Maria)
Caruso (Enrico)
Kirkby (Emma)
Tauber (Richard)
Watson (Russell)

7
Caballé (Montserrat)
Domingo (Placido)
Ferrier (Kathleen)
Hammond (Joan)
Jenkins (Catherine)
Lehmann (Lotte)
Nilsson (Birgit)
Sargent (Malcolm)
Tebaldi (Renate)
Wallace (Ian)

8
Björling (Jussi)
Boccelli (Andrea)
Carreras (José)
Flagstad (Kirsten)

9
Brannigan (Owen)
Chaliapin (Feodor)

McCormack (John)
Pavarotti (Luciano)

10
Soderstrom (Elizabeth)
Sutherland (Joan)

11
Schwarzkopf (Elizabeth)

2+ words
Los Angeles (Victoria de)
Te Kanawa (Kiri).

FAMOUS POPULAR SINGERS

3
Ant (Adam)
Day (Doris)
Lee (Peggy)
Ray (Johnnie)
Vee (Bobby)

4
Anka (Paul)
Baez (Joan)
Bono
Bush (Kate)
Cash (Johnny)
Cher
Cole (Nat King)
Como (Perry)
Dion (Celine)
Dury (Ian)
Eddy (Duane)
Fame (Georgie)
Ford (Tennessee Ernie)
Fury (Billy)
Gaye (Marvin)
Idol (Billy)
Ives (Burl)
Joel (Billy)
John (Elton)
Keel (Howard)
King (B.B./Carole)
Kitt (Eartha)
Lulu

Lynn (Vera)
Piaf (Edith)
Ross (Diana)
Shaw (Sandie)

5
Adams (Bryan)
Allen (Chesney)
Autry (Gene)
Berry (Chuck)
Black (Cilla)
Bolan (Marc)
Boone (Pat)
Bowie (David)
Brown (James)
Clark (Dave/Petula)
Cohen (Leonard)
Darin (Bobby)
Davis (Sammy)
Dylan (Bob)
Essex (David)
Faith (Adam)
Ferry (Brian)
Harry (Debbie)
Haley (Bill)
Holly (Buddy)
Jones (Quincy/Tom)
Laine (Frankie)
Lewis (Huey/Jerry Lee)
Lloyd (Marie)
Moyet (Alison)
Ocean (Billy)
Paige (Elaine)
Price (Alan)
Proby (P.J.)
Sayer (Leo)
Seger (Bob)
Simon (Carly/Paul)
Smith (Bessy)
Sting
Tormé (Mel)
Young (Neil/Paul)

6
Avalon (Frankie)
Baldry (Long John)
Bassey (Shirley)
Burdon (Eric)

Cocker (Joe)
Cooper (Alice)
Coward (Noel)
Crosby (Bing)
Dekker (Desmond)
Denver (John)
Easton (Sheena)
Fields (Gracie)
Fisher (Eddie)
Formby (George)
Geldof (Bob)
Gentry (Bobby)
Hooker (John Lee)
Jagger (Mick)
Jolson (Al)
Joplin (Janis)
Kramer (Billy J.)
Lauper (Cindie)
Lennon (John)
Lennox (Annie)
Marley (Bob)
Martin (Dean)
Mathis (Johnny)
Nelson (Ricky/Willie)
Osmond (Donny)
Parton (Dolly)
Pitney (Gene)
Prince
Reeves (Jim)
Ritchie (Lionel)
Sedaka (Neil)
Seeger (Pete)
Simone (Nina)
Sledge (Percy)
Steele (Tommy)
Summer (Donna)
Tilley (Vesta)
Trenet (Charles)
Turner (Tina)
Twitty (Conway)
Valens (Ritchie)
Waters (Muddy)
Womack (Bobby)
Wonder (Stevie)

7
Andrews (Julie)
Astaire (Fred)

Bennett (Tony)
Cassidy (David)
Charles (Ray)
Checker (Chubby)
Clapton (Eric)
Clooney (Rosemary)
Cochran (Eddy)
Collins (Judy/Phil)
Diamond (Neil)
Diddley (Bo)
Donegan (Lonnie)
Donovan
Francis (Connie)
Gabriel (Peter)
Garland (Judy)
Guthrie (Woody)
Hendrix (Jimi)
Holiday (Billie)
Houston (Whitney)
Jackson (Janet/Michael)
Madonna
Manilow (Barry)
Mercury (Freddie)
Michael (George)
Minogue (Kylie)
Orbison (Roy)
Perkins (Carl)
Pickett (Wilson)
Presley (Elvis)
Preston (Billy)
Redding (Otis)
Richard (Cliff)
Robeson (Paul)
Shannon (Del)
Shapiro (Helen)
Sinatra (Frank)
Stevens (Cat)
Stewart (Rod)
Vaughan (Frankie/Sarah)
Vincent (Gene)
Wakeman (Rick)
Warwick (Dionne)
Wynette (Tammy)

8
Aznavour (Charles)
Bygraves (Max)
Campbell (Glen)

Costello (Elvis)
Dietrich (Marlene)
Flanagan (Bud)
Flanders (Michael)
Franklin (Aretha)
Hamlisch (Marvin)
Harrison (George)
Iglesias (Julio)
Minnelli (Liza)
Mitchell (Joni)
Morrison (Van)
Oldfield (Mike)
Osbourne (Ozzy)
Rafferty (Gerry)
Ronstadt (Linda)
Vandross (Luther)
Williams (Andy/Robbie)

9
Armstrong (Louis)
Belafonte (Harry)
Chevalier (Maurice)
Echobelly
Faithfull (Marianne)
Garfunkel (Art)
Leadbelly
McCartney (Paul)
O'Sullivan (Gilbert)
Streisand (Barbara)

10
Fitzgerald (Ella)
Washington (Dinah)

11
Armatrading (Joan)
Springfield (Dusty)
Springsteen (Bruce)

2+ words
Boy George
Little Eva
Meat Loaf
Newton-John (Olivia)

SNAKES

3
asp
boa

4
naga

5
adder
cobra
krait
mamba
viper

6
python

7
rattler
serpent

8
anaconda
moccasin
ophidian
slowworm

9
boomslang

10
bushmaster
copperhead
sidewinder

11
constrictor
cottonmouth
rattlesnake

2+ words
coral snake
fer-de-lance
garter snake
grass snake
king cobra
pit viper
puff adder
ring snake
sand snake
water snake

SOUNDS

3
baa
bay
boo
caw
coo
cry
din
hum
mew
moo
pip
pop
rap
row
tap
yap

4
bang
bark
bawl
beat
beep
blow
bong
bonk
boom
bray
bump
buzz
call
chug
clap
clop
ding
dong
echo
gasp
hiss
honk
hoot
howl
moan

note
oink
peal
peep
ping
plop
purl
purr
rasp
ring
roar
sigh
slam
thud
tick
ting
toll
tone
toot
wail
wham
whiz
woof
yell
yelp

5
bleat
bleep
cheep
chime
chink
chirp
clang
clash
click
clink
cluck
clunk
crack
crash
croak
drone
groan
growl
grunt
knell
miaow

music
neigh
noise
pluck
plunk
quack
shout
slurp
smash
snarl
splat
swish
throb
thrum
thump
trill
twang
tweet
whine
whirr
whoop

6
babble
bellow
burble
crunch
giggle
gurgle
jangle
jingle
murmur
mutter
patter
racket
rattle
rumble
rustle
scream
shriek
sizzle
splash
squawk
squeak
squeal
squish
swoosh
thwack

timbre
tinkle
titter
tootle
warble
wheeze
whinny
whoosh

7
catcall
chatter
chirrup

chortle
chuckle
crackle
screech
sniffle
snigger
squelch
thunder
trumpet
twitter
whimper
whisper
whistle

8
splutter
ticktock

9
caterwaul
resonance

SPACE

Space
Terms used in space
exploration

SPACE

3
gap

4
area
hole
room
void

5
blank
break
pause
place
scope

6
cosmos
lacuna
leeway
margin
period
vacuum
window

7
expanse
freedom
headway
heavens
legroom
liberty
opening

8
aperture
capacity
headroom

interval
latitude
universe

9
clearance
dimension
elbowroom
expansion
extension

10
dimensions
interstice

TERMS USED IN SPACE EXPLORATION

3
ESA
EVA
LEM
Mir
pod

4
dock
NASA

5
lunar
orbit
probe
Soyuz

6
Apollo
lander
launch
module
rocket
Salyut
Skylab
Viking
Vostok

7
capsule
Galileo
Mariner
shuttle
orbiter
Sputnik
Voyager

8
Atlantis
Columbia
Explorer
moonshot
moonwalk
nosecone
spaceman

9
astrodrome
astronaut
cosmonaut
countdown
Discovery
launchpad
satellite
spacecrew
spaceship
spacesuit
spacewalk

10
Challenger
spacecraft
spacewoman
splashdown

2+ words
blast off
booster rocket
command module
launch vehicle
lift-off
lunar module
re-entry

SPICES

4
mace

5
chili
clove
cumin
curry

6
chilli
garlic

ginger
nutmeg
pepper

7
aniseed
caraway
cayenne
mustard
oregano
paprika
pimento
saffron

8
allspice
cardamom
cardamum
cinnamon
tarragon
turmeric

9
coriander

SPORT

Sports
Famous sportsmen and
sportswomen
Terms used in sport
See also **CRICKET,**
FOOTBALL, GOLF,
RACE/RACING

SPORTS

2
RU

4
golf
judo
polo
pool

5
bowls
fives
kendo
rugby

6
aikido
boules
boxing
discus
diving
hockey
hurley
karate
pelota
racing
riding
rowing
savate
shinty
skiing
soccer
squash
tennis

7
angling
archery
bowling
cricket
croquet
curling
cycling
fencing
fishing
gliding
hunting
hurling
javelin
jogging
jujitsu
karting
netball
rackets
running
sailing
skating
snooker
surfing
walking

8
baseball
biathlon
canoeing
coursing
climbing
falconry
football
handball
hardball
hurdling
korfball
lacrosse
langlauf
marathon
petanque
rallying
rounders
shooting
sledging
softball
speedway

swimming
trotting
yachting

9
athletics
badminton
billiards
bobsleigh
canyoning
decathlon
motocross
parapente
skydiving
triathlon
wrestling

10
basketball
foxhunting
gymnastics
heptathlon
kickboxing
volleyball

11
basejumping
bobsledding
parachuting
pentathlon
tobogganing
waterskiing
windsurfing

12
bullfighting
cockfighting
orienteering
snowboarding
steeplechase
trampolining
wakeboarding

13
skateboarding
weightlifting

14
mountaineering

2+ words
cross-country
dog racing
hang-gliding
high jump
ice dancing
ice hockey
ice skating
kung-fu
long jump
para-gliding
ping-pong
pole vault
pot-holing
sail-boarding
show-jumping
sky-diving
stool ball
table-tennis
T'ai chi
water polo

FAMOUS SPORTSMEN AND
SPORTSWOMEN

3
Ali (Muhammad, boxer)
Coe (Sebastian, runner)
Law (Denis, footballer)

4
Amis (Dennis, cricketer)
Ashe (Arthur, tennis
player)
Best (George, footballer)
Borg (Bjorn, tennis
player)
Clay (Cassius, see Ali)
Cram (Steve, runner)
Dean (Dixie, footballer)
Duke (Geoff, racing
motorcyclist)
Figo (Luis, footballer)
Graf (Steffi, tennis player)
Hall (Wesley, cricketer)

Hill (Damon/Graham,
racing drivers)
Hoad (Lew, tennis player)
Hunt (James, racing
driver)
John (Barry, rugby player)
Khan (Imran, cricketer)
King (Billie Jean, tennis
player)
Lamb (Allan, cricketer)
Lara (Brian, cricketer)
Lock (Tony, cricketer)
Lomu (Jonah, rugby
player)
Lyle (Sandy, golfer)
Moss (Stirling, racing
driver)
Owen (Michael,
footballer)
Pele (footballer)
Rees (Dai, golfer)
Rush (Ian, footballer)
Snow (John, cricketer)
Wade (Virginia, tennis
player)

5
Adams (Tony, footballer)
Banks (Gordon,
footballer)
Blake (Peter, yachtsman)
Blyth (Chey, yachtsman)
Bruno (Frank, boxer)
Budge (Donald, tennis
player)
Bueno (Maria, tennis
player)
Busby (Matt, footballer)
Clark (Jim, racing driver)
Close (Brian, cricketer)
Court (Maragaret, tennis
player)
Curry (John, ice skater)
Davis (Steve, snooker
player)
Evans (Godfrey, cricketer)
Evert (Christine, tennis
player)

Faldo (Nick, golfer)
Giggs (Ryan, footballer)
Going (Sid, rugby player)
Gooch (Graham,
cricketer)
Gough (Darren, cricketer)
Gower (David, cricketer)
Grace (W.G., cricketer)
Greig (Tony, cricketer)
Henri (Thierry,
footballer)
Hobbs (Jack, cricketer)
Hogan (Ben, golfer)
Hurst (Geoff, footballer)
Jeeps (Dickie, rugby
player)
Knott (Alan, cricketer)
Laker (Jim, cricketer)
Lauda (Niki, racing
driver)
Laver (Rod, tennis player)
Lewis (Carl, athlete)
Lewis (Lennox, boxer)
Lloyd (Clive, cricketer)
Locke (Bobby, golfer)
Louis (Joe, boxer)
Meads (Colin rugby
player)
Moore (Bobby, footballer)
Ovett (Steve, runner)
Owens (Jesse, athlete)
Perry (Fred, tennis
player)
Revie (Don, footballer)
Seles (Monica, tennis
player)
Senna (Ayrton, racing
driver)
Sheen (Barry, racing
motorcyclist)
Smith (Harvey,
showjumper)
Snead (Sam, golfer)
Spitz (Mark, swimmer)
Stein (Jock, footballer)
Tyson (Mike, boxer)
Viren (Lasse, runner)
Walsh (Courtney, cricketer)

Warne (Shane, cricketer)
Waugh (Mark/Steve, cricketers)
Wills (Helen, tennis player)
Woods (Tiger, golfer)

6
Agassi (André, tennis player)
Alliss (Peter, golfer)
Bailey (Trevor, cricketer)
Barker (Sue, tennis player)
Becker (Boris, tennis player)
Bedser (Alec/Eric, cricketers)
Benaud (Richie, cricketer)
Border (Allan, cricketer)
Botham (Ian, cricketer)
Broome (David, showjumper)
Brough (Louise, tennis player)
Bugner (Joe, boxer)
Button (Jensen, racing driver)
Carson (Willy, jockey)
Cawley (Evonne, tennis player)
Cotton (Henry, golfer)
Cruyff (Johann, footballer)
Dexter (Ted, cricketer)
Edberg (Stefan, tennis player)
Edrich (Bill/John, cricketers)
Fangio (Juan, racing driver)
Fraser (Dawn, swimmer)
Ginola (David, footballer)
Hadlee (Richard, cricketer)
Haynes (Johnny, footballer)
Hendry (Stephen, snooker player)
Henman (Tim, tennis player)
Hingis (Martina, tennis player)
Hoddle (Glen, footballer)
Holmes (Kelly, runner)
Hutton (Len, cricketer)
Kanhai (Rohan, cricketer)
Karpov (Anatoly, chess player)
Keegan (Kevin, footballer)
Korbut (Olga, gymnast)
Langer (Bernhard, golfer)
Lillee (Dennis, cricketer)
Miller (Keith, cricketer)
Morgan (Cliff, rugby player)
Murray (Andrew, tennis player)
Norman (Greg, golfer)
Palmer (Arnold, golfer)
Player (Gary, golfer)
Ramsey (Alf, footballer)
Rhodes (Wilfred, cricketer)
Robson (Bobby/Brian, footballer)
Rooney (Wayne, footballer)
Smythe (Pat, showjumper)
Sobers (Gary, cricketer)
Statham (Brian, cricketer)
Taylor (Roger, tennis player)
Titmus (Fred, cricketer)
Tunney (Gene, boxer)
Weekes (Everton, cricketer)
Wenger (Arsène, footballer)
Willis (Bob, cricketer)
Wright (Billy, footballer)
Zidane (Zinadine, footballer)

7
Ambrose (Curtley, cricketer)
Beckham (David, footballer)
Bennett (Phil, rugby player)
Boycott (Geoffrey, cricketer)
Brabham (Jack, racing driver)
Bradman (Donald, cricketer)
Bristow (Eric, darts player)
Cantona (Eric, footballer)
Carling (Will, rugby player)
Carnera (Primo, boxer)
Compton (Denis, cricketer)
Connors (Jimmy, tennis player)
Cowdrey (Colin, cricketer)
Dempsey (Jack, boxer)
Elliott (Herb, runner)
Federer (Roger, tennis player)
Fischer (Bobby, chess player)
Frazier (Joe, boxer)
Goodhew (Duncan, swimmer)
Greaves (Jimmy, footballer)
Gunnell (Sally, runner)
Hammond (Wally, cricketer)
Higgins (Alex 'Hurricane', snooker player)
Hussain (Nasser, cricketer)
Jacklin (Tony, golfer)
Jardine (Douglas, cricketer)
Johnson (Ben, runner)

Larwood (Harold, cricketer)
Lenglen (Suzanne, tennis player)
Lineker (Gary, footballer)
Mansell (Nigel, racing driver)
McBride (Willie John, rugby player)
McCoist (Ally, footballer)
McEnroe (John, tennis player)
Piggott (Lester, jockey)
Rivaldo (footballer)
Ronaldo (footballer)
Sampras (Pete, tennis player)
Scholes (Paul, footballer)
Shearer (Alan, footballer)
Shilton (Peter, footballer)
Spassky (Boris, chess player)
Stewart (Alec cricketer)
Stewart (Jackie, racing driver)
Surtees (John, racing driver and motorcyclist)
Thomson (Jeff, cricketer)
Trevino (Lee, golfer)
Trueman (Fred, cricketer)
Woosnam (Ian, golfer)
Winkler (Hans, showjumper)
Worrell (Frank, cricketer)
Zatopek (Emil, runner)

8
Agostini (Giacomo, racing motocyclist)
Atherton (Michael, cricketer)
Baiocchi (Hugh, golfer)
Bergkamp (Denis, footballer)
Brooking (Trevor, footballer)
Chappell (Greg/Ian, cricketers)

Charlton (Bobby/Jack, footballers)
Christie (Linford, runner)
Comaneci (Nadia, gymnast)
Dalglish (Kenny, footballer)
Docherty (Tommy, footballer)
Ferguson (Alex, footballer)
Gavascar (Sunil, cricketer)
Graveney (Tom, cricketer)
Hailwood (Mike, racing motorcyclist)
Hakkinen (Tino, racing driver)
Hawthorn (Mike, racing driver)
Klinsman (Jurgen, footballer)
Korchnoi (Victor, chess player)
Lindwall (Ray, cricketer)
Maradona (Diego, footballer)
Marciano (Rocky, boxer)
Marshall (Clive, cricketer)
Matthews (Stanley, footballer)
Newcombe (John, tennis player)
Nicklaus (Jack, golfer)
Olazabal (José, golfer)
Phillips (Zara, showjumper)
Redgrave (Steve, rower)
Richards (Gordon, jockey)
Richards (Viv, cricketer)
Robinson (Sugar Ray, boxer)
Rosewall (Ken, tennis player)
Rusedski (Greg, tennis player)
Sullivan (John, boxer)
Thompson (Daley, athlete)

Williams (J.P.R., rugby player)
Williams (Serena/Venus, tennis players)

9
Bannister (Roger, runner)
Beardsley (Peter, footballer)
Bonington (Chris, mountaineer)
Coulthard (David, racing driver)
Davenport (Lindsay, tennis player)
D'Oliviera (Basil, cricketer)
Gascoigne (Paul, footballer)
Goolagong (Evonne, tennis player)
Llewellyn (Harry, showjumper)
Lofthouse (Nat, footballer)
Radcliffe (Paula, runner)
Schmeling (Max, boxer)
Sutcliffe (Herbert, cricketer)
Underwood (Derek, cricketer
Whitbread (Fatima, athlete)
Wilkinson (Johnny, rugby player)

10
Fittipaldi (Emerson, racing driver)
Sheringham (Teddy, footballer)
Schumacher (Michael, racing driver)
Villeneuve (Jacques, racing driver)

11
Ballesteros (Seve, golfer)

Beckenbauer (Franz, footballer)
Constantine (Learie, cricketer)
Illingworth (Ray, cricketer)
Lonsborough (Anita, swimmer)
Navratilova (Martina, tennis player)
Weissmuller (Johnny, swimmer)

TERMS USED IN SPORT

3
ace
bat
bet
bob
bow
box
bye
cue
cup
dan
die
gym
jog
lob
mat
net
oar
out
par
peg
put
rod
run
set
ski
tag
tee
tie
try
win
won

4
bait
ball
bias
bite
boat
club
dive
draw
épee
foil
fore
foul
gala
game
heat
hunt
jack
judo
love
luge
meet
miss
odds
pace
pike
play
pool
punt
race
ride
ring
rink
shot
side
skip
spar
swim
team
toss
tote
trap
trot
tuck
turf
volt
walk
whip

wide
xyst
yoga

5
arena
bench
bogey
boule
boxer
caddy
champ
chase
cheat
coach
derby
deuce
diver
drawn
drive
dummy
extra
field
fluke
hobby
judge
links
loser
lucky
lunge
match
miler
mount
pacer
piste
pitch
point
prize
quits
racer
reins
relay
rider
rifle
rodeo
score
scrum
skate

skier
slice
slide
slosh
spoon
spurt
stalk
stand
start
stunt
swing
throw
touch
track
train
trial
trump
vault
wager
yacht

6

archer
bowman
caddie
course
defeat
driver
falcon
fencer
finish
gillie
hammer
hunter
hurdle
jockey
jumper
kicker
lariat
league
loader
manege
marker
mashie
outing
outrun
pacing
paddle

pistol
player
punter
putter
racing
racket
record
rubber
rugger
runner
scorer
second
skater
slalom
stroke
thrash
thrust
tierce
travel
trophy
umpire
unfair
venery
victor
winner

7

acrobat
allonge
amateur
archery
athlete
average
bathing
batsman
batting
beagles
benefit
bicycle
chicane
contest
cyclist
decider
doubles
dribble
driving
forward
fouling

gymnast
harrier
hurdler
niblick
oarsman
oarsmen
outdoor
outride
pitcher
playing
putting
rambler
referee
regatta
scoring
scratch
sculler
singles
stadium
starter
tourney
trained
trainer
trapeze
trounce
vaulter
wargame
weights
winning

8

champion
cheating
division
exercise
gymkhana
handicap
movement
olympiad
olympics
outsider
pugilism
pugilist
sparring
sporting
sprinter
teamwork
toboggan

training
tricycle
umpiring
vaulting
walkover

9

acrobatic
advantage
bullfight
challenge
cockfight
contender
cricketer
dumbbells
favourite
gymnasium
gymnastic
horserace
overmatch
pacemaker
programme
racehorse
scorching
scorecard
sportsman
stopwatch
timekeeper
untrained
yachtsman

10

acrobatics
battledore
challenger
competitor
feathering
grandstand
racecourse
raceground
recreation
scoreboard
somersault
sweepstake
tournament
victorious

11

atheleticism
competition
competitive
heavyweight
lightweight
prizewinner
shuttlecock
springboard
totalisator
toxophilite

12

bantamweight
championship
horsemanship
professional

2+ words

boat race
cup tie
cup winner
dead heat
decoy duck
dirt track
diving board
drawn game
fox chase
fox hunt
full back
go-kart
golf bag
golf ball
golf club
keep fit
last lap
love all
love game
mixed doubles
paper chase
play-off
point-to-point
prize ring
relay race
ski jump
top spin
toss-up
water jump
whipper-in
work-out

TELEVISION AND RADIO

Terms connected with TV and radio
TV and radio personalities
TV and radio shows

TERMS CONNECTED WITH TV AND RADIO

2
AF
AM
CB
FM
LW
MW
OB
SW

3
air
BBC
box
DAB
DVD
ITV
mic
PAL
set
Sky
UHF
VCR
VHF

4
band
boom
dish
Emmy
host
live
pips
quiz
shot
show
soap

tape
tube
view
zoom

5
cable
NICAM®
panel
telly
tuner
video

6
aerial
anchor
Ceefax®
colour
screen
remote
repeat
replay
serial
series
signal
sitcom
static
stereo
studio
tuning
viewer
zapper

7
booster
carrier
channel
compere
digital
hostess
speaker
station
trailer
trannie
viewing
Walkman®

8
contrast
epilogue
Freeview
newscast
receiver
sideband
subtitle
Teletext
transmit
waveband
wireless

9
amplifier
anchorman
announcer
bandwidth
broadcast
cameraman
interlude
presenter
programme
satellite

10
brightness
commentary
commentate
Eurovision
miniseries
monochrome
newscaster
newreader
telecamera
transistor
weatherman

11
anchorwoman
broadcaster
commentator
documentary
loudspeaker
transmitter
weathergirl

12
interference
transmission

2+ words
black-and-white
cathode-ray tube
chat show
classic serial
commentary box
crystal set
flat screen
ghetto-blaster
Home Service
Light Programme
off the air
on the air
outside broadcast
phone-in
prime time
reality TV/television
red button
signature tune
small screen
talk show
time signal
walkie-talkie
wide screen

TV AND RADIO
PERSONALITIES

3
Fry (Stephen)
Ray (Ted)

4
Adie (Kate)
Bell (Martin)
Cook (Peter/Roger)
Ford (Anna)
Hall (Henry)
Hill (Benny)
Hope (Bob)
Lowe (Arthur)
Mayo (Simon)
Muir (Frank)
Peel (John)

Ross (Jonathan)
Snow (John)
Took (Barry)
Wise (Ernie)

5
Allen (Dave)
Baker (Richard)
Benny (Jack)
Burns (George)
Bruce (Fiona)
Cooke (Alistair)
Elton (Ben)
Evans (Chris)
Frost (David)
Goody (Jade)
Grade (Lew/Michael)
Horne (Kenneth)
James (Clive/Sid)
Moore (Dudley)
Reith (Lord [John])
Palin (Michael)
Smith (Delia)
Sykes (Eric)
Wogan (Terry)
Worth (Harry)

6
Arlott (John)
Barker (Ronnie)
Cleese (John)
Cotton (Billy)
Hansen (Alan)
Morley (Robert)
Motson (John)
Norden (Dennis)
Norton (Graham)
Paxman (Jeremy)
Savile (Jimmy)
Weldon (Huw)

7
Andrews (Eamonn)
Bentine (Michael)
Dimbleby
(David/Jonathan/Richard)
Edwards (Jimmy)
Enfield (Harry)

Feldman (Marty)
Freeman (Alan)
Hancock (Tony)
Handley (Tommy)
Harding (Gilbert)
Jacques (Hattie)
Johnson (Brian)
Parsons (Nicholas)
Rantzen (Esther)
Rushton (Willie)
Secombe (Harry)
Sellers (Peter)
Sherrin (Ned)

8
Brambell (Wilfred)
Bygraves (Max)
Clarkson (Jeremy)
Connolly (Billy)
Craddock (Fanny)
Forsythe (Bruce)
Grenfell (Joyce)
Humphrys (John)
Milligan (Spike)
Naughtie (James)
Williams (Kenneth)

9
Blackburn (Tony)
Gascoigne (Bamber)
Lyttleton (Humphry)
MacDonald (Trevor)
MacGregor (Sue)
Monkhouse (Bob)
Morecambe (Eric)
Parkinson (Michael)

10
Titchmarsh (Alan)
Whitehouse (Paul)

12
Attenborough (David)
Wolstenholme (Kenneth)

TV AND RADIO SHOWS

4
Bill (The)
ITMA
Lost

5
Bread
Frost
Morse
Today

6
Dallas

7
Archers (The)
Bagpuss
Wombles (The)

8
Bergerac
Kavanagh

9
Brookside
Emmerdale
Heartbeat
Newsnight

10
Neighbours

11
Butterflies

2+ words
Beyond Our Ken
Big Brother
Coronation Street
East Enders

Gardener's World
Goon Show (The)
Hancock's Half Hour
Just a Minute
Listen with Mother
Only Fools and Horses
Round the Horne
Steptoe and Son
Take It From Here
The Good Life
Woman's Hour
Workers' Playtime
Yes Minister

THEATRE

Plays
Playwrights
Famous theatres
Theatrical terms
See also SHAKESPEARE

PLAYS

3
Fen (Chrchill)

4
Loot (Orton)
Ross (Rattigan)

5
Faust (Goethe)
Medea (Euripides)
Roots (Wesker)

6
Egmont (Goethe)
Ghosts (Ibsen)
Hamlet (Shakespeare)
Phèdre (Racine)
Plenty (Hare)
Sleuth (Anthony Shaffer)
Strife (Galsworthy)
Thark (Travers)

7
Amadeus (Peter Shaffer)
Arcadia (Stoppard)
Athalie (Racine)
Candida (Shaw)
Electra (Sophocles)
Galileo (Brecht)
Jumpers (Stoppard)
Macbeth (Shakespeare)
Othello (Shakespeare)
Volpone (Jonson)

8
Antigone (Sophocles)
Hysteria (Johnson)
Pericles (Shakespeare)

Tartuffe (Molière)

9
Cavalcade (Coward)
Cymbeline (Shakespeare)
Pygmalion (Shaw)

10
Andromaque (Racine)
Coriolanus (Shakespeare)

2+ words
Dr Faustus (Marlow)
Hay Fever (Coward)
Journey's End (Sherriff)
King John (Shakespeare)
King Lear (Shakespeare)
Look Back in Anger
(Osborne)
Maria Stuart (Schiller)
Noises Off (Frayn)
Peter Pan (Barrie)
Private Lives (Coward)
Saint Joan (Shaw)
The Alchemist (Jonson)
The Birds (Aristophanes)
The Birthday Party
(Pinter)
The Cherry Orchard
(Chekhov)
The Devils (Whiting)
The Crucible (Miller)
The Frogs (Aristophanes)
The Hostage (Behan)
The Lark (Anouilh)
The Maids (Genet)
The Mousetrap (Christie)
The Rivals (Sheridan)
The Room (Pinter)
The Seagull (Chekhov)
The Way of the World
(Congreve)
Top Girls (Churchill)

PLAYWRIGHTS

2
Fo (Dario, Italian)

3
Fry (Christopher, UK)
Gay (John, UK)
Kyd (Thomas, UK)

4
Behn (Aphra, English)
Bolt (Robert, UK)
Bond (Edward, UK)
Ford (John, English)
Gems (Pam, UK)
Gray (Simon, UK)
Hall (Willis, UK)
Hare (David, UK)
Hart (Moss, US)
Hugo (Victor, French)
Rowe (Nicholas, UK)
Shaw (George Bernard,
Irish)
Vega (Lope de, Spanish)

5
Albee (Edward, US)
Arden (John, UK)
Behan (Brendan, Irish)
Eliot (T.S., UK)
Frayn (Michael, UK)
Friel (Brian, Irish)
Genet (Jean, French)
Gogol (Nikolai, Russian)
Havel (Vaclav, Czech)
Ibsen (Henrik,
Norwegian)
Jarry (Alfred, French)
Jones (LeRoi, US)
Lorca (Garcia, Spanish)
Mamet (David, US)
Odets (Clifford, US)
Orton (Joe, UK)
Synge (John, Irish)
Wilde (Oscar, Irish)

6
Barrie (JM, UK)
Brecht (Berthold,
German)
Coward (Noel, UK)
Dryden (John, English)

Frisch (Max, Swiss)
Fugard (Athol, South African)
Goethe (J.W. von, Ger)
Jonson (Ben, English)
Kleist (Heinrich von, German)
Miller (Arthur, US)
Musset (Alfred de, French)
O'Casey (Sean, Irish)
O'Neill (Eugene, US)
Pinero (Arthur Wing, UK)
Pinter (Harold, UK)
Racine (Jean, French)
Sardou (Victorien, French)
Sartre (J-P, French)
Seneca (Roman)
Thomas (Brandon, UK)
Wesker (Arnold, UK)
Wilder (Thornton, US)

7
Anouilh (Jean, French)
Beckett (Samuel, Irish)
Bennett (Alan, UK)
Büchner (Georg, German)
Chekhov (Anton, Russian)
Feydeau (Georges, French)
Gilbert (W.S., UK)
Goldoni (Carlo, Italian)
Hampton (Christopher, UK)
Hellman (Lillian, US)
Ionesco (Eugene, French)
Johnson (Terry, UK)
Kaufman (George S., US)
Labiche (Eugène, French)
Lessing (Gottfried, German)
Marlowe (Christopher, English)
Molière (Jean-Baptiste Poquelin, French)

Osborne (John, UK)
Plautus (Roman)
Rostand (Edmond, French)
Scarron (Paul, French)
Shaffer (Peter/Anthony, UK)
Shepard (Sam, US)
Terence (Roman)
Travers (Ben, UK)
Webster (John, English)
Whiting (John, UK)

8
Beaumont (Francis, English)
Calderon (Pedro, Spanish)
Christie (Agatha, UK)
Claudel (Paul, French)
Cocteau (Jean, French)
Congreve (William, Irish)
Etherege (George, English)
Farquhar (George, Irish)
Marivaux (Pierre French)
Menander (Greek)
Mortimer (John, UK)
Rattigan (Terence, UK)
Schiller (Friedrich, German)
Sheridan (Richard Brinsley, Irish)
Sherriff (R.C., UK)
Stoppard (Tom, UK)
Vanbrugh (John, English)
Williams (Tennessee, US)

9
Aeschylus (Greek)
Ayckbourn (Alan, UK)
Bleasdale (Alan, UK)
Corneille (Pierre, French)
Churchill (Caryl, UK)
Euripides (Greek)
Giraudoux (Jean, French
Goldsmith (Oliver, Irish)
Hauptmann (Gerhard,

German)
Middleton (Thomas, English)
Priestley (J.B., UK)
Sophocles (Greek)
Wycherley (William, English)

10
Dürrenmatt (Friedrich, Swiss)
Galsworthy (John, UK)
Pirandello (Luigi, Italian)
Schnitzler (Arthur, Austrian)
Strindberg (August, Swedish)
Waterhouse (Keith UK)

11
Grillparzer (Franz, Austrian)
Shakespeare (William, English)

12
Aristophanes (Greek)
Beaumarchais (Pierre, French)

FAMOUS THEATRES

3
Pit (Barbican)

4
Swan (Stratford)

5
Abbey (Dublin)
Globe
Lyric
Savoy

6
Albery
Apollo
Comedy

Lyceum
Queen's
Strand

7
Adelphi
Aldwych
Mermaid
Olivier
Phoenix
Prince's
Variety

8
Barbican
Coliseum
Dominion
National (Theatre)
Victoria
Windmill
Wyndham's

9
Cottesloe
Criterion
Haymarket
Lyttleton
Palladium
Whitehall

10
Hippodrome
Piccadilly

11
Ambassadors
Shaftesbury

2+ words
La Scala (Milan)
Covent Garden
Drury Lane
Old Vic
Royal Court
Royal Shakespeare
Sadler's Wells
Young Vic
Yvonne Arnaud

THEATRICAL TERMS

2
No
on

3
act
ASM
bow
box
cue
fan
gag
ham
hit
mug
Noh
off
pit
rep
RSC
run
set
tag
wig

4
bill
book
busk
cast
clap
crew
dark
diva
duet
exit
flat
flop
foil
gala
gods
hero
idol
joke
lead
line

mask
mike
mime
mute
part
plot
prop
rave
role
show
skit
solo
spot
star
team
turn
wing

5
actor
agent
angel
apron
aside
clown
comic
debut
decor
drama
enact
farce
flies
foyer
heavy
hokum
house
lines
mimer
mimic
opera
panto
piece
props
revue
scene
stage
stall
usher

wings

6
acting
action
appear
backer
ballet
barker
boards
buskin
chorus
circle
circus
claque
comedy
critic
dancer
direct
effect
encore
finale
flyman
fringe
Kabuki
lights
masque
method
motley
mummer
nautch
number
parody
patron
patter
player
podium
prompt
puppet
recite
repeat
satire
script
season
sketch
speech
stalls
stooge

talent
ticket
tights
timing
tinsel
troupe
writer

7
acrobat
actress
amateur
balcony
benefit
booking
buffoon
cabaret
callboy
cartoon
casting
catcall
catwalk
charade
chorine
circuit
commere
company
compere
concert
console
costume
curtain
dancing
deadpan
farceur
gallery
heroine
ingenue
juggler
leotard
matinee
mimicry
mummery
musical
mystery
onstage
overact
pageant

perform
Pierrot
players
playing
playlet
portray
prelude
present
preview
produce
recital
reciter
reprise
resting
revival
rostrum
scenery
showbiz
showman
sponsor
stadium
stagery
staging
stardom
starlet
support
tableau
theatre
tragedy
trilogy
trouper
tumbler
upstage
variety
vehicle

8
applause
artistry
audience
audition
backdrop
Broadway
burletta
carnival
clapping
clowning
coliseum

comedian
conjurer
costumer
coulisse
dialogue
director
disguise
dramatic
duologue
entr'acte
entrance
epilogue
farceuse
fauteuil
festival
interval
juggling
libretto
magician
morality
offstage
operatic
operetta
overture
parterre
pastoral
platform
playbill
playgoer
premiere
producer
prologue
prompter
protasis
rehearse
scenario
showbill
stagebox
straight
stripper
thespian
tragical
travesty
typecast
wardrobe
wigmaker

9
backcloth
backstage
barnstorm
burlesque
character
cloakroom
Columbine
conjuring
costumier
coulisses
criticism
cyclorama
discovery
downstage
dramatics
dramatist
dramatize (dramatise)
entertain
floorshow
Harlequin
impromptu
interlude
limelight
melodrama
monodrama
monologue
orchestra
pantaloon
pantomime
performer
Pierrette
playhouse
portrayal
programme
publicity
punchline
quartette
rehearsal
repertory
represent
slapstick
soliloquy
soubrette
spectacle
spectator
spotlight
stagehand

tragedian
usherette
wisecrack

10
afterpiece
appearance
auditorium
comedienne
comedietta
continuity
denouement
dramaturge
dramaturgy
fantoccini
footlights
hippodrome
histrionic
impresario
intermezzo
legitimate
librettist
marionette
masquerade
microphone
performing
playwright
production
properties
proscenium
Pulcinella
recitation
repertoire
repetiteur
stagecraft
striptease
substitute
tearjerker
theatrical
understudy
vaudeville

11
accompanist
balletomane
barnstormer
electrician
entertainer

equilibrist
funambulist
greasepaint
histrionics
illusionist
impersonate
legerdemain
pantomimist
performance
protagonist
psychodrama
Punchinello
showmanship
spectacular
terpsichore
thaumaturgy
theatregoer
theatricals
tragedienne
tragicomedy
unrehearsed
ventriloquy

12
amphitheatre
dramaturgist
extravaganza
harlequinade
impersonator
introduction
melodramatic
scriptwriter

2+ words
actor-manager
ad lib
all-star cast
art director
big top
bit part
bit player
black comedy
box office
chorus boy
chorus girl
comic opera
concert hall
crowd scene

disc jockey
double act
double bill
drama critic
drama group
drama school
dress circle
dressing room
drop scene
dumb show
exeunt omnes
exotic dancer
fan club
fire curtain
first night
first-nighter
full house
funny man
gala night
get the bird
Grand Guignol
Greek chorus
guest star
ham actor
high comedy
in the round
in the wings
junior lead
juvenile lead
kitchen-sink
leading lady
leading man
light comedy
long run
love scene
low comedy
make-up
make-up artist
male lead
method acting
method actor
minor role
minstrel show
miracle play
modern ballet
morality play
music drama
music hall

name in lights
new wave
on cue
on stage
on tour
one act play
opera bouffe ·
opera glasses
opera singer
orchestra pit
Passion play
pit-stalls
prima donna
principal boy
problem play
prompt-book
prompt-box
Punch and Judy
puppet show
rave notice
rave review
re-enact
ring down
ring up
scene change
scene painter
scene shifter
scene stealer
set designer
set piece
set the scene
show business
show-stopper
side show
smash hit
song and dance
sound effect(s)
sound effects
spear carrier
stage design
stage door
stage effect
stage fright
stage left
stage manager
stage play
stage right
stage whisper

stage-struck
stand-in
star billing
star player
star quality
star turn
starring role
star-studded

steal the show
stock company
straight part
take a part
talent scout
theatre land
top of the bill
upper circle

variety act
variety show
walk-on
walk-on part
warm-up
West End
word-perfect

TOOLS

A tool
Types of tool

A TOOL

5
gizmo
means

6
device
gadget

7
utensil

9
apparatus
implement

10
instrument

11
contrivance

TYPES OF TOOL

3
awl
axe
bit
bob
die
hod
hoe
jig
key
loy
nut
peg
pen
pin
ram
saw
set

tap

4
adze
bill
bolt
brad
burr
clip
comb
file
fork
gaff
hook
hose
iron
jack
last
lead
lens
mace
maul
nail
pole
pick
plug
prod
rake
rasp
rose
rule
shim
size
slot
spud
stud
tack
trap
vice

5
anvil
auger
besom
bevel
blade
borer
brace

brand
brush
burin
chuck
clamp
clasp
cleat
clout
corer
croze
cupel
dolly
dowel
drill
flail
float
gavel
gouge
hoist
jemmy
knife
level
lever
parer
plane
plumb
probe
prong
punch
razor
rivet
ruler
scale
scoop
screw
shave
sieve
snips
spade
spike
spile
spoon
stamp
steel
strop
style
tongs
wedge

wrest

6
barrow
beetle
bodkin
broach
chaser
chisel
cotter
dibber
dibble
filter
flange
folder
fraise
funnel
gimlet
grater
graver
hackle
hammer
jigger
jigsaw
ladder
lancet
mallet
marker
mortar
needle
nozzle
opener
paddle
pallet
pencil
pestle
pitsaw
pliers
plough
pulley
rabbet
rammer
reamer
riddle
ripsaw
roller
rubber
sander

screen
scribe
scythe
shears
shovel
sickle
sifter
skewer
sledge
slicer
spacer
square
staple
stylus
tamper
tracer
trowel
washer
wimble
wrench

7
ammeter
backsaw
balance
bandsaw
bearing
bellows
bolster
bradawl
buzzsaw
caltrop
capstan
chopper
cleaver
clipper
compass
coulter
counter
crampon
crowbar
cuvette
divider
forceps
fretsaw
grapnel
grapple
hacksaw

handsaw
hatchet
hobnail
jointer
mandrel
mattock
nippers
pickaxe
pincers
plummet
plunger
poleaxe
scalpel
scraper
scriber
shackle
spanner
sprayer
stapler
thimble
trestle
trimmer
vernier
whipsaw
whittle

8
billhook
blowlamp
blowpipe
boathook
bootjack
bootlast
chainsaw
corundum
handmill
oilstone
penknife
picklock
polisher
puncheon
sawhorse
scissors
strickle
stripper
tweezers
windlass

9
altimeter
barometer
baseplate
callipers
corkscrew
compasses
handspike
megaphone
metronome
periscope
pitchfork
plumbline
retractor
sandpaper
secateurs
sharpener
steelyard
whetstone

10
grindstone
guillotine

micrometer
paintbrush
pantograph
protractor
spokeshave
stepladder
tenterhook
theodolite
thermostat
turnbuckle

11
carborundum
countersink
ploughshare
screwdriver
thermometer

2+ words
bow-saw
centre-bit
feeler-gauge
foot-pump

glass-cutter
grease-gun
hand-pump
jack-knife
jack-plane
lazy-tongs
monkey wrench
paint-roller
paper-knife
pinking-iron
pipe wrench
pruning-hook
set-square
sheath-knife
slide rule
spirit level
tenon-saw
tin-opener
tommy-bar
try square
T-square

TOWNS

A city/a town
Ancient cities
Towns and cities of the world
See also **ENGLAND,**
SCOTLAND, WALES

A CITY/ A TOWN

2
EC
LA
NY

4
burg

5
burgh

7
borough

9
community

10
metropolis
settlement

11
conurbation

12
municipality

ANCIENT CITIES

2
Ur (Bible)

4
Rome
Troy (Greek myth)

5
Petra (Jordan)

6
Athens (Greece)
Sparta (Greece)
Thebes (Greece)

7
Babylon
Ephesus
Knossos (Crete)
Mycenae (Greece)

8
Carthage

TOWNS AND CITIES OF
THE WORLD

3
Aix (France)
Ayr (UK)
Ely (UK)
Fez (Morocco)
Pau (France)
Rio (Brazil)
Rye (UK)

4
Aden (Yemen)
Agra (India)
Albi (France)
Baku (Azerbaijan)
Bari (Italy)
Bath (UK)
Bern (Switzerland)
Bray (Ireland/UK)
Brno (Czech Rep.)
Bude (UK)
Bury (UK)
Caen (France)
Cali (Colombia)
Clun (UK)
Cobh (Ireland)
Cork (Ireland)
Deal (UK)
Diss (UK)
Eton (UK)
Gary (USA)
Gaza (Israel)

Giza (Egypt)
Graz (Austria)
Hove (UK)
Hull (UK)
Hyde (UK)
Ince (UK)
Kiev (Ukraine)
Kobi (Japan)
Laon (France)
Lima (Peru)
Linz (Austria)
Lodz (Poland)
Looe (UK)
Lvov (Ukraine)
Lyon (France)
Metz (France)
Nice (France)
Oban (UK)
Omsk (Russia)
Oran (Algeria)
Oslo (Norway)
Perm (Russia)
Pisa (Italy)
Reno (USA)
Riga (Latvia)
Rome (Italy)
Ross (UK)
Ryde (UK)
Troy (USA)
Tver (Russia)
Tyre (Lebanon)
Vigo (Spain)
Waco (USA)
Ware (UK)
Wick (UK)
Xian (China)
York (UK)

5
Abuja (Nigeria)
Adana (Turkey)
Ajmer (India)
Alloa (UK)
Alton (UK)
Alwar (India)
Arhus (Denmark)
Arles (France)
Arras (France)

Aswan (Egypt)
Bacup (UK)
Banff (UK)
Basel (Switzerland)
Basle (Switzerland)
Basra (Iraq)
Belem (Brazil)
Breda (Netherlands)
Brest (Belarus/France)
Cadiz (Spain)
Cairo (Egypt)
Chard (UK)
Cowes (UK)
Crewe (UK)
Cuzco (Peru)
Dakar (Senegal)
Delhi (India)
Derby (UK)
Derry (N. Ireland)
Dhaka (Bangladesh)
Dijon (France)
Douai (France)
Dover (UK)
Elgin (UK)
Epsom (UK)
Essen (Germany)
Evian (France)
Frome (UK)
Genoa (Italy)
Ghent (Belgium)
Goole (UK)
Hague, The (Netherlands)
Haifa (Israel)
Halle (Germany)
Huambo (Angola)
Hythe (UK)
Izmir (Turkey)
Kandy (Sri Lanka)
Kazan (Russia)
Kyoto (Japan)
Lagos (Nigeria)
Larne (N. Ireland)
Leeds (UK)
Leigh (UK)
Lewes (UK)
Liège (Belgium)
Lille (France)
Lobito (Angola)

Louth (UK)
Luanda (Angola)
Luton (UK)
Luxor (Egypt)
Lyons (France)
Mainz (Germany)
Malmo (Sweden)
March (UK)
Mecca (Saudi Arabia)
Medan (Indonesia)
Miami (USA)
Milan (Italy)
Minsk (Belarus)
Mosul (Iraq)
Nancy (France)
Newry (N. Ireland)
Nimes (France)
Omagh (N. Ireland)
Omaha (USA)
Osaka (Japan)
Ostia (Italy)
Otley (UK)
Padua (Italy)
Palma (Majorca)
Paris (France)
Parma (Italy)
Patna (India)
Perth (Australia, Scotland)
Poole (UK)
Poona (India)
Posen (Poland)
Pskov (Russia)
Quito (Ecuador)
Rabat (Morocco)
Reims (France)
Rieti (Italy)
Ripon (UK)
Rouen (France)
Rugby (UK)
Salem (USA)
Selby (UK)
Selma (USA)
Seoul (S Korea)
Sidon (Lebanon)
Siena (Italy)
Simla (India)
Sligo (Ireland)
Sofia (Bulgaria)

Split (Croatia)
Stoke (UK)
Surat (India)
Tenby (UK)
Thame (UK)
Tokyo (Japan)
Tours (France)
Trent (Italy)
Trier (Germany)
Tring (UK)
Truro (UK)
Tulsa (USA)
Turin (Italy)
Vence (France)
Vichy (France)
Wells (UK)
Wigan (UK)
Worms (Germany)
Wutan (China)
Yalta (Ukraine)
Ypres (Belgium)

6

Aachen (Germany)
Abadan Iran)
Albany (USA)
Aleppo (Syria)
Amalfi (Italy)
Amiens (France)
Ankara (Turkey)
Anshan (China)
Antrim (N. Ireland)
Arklow (Ireland)
Arnhem (Netherlands)
Ashton (UK)
Asmara (Eritrea)
Athens (Greece)
Austin (USA)
Bamako (Mali)
Bangor (UK, USA)
Banjul (Gambia)
Bantry (Ireland)
Barrow (UK)
Batley (UK)
Bayeux (France)
Beirut (Lebanon)
Bergen (Norway)
Berlin (Germany)

Bhopal (India)
Bilbao (Spain)
Biloxi (USA)
Bissau (Guinea-Bissau)
Bochum (Germany)
Bodmin (UK)
Bognor (UK)
Bogota (Colombia)
Bolton (UK)
Bombay (India)
Bootle (UK)
Boston (USA)
Bremen (Germany)
Bruges (Belgium)
Buxton (UK)
Cairns (Australia)
Calais (France)
Cannes (France)
Canton (China)
Carlow (Ireland)
Cassel (Germany)
Cromer (UK)
Dallas (USA)
Danzig (Poland)
Darwin (Australia)
Dayton (USA)
Denver (USA)
Dieppe (France)
Dodoma (Tanzania)
Dublin (Ireland)
Dudley (UK)
Dundee (UK)
Durban (South Africa)
Durham (UK)
Erfurt (Germany)
Exeter (UK)
Fresno (USA)
Fushun (China)
Galway (Ireland)
Gdansk (Poland)
Geneva (Switzerland)
Granada (Spain)
Hamlin (Germany)
Harare (Zimbabwe)
Harlow (UK)
Havana (Cuba)
Havant (UK)
Henley (UK)

Hexham (UK)
Hobart (Australia)
Howrah (India)
Ilkley (UK)
Indore (India)
Irvine (USA)
Jaipur (India)
Jarrow (UK)
Jeddah (Saudi Arabia)
Jhansi (India)
Juarez (Mexico)
Kanpur (India)
Kassel (Germany)
Kendal (UK)
Kirkuk (Iraq)
Kohima (India)
Krakow (Poland)
Lahore (Pakistan)
Lanark (UK)
Leiden (Netherlands)
Leyden (Netherlands)
Lisbon (Portugal)
London (UK)
Luanda (Angola)
Lubeck (Germany)
Lublin (Poland)
Ludlow (UK)
Lusaka (Zambia)
Mackay (Australia)
Madras (India)
Madrid (Spain)
Malabo (Equatorial
Guinea)
Malaga (Spain)
Manaus (Brazil)
Maputo (Mozambique)
Maseru (Lesotho)
Medina (Saudi Arabia)
Meerut (India)
Mobile (USA)
Moscow (Russia)
Mukden (China)
Multan (Pakistan)
Mumbai (India)
Munich (Germany)
Mysore (India)
Nagoya (Japan)
Nagpur (India)

Nantes (France)
Naples (Italy)
Nassau (USA)
Newark (USA)
Newark (UK)
Niamey (Niger)
Oakham (UK)
Odense (Denmark)
Odessa (Ukraine)
Oldham (UK)
Oporto (Portugal)
Orange (France)
Ostend (Belgium)
Ottawa (Canada)
Oxford (UK)
Peking (China)
Peoria (USA)
Prague (Czech Rep.)
Puebla (Mexico)
Quebec (Canada)
Quetta (Pakistan)
Rampur (India)
Recife (Brazil)
Redcar (UK)
Regina (Canada)
Rheims (France)
Riyadh (Saudi Arabia)
Romsey (UK)
Samara (Russia)
Settle (UK)
Seville (Spain)
Siraz (Iran)
Skopje (Macedonia)
Smyrna (Turkey)
Soweto (South Africa)
Stroud (UK)
Sydney (Australia)
Tabriz (Iran)
Taipei (Taiwan)
Tehran (Iran)
Thebes (Ancient Greece)
Thirsk (UK)
Tobruk (Libya)
Toledo (Spain)
Topeka (USA)
Totnes (UK)
Toulon (France)
Treves (Germany)

Tsinan (China)
Tucson (USA)
Varna (Bulgaria)
Venice (Italy)
Verdun (France)
Verona (Italy)
Vienna (Austria)
Warsaw (Poland)
Whitby (UK)
Widnes (UK)
Yeovil (UK)
Zagreb (Croatia)
Zurich (Switzerland)

7

Abidjan (Ivory Coast)
Airdrie (UK)
Ajaccio (France)
Alencon (France)
Algiers (Algeria)
Alnwick (UK)
Anaheim (USA)
Andover (UK)
Antwerp (Belgium)
Appleby (UK)
Arundel (UK)
Ashford (UK)
Athlone (Ireland)
Atlanta (USA)
Auxerre (France)
Avignon (France)
Badajoz (Spain)
Baghdad (Iraq)
Banbury (UK)
Bandung (Indonesia)
Bayonne (France)
Beccles (UK)
Bedford (UK)
Beijing (China)
Belfast (N. Ireland)
Benares (India)
Berwick (UK)
Bexhill (UK)
Bologna (Italy)
Bolzano (Italy)
Boulder (USA)
Bourges (France)
Breslau (Poland)

Bristol (UK)
Brixham (UK)
Buffalo (USA)
Burnley (UK)
Burslem (UK)
Calgary (Canada)
Caracas (Venezuela)
Cardiff (UK)
Chatham (UK)
Cheadle (UK)
Chesham (UK)
Chester (UK)
Chicago (USA)
Chorley (UK)
Clacton (UK)
Coblenz (Germany)
Cologne (Germany)
Colombo (Sri Lanka)
Conakry (Guinea)
Concord (USA)
Cordoba (Argentina,
Spain)
Corinth (Greece)
Corunna (Spain)
Cotonou (Benin)
Crawley (UK)
Croydon (UK)
Detroit (USA)
Devizes (UK)
Donetsk (Ukraine)
Dorking (UK)
Douglas (UK)
Dresden (Germany)
Dundalk (Ireland)
Dunkirk (France)
Evesham (UK)
Exmouth (UK)
Falkirk (UK)
Fareham (UK)
Farnham (UK)
Geelong (Australia)
Glasgow (UK)
Glossop (UK)
Gosport (UK)
Grimsby (UK)
Gwalior (India)
Halifax (Canada)
Halifax (UK)

Hamburg (Germany)
Hampton (USA)
Hanover (Germany)
Harwich (UK)
Hitchin (UK)
Homburg (Germany)
Honiton (UK)
Hornsea (UK)
Horsham (UK)
Houston (USA)
Ipswich (UK)
Irkutsk (Russia)
Isfahan (Iran)
Jackson (USA)
Jakarta (Indonesia)
Jodhpur (India)
Karachi (Pakistan)
Karbala (Iraq)
Keswick (UK)
Kildare (Ireland)
Kinross (UK)
Koblenz (Germany)
Kottbus (Germany)
Kunming(China)
Lanchow (China)
Lancing (UK)
Leipzig (Germany)
Limoges (France)
Lincoln (USA)
Lincoln (UK)
Lourdes (France)
Lucerne (Switzerland)
Lucknow (India)
Madison (USA)
Malvern (UK)
Mansura (Egypt)
Margate (UK)
Masshad (Iran)
Matlock (UK)
Mbabane (Swaziland)
Melrose (UK)
Memphis (USA)
Memphis (Egypt)
Messina (Italy)
Modesto (USA)
Mombasa (Kenya)
München (Germany)
Münster (Germany)

Nairobi (Kenya)
Nanking (China)
Newbury (UK)
Newport (UK)
Nicosia (Cyprus)
Norwich (UK)
Oakland (USA)
Orlando (USA)
Orleans (France)
Paisley (UK)
Palmyra (Syria)
Peebles (UK)
Penrith (UK)
Phoenix (USA)
Piraeus (Greece)
Potsdam (Germany)
Preston (UK)
Rainham (UK)
Ravenna (Italy)
Reading (UK)
Redhill (UK)
Redruth (UK)
Reigate (UK)
Renfrew (UK)
Ristick (Germany)
Rodrion (Argentina)
Romford (UK)
Runcorn (UK)
Salerno (Italy)
Salford (UK)
Seattle (USA)
Selkirk (UK)
Shipley (UK)
Skipton (UK)
Swanage (UK)
Swansea (UK)
Swindon (UK)
Swinton (UK)
Tallinn (Estonia)
Tangier (Morocco)
Taunton (UK)
Teheran (Iran)
Telford (UK)
Tetbury (UK)
Toronto (Canada)
Torquay (UK)
Trieste (Italy)
Tripoli (Lebanon)

Tripoli (Libya)
Uppsala (Sweden)
Utrecht (Netherlands)
Ventnor (UK)
Vilnius (Lithuania)
Walsall (UK)
Wantage (UK)
Warwick (UK)
Watford (UK)
Wexford (Ireland)
Windsor (UK)
Wisbech (UK)
Worksop (UK)
Wrexham (UK)
Yakutsk (Russia)
Yaoundé (Cameroun)

8
Aberdeen (UK)
Abingdon (UK)
Acapulco (Mexico)
Adelaide (Australia)
Alfreton (UK)
Alicante (Spain)
Amritsar (India)
Arbroath (UK)
Argatala (India)
Augsburg (Germany)
Bakewell (UK)
Ballarat (Australia)
Barnsley (UK)
Belgrade (Serbia)
Bergerac (France)
Berkeley (USA)
Besancon (France)
Beverley (UK)
Biarritz (France)
Bicester (UK)
Bideford (UK)
Bolsover (UK)
Bordeaux (France)
Boulogne (France)
Bradford (UK)
Brasilia (Brazil)
Bridport (UK)
Brighton (UK)
Brisbane (Australia)
Budapest (Hungary)

Bulawayo (Zimbabwe)
Calcutta (India)
Canberra (Australia)
Cardigan (UK)
Carlisle (UK)
Caterham (UK)
Cawnpore (India)
Chamonix (France)
Chartres (France)
Chemnitz (Germany)
Chepstow (UK)
Chertsey (UK)
Columbus (USA)
Coventry (UK)
Crediton (UK)
Damascus (Syria)
Dartford (UK)
Daventry (UK)
Dewsbury (UK)
Djibouti (Djibouti)
Dortmund (Germany)
Drogheda (Ireland)
Dumfries (UK)
Edmonton (Canada)
Falmouth (UK)
Freetown (Sierra Leone)
Freiburg (Germany)
Gaborone (Botswana)
Goteborg (Sweden)
Grantham (UK)
Greenock (UK)
Grenoble (France)
Hamilton (Canada)
Hannover (Germany)
Hastings (UK)
Hatfield (UK)
Helsinki (Finland)
Hereford (UK)
Hertford (UK)
Hinckley (UK)
Holbeach (UK)
Honolulu (USA)
Ilkeston (UK)
Ismailia (Egypt)
Istanbul (Turkey)
Jamalpur (India)
Kawasaki (Japan)
Keighley (UK)

Khartoum (Sudan)
Kilkenny (Ireland)
Kingston (Canada)
Kinshasa (Congo)
Kirkwall (UK)
Lausanne (Switzerland)
Lechlade (UK)
Lilongwe (Malawi)
Limerick (Ireland)
Listowel (Ireland)
Mannheim (Germany)
Medellin (Colombia)
Monmouth (UK)
Monrovia (Liberia)
Montreal (Canada)
Montrose (UK)
N'Djamena (Chad)
Nagasaki (Japan)
Nantwich (UK)
Newhaven (UK)
Nijmegen (Netherlands)
Novgorod (Russia)
Nuneaton (UK)
Nürnberg (Germany)
Oswestry (UK)
Pamplona (Spain)
Pasadena (USA)
Pembroke (UK)
Penzance (UK)
Peshawar (Pakistan)
Plymouth (UK)
Portland (USA)
Pretoria (South Africa)
Ramsgate (UK)
Redditch (UK)
Richmond (UK/USA)
Rochdale (UK)
Roxburgh (UK)
Salonika (Greece)
Salvador (Brazil)
Salzburg (Austria)
Sandwich (UK)
Santiago (Chile)
Schwerin (Germany)
Sedbergh (UK)
Semarang (Indonesia)
Shanghai (China)
Shanklin (UK)

Shenyang (China)
Skegness (UK)
Sleaford (UK)
Smolensk (Russia)
Soissons (France)
Southend (UK)
Spalding (UK)
Srinagar (India)
Stafford (UK)
Stamford (UK/USA)
Stirling (UK)
Stockton (UK)
Surabaj (Indonesia)
Syracuse (USA)
Syracuse (Italy)
Tamworth (UK)
Tangier (Morocco)
Tashkent (Uzbekistan)
Thetford (UK)
Tientsin (China)
Timbuktu (Mali)
Tiverton (UK)
Toulouse (France)
Trentino (Italy)
Uxbridge (UK)
Valencia (Spain)
Varanasi (India)
Veracruz (Mexico)
Victoria (Canada)
Wallasey (UK)
Wetherby (UK)
Weymouth (UK)
Winnipeg (Canada)
Worthing (UK)
Yarmouth (UK)
Yokohama (Japan)
Zaragoza (Spain)

9

Abbeville (France)
Agrigento (Italy)
Ahmadabad (India)
Aldeburgh (UK)
Aldershot (UK)
Allahabad (India)
Amsterdam(Netherlands)
Anchorage (USA)
Arlington (USA)

Aylesbury (UK)
Baltimore (USA)
Bangalore (India)
Barcelona (Spain)
Beersheba (Israel)
Blackburn (UK)
Blackpool (UK)
Blandford (UK)
Bracknell (UK)
Braintree (UK)
Brunswick (Germany)
Bucharest (Romania)
Bujumbura (Burundi)
Cambridge (USA)
Cartagena (Spain)
Cartegena (Colombia)
Cherbourg (France)
Chungking (China)
Cleveland (USA)
Clitheroe (UK)
Coleraine (N. Ireland)
Darmstadt (Germany)
Dartmouth (UK)
Devonport (UK)
Doncaster (UK)
Dordrecht (Netherlands)
Droitwich (UK)
Dubrovnik (Croatia)
Dumbarton (UK)
Dunkerque (France)
Dunstable (UK)
Edinburgh (UK)
Eindhoven (Netherlands)
Ellesmere (UK)
Fairbanks (USA)
Faversham (UK)
Fleetwood (UK)
Frankfurt (Germany)
Fremantle (Australia)
Galveston (USA)
Gateshead (UK)
Godalming (UK)
Gravesend (UK)
Guildford (UK)
Harrogate (UK)
Haslemere (UK)
Hiroshima (Japan)
Hyderabad (India)

Hyderabad (Pakistan)
Immingham (UK)
Innsbruck (Austria)
Inverness (UK)
Islamabad (Pakistan)
Jerusalem (Israel)
Kettering (UK)
Killarney (Ireland)
Kimberley (South Africa)
Ladysmith (South Africa)
Lancaster (UK)
Leicester (UK)
Lexington (USA)
Lichfield (UK)
Liverpool (UK)
Lowestoft (UK)
Magdeburg (Germany)
Maidstone (UK)
Mansfield (UK)
Maracaibo (Venezuela)
Marrakesh (Morocco)
Marseille (France)
Melbourne (Australia)
Milwaukee (USA)
Mogadishu (Somalia)
Monterrey (Mexico)
Nashville (USA)
Newcastle (Australia)
Newcastle (UK)
Newmarket (UK)
Nuremberg (Germany)
Palembang (Indonesia)
Pickering (UK)
Portadown (N. Ireland)
Princeton (USA)
Rochester (USA)
Rochester (UK)
Roscommon (Ireland)
Rotherham (UK)
Rotterdam (Netherlands)
Salisbury (UK)
Samarkand (Uzbekistan)
Santander (Spain)
Saragossa (Spain)
Saskatoon (Canada)
Sevenoaks (UK)
Sheerness (UK)
Sheffield (UK)

Sherborne (UK)
Southwell (UK)
Southwold (UK)
Stevenage (UK)
Stockholm (Sweden)
Stockport (UK)
Stranraer (UK)
Stratford (UK)
Stuttgart (Germany)
Tavistock (UK)
Tenterden (UK)
Tipperary (Ireland)
Tobermory (UK)
Tombstone (USA)
Tonbridge (UK)
Towcester (UK)
Trondheim (Norway)
Tynemouth (UK)
Ulverston (UK)
Uppingham (UK)
Uttoxeter (UK)
Vancouver (Canada)
Wakefield (UK)
Waterford (Ireland)
Weybridge (UK)
Wiesbaden (Germany)
Wokingham (UK)
Worcester (UK)
Wuppertal (Germany)

10

Accrington (UK)
Altrincham (UK)
Barnstaple (UK)
Billericay (UK)
Birkenhead (UK)
Birmingham (USA)
Birmingham (UK)
Bratislava (Slovakia)
Bridgnorth (UK)
Bridgwater (UK)
Buckingham (UK)
Canterbury (UK)
Casablanca (Morocco)
Chandigarh (India)
Charleston (USA)
Chelmsford (UK)
Cheltenham (UK)

Chichester (UK)
Chittagong (Bangladesh)
Cincinatti (USA)
Colchester (UK)
Copenhagen (Denmark)
Darjeeling (India)
Darlington (UK)
Dorchester (UK)
Düsseldorf (Germany)
Eastbourne (UK)
Folkestone (UK)
Gillingham (UK)
Gloucester (UK)
Gothenburg (Sweden)
Harrisburg (USA)
Hartlepool (UK)
Heidelberg (Germany)
Huntingdon (UK)
Ilfracombe (UK)
Kalgoorlie (Australia)
Kenilworth (UK)
Kilmarnock (UK)
Launceston (Australia)
Launceston (UK)
Leamington (UK)
Leominster (UK)
Libreville (Gabon)
Louisville (USA)
Maastricht (Netherlands)
Maidenhead (UK)
Malmesbury (UK)
Manchester (UK)
Marseilles (France)
Montelimar (France)
Montgomery (USA)
Motherwell (UK)
Nottingham (UK)
Palmerston (Australia)
Piitsburgh (USA)
Pontefract (UK)
Portsmouth (UK)
Providence (USA)
Rawalpindi (Pakistan)
Sacramento (USA)
Shrewsbury (UK)
Strasbourg (France)
Sunderland (UK)
Tananarive (Madagascar)

Valparaiso (Chile)
Versailles (France)
Warrington (UK)
Washington (USA)
Whitstable (UK)
Winchester (UK)
Woolongong (Australia)
Workington (UK)

11
Brazzaville (Congo)
Albuquerque (USA)
Armentières (France)
Basingstoke (UK)
Berkhamstead (UK)
Bournemouth (UK)
Bridlington (UK)
Chattanooga (USA)
Chelyabinsk (Russia)
Cleethorpes (UK)
Dunfermline (UK)
Enniskillen (N. Ireland)
Grahamstown (South Africa)
Kaliningrad (Russia)
Londonderry (N. Ireland)
Lutterworth (UK)
Mablethorpe (UK)
Manningtree (UK)
Marlborough (UK)
Minneapolis (USA)
Montpellier (France)
Novosibirsk (Russia)
Petersfield (UK)
Saarbrücken (Germany)
Scarborough (UK)
Shaftesbury (UK)
Southampton (UK)
Springfield (USA)
Thessaloniki (Greece)
Trincomalee (Sri Lanka)
Westminster (UK)

12
Antananarivo (Madagascar)
Bloemfontein (South Africa)

Chesterfield (UK)
Christchurch (UK)
Gainsborough (UK)
Huddersfield (UK)
Indianapolis (USA)
Johannesburg (South Africa)
Loughborough (UK)
Macclesfield (UK)
Peterborough (UK)
Philadelphia (USA)
Shoeburyness (UK)

13
Boroughbridge (UK)
Brightlingsea (UK)
Charlottetown (Canada)
Godmanchester (UK)
Kidderminster (UK)
Knaresborough (UK)
Littlehampton (UK)
Middlesborough (UK)
Northallerton (UK)
Wolverhampton (UK)

2+ words
Addis Ababa (Ethiopia)
Atlantic City (USA)
Baden Baden (Germany)
Baha Blanca (Argentina)
Baton Rouge (USA)
Bishop Auckland (UK)
Bognor Regis (UK)
Buenos Aires (Argentina)
Burton-on-Trent (UK)
Bury St Edmunds (UK)
Cape Town (South Africa)
Dar es Salaam (Tanzania)
Des Moines (USA)
El Paso (USA)
Fort Worth (USA)
Hemel Hempstead (UK)
Hong Kong (China)
Kansas City (USA)
King's Lynn (UK)
Las Vegas (USA)

Le Havre (France)
Le Mans (France)
Little Rock (USA)
Long Beach (USA)
Los Angeles (USA)
Lyme Regis (UK)
Lytham St Annes (UK)
Melton Mowbray (UK)
Merthyr Tidfil (UK)
Mexico City (Mexico)
Milton Keynes (UK)
New Haven (USA)
New Orleans (USA)
New York (USA)
Newton Abbot (UK)
Niagara Falls (Canada)
Palm Springs (USA)
Palo Alto (USA)
Port Louis (Mauritius)
Port Said (Egypt)
Porto Alegre (Brazil)
Rio de Janeiro (Brazil)
Saffron Walden (UK)
San Antonio (USA)
San Diego (USA)
San Francisco (USA)
San Jose (USA)
Santa Ana (USA)
Santa Fe (USA)
Sao Paulo (Brazil)
South Shields (UK)
St Albans (UK)
St Austell (UK)
St Etienne (France)
St Helens (UK)
St Ives (UK)
St Johns (Canada)
St Leonards (UK)
St Louis (USA)
St Malo (France)
St Neots (UK)
St Paul (USA)
St Petersburg (Russia)
St Tropez (France)
Thunder Bay (Canada)
Tunbridge Wells (UK)

TREES

TYPES OF TREE

2
bo
ti

3
ash
asp
bay
ban
box
elm
fig
fir
gum
jak
koa
oak
sal
tea
ule
wax
yew

4
acer
akee
aloe
bael
bhel
coco
cola
dali
date
dhak
dita
doum
gean
holm
ilex
kaki
kava
kola
lana
lime
nipa
palm
pear
pine
plum
poon
rata
rose
sago
shea
sorb
teak
teil
titi
toon
upas

5
abele
abies
alder
apple
areca
aspen
balsa
beech
birch
boree
bunya
cacao
carob
cedar
ebony
elder
fever
flame
guava
hazel
holly
iroko
judas
karri
kauri
larch
lemon
lilac
mango
maple
myall
ngaio
nikau
nyssa
olive
osier
papaw
peach
pecan
pipal
plane
rohan
rowan
sassy
sumac
taxus
tikul
tilia
tuart
tulip
withy
yacca
zamia

6
acacia
acajou
almond
antiar
bamboo
banana
banyan
baobab
bonsai
cashew
cassia
cerris
cherry
citrus
coffee
cornel
damson
datura
deodar
durian
fustic
ginkgo

gomuti
gopher
jarrah
jujube
jupati
kamala
laurel
linden
litchi
locust
loquat
mallee
medlar
mimosa
obeche
orange
peepul
poplar
quince
rattan
rubber
sallow
sandal
sapele
sapota
sappan
spruce
sumach
tupelo
walnut
wattle
willow
yarran

7

ailanto
amboina
amboyna
apricot
arbutus
bebeeru
cajuput
camphor
canella
catalpa
champak
coconut
coquito

cypress
dogwood
durmast
filbert
hickory
kumquat
juniper
madrona
marasca
mazzard
mesquit
moriche
palmyra
paxiuba
platane
pollard
quassia
redwood
robinia
sequoia
seringa
service
shittah
soursop
talipot
varnish
wallaba

8

basswood
beefwood
bergamot
blackboy
calabash
carnauba
chestnut
cinchona
coolabah
corkwood
crabwood
guaiacum
hawthorn
hornbeam
ironwood
kingwood
laburnum
magnolia
mahogany

mangrove
mesquite
mulberry
oleaster
palmetto
pinaster
quandong
raintree
rambutan
rosewood
sweetsop
sycamore
tamarack
tamarind
tamarisk
umbrella

9

ailanthus
araucaria
bearberry
blackwood
buckthorn
carambola
chinkapin
deciduous
evergreen
hackberry
jacaranda
kurrajong
macadamia
marmalade
monkeypot
naseberry
paperbark
persimmon
pistachio
poinciana
quebracho
sapodilla
sassafras
satinwood
stinkwood
terebinth
whitebeam
whitewood
wineberry
zebrawood

10
blackthorn
breadfruit
calamondin
chinquapin
cottonwood
eucalyptus
greenheart
hackmatack
mangosteen
quickthorn
sandalwood
sappanwood

11
bottlebrush
chaulmougra
chokecherry
flamboyante
gingerbread
liquidambar
pomegranate

2+ words
bog-oak
copper beech
date-palm
fan-palm
holly oak
holm-oak
mako-mako

monkey puzzle
mountain ash
oil-palm
rain tree
red-bud
red-gum
red-oak
sago-palm
scots pine
sitka spruce
swamp oak
turkey oak
wax-palm
witch-elm
wych-elm
yellow-wood
ylang-ylang

USA

States of the USA
Towns and Cities of the USA

STATES OF THE USA

State	Abbr	Zip code	Capital
Alabama	ALA	AL	Montgomery
Alaska	ALAS	AK	Juneau
Arizona	ARIZ	AZ	Phoenix
Arkansas	ARK	AR	Little Rock
California	CALIF	CA	Sacramento
Colorado	COLO	CO	Denver
Connecticut	CONN	CT	Hartford
Delaware	DEL	DE	Dover
District Of Columbia	DC	DC	Washington
Florida	FLA	FL	Tallahassee
Georgia	GA	GA	Atlanta
Hawaii	HI	HI	Honolulu
Idaho	IDA	ID	Boise
Illinois	ILL	IL	Springfield
Indiana	IND	IN	Indianapolis
Iowa	IA	IA	Des Moines
Kansas	KANS	KS	Topeka
Kentucky	KY	KY	Frankfort
Louisiana	LA	LA	Baton Rouse
Maine	ME	ME	Augusta
Maryland	MD	MD	Annapolis
Massachusetts	MASS	MA	Boston
Michigan	MICH	MI	Lansing
Minnesota	MINN	MN	St Paul
Mississippi	MISS	MS	Jackson
Missouri	MO	MO	Jefferson City
Montana	MONT	MT	Helena
Nebraska	NEBR	NE	Lincoln
Nevada	NEV	NV	Carson City
New Hampshire	NH	NH	Concord
New Jersey	NJ	NJ	Trenton
New Mexico	N MEX	NM	Santa Fe
New York	NY	NY	Albany
North Carolina	NC	NC	Raleigh
North Dakota	N DAK	ND	Bismarck
Ohio	OH	OH	Columbus
Oklahoma	OKLA	OK	Oklahoma City
Oregon	OREG	OR	Salem
Pennsylvania	PENN	PA	Harrisburg
Rhode Island	RI	RI	Providence

State	Abbr	Zip code	Capital
South Carolina	SC	SC	Columbia
South Dakota	S DAK	SD	Pierre
Tennessee	TENN	TN	Nashville
Texas	TEX	TX	Austin
Utah	UT	UT	Salt Lake City
Vermont	VT	VT	Montpelier
Virginia	VA	VA	Richmond
Washington	WASH	WA	Olympia
West Virginia	WVA	WV	Charleston
Wisconsin	WISC	WI	Madison
Wyoming	WYO	WY	Cheyenne

TOWNS AND CITIES IN THE USA

4
Gary
Lima
Reno
Troy
Waco

5
Akron
Miami
Omaha
Salem
Selma
Tulsa

6
Albany
Austin
Bangor
Biloxi
Boston
Dallas
Dayton
Denver
Fresno
Irvine
Mobile
Nassau
Newark
Peoria
Topeka
Tucson

7
Anaheim
Atlanta
Boulder
Buffalo
Chicago
Concord
Detroit
Hampton
Houston
Jackson
Lincoln
Madison
Memphis
Modesto
Oakland
Orlando
Phoenix
Seattle

8
Berkeley
Columbus
Honolulu
Pasadena
Portland
Richmond
Stamford
Syracuse

9
Anchorage
Arlington
Baltimore
Cambridge
Cleveland
Fairbanks
Galveston
Lexington
Milwaukee
Nashville
Princeton
Rochester
Tombstone

10
Birmingham
Charleston
Cincinatti
Harrisburg
Louisville
Montgomery
Piitsburgh
Providence
Sacramento
Washington

11
Albuquerque
Chattanooga
Minneapolis
Springfield

12
Indianapolis
Philadelphia

2+ words
Atlantic City
Baton Rouge

Des Moines
El Paso
Fort Worth
Kansas City
Las Vegas
Little Rock
Long Beach
Los Angeles
New Haven

New Orleans
New York
Palm Springs
Palo Alto
San Antonio
San Diego
San Francisco

San Jose
Santa Ana
Santa Fe
St Paul
St Louis

VEGETABLES

TYPES OF VEGETABLE

3
cos
cep
dal
oca
pea
soy
udo
yam

4
bean
beet
cole
corn
dhal
eddo
kale
kohl
leek
neep
okra
rape
soya
spud
taro

5
chard
chive
colza
cress
gumbo
laver
maize
navew
onion
orach
pease
pulse
savoy
swede
tuber

6
batata
carrot
celery
endive
fennel
frijol
garlic
legume
lentil
manioc
marrow
murphy
pepper
potato
pratie
radish
runner
sprout
squash
tomato
turnip

7
avocado
cabbage
cassava
chicory
gherkin
lettuce
parsnip
pimento
pumpkin
salsify
seakale
seaweed
shallot
spinach
truffle

8
beetroot
borecole
brassica
broccoli
capsicum
celeriac
chickpea

colerape
colewort
cucumber
eggplant
eschalot
kohlrabi
mushroom
rutabaga
samphire
scallion
zucchini

9
artichoke
asparagus
aubergine
calabrese
courgette
flageolet
radicchio
sweetcorn
mangetout

10
butterbean
sauerkraut

11
cauliflower

2+ words
broad bean
brussels sprout
curly-kale
French bean
globe artichoke
green pepper
red pepper
runner bean
spring greens
spring onion

VEHICLES

TYPES OF VEHICLE

2
RV

3
BMX
bus
cab
car
dan
fly
gig
HGV
JCB
jet
LMS
rig
SUV
van

4
auto
biga
bike
cart
drag
dray
duck
heap
jeep
limo
loco
luge
mini
pram
shay
skis
sled
tank
taxi
tram
trap
tube
wain

whim

5
artic
bandy
bogey
brake
buggy
caddy
chair
coach
coupe
crate
cycle
dandy
dilly
float
lorry
metro
moped
motor
palki
plane
pulka
ratha
sedan
sulky
tonga
train
trike
truck
wagon

6
banger
barrow
beetle
berlin
bowser
calash
camion
camper
chaise
dennet
digger
dodgem
doolie
drosky

engine
estate
fiacre
gharry
gingle
hansom
hearse
hotrod
jalopy
jampan
jigger
jitney
landau
limber
litter
oxcart
pochay
pulkha
random
saloon
skibob
Skidoo
sledge
sleigh
Snocat®
spider
surrey
tandem
tender
tourer
troika
waggon
weasel
wheels

7
autobus
autocar
balloon
bicycle
britzka
caboose
cacolet
caravan
caravel
cariole
caroche
chariot

chopper
crawler
dogcart
droshky
fourgon
gritter
growler
gyrocar
hackery
hackney
hardtop
haywain
helibus
kibitka
minibus
minicab
minicar
omnibus
pedicab
pedrail
phaeton
pullman
railbus
railcar
scooter
sidecar
taxicab
tilbury
tipcart
tonneau
tractor
trailer
tramcar
trishaw
trolley
trundle
tumbrel
tumbril
turnout
voiture

8
barouche
bendibus
brakevan
britzska
brougham
cablecar

carriage
carriole
carryall
carrycot
clarence
curricle
dragster
dustcart
equipage
fastback
golfcart
handcart
jetliner
motorbus
motorcar
pushcart
quadriga
rickshaw
roadster
rockaway
runabout
sociable
stanhope
tarantas
toboggan
tricycle
unicycle
victoria

9
ambulance
amphibian
applecart
automatic
bandwagon
bobsleigh
buckboard
bulldozer
cabriolet
charabanc
diligence
Dormobile®
Gladstone
hatchback
landaulet
limousine
monocycle
motorbike

motorcade
muletrain
palanquin
scrambler
skimobile
streetcar
stretcher
tarantass
wagonette

10
automobile
boneshaker
convertible
conveyance
hobbyhorse
hovercraft
jinricksha
juggernaut
knockabout
locomotive
motorcoach
motorcycle
roadroller
snowmobile
snowplough
spacecraft
stagecoach
timwhiskey
velocipede
voiturette
waggonette
wheelchair

11
caterpillar
landaulette
quadricycle
steamroller
transporter
trolleybus
wheelbarrow

12
autorickshaw
pantechnicon
perambulator

2+ words

armoured car
baby buggy
baby carriage
bath chair
beach buggy
Black Maria
boat train
box wagon
breakdown van
brewer's dray
bubble car
bullock cart
bumper car
Cape cart
cattle car
chapel cart
coach-and-four
coach-and-pair
cycle car
delivery van
dining car
dodgem car
donkey cart
dune buggy
estate car
express train
fire engine
fly coach
four wheeler
four-by-four
four-in-hand
furniture van
glass coach
go-cart
goods train
goods truck

goods van
goods wagon
guard's van
gun-carriage
hackney cab
hackney coach
half-track
hand barrow
hansom cab
horse litter
ice skates
ice yacht
invalid cab
invalid chair
jaunting car
Land Rover
low-loader
luggage train
magic carpet
mail car
mail cart
mail coach
mail phaeton
mail train
mail-van
milk cart
milk float
milk train
mobile home
motor lorry
motor scooter
moving van
old crock
paddy wagon
pony engine
post chaise
post-chaise

prison van
pullman car
quad bike
racing car
railway train
rally car
rocket car
saloon car
sand yacht
scout car
sedan chair
sleeping car
smoking car
sports car
spring cart
state coach
state landau
steam car
steam engine
stock car
stretch limo
swamp buggy
three-in-hand
three-wheeler
tin lizzie
tip-up lorry
touring car
tramway car
trolley bus
trolley car
vis-à-vis
waggon train
wagon-lit
war chariot
water cart
watering cart

VOLCANOES

*VOLCANOES OF THE
WORLD*

3
Aso (Japan)
Awu (Indonesia)

4
Etna (Sicily)
Fogo (Cape Verde)
Fuji (Japan)
Gede (Indonesia)
Kaba (Indonesia)
Laki (Iceland)
Nila (Indonesia)
Poas (Costa Rica)
Taal (Philippines)

5
Agung (Indonesia)
Asama (Japan)
Askja (Iceland)
Dempo (Indonesia)
Fuego (Guatemala)
Hekla (Iceland)
Katla (Iceland)
Manam (Papua New
Guinea)
Mayon (Philippines)
Noyoe (Iceland)
Okmok (USA)
Paloe (Indonesia)
Pelee (Martinique)
Spurr (USA)

6
Alcedo (Galapagos)
Ambrim (Vanuata)
Buleng (Indonesia)
Colima (Mexico)
Dukono (Indonesia)
Erebus (Antartica)
Izalco (El Salvador)

Katmai (USA)
Lascar (Chile)
Lassen (USA)
Llaima (Chile)
Lopevi (Vanuatu)
Marapi (Indonesia)
Martin (USA)
Meakan (Japan)
Merapi (Indonesia)
Oshima (Japan)
Pacaya (Guatemala)
Pavlof (USA)
Puracé (Colombia)
Sangay (Ecuador)
Semeru (Indonesia)
Slamat (Indonesia)
Tacana (Guatemala)
Unauna (Indonesia)

7
Atitlan (Guatemala)
Barcena (Mexico)
Bulusan (Philippines)
Didicas (Philippines)
Galeras (Colombia)
Jorullo (Mexico)
Kilauea (USA)
Ometepe (Nicaragua)
Puyehue (Chile)
Ruapehu (New Zealand)
Sabrina (Azores)
Soputan (Indonesia)
Surtsey (Iceland)
Ternate (Indonesia)
Tjareme (Indonesia)
Tokachi (Japan)
Torbert (USA)
Trident (USA)
Vulcano (Italy)

8
Bogoslof (USA)
Cotopaxi (Ecuador)
Demavend (Iran)
Fonualei (Tonga)
Fujiyama (Japan)

Krakatoa (Indonesia)
Krakatau (Indonesia)
Rindjani (Indonesia)
Sangeang (Indonesia)
Tarawera (New Zealand)
Vesuvius (Italy)
Yakedake (Japan)

9
Amburombu (Indonesia)
Cleveland (USA)
Coseguina (Nicaragua)
Cotacachi (Ecuador)
Gamkonora (Indonesia)
Grimsvotn (Iceland)
Momotombo
(Nicaragua)
Ngauruhoe (New
Zealand)
Paricutin (Mexico)
Rininahue (Chile)
Santorini (Greece)
Stromboli (Italy)
Tongariro (New
Zealand)

10
Acatenango (Guatemala)
Capelinhos (Azores)
Guallatiri (Azores)
Miyakejima (Japan)
Nyamiagira (Congo)
Nyiragongo (Congo)
Shishaldin (USA)
Tungurahua (Ecuador)
Villarrica (Chile)

11
Kilimanjaro (Tanzania)
Tupungatito (Chile)

12
Huainaputina (Peru)
Popocatepetl (Mexico)

2+ words
Mount St Helens (USA)

WALES/WELSH

Famous Welshmen and Welshwomen
Towns and cities in Wales
See also **COUNTIES**

FAMOUS WELSHMEN AND WELSHWOMEN

4
John (Augustus/Gwen, painters)
John (Barry, rugby player)
Rees (Angharad, actress)

5
Baker (Kenneth, politician)
Baker (Stanley, actor)
Bevan (Aneurin, politician)
Evans (Geraint, singer)
Evans (Gwynfor, politician)
Giggs (Ryan, footballer)
Ifans (Rhys, actor)
Johns (Glynis/Mervyn, actors)
Jones (Terry, actor and author)
Jones (Tom, singer)
Lloyd (Sian, broadcaster)
Madoc (Philip, actor)
Pryce (Jonathan, actor)

6
Bassey (Shirley, singer)
Burton (Richard, actor)
Church (Charlotte, singer)
Dalton (Timothy, actor)
Davies (Lynn, athlete)
French (Dawn, comedienne)
Hislop (Ian, journalist)
Hopkin (Mary, singer)
Howard (Michael, politician)
Hughes (Mark, footballer)
Morgan (Cliff, rugby player)
Morgan (Rhodri, First Minister)
Terfel (Bryn, singer)

7
Bennett (Phil, rugby player)
Charles (John, footballer)
Edwards (Huw, broadcaster)
Hopkins (Anthony, actor)
Houston (Donald/Glyn, actors)
Jackson (Colin, athlete)
Jenkins (Karl/Katherine, musicians)
Jenkins (Roy, politician)
Kinnock (Neil, politician)
Milland (Ray, actor)
Secombe (Harry, comedian)
Stanley (Henry Morton, explorer)
Toshack, John, footballer)
Wheldon (Huw, broadcaster)
Woosnam (Ian, golfer)

8
Griffith (Hugh/Kenneth, actors)
Humphrys (John, broadcaster)
Lawrence (T.E., soldier and author)
Phillips (Siân, actress)
Williams (Emlyn, actor and writer)
Williams (J.P.R., rugby player)
Williams (Rowan, Archbishop of Canterbury)

9
Greenaway (Peter, film director)

2+ words
Lloyd George (David, prime minister)
Rhys Jones (Griff, comedian)
Zeta-Jones (Catherine, actress)

TOWNS AND CITIES IN WALES

4
Bala
Holt
Mold
Pyle
Rhyl

5
Barry
Chirk
Conwy
Flint
Neath
Nevin
Tenby
Towin

6
Amlwch
Bangor
Brecon
Builth
Conway
Ruabon
Ruthin

7
Carbury
Cardiff
Cwmbran
Denbugh
Maesteg
Newport

Newtown
Swansea
Wrexham

8
Aberavon
Aberdare
Abergele
Bramouth
Bridgend
Caerleon
Cardigan
Chepstow
Dolgelly
Hawarden
Holyhead
Holywell
Kidwelly
Knighton
Lampeter
Llandaff
Llanelli
Llanelly
Llanrwst
Monmouth
Pembroke
Pwllheli

Rhayader
Skerries
Skifness
Talgarth
Tredegar
Tregaron

9
Aberaeron
Aberdovey
Aberffraw
Beaumaris
Bodlondes
Carnavon
Criccieth
Festiniog
Fishguard
Llanberis
Llandudno
Pontypool
Porthcawl
Portmadoc
Welshpool

10
Caernarfon
Caernavon

Carmathen
Crickhowel
Ffestiniog
Llandovery
Llanfyllin
Llangadock
Llangollen
Llanidloes
Montgomery
Plinlimmon
Pontypridd
Presteigne

11
Abergavenny
Aberystwyth
Llantrisant
Machynlleth
Oystermouth

13
Haverfordwest

2+ words
Merthyr Tydfil
Port Talbot
St Davids

WEAPONS

TYPES OF WEAPON

3
arm
axe
bow
gat
gun
rod
RPG
SAM
TNT

4
ball
barb
bill
bolt
bomb
bren
club
Colt®
cosh
dart
dirk
épée
foil
ICBM
kris
mace
mine
MIRV
pike
sten
whip

5
arrow
baton
bolas
blade
knife
knout
kukri
lance
lasso

Luger®
Maxim
panga
pilum
rifle
sabre
sharp
shell
sling
spear
sword

6
airgun
Bofors®
bullet
cannon
cudgel
dagger
Exocet
Mauser®
mortar
musket
napalm
parang
pistol
pompom
rapier
rocket
Semtex®
Webley®

7
assegai
bayonet
bazooka
blowgun
bombard
caliver
caltrop
carbine
cutlass
grenade
halberd
handgun
harpoon
hatchet
javelin

longbow
machete
missile
poniard
shotgun
sidearm
torpedo
trident
Walther®
warhead

8
arbalest
Armalite®
arquebus
ballista
basilisk
blowpipe
bludgeon
catapult
claymore
crossbow
culverin
falchion
howitzer
landmine
Oerlikon
ordnance
partisan
repeater
revolver
scimitar
shrapnel
stiletto
tomahawk

9
artillery
automatic
battleaxe
boomerang
derringer
deterrent
doodlebug
flintlock
gelignite
grapeshot
gunpowder

matchlock
slingshot
trebuchet
truncheon

10
broadsword
fieldpiece
incendiary
knobkerrie
nightstick
peacemaker
shillelagh
Winchester

11
blockbuster
blunderbuss
Kalashnikov

12
mitrailleuse

13
knuckleduster

2+ words
A-bomb
booby trap
brass knuckles
breech-loader
cruise missile
depth-charge
flame-thrower
flick-knife
fowling-piece
guided missile
H-bomb
Lee-Enfield

letter bomb
life-preserver
limpet mine
machine gun
Martini-Henry
muzzle-loader
pop-gun
pump-gun
scatter-gun
six-gun
six-shooter
skean-dhu
smart bomb
submachine-gun
sword-stick
tommy-gun

WEATHER

Cloud
Weather words
Winds
Winds in classical
mythology

CLOUD

3
fog

4
blur
haze
mist
rack
scud

5
anvil
gloom
sheet

6
cirrus
nimbus
vapour

7
cumulus
stratus

11
altocumulus
altostratus

12
cirrocumulus
cirrostratus
cumulonimbus

2+ words
mackerel sky

WEATHER WORDS

3
dew
dry
eye
fog
ice
icy
low
sun
wet

4
back
calm
cool
damp
dull
gale
gust
hail
haze
heat
high
mild
mist
pour
rain
smog
snow
thaw
veer
warm
wind

5
above
below
clear
close
cloud
foggy
front
frost
gusty
heavy
light

misty
muggy
rainy
shine
sleet
slush
snowy
storm
sunny
windy

6
arctic
autumn
breeze
bright
chilly
cloudy
deluge
freeze
frosty
isobar
mizzle
normal
shower
spring
squall
stormy
sultry
summer
torrid
trough
winter
wintry

7
backing
Celsius
climate
cyclone
degrees
drizzle
drought
fogbank
freshen
hailing
insular
monsoon

onshore
pouring
rainbow
raining
settled
showery
snowing
squally
summery
tempest
thermal
thunder
tornado
tsunami
typhoon
veering
wintery

8
autumnal
blizzard
climatic
cyclonic
doldrums
downpour
easterly
fogbound
forecast
heatwave
maritime
occluded
offshore
overcast
raindrop
rainfall
snowfall
sunshine
thundery
tropical
sunshine
westerly

9
barometer
cloudless
drizzling
hailstorm
hoarfrost

hurricane
lightning
northerly
snowstorm
southerly
updraught
whirlwind

10
anemometer
atmosphere
centigrade
changeable
convection
depression
Fahrenheit
forecaster
frostbound
prevailing
waterspout

11
anticyclone
atmospheric
temperature
thunderbolt
thunderclap
troposphere
turbulence

12
anticyclonic
condensation
meteorology
stratosphere
thundercloud
thunderstorm

2+ words
black ice
cold snap
dust devil
global warming
heat haze
sand storm
sea breeze

WINDS

4
bise (Alps)
bora (Adriatic)
eddy
föhn (Alps)
gale
gust
helm (Lake District)
puna (Peru)

5
blast
chili (North Africa)
gibli (North Africa)
norte (Mexico)
storm
trade (tropics)
zonda (Argentina)

6
baguio (Philippines)
ghibli (North Africa)
samoon (Iran)
simoom (Arabia)
simoon (Arabia)
solano (Spain)

7
chinook (Rockies)
etesian (Mediterranean)
gregale (Mediterranean)
meltemi (Mediterranean)
mistral (Southern France)
monsoon (Indian ocean)
pampero (Andes)
sirocco (Mediterranean)

8
easterly
levanter (Mediterranean)
scirocco (Mediterranean)
westerly
williwaw (South America)

9
harmattan (West Africa)

libecchio
(Mediterranean)
northerly
southerly

10
tramontana (Italy)

12
brickfielder (Australia)

2+ words
berg wind (South Africa)
Cape doctor (South
Africa)
Santa Anna (USA)
trade wind (tropics)

*WINDS IN CLASSICAL
MYTHOLOGY*

4
Afer (south west)
Libs (south west)

5
Eurus (east)
Notus (south

6
Aquilo (north)
Auster (south)
Boreas (north)
Caurus (north west)

Kaikas (north east)
Zephyr (west)

7
Africus (south west)

8
Favonius (west)
Zephyrus (west)

9
Thrascias (north west)

WINE

3
red
sec
vin

4
Asti
brut
Cava
Fino
hock
port
rosé
sack
sake
sekt
vino

5
Anjou
blanc
Fitou
Macon
Médoc
Mosel
negus
plonk
Rhine
Rioja
Soave
Tokay
white

6
Alsace
Barolo
Barsac
Beaune
bubbly

Claret
Graves
Merlot
Saumur
sherry
Shiraz

7
Chablis
Chianti
Cinsaut
Madeira
Malmsey
Margaux
Marsala
Moselle
retsina
Rhenish
Sangria
Vouvray

8
Bordeaux
Burgundy
cabernet
champers
Frascati
Montilla
Muscadel
Muscadet
Pinotage
Riesling
Sancerre
Santenay
Semillon
Spätlese
Spumanate
Sylvaner

9
Bardolino
Champagne
Hermitage
Lambrusco
Meursault
Minervois
ordinaire
Sauternes
Sauvignon
sparkling
Zinfandel

10
Beaujolais
Chambertin
Chardonnay
Constantia
Hochheimer
Manzanilla
Montrachet
Piesporter

11
Amontillado
Monbazillac
Niersteiner
Rudesheimer

12
Valpolicella

13
Liebfraumilch

2+ words
Châteauneuf du Pape
Côtes du Rhône
Côte d'Or
Nuits St George
Pouilly Fuissé
St Emilion

WRITERS

Writer
Famous children's writers
Famous writers

WRITER

3
ink
pen

4
biro
hack
poet

5
clerk
quill

6
author
journo
pencil
scribe

7
diarist

8
essayist
novelist

9
columnist
dramatist
penpusher
scribbler
secretary
wordsmith

10
journalist
playwright

FAMOUS CHILDREN'S WRITERS

4
Baum (L. Frank, *Wizard of Oz*)
Bond (Michael, *Paddington Bear*)
Dahl (Roald, *Charlie and the Chocolate Factory*)
Lear (Edward, *nonsense poems*)
Todd (Barbara Euphan, *Worzel Gummidge*)

5
Adams (Richard, *Watership Down*)
Asch (Frank, *Happy Birthday Moon*)
Awdry (Rev. W. *Thomas the Tank Engine*)
Blume (Judy, *Iggie's House*)
Grimm (Brothers, Jakob/Wilhelm, *Fairy Tales*)
Lively (Penelope, *Ghost of Thomas Kempe*)
Lewis (C. S., *Narnia*)
Milne (A. A., *Winnie the Pooh*)
Zeuss (Dr., *Cat in the Hat*)

6
Alcott (Luisa M., *Little Women*)
Barrie (J.M., *Peter Pan*)
Blyton (Enid, *Noddy, Famous Five*)
Garner (Alan, *Weirdstone of Brisingamen*)
Harris (Joel Chandler, *Uncle Remus*)
Hughes (Thomas, *Tom Brown's Schooldays*)
Kipling (Rudyard, *Jungle Book*)
Nesbit (E[dith], *Railway Children*)
Potter (Beatrix, *Peter Rabbit*)
Sewell (Anna, *Black Beauty*)
Uttley (Alison, *Little Grey Rabbit*)
Wilder (Laura Ingalls, *Little House on the Prairie*)
Wilson (Jacqueline, *Girls in Love*)

7
Bagnold (Enid, *National Velvet*)
Burnett (Frances Hodgson, *The Secret Garden*)
Carroll (Lewis, *Alice in Wonderland*)
Grahame (Kenneth, *Wind in the Willows*)
Kästner (Erich, *Emil and the Detectives*)
Lofting (Hugh, *Dr Doolittle*)
Marryat (Captain F., *Children of the New Forest*)
Pullman (Philip, *His Dark Materials*)
Ransome (Arthur, *Swallows and Amazons*)
Rowling (J.K., *Harry Potter*)

8
Andersen (Hans Christian, *Fairy Tales*)
Crompton (Richmal, *Just William*)
Kingsley (Charles, *Water Babies*)
Lindgren (Astrid, *Pippi Longstocking*)
Perrault (Charles, *Tales of Mother Goose*)
Richards (Frank, *Billy Bunter*)

10
Ballantyne (R.M., *Coral Island*)
Buckeridge (Anthony, *Jennings*)
Hargreaves (Roger, *Mr Men*)
Williamson (Henry, *Tarka the Otter*)

2+ words
King Smith (Dick, *The Sheep-pig*)

FAMOUS WRITERS

2
Fo (Dario, Italian dramatist)

3
Eco (Umberto, Italian novelist)
Fry (Christopher, UK dramatist)
Gay (John, UK dramatist)
Kyd (Thomas, UK dramatist)
Poe (Edgar Allen, US poet)
Pye (Henry, UK poet)
Sue (Eugène, French novelist)

4
Agee (James, US novelist)
Amis (Kingsley/Martin, UK novelists)
Behn (Aphra, English dramatist)
Benn (Gottfried, German poet)
Böll (Heinrich, German novelist)
Bolt (Robert, UK dramatist)
Bond (Edward, UK dramatist)

Buck (Pearl S., US novelist)
Cary (Joyce, UK novelist)
Cruz (Juana, Mexican poet)
Ford (Ford Madox, UK novelist)
Ford (John, English dramatist)
Gems (Pam, UK dramatist)
Gide (André, French novelist)
Gray (Simon, UK dramatist/ Thomas, UK poet)
Gunn (Thom, UK/US poet)
Hall (Willis, UK dramatist)
Hare (David, UK dramatist)
Hart (Moss, US dramatist)
Hill (Geoffrey, UK poet)
Hogg (James, Scottish poet)
Hood (Thomas, UK poet)
Hope, Anthony (UK novelist)
Hugo (Victor, French poet, novelist and dramatist)
Hunt (Leigh, UK poet)
King (Stephen, US novelist)
Lamb (Charles, UK essayist)
Lear (Edward, UK humorous poet)
Livy (Roman historian)
Loti (Pierre, French novelist)
Mann (Thomas, German novelist)
Muir (Edwin, UK poet)
Nash (Ogden, US humorist)

Ovid (Roman poet)
Owen (Wilfred, UK poet)
Pope (Alexander, UK poet)
Rhys (Jean, UK novelist)
Roth (Philip, US novelist)
Rowe (Nicholas, UK dramatist)
Sade (Marquis de, French novelist)
Sadi (Persian poet)
Saki (*H. H. Munro*, UK novelist)
Sand (Georges, French novelist)
Seth (Vikram, Indian novelist)
Shaw (George Bernard, Irish dramatist)
Snow (C. P., UK novelist)
Tate (Allen, US poet)
Tate (Nahum, English poet)
Vega (Lope de, Spanish dramatist)
Wain (John, UK novelist and poet)
Webb (Mary, UK novelist)
West (Rebecca, UK novelist)
Wren (P. C., UK novelist)
Zola (Emile, French novelist)

5
Adams (Henry, US historian/Richard, UK novelist)
Albee (Edward, US dramatist)
Arden (John, UK dramatist)
Auden (W. H., UK poet)
Babel (Isaac, Russian short-story writer)
Barth (John, US novelist)
Bates (H. E., UK novelist)

Behan (Brendan, Irish dramatist)

Benét (Stephen, US novelist)

Blake (William, UK poet)

Bowen (Elizabeth, UK novelist)

Burns (Robert, Scottish poet)

Butor (Michel, French novelist)

Byatt (A.S., UK novelist)

Byron (Lord George Gordon, UK poet)

Camus (Albert, French novelist)

Carew (Thomas, English poet)

Carey (Peter, Australian novelist)

Clare (John, UK poet)

Colum (Padraic, Irish poet)

Crane (Hart, US poet)

Crane (Stephen, US novelist)

Dante (Alighieri, Italian poet)

Defoe (Daniel, UK novelist)

Donne (John, English poet)

Doyle (Roddy, Irish novelist)

Dumas (Alexandre, French novelist)

Duras (Marguerite, French novelist)

Eliot (George, *Mary Anne Evans*, UK novelist)

Eliot (T. S., US/UK poet and dramatist)

Frayn (Michael, UK dramatist)

Friel (Brian, Irish dramatist)

Frost (Robert, US poet)

Genet (Jean, French dramatist)

Gogol (Nikolai, Russian dramatist and novelist)

Gorki (Maxim, Russian novelist)

Gosse (Edmund, UK critic)

Gower (John, English poet)

Grass (Günther, German novelist)

Hafiz (Persian poet)

Hardy (Thomas, UK novelist and poet)

Harte (Brett, US short-story writer novelist)

Havel (Vaclav, Czech dramatist)

Heine (Heinrich, German poet)

Henry (O., *William Sidney Porter*, US short story writer)

Hesse (Hermann, German novelist)

Homer (Greek poet)

Ibsen (Henrik, Norwegian dramatist)

James (Henry, US/UK novelist)

James (P. D., UK novelist)

Jarry (Alfred, French dramatist)

Jones (LeRoi, US dramatist)

Joyce (James, Irish novelist)

Kafka (Franz, Czech novelist)

Keats (John, UK poet)

Kesey (Ken, US novelist)

Keyes (Sidney, UK poet)

Lewis (Sinclair, US/Wyndham, UK novelists)

Lodge (David, UK novelist)

Lorca (Federico Garcia, Spanish poet and

dramatist)

Lowry (Malcolm, UK novelist)

Lucan (Roman poet)

Mamet (David, US dramatist)

Marot (Clément, French poet)

Marsh (Ngaio, New Zealand novelist)

Moore (Marianne, US/Thomas, Irish poets)

Musil (Robert, Austrian novelist)

Noyes (Alfred, UK poet)

Odets (Clifford, US dramatist)

Orczy (Baroness, UK novelist)

Orton (Joe, UK dramatist)

Paton (Alan, South African novelist)

Peake (Mervyn, UK novelist)

Péguy (Charles, French poet)

Perse (St Jean, French poet)

Plath (Sylvia, US poet)

Pound (Ezra, US poet)

Powys (John Cowper, UK novelist)

Prior (Matthew, UK poet)

Rilke (Rainer Maria, Austrian poet)

Sachs (Hans, German poet)

Sagan (Françoise, French novelist)

Scott (Walter, Scottish novelist and poet)

Shute (Neville, Australian novelist)

Smith (Stevie, UK poet)

Smith (Zadie, UK novelist)

Spark (Muriel, UK

novelist)
Storm (Theodor, German novelist)
Stowe (Harriet Beecher, US novelist)
Swift (Graham, UK novelist)
Swift (Jonathan, Irish satirist)
Synge (John, Irish dramatist)
Tasso (Torquato, Italian poet)
Twain (Mark, US novelist)
Varro (Marcus Terentius, Roman poet)
Verne (Jules, French novelist)
Vidal (Gore, US novelist)
Vigny (Alfred de, French poet)
Watts (Isaac, UK poet)
Waugh (Evelyn, UK novelist)
Wells (H.G., UK novelist)
White (Patrick, Australian novelist)
Wilde (Oscar, Irish dramatist)
Wolfe (Thomas, US novelist)
Woolf (Virginia, UK novelist)
Wyatt (Thomas, English poet)
Yeats (W.B., Irish poet)
Yonge (Charlotte, UK novelist)

6
Aldiss (Brian, UK novelist)
Asimov (Isaac, US novelist)
Atwood (Margaret, Canadian novelist)
Austen (Jane, UK

novelist)
Austin (Alfred, UK poet)
Balzac (Honoré de, French novelist)
Barrie (JM, UK dramatist)
Belloc (Hilaire, UK poet and essayist)
Bellow (Saul, US novelist)
Bierce (Ambrose, US writer)
Binchy (Maeve, Irish novelist)
Binyon (Robert, UK poet)
Bishop (Elizabeth, US poet)
Borges (Jorge Luis, Argentine novelist)
Braine (John, UK novelist)
Brecht (Berthold, German dramatist)
Bronte (Ann/Charlotte, Emily, UK novelists)
Brooke (Rupert, UK poet)
Bryant (William Cullens, US poet)
Buchan (John, UK novelist)
Bunyan (John, English religious writer)
Burney (Fanny, UK novelist)
Butler (Samuel, UK novelist)
Camoes (Luis de, Portuguese poet)
Capote (Truman, US novelist)
Céline (Louis, French poet)
Conrad (Joseph, UK novelist)
Cooper (James Fenimore, US novelist)
Coward (Noel, UK dramatist)

Cowley (Abraham, English poet)
Cowper (William, UK poet)
Crabbe (George, UK poet)
Cronin (A.J., UK novelist)
Daudet (Alphonse, French novelist)
Dobson (Henry, UK poet)
Dowson (Ernest, UK poet)
Dryden (John, English dramatist and poet)
Dunbar (William, Scottish poet)
Eluard (Paul, French poet)
Eusden (Laurence, UK poet)
Fowles (John, UK novelist)
France (Anatole, French novelist)
Fraser (George Macdonald, UK novelist)
Frisch (Max, Swiss dramatist)
Fugard (Athol, South African dramatist)
Fuller (Roy, UK poet)
George (Stefan, German poet)
Gibbon (Edward, UK historian)
Goethe (J.W. von, German poet and dramatist)
Graves (Robert, UK poet and novelist)
Greene (Graham, UK novelist)
Hailey (Arthur, US novelist)
Hamsun (Knut, Norwegian novelist)

Harris (Joel Chandler, US novelist)
Heaney (Seamus, Irish poet)
Heller (Joseph, US novelist)
Hesiod (Greek poet)
Horace (Roman poet)
Hughes (Richard, UK novelist)
Hughes (Ted, UK poet)
Huxley (Aldous, UK novelist)
Irving (Washington, US novelist)
Jonson (Ben, English dramatist and poet)
Kleist (Heinrich von, German dramatist)
Laclos (Pierre Choderlos de, French novelist)
Landor (Walter Savage, UK poet)
Larkin (Philip, UK poet)
London (Jack, US novelist)
Lowell (Amy/ James Russell/Robert, US poets)
Mailer (Norman, US novelist)
Malory (Thomas, English writer)
McEwan (Ian, UK novelist)
Millay (Edna St Vincent, US poet)
Miller (Arthur, US dramatist)
Miller (Henry, US novelist)
Milton (John, English poet)
Motion (Andrew, UK poet)
Musset (Alfred de, French dramatist and poet)
Neruda (Pablo, Chilean poet)

Nerval (Gérard de, French poet)
O'Brien (Edna/Flann, Irish novelists)
O'Casey (Sean, Irish dramatist)
O'Neill (Eugene, US dramatist)
Orwell (George, UK novelist)
Parker (Dorothy, US humourist)
Pindar (Greek poet)
Pinero (Arthur Wing, UK dramatist)
Pinter (Harold, UK dramatist)
Porter (Katherine Anne, US novelist)
Powell (Anthony, UK novelist)
Proust (Marcel, French novelist)
Racine (Jean, French dramatist)
Ransom (John Crowe, US poet)
Runyon (Damon, US humorist)
Sappho (Greek poet)
Sardou (Victorien, French dramatist)
Sartre (Jean-Paul, French novelist)
Seneca (Roman dramatist)
Sidney (Sir Philip, English poet)
Singer (Isaac Bashevis, US novelist)
Sterne (Laurence, UK novelist)
Stoker (Bram, Irish novelist)
Thomas (Brandon, UK dramatist)
Thomas (Dylan, Welsh poet/Edward, English poet)

Updike (John, US novelist)
Valéry (Paul, French poet)
Villon (François, French poet)
Virgil (Roman poet)
Warton (Thomas, UK poet)
Wesker (Arnold, UK dramatist)
Wilder (Thornton, US dramatist)
Wilson (Angus, UK novelist)
Wright (Richard, US novelist)

7

Ackroyd (Peter, UK novelist)
Addison (Joseph, UK poet)
Alcaeus (Greek poet)
Allende (Isabel, Chilean novelist)
Anouilh (Jean, French dramatist)
Ariosto (Ludovico, Italian poet)
Balchin (Nigel, UK novelist)
Baldwin (James, US novelist)
Beckett (Samuel, Irish dramatist and novelist)
Bennett (Alan, UK dramatist)
Bennett (Arnold, UK novelist)
Bentley (Edmund Clerihew, UK poet)
Blunden (Edmund, UK poet)
Boileau (Nicolas, French poet)
Boswell (James, Scottish biographer)
Bridges (Robert, UK

poet)
Büchner (Georg, German dramatist)
Burgess (Anthony, UK novelist)
Caedmon (Old English poet)
Chapman (George, English poet)
Chaucer, Geoffrey, English poet)
Chekhov (Anton, Russian dramatist)
Chénier (André, French poet)
Cleland (John, UK novelist)
Coetzee (J.M., South African novelist)
Colette (French novelist)
Collins (Wilkie, UK novelist)
Collins (William, UK poet)
Crashaw (Richard, English poet)
Dickens (Charles, UK novelist)
Douglas (Keith, UK poet)
Drabble (Margaret, UK novelist)
Drayton (Michael, English poet)
Dreiser (Theodore, US novelist)
Duhamel (Georges, French novelist)
Durrell (Lawrence, UK novelist)
Emerson (Ralph Waldo, US philosopher and poet)
Feydeau (Georges, French dramatist)
Flecker (James Elroy, UK poet)
Fleming (Ian, UK novelist)
Forster (E.M., UK

novelist)
Gaskell (Elizabeth, UK novelist)
Gautier (Théophile, French poet)
Gilbert (W.S., UK comic dramatist)
Gissing (George, UK novelist)
Golding (William, UK novelist)
Goldoni (Carlo, Italian dramatist)
Grisham (John, US novelist)
Haggard (Rider, UK novelist)
Hammett (Dashiell, US novelist)
Hampton (Christopher, UK dramatist)
Hartley (L.P., UK novelist)
Hellman (Lillian, US dramatist)
Herbert (George, English poet)
Herrick (Robert, English poet)
Hopkins (Gerard Manley, UK poet)
Housman (A.E., UK poet)
Ionesco (Eugene, French dramatist)
Jeffers (Robinson, US poet)
Johnson (Lionel, UK poet/Terry UK dramatist)
Johnson (Dr Samuel, UK poet and essayist)
Juvenal (Roman satirical poet)
Kaufman (George S., US dramatist)
Kerouac (Jack, US novelist)
Khayyam (Omar, Persian poet)

Kipling (Rudyard, UK poet)
Labiche (Eugène, French dramatist)
Lessing (Doris, UK novelist)
Lessing (Gottfried, German dramatist)
Lindsay (Vachel, US poet)
Malraux (André, French novelist)
Manzoni (Alessandro, Italian novelist)
Marlowe (Christopher, English dramatist)
Martial (Roman poet)
Marvell (Andrew, English poet)
Maugham (Somerset, UK novelist)
Mauriac (François, French novelist)
McGough (Roger, UK poet)
Merimée (Prosper, French novelist)
Mistral (Frédéric, Provencal French poet)
Molière (Jean-Baptiste Poquelin, French dramatist)
Moravia (Alberto, Italian novelist)
Murdoch (Iris, UK novelist)
Nabokov (Vladimir, US novelist)
Naipaul (V.S., West Indian novelist)
Newbolt (Sir Henry, UK poet)
Osborne (John, UK dramatist)
Peacock (Thomas Love, UK novelist)
Plautus (Roman dramatist)
Prévert (Jacques, French

novelist)

Pushkin (Alexander, Russian poet)

Pynchon (Thomas, US novelist)

Queneau (Raymond, French novelist)

Rimbaud (Arthur, French poet)

Rolland (Romain, French novelist)

Romains (Jules, French novelist)

Ronsard (Pierre de, French poet)

Rostand (Edmond, French dramatist)

Roussel (Raymond, French novelist)

Rushdie (Salman, UK novelist)

Sassoon (Siegfried, UK poet)

Scarron (Paul, French dramatist)

Shaffer (Peter/Anthony, UK dramatists)

Shelley (Mary, UK novelist)

Shelley (Percy Bysshe, UK poet)

Shepard (Sam, US dramatist)

Simenon (Georges, Belgian novelist)

Sitwell (Dame Edith, UK poet)

Skelton, John, English poet)

Southey (Robert, UK poet)

Spender (Stephen, UK poet)

Stevens (Wallace, UK poet)

Surtees (Robert, UK novelist)

Terence (Roman

dramatist)

Thurber (James, US humorist)

Tolkien (J.R.R., UK novelist)

Tolstoy (Leo, Russian novelist)

Travers (Ben, UK dramatist)

Vaughan (Henry, English poet)

Wallace (Edgar, UK/Lew US novelist)

Webster (John, English dramatist)

Wharton (Edith, US novelist)

Whiting (John, UK dramatist)

Whitman (Walt, US poet)

Wyndham (John, UK novelist)

8

Anacreon (Greek poet)

Barbusse (Henri, French novelist)

Beaumont (Francis, English dramatist)

Beauvoir (Simone de, French novelist)

Bernanos (Georges, French novelist)

Berryman (John, US poet)

Betjeman (John, UK poet)

Bradbury (Ray, US novelist)

Brookner (Anita, UK novelist)

Browning (Robert, UK poet)

Calderon (Pedro, Spanish dramatist)

Campbell (Roy, South African poet)

Catullus (Roman poet)

Chandler (Raymond, US novelist)

Christie (Agatha, UK novelist)

Claudel (Paul, French dramatist)

Claudian (Roman poet)

Cocteau (Jean, French dramatist)

Congreve (William, Irish dramatist)

Constant (Benjamin, French novelist)

cummings (e.e., US poet)

Davenant (Sir William, English poet)

Disraeli (Benjamin, UK novelist)

Etherege (George, English dramatist)

Farquhar (George, Irish dramatist)

Faulkner (William, US novelist)

Fielding (Henry, UK novelist)

Flaubert (Gustave, French novelist)

Forester (C.S., UK novelist)

Ginsberg (Allen, US poet)

Goncourt (Edmond/Jules de, French novelists)

Henryson (Robert, Scottish poet)

Huysmans (Joris Karl, French novelist)

Keneally (Thomas, Australian novelist)

Kingsley (Charles, UK novelist)

Lawrence (D. H., UK novelist and poet)

Lawrence (T.E., UK soldier and writer)

Macleish (Archibald, US poet)

Malherbe (François de, French poet)

Mallarmé (Stéphane,

French poet)
Marivaux (Pierre, French dramatist)
Marquand (J.P., US novelist)
McCarthy (Mary, US novelist)
Melville (Herman, US novelist)
Menander (Greek dramatist).
Meredith (George, UK novelist)
Mitchell (Margaret, US novelist)
Mortimer (John, UK dramatist and novelist)
Ondaatje (Michael, Canadian novelist)
Petrarch (Francesco, Italian poet)
Philemon (Greek poet)
Rattigan (Terence, UK dramatist)
Rossetti (Dante Gabriel/Christina, UK poets)
Salinger (J.D., US novelist)
Sandburg (Carl, US poet)
Schiller (Friedrich, German dramatist and poet)
Sheridan (Richard Brinsley, Irish dramatist)
Sherriff (R.C., UK dramatist)
Sillitoe (Alan, UK novelist)
Sinclair (Upton, US novelist)
Smollett (Tobias, UK novelist)
Spillane (Mickey, US novelist)
Stendhal (Henri Beyle, French novelist)
Stoppard (Tom, UK

dramatist)
Suckling (John, English poet)
Tennyson (Alfred Lord, UK poet)
Traherne (Thomas, English poet)
Trollope (Anthony/ Joanna, UK novelists)
Turgenev (Ivan, Russian novelist)
Vanbrugh (John, English dramatist)
Verlaine (Paul, French poet)
Voltaire (François-Marie Arouet, French novelist)
Vonnegut (Kurt, US novelist)
Williams (Tennessee, US dramatist)
Williams (William Carlos, US poet)

9
Aeschylus (Greek dramatist)
Akhmatova (Anna, Russian poet)
Allingham (Marjorie, UK novelist)
Ayckbourn (Alan, UK dramatist)
Blackmore (R.D., UK novelist)
Bleasdale (Alan, UK dramatist)
Burroughs (Edgar Rice/William, US novelists)
Cervantes (Miguel de, Spanish novelist)
Churchill (Caryl, UK dramatist)
Coleridge (Samuel Taylor, UK poet)
Corneille (Pierre, French dramatist)

D'Annunzio (Gabriele, Italian poet)
Dickinson (Emily, US poet)
Euripides (Greek dramatist)
Froissart (Jean, French chronicler)
Giraudoux (Jean, French dramatist)
Goldsmith (Oliver, Irish dramatist)
Hauptmann (Gerhard, German dramatist)
Hawthorne (Nathaniel, US novelist)
Hemingway (Ernest, US novelist)
Highsmith (Patricia, US novelist)
Hölderlin (Friedrich, German poet)
Isherwood (Christopher, UK novelist)
Lamartine (Alphonse de, French poet)
Lampedusa (Giuseppe di, Italian novelist)
Lermontov (Mikhail, Russian poet)
Linklater (Eric, UK novelist)
Llewellyn (Richard, UK novelist)
Lucretius (Roman poet)
Mansfield (Katherine, New Zealand short-story writer)
Masefield (John, UK poet)
Maupassant (Guy de, French novelist)
McCullers (Carson, US novelist)
Middleton (Thomas, English dramatist)
Monsarrat (Nicholas, UK novelist)

O'Flaherty (Liam, Irish novelist)

Pasternak (Boris, Russian novelist)

Pratchett (Terry, UK novelist)

Priestley (J.B., UK dramatist and novelist)

Pritchett (V.S., UK novelist)

Rochester (John Wilmot, English poet)

Sophocles (Greek dramatist)

Steinbeck (John, US novelist)

Stevenson (Robert Louis, UK novelist)

Swinburne (Algernon Charles, UK poet)

Thackeray (William Makepeace, UK novelist)

Wodehouse (P.G., UK novelist)

Wycherley (William, English dramatist)

10

Bainbridge (Beryl, UK novelist)

Baudelaire (Charles, French poet)

Chesterton (G.K., UK novelist, essayist and poet)

Dürrenmatt (Friedrich, Swiss dramatist)

Fitzgerald (Edward, UK poet)

Fitzgerald (Scott, US novelist)

Galsworthy (John, UK novelist and dramatist)

Longfellow (Henry Wadsworth, US poet).

Mandelstam (Osip, Russian poet)

Pirandello (Luigi, Italian dramatist)

Propertius (Sextus, Roman poet)

Richardson (Samuel, UK novelist)

Schnitzler (Arthur, Austrian dramatist)

Strindberg (August, Swedish dramatist)

Theocritus (Greek poet)

Waterhouse (Keith, UK dramatist)

Wordsworth (William, UK poet)

11

Apollinaire (Guillaume, French poet)

Dostoievski (Fyodor, Russian novelist)

Grillparzer (Franz,

Austrian dramatist)

Montherlant (Henry de, French novelist)

Shakespeare (William, English dramatist and poet)

Yevtushenko (Yevgeny, Russian poet)

12

Aristophanes (Greek dramatist)

Beaumarchais (Pierre, French dramatist)

Solzhenitsyn (Aleksandr, Russian novelist)

2+ words

Conan Doyle (Arthur, UK novelist)

Day Lewis (Cecil, UK poet)

de la Mare (Walter, UK poet)

Du Maurier (Daphne, UK novelist)

La Fontaine (Jean de, French poet)

Le Carré (John, UK novelist)

Saint-Exupery (Antoine de, French novelist)